Critical Issues in Tourism

Critical Issues in Tourism:

a geographical perspective

Second Edition

Gareth Shaw and Allan M. Williams

First edition published 1994
Reprinted 1994, 1995, 1996, 1997, 1998, 2000

Second edition published 2002

Blackwell Publishers Ltd
108 Cowley Road
Oxford OX4 1JF, UK

Blackwell Publishers Inc.
350 Main Street
Malden, Massachusetts 02148, USA

British Library Cataloguing in Publication Data
A CIP catalogue record for this book is available from the British Library

Library of Congress Cataloging in Publication Data
Shaw, Gareth.
    Critical issues in tourism : a geographical perspective / Gareth Shaw and Allan M. Williams.—2nd ed.
        p. cm.
Includes bibliographical references (p.) and index.
    ISBN 0–631–22413–0 (hbk : alk. paper)—ISBN 0–631–22414–9 (pbk : alk. paper)
1. Tourism.   I. Williams, Allan M.   II. Title.
G155.A1 S48 2002
338.4′791—dc21

                                                                                2001004193

Typeset in 10.5 on 12 pt Imprint
by Best-set Typesetter Ltd., Hong Kong
Printed and bound in Great Britain
by TJ International Ltd, Padstow, Cornwall

This book is printed on acid-free paper

Contents

Tables

Boxes

Figures

Plates

Preface to the Second Edition

The first edition of this book was published in 1994 and preparing the second edition has provided an opportunity both to revise and update our exploration of critical issues in tourism, viewed from a geographical perspective. Above all, we have been impressed by the massive increase of activity within this field during the intervening years, and the increasing theorization of the subject, alongside the rich tradition of empirical and case study research. In many ways, however, the aims of the second edition remain essentially the same as those of the first.

First, the book emphasizes the need to analyze tourism within the context of leisure as a whole; this is important given the traditional segmentation of the literature in these two fields. Second, we have attempted to link some of the issues in tourism to wider issues in the social science literature. Implicitly, this is what de Kadt (1979) was calling for when he warned researchers against concentrating on the "unique" problems associated with tourism. The holistic nature of much of the recent development of critical social science has been particularly helpful in widening the analytical frame of reference. But at the same time, we have found that tourism researchers have striven to reach across the disciplinary divides to engage with some of the theoretical debates in other social sciences in recent years. There are still yawning chasms in some areas of research, but bridges are being built. It is unfortunate that most of these bridges carry one way traffic, for the growing engagement of tourism researchers with debates in geography, sociology, and psychology has not always been reciprocated. Third, we sought to link the analyses of production and consumption by examining how these come together to produce particular types of tourism environments (Part III). In this volume it is not possible to be comprehensive in this respect and, instead, we concentrate on rural, urban, and mass tourism environments. The actual form that any one of these tourism environments assumes in a particular locality is, of course, contingent. Our aim, therefore, has been to identify relevant issues in each case rather than to prescribe their characteristics in any deterministic sense. Our overall approach is broadly set within a political economy perspective, but we draw on behavioralist and cultural interpretations to explore these issues in detail.

In terms of geographical coverage we have principally focused the book on the tourism and leisure of the developed capitalist societies. We, therefore, make scant reference to tourism in the former state socialist countries, and are mainly concerned with the Less Developed Countries in so far as they are locked into tourism relationships with the more developed economies. The book, therefore, does not claim to provide a comprehensive perspective on tourism or tourism geography. Instead, our aim is to review some of the critical issues in the geography of tourism production and consumption which have been, are, or should be important objects of analysis.

The second edition marks a significant revision. The final chapter represents a totally new addition to the book. In place of the general consideration of the emergence of new forms of tourism in the conclusion to the first edition, we have instead included a chapter which focuses on environmental issues and sustainability. This very much reflects the ascendancy of this ideological framework in many aspects of tourism research and policy in recent years, and our belief that the subject needs critical engagement. In particular, we emphasize the need to approach the subject in the context of a broader understanding of production and consumption issues. Elsewhere, we have revised the text to varying degrees as appropriate. In places, we have added new sections, revised our lines of arguments, or simply updated some of the illustrations. The value of these refinements is, of course, for others to judge.

Finally, we wish to acknowledge the help and support of a number of people in particular without whom this book could not have been produced. Cathy Aggett and Jan Thatcher provided invaluable support in word-processing and coordinating the production of the new manuscript, while Terry Bacon, Helen Jones, Sue Rouillard, and Andrew Teed took on the task of producing illustrations for this edition.

Gareth Shaw and Allan M. Williams
Exeter, March 2001

Part I

An Approach to Tourism

1

Introduction

This book explores a number of critical issues in the geography of tourism. It focuses on some of the central concerns of geography – space, place, and the environment – but advocates a flexible approach to disciplinary boundaries. This is particularly important because tourism has too often been abstracted from wider social and spatial relationships, so that there has been a failure to understand how it is shaped by and contributes to wider economic, political, social, and cultural structures and relationships in society. There is, therefore, a need for a holistic approach, and a willingness to integrate many of the traditional concerns of tourism studies – for example, tourist behavior, host–guest relationships, and the structure and evolution of resorts – with wider debates about societal change. These can be approached from a number of different perspectives but, as is explained at the end of this chapter, we focus on production and consumption issues, within a broadly political economy framework, albeit cognizant of the importance of cultural interpretations and studies of individual behavior. First, however, tourism has to be located in relation to the wider practises of leisure and mobility in contemporary society, and this necessarily requires that we consider definitional issues.

Tourism, Leisure, and Mobility: Definitions and Relationships

Urry (1995: 129) memorably has written that the consumption of leisure-related activities "cannot be separated from the social relations in which they are embedded." In context of this book, we emphasize that tourism needs to be seen in context of overall leisure behavior –

home based leisure, neighborhood or locality based tourism, and day trips can both complement and contradict the aims and practices of tourism. Moreover, tourism has to be seen in relation to the many different types of mobility: it is a form of circulation, of varying duration, but one that is different from other forms of circulation such as shopping trips, or labor migration. First, however, we consider the relations between tourism and leisure.

One way in which we can approach this issue is through definitions. This is more difficult than first appears as there are a number of definitions of both concepts. Turning first to leisure, there are three main competing definitions (see de Grazia 1984; Kelly 1982; Patmore 1983: 5–6; Stockdale 1985: 13–14). These are based on temporality, activities or practises, and experiences:

- In the first definition, leisure is juxtaposed with time that is functionally obligated to work, to biological needs such as eating or sleeping, or to other commitments such as travel to work. The residual time is considered to be free time and this is equated with leisure. It is notoriously difficult to pin down such free time empirically, given the subjectivity implicit in the notion of obligation. Nevertheless, one survey suggested that in the European Union 15.7 percent of an individual's time, on average, is free time (figure 1.1). The ambiguous notion of free time is usually used in the sense of "freedom from" obligations such as work. This is a negative definition which is quite different from the concept of "freedom to" enjoy leisure; hence Rojek (1985: 13) states that "the concept of free time has no intrinsic meaning" with respect to leisure. It ignores the quality of the time available – whether it is fragmented, or whether you are on standby care duty for family or others – and the resources that are necessary to allow participation in many forms of leisure. At one level, these differences are shaped by human agency which accounts for some individual variation in leisure practices. But Rojek, as does Urry (1995), directs us to the social relations of leisure (and tourism). Freedom to enjoy leisure has structural determinants such as class, life cycle, race, and gender. For example, the role of married women in the dual labor force (the home and the formal labor market or the external workplace) means that their quality of time is more fragmented, as well as more spatially and socially constrained than is the time available to married men (Hudson and Williams 1989: 112–15).
- The second definition assumes that leisure is the time when leisure activities are undertaken. This overlaps with the definition of recreation as the activities undertaken during leisure time. In this definition leisure takes on a strictly objective form – it is a list of activities

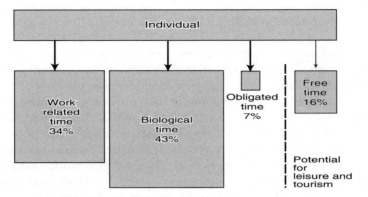

Figure 1.1   *Idealized use of time in the developed countries*
Source: modified from WTO (1983)

prescribed by an external agent such as a researcher or government department. Apart from some circularity in the argument, this definition is unsatisfactory because it assumes a false objectivity. Activities such as gardening or do-it-yourself home repairs can be regarded either as leisure or obligations: it all depends on values and motivations.

- In response to criticism of these approaches, a third perspective argues that leisure is an attitude of mind (for example, Iso-Ahola 1980). It is the perception of activities by individuals which is important, for leisure is rooted in enjoyment, well-being, and personal satisfaction. Kelly (1982: 7) catches the essence of this definition: "Leisure is defined by the use of time, not the time itself. It is distinguished by the meaning of the activity not its form." Walking may be an important leisure activity for some but may be abhorred by others. Similarly, some fortunate individuals experience paid work as leisure. In general, this approach implies that leisure activities are freely entered into and yield personal satisfaction. However, this notion can be misleading for it exaggerates the voluntary nature of activities and ignores the fact that there are socially constructed boundaries to individual choices, based on social position, expectations, and socialization. Wealth, income, gender, race, and other structural characteristics influence how activities are experienced. As Featherstone (1987: 115) states, "The significance and meaning of a particular set of leisure choices . . . can only be made intelligible by inscribing them on a map of the class-defined social field of leisure and life-style practices in which their meaning and significance is relationally defined with reference to structured oppositions and differences." This experiential definition, set in context of social relations, informs this book.

The definition of tourism is also problematic. Gunn (1988), for example, considers that tourism includes all traveling except commuting. This is too all-embracing for it would involve not only all out-of-home recreation but also traveling for such purposes as visiting doctors. In other words, it fails to differentiate tourism from other forms of mobility. Another definition stresses that tourism involves traveling away from home for leisure purposes. It is therefore seen as a subset of leisure and of recreation. For example, Kelly (1985) writes that tourism is "recreation on the move, engaging in activity away from home in which the travel is at least part of the satisfaction sought." There is ambiguity here in that it is not clear whether "away from home" begins at the front door, involves a substantial journey of a minimum length or implies an overnight stay away from home.

Another definition, necessarily arbitrary, is the practical definition preferred by international bodies such as the World Tourism Organization, whereby tourism includes all travel that involves a stay of at least one night, but less than one year, away from home. This therefore includes travel for such purposes as visiting friends or relatives, or to undertake business activities. It is a definition based on the duration rather than the motivations for mobility. This definition has the advantage of being relatively easily measurable, which gives it apparent objectivity. However, it stands in contrast to the experiential definition of leisure. Nevertheless, it is the definition most commonly in use within the literature on tourism. More importantly, we do not believe that pleasure tourism can be studied in isolation from other forms of tourism such as business travel. The economics of the air travel and the accommodation industries, for example, are based on the carriage of both business and holiday tourists. The structure of the tourism industry can no more be understood solely through a study of pleasure tourism than it can through a study of tourism in isolation of leisure. Furthermore, mobility has become increasingly multi-purpose. It is common for business tourists to enjoy leisure activities during their trips. Tourism also blurs with labor migration in the case of, for example, the tourist-worker, who funds his or her travels through periodic bouts of paid employment (see Williams and Hall 2000).

The last point raises the issue of the duration of the trip. Most definitions emphasize that tourism is characterized by non-permanent moves, an intention to return home within a relatively short time period, and a purpose other than taking up permanent residence or employment. This is problematic given that there is no clear conceptualization of "permanence," and instead the pragmatic device of absence from home for at least one night but for less than twelve months is adopted both by academics and by many statistical bodies (Williams and Hall 2000). Bell and Ward (2000: 88) have provided useful guidance on this topic. For them, "Tourism represents one form of circulation, or temporary population movement. Temporary movements and permanent migration, in turn, form part of the same continuum of population mobility in time and space." They focus on the essential characteristics of temporary mobility and permanent migration. Permanent migration implies no intention to return, involves a lasting relocation, a single transition, and arrival in a destination has only minor seasonality. In contrast, temporary migrants may plan to return home, have varying duration of stay, generally are involved in repeat movements, and their arrival tends to have a strong seasonal distribution. Another difference is that the place of "usual residence" is a central feature of permanent migration but not of temporary migration. Bell and Ward try to locate the different types of mobility in a two dimensional space. This is most effective at the two poles. Permanent moves are measured in years and occur at different scales, for different purposes. At the other extreme is mobility which does not involve overnight stays, such as shopping and commuting. Between these poles, the different forms of temporary mobility tend to be blurred in terms of scale and time so that temporary mobility is best viewed as "a sequence of intersecting and overlapping layers, of varying intensity and spatial extent, each representing a different form of mobility behaviour" (Bell and Ward 2000: 93). Attempts to produce a definition based on motivations are no more successful, for they conclude that both temporary and permanent mobility can be for consumption or production reasons, or for a combination of these. Ultimately, therefore, while the discussion of temporary mobility is useful as a way of contextualizing the definition of tourism, it does not actually provide a working definition.

The approach taken in this book is to focus mainly on the leisure tourist. We also argue that this phenomenon can not be adequately understood without considering either leisure as a whole, or tangential and sometimes overlapping forms of mobility such as business tourism (see figure 1.2). We consider that an overnight stay is essential to be considered a tourist, but note that this is a problematic notion: there are considerable differences between children staying overnight with nearby friends, and long distance long-duration holiday makers. The statistics in this area are, of course, a veritable minefield, and of necessity we have had to draw on sources using many different definitions. Therefore particular care is required in contextualizing the statistics, let alone in pursing our objective of studying tourism within its wider social relations. We therefore advocate flexibility around the notion of

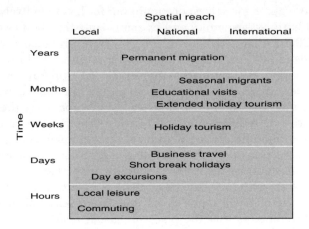

Figure 1.2 *Situating tourism in relation to leisure and mobility: temporal and spatial dimensions*

Source: elaboration of a model by Bell and Ward (2000)

the tourist as an overnight visitor mainly or partly for pleasure purposes rather than a rigid adherence to any one definition.

Despite the problems inherent in this flexible approach to definitional issues, we believe this is important. Much of the previous literature on tourism, leisure, and recreation has developed as separate strands of research and teaching, often with very few points of contacts (see Fedler 1987). One of the aims of this book is to help rectify this imbalance. We would not go so far as to agree with Jansen-Verbeke and Dietvorst (1987: 263) that "in the perception of the individual at least, the distinction between recreation and tourism is becoming irrelevant," but the perceptions are increasingly mutually informing. There are a number of points at which tourism and (non-tourism) leisure are interrelated, and neither can be adequately understood without reference to the other.

First, they are tied together in the same *time–space framework*. Individuals' lives, seen as trajectories through time, have a certain structure. Work and other functional obligations mean that there is a rhythm to the time available for leisure – at least for most people. The total amount and the quality of time (degree of fragmentation, possibility of interruptions by functional obligations such as family care, etc.) available for leisure and tourism varies through the day, the week, the year and the life-course. Work and family/household obligations are the most important influences but these are not deterministic. Human agency is important. Most individuals have the potential to vary the amount of time they devote to leisure, by reorganizing the time that they spend on other activities. As tourism involves a minimum of one night spent away from home, this activity is only possible during certain blocks of the time available for leisure. While this is absolutey irreducible, the propensity to participate in tourism during particular time periods is relational. It depends in part on the individual (motivations to overcome obstacles to tourism), or the life cycle (whether you are free from obligations and can depart at short notice). But it is also to be understood within social structures and the distribution of income and mobility resources across society. The use made of time is also related to economic development and technological changes. For example, technological advances in travel may facilitate short tourism breaks.

Tourism and non-tourism leisure also make demands upon the same *household budget*. If the disposable income available is inadequate to satisfy both sets of demand, then they are in a substitutional relationship. The degree of substitution depends in part on the motivations of the individual. For example, the desire to discover new places via tourism is not easily substituted by locally-based recreation. But there is reasonable substitutability between playing golf while on holiday and doing so locally. The degree of substitutability changes over time in response to changes in both the total household budget, and the demand for tourism and leisure. It is not only a matter of income elasticities of demand (changes in the amounts purchased as income changes) but also to shifts in values and motivations which are both intrinsic and external to the individual (see chapter 3).

Tourism and leisure are also inter-related because their practices often occupy the same *shared spaces*. This is particularly evident in those places that are not highly specialized in tourism, that is the resorts. Thus the streets of Rome, Sydney, or New York may, at any one time, be filled with a medley of short break leisure tourists, business tourists taking a break before they fly home after business meetings, day excursionists from the surrounding region, and local residents. At one level, their enjoyment of these spaces are mutually dependent: the economies of scale and scope that support many facilities (whether museums, theatres, or restaurants) may well depend on the critical market mass created by their combined expenditures. And it is the presence of "others" which not only creates the sense of place (for example, a feeling of vibrancy) but also signifies that these are the places to visit and to be seen to visit. Yet on the other hand, their practices may be incompatible and these can become contested spaces and places: the streets and the public transport can become congested and uncomfortable; aggregate demand may inflate prices for meals, services and labor; and the late night practises of one group may clash with the sleeping practises of others.

Finally, the objects of both tourism and local leisure activities are *socially constructed* (Urry 1990). It is sometimes suggested that their respective constructions are not only independent but diagonally opposed. Gunn (1988: 13), for example, states that "Because recreation is value-loaded (healthful, purposeful), its proponents often view tourism, with its emphasis on consumerism and commercialism, as an adversary." However, in reality their social constructions are linked. For example, enjoyable holiday experiences may become incorporated into the social construction of what constitutes desirable local leisure practises. Examples include the demand for and investment in dry ski slopes and outdoor bistros in an attempt to simulate some of the conditions, practises, and experiences of holidays in the Alps and the Mediterranean. Moreover, these inter-relationships flow in both directions and local leisure experiences and practices may inform the social construction of tourism. For example, the importance attached to at-home electronic entertainment equipment may create an expectation that television sets, and even videos, should be provided in tourist accommodation. More fundamentally, Urry (1990) argues that innovations in local leisure – such as theme parks and leisure centres – have contributed to British seaside holiday resorts losing their exotic allure, appearing to offer everyday experiences instead. Whether the increasingly sophisticated theming and internationalization of many parks and shopping malls, let alone the growth of "virtual tourism" via the Internet, will, in time, make many international resorts seem "everyday" remains open to question.

The relationship between tourism and locally-based leisure is not fixed. It is culturally and economically contingent. The expectations of participation in leisure and tourism, as well as the economics of their supply, change over time and between societies; this is only to be expected as they are socially-constructed practices. The values attached to home versus travel, the shift from single-place dominated lives to multiple-place lives (notably via second homes) and the resources available for the purchase of increasingly commodified tourism and leisure practices are constantly changing. It therefore follows that the relationship between tourism and leisure is not only place specific but also historically specific (Rojek 1985: 23–9).

Until the twentieth century, for example, the costs of travel, the limited availability of holidays, and the absolute levels of incomes meant that tourism was essentially a preserve of the upper classes and some of the middle classes, even in the most developed countries. There was, therefore, a clear class basis as to who could subsequently participate in both tourism and leisure. The relationship between tourism and leisure has been affected by what has been termed "time deepening." There are three aspects of time-deepening: "undertaking an activity more quickly or satisfying some need through an activity more quickly, undertaking more than one activity simultaneously, and using time more precisely" (Golbey 1985: 19). This is evident in the post-1950 expansion of mass consumption in the developed countries which saw an increase not only in the number of goods people owned but also in the number and range of leisure activities in which they participated. This was facilitated by improvements in personal mobility, especially the extension of car ownership, but also by changes in the popular appreciation that tourism and leisure were critical components in social well-being, a theme that we return to later in this chapter. There were further changes in the 1960s with the growth of mass international tourism, particularly from Europe and the USA. At first, the destination countries were mainly the Caribbean or other European countries. However, by the 1980s mass tourism from Europe and North America, and from new countries of origin such as Japan and the Newly Industrialized Countries (NICs), was being extended to an increasingly global range of destinations. This had implications for the key relationship between tourism and leisure that we identified above: time–space frameworks, household budgets, shared spaces and their social construction.

One of the central contentions of this volume is the need to place the study of tourism in the context of leisure. The following section addresses this through an exploration of their interrelationship in terms of economic development, the quality of life and lifestyles, and culture. This discussion also serves to emphasize that tourism is not a peripheral aspect of local, national, or global economies and societies. Instead, it is increasingly central to all of these.

Tourism and Leisure: Economy, Society, and Culture

Economic structures: commodification and privatization

The service sector has increased in importance, in both absolute and relative terms, in most economies in recent decades (Knox and Agnew 1998: chapter 7). While this is often linked to the process of de-industrialization, this is an ethnocentric view founded in the experiences of the developed countries. For example, because of the impact of technological change, many of the more recently industrialized countries have not developed extensive manufacturing employment despite the importance of this sector in production terms (Urry 1987: 5–6). In addition, some less developed countries have based their development strategies on the service industries – whether off-shore financial services as in the Bahamas, or tourism as in the Seychelles.

The research neglect of the service sector has been remedied to some extent in recent years. In particular, the producer services have been extensively analysed in respect of their role in capital accumulation and uneven development (for example, Marshall 1989). However, the consumer services have tended to be ignored, despite the fact that they consistently feature among the most rapid growth sectors in most developed countries (see Urry 1987: 11). The economic role of tourism and leisure can be examined in a number of ways but here we emphasize output, employment, inter-firm linkages, trade, "sustainability" costs, and place images.

1. Tourism and leisure services are a significant component of production in many economies. In 1985, international and domestic tourism accounted for global expenditure equivalent to $1,800 billion (Gunn 1988: 3), and the leisure industries for an even higher level. In 1999 international tourism alone accounted for receipts of $455 bn. (World Tourism Organization 2000a). Moreover, this is also one of the most rapidly expanding sectors in the world economy. In practise, it is difficult to disentangle their output and employment in most statistical data series. Accommodation services are one of the few sectors which specifically cater for overnight visitors, but even this sector is not exclusively dedicated to this market segment. For example, hotels may host conferences, or receptions attended predominantly by local residents.

2. Tourism and leisure are also important elements in labor markets, with tourism accounting for more than one million jobs in the UK alone. Although there is a considerable debate about the nature of tourism employment (Williams and Shaw 1988, 1998), this has not diminished its attraction to policy makers responding to the recurrent crises of unemployment in capitalist economies. Again, tourism and leisure employment are often inter-twined with jobs in catering, in particular, being supported by their expenditure. However, as noted earlier, the temporality of service provision is different in the tourism and leisure sector, with seasonality being far more prominent in the former. The extent to which they are complementary is, however, contingent on the nature of the tourism product which largely determines the inflows of tourists.

3. Tourism and leisure firms are characterized by inter-firm linkages, and these may be within or beyond the sector. There may be complementary (backward, forward, or horizontal linkages), or competitive (as in negative externalities, labor market shortages, and land price inflation). These can be quantified in various ways, but multiplier studies mostly indicate that tourism and leisure firms have a significant impact on other firms in their local economies.

As catering tends to be more important in tourism than in leisure provision, the former tends to have stronger links to the agricultural sector. Tourism also has specific links to inter-regional transport firms, and to some forms of furniture producers (notably bedroom furniture) that are insignificant in the remainder of the leisure sector. However, they also have overlapping linkages, for example to leisure retailing and to intra-regional transport firms, as well being mutually inter-linked: tourists may use leisure facilities, such as parks and swimming pools, that were mainly constructed for local residents, while local residents may visit theme parks that were developed for the tourism market.

4. Tourism, given the definition adopted in this book, is necessarily a non-basic economic sector, in the sense that it relies on exports or, more precisely, generates external income for an area. In other words, tourism can be a significant element in an area's trade. This has long been recognized in the analysis of international tourism (see Shaw and Williams 1998b). But it is also important in the trade of regions and localities, and this is explicitly recognized in many local and regional economic development strategies, which are centered on the capacity of tourism to attract external expenditure (Townsend 1992). The fact that tourism attractions are socially-constructed rather than "natural" or given, means that tourism features in the economic policies of most sub-national areas in the developed economies (Williams and Shaw 1998). Leisure activities that predominantly serve local residents do not, by definition, generate external income. However, as noted earlier, the two sectors are linked by the shared use of some facilities.

5. Tourism and leisure developments can have major local environmental and social impacts. These range from congestion costs, to pollution, to crime, and social disruption. Not all of these are easily quantified, but this does not allow us to ignore the economic costs and benefits that may be implicit in them: cleaning up litter, policing, and longer journey times, for example. These can be conceptualized as "sustainability costs" of tourism and leisure: that is the full social costs of non-sustainable development. While these impacts are mostly seen as costs (Mathieson and Wall 1982), they can have positive economic impacts, creating jobs in the cleansing services and the police, or leading to investment in the transport system, which benefits both locals and tourists. There is a tendency to associate high sustainability costs with mass tourism but the real picture is more complex: for the total sustainability costs of mass tourism may be less than the accumulated costs of the same number of tourists dispersed over a much wider geographical area (causing congestion on narrow rural roads, directly impacting on

the lives of far larger numbers of areas and residents, etc). Leisure activities by local residents also have sustainability costs: for example, the impacts of golf course development on water supply and ecosystems vegetation is indifferent to whether the golfer is a tourist or a local resident. Similarly, football matches can cause as much if not more congestion in the transport system as periodic influxes of tourists. In some instances, the sustainability costs generated by tourism and local leisure activities are mutually reinforcing; for example, those associated with major night clubs such as the Hacienda in London which became cultural icons drawing in customers or participants from beyond the immediate locality. Only the inter-regional transport sustainability costs of tourism may differ from those of the local leisure participant in this case.

6. Leisure, and tourism, in particular, can also play a critical role in the reconstruction of place identities and images. Outstanding examples include the waterfront redevelopment in cities such as Baltimore, Liverpool, and Sydney. This works at several levels: urban regeneration schemes may be predicated on tourism income generation (directly and via tax returns), while media coverage of and direct tourist visits to the tourism sites will reinforce changes in place identities. These regeneration zones also become sites for local leisure, whether as a landscape to be simply gazed on or a series of specific attractions. Thus in Liverpool, renovated docks have become an attraction in their own right as well as housing a branch of the Tate collection. But Sydney and Barcelona probably provide the best examples of this phenomenon. They hosted successful Olympic Games which generated additional investment to reinforce existing economic regeneration strategies, created new sporting and hospitality facilities which would become available for local use, attracted world-wide media attention, projected strong and positive place images, and enhanced the self confidence and identities of their citizens.

While tourism consumption has attracted increasing interest in recent years (Urry 1995), there is continuing neglect of tourism production (Debbage and Daniels 1998). The geography of the production of leisure and tourism services does share many features with other sectors (Agarwal et al. 2000); for example, changes in the labor process, the transnationalization of capital, and shifts to more flexible production. While there has been some empirical work on the supply side of these industries (see ch. 8), they are still absent from many of the major theoretical debates that characterize economic geography (Agarwal et al. 2000). More than a decade ago, Urry (1987: 22–3) argued that there was a need to situate tourism in relation to the debates on restructuring. In particular, he stressed the need to address the issues of partial self-provisioning, investment and technical change, rationalization, changing labor inputs, quality enhancement, and centralization. There has been little advancement of our understanding of most of these areas in the intervening years. And yet there are a number of significant and distinctive aspects of the production of tourism and leisure services that merit attention. Here we consider what can be termed the property rights relating to tourism and leisure and, in order to simplify the discussion, we consider three features: household production, commodification, and state intervention and marketization.

First, despite the commodification of tourism and leisure, these services are usually produced through a composite mix of the formal economy, informal (non-household) production and household production. These sectors are not insulated from each other but are linked by flows of money, goods, services, and labor. For example, the informal economy may produce pirate videos, and the household may use these in providing leisure at home, while being sold alongside legal videos. But an important, if not unique feature of tourism and leisure is the significant role of household production. Households continue to produce their own leisure and tourism experiences such as family games or outings. This can be related to Gershuny and Miles' (1983) concept of the self-service economy whereby there is substitution of goods (such as videos) to be used at home in place of externally provided services (such as cinema attendance). Additionally, individuals within the household may take on the role of unpaid travel agent, in assembling a "package" of commercial components for a holiday. And households – especially families – are at the heart of leisure and tourism as a shared experience for many, particularly at some stages of the family life cycle. Households therefore may provide alternative or complementary bases for the production of leisure and tourism services. In some cases, holiday visits to certain places can only become possible through a combination of these forms of production; for example, self provisioning by a household in commercially-rented self-catering accommodation.

Secondly, although household production and the use of non-charging attractions (beaches or mountains, for example) are still important, tourism and leisure are subject to commodification. Newman (1983: 100) argues that "On the one hand, leisure time appears as a form of free time, holding out the promise of spontaneity and periodic liberalisation. On the other, leisure is seen as assimilated into the values prevailing elsewhere, and hence is equally marked by the materialist imperative motivating consumption and work." Informally-organized leisure pursuits are increasingly being converted into traded products and services. For example, walkers are confronted with more opportunities to buy specialized equipment: specialized weatherproof clothing, shoes, and books of guided walks replace everyday clothing and shoes, and informal knowledge of walks and trails. Moreover, the growth of electronic equipment for in-home entertainment has been truly remarkable, creating waves of new opportunities for the realization of profits by private capital. Videos, PC based electronic games, and mobile form messaging all represent this tendency. In addition, Harvey (1987: 273–6) argues that cultural and symbolic capital have become more significant, and this has contributed to strong growth in consumer expenditure, especially by the expanding new middle class. In other words this is investment of time and capital in the consumption and collection of commodities and positionality goods, which are intended manifestly to demonstrate taste or status. In other words, private capital exploits the fact that the ownership of certain goods (or participating in certain activities) comes not only directly from these but also from their conspicuous consumption.

A third feature is the changing role of the state in tourism provision. Private capital cannot guarantee the sustained production of the tourism and leisure services that a society values and, to some extent, needs for its reproduction. There is, therefore, marked state intervention in their production in most capitalist societies, as well as in state socialist societies where they form an important element of state ideology (Williams and Balaz 2000a). State intervention comes in many forms including subsidies to, or the ownership of, accommodation and transport facilities, as well as regulation of quality standards, and the enforcement of health and safety standards. In reality, in both the capitalist economies and the state socialist ones, service provision tends to be a public–private mix. However, this balance has been changing in recent decades. Capitalist societies have witnessed a rolling back of the frontiers of the state which has seen greater marketization of provision. This may involve outright privatization of leisure services (Rojek 1985: 19), such as leisure centres in the UK or the state owned *parador* hotels in Spain, as well as the marketization of publicly owned services by charging for their use (for example, museums) or tendering for their catering facilities. The change has been even more marked in the state socialist societies, whether in Eastern Europe or in China, were publicly-owned facilities have been privatized, at the same time as the establishment of new private firms has been liberalized (Williams and Balaz 2000b).

These are not the only distinctive features of tourism and leisure production. There are also distinctive spatiality and temporality features. Tourism experiences are place and time specific: they are enjoyed at particular sites, and can not be deferred or geographically dispersed. There are some exceptions to this, notably the pleasure that comes from planning a tourism trip, and in reliving the experience afterwards, through talking about the visit with others, aided by souvenirs and photographs. Crang (1999) refers to the way in which these "gathered" images are embodied: memories and knowledge are reworked in embodied ways and used in friendships. There is also the growth of "virtual tourism," enjoyed through the web and multimedia. But most tourism experiences are still enjoyed at particular places and tourism services have to be provided at the moment of the tourist interactions at those sites. This has important implications for the geography of tourism production which we return to later. Leisure activities have more flexibility and there is usually a range of places where particular leisure activities can be undertaken, and far less temporal constraints on their enjoyment, even if individuals are still bounded by obligated, biological and work related time (figure 1.1).

In summary, then, as argued earlier, the production of most local leisure and tourism services are interdependent. Their facilities are rarely exclusive to either tourism or non-tourism market segments, with a few exceptions such as accommodation. In addition, many large companies, such as Bass (UK) have diversified activities (pubs and hotels), which extend across both market segments. Moreover, the continuing role of the household as a centre of tourism and leisure activities, despite processes of commodification, marketization, and privatization, also contributes to this interdependency.

Social well being, and life styles

Social well being and quality of life are terms open to a variety of interpretations, but they centre on the satisfaction that people obtain from their lives. This can be measured both subjectively and in terms of objective indicators. Subjective research on the quality of life tends to identify leisure as an important element, but secondary to such items as health, family life, and marriage (for example, Andrews and Withey 1976). Clearly, tourism and leisure come relatively high up in Maslow's (1954) hierarchy of needs: it figures among "self-actualization" and "esteem" at the apex of the pyramid rather than among the "physiological needs" such as hunger and shelter at its base. But this argument is somewhat misleading for terms such as social exclusion, disadvantage, and deprivation are relational concepts. For example, detailed empirical research in the UK confirms the "existence of identifiable groups who suffer leisure disadvantage or even privation, often in the context of economic constraints and limited job satisfaction" (Stockdale 1985: 117). There is also the need to look at the wider ramifications of leisure. Smith (1987: 83) for example, argues that leisure serves two fundamental needs: "the need for the leisure space in which to construct ongoing close relationships, and also the need for the leisure space to renew individual energy and potential."

This is reflected in the role of state provision in leisure and, in some countries, in social tourism programmes (see chapter 3). This is most clearly evident in the former state socialist economies of Central and Eastern Europe. For example, in the former Czechoslovakia, most workers were provided with annual holidays in low cost provision by their employers or trade unions, and these were held to be important in the reproduction of the labor force, and in reinforcing collectivism (Williams and Balaz 2001). But capitalist economies, such as Switzerland, have also operated social tourism programmes, providing holiday vouchers to the most disadvantaged groups in society. Arguably this can be related to the concept of citizenship, centring on the rights and obligations of individual citizens in their relationships to the state and to civil society. In the more developed countries, where basic needs have mostly been assured, a case can be made that all citizens have a right to a holiday, as part of their entitlement to a minimum quality of life. There is also the counter argument that citizenship implies certain obligations, such as being "responsible" in their behavior as tourists in respect of the environment and other tourists/hosts (see chapter 12).

Geographers have contributed to the debate on the quality of life and social well being. There have been a number of attempts to derive objective measures of these concepts and to use such social indicators to measure spatial variations in their distribution. These include both indirect measures pertaining to leisure and tourism – such as over-crowding and car ownership – and direct measures. With regard to the latter, Knox (1974) includes the availability of public libraries and cinemas in his synthetic index of "the level of living." This is then used to map out the spatial distribution of the level of living in the UK, which highlights both rural–urban and north–south differences. Such an approach is essentially descriptive, and although later attempts have been made to ground this work in theories of social and economic differentiation (Coates et al. 1977; Smith, D. M. 1977) these have not been entirely successful. Not least the approach is subject to two fundamental criticisms: first, that the quality of life is essentially a subjective matter and that it is therefore not amenable to objective statistical analysis; and second, that the spatial focus has diverted attention from social differences in the quality of life. There is a thesis that developed countries have been moving towards being "leisure democracies" (for example, see Golbey 1985: 38). This takes the view that people's leisure activities are determined less by status and income and more by personality and individual lifestyle. While there are such tendencies, and this has been borne out by market research (see chapter 4), we contend that gender, race, life-cycle, and other social relationships – in combination – are critical filters that condition social access to tourism and leisure (see chapter 3).

These different structural determinants of access to leisure and tourism do not operate independently. The class experience of leisure is conditioned by gender, stage of life-cycle, race, and location. There really are differences in the leisure and tourism experiences of the working class in different regions within any one country, let alone internationally. And it is obvious that age, the existence of dependants, gender, and race (still little researched) influence not only the availability and the quality of time available for tourism and leisure, but also the types of activities that can be experienced. But, as argued elsewhere, we do believe that "whilst class does not have a simplistic deterministic influence, it does have a determinate one" (Hudson and Williams 1995: 16). A high level of disposable income, for example, provides a means to compensate for some of the systematic leisure disadvantages of being a woman, being elderly, being black or living in a poorly serviced area. Being born into a class influences, early tourism and leisure experiences, expectations, and the opportunities that are available in later life. "In short, while class is not the only dimension of social structure and division, and other non-class divisions are not reducible to it, it does none the less impinge strongly on and interact with them" (Hudson and Williams 1995: 17). This is why leisure and tourism are important elements of the quality of life.

However, leisure and tourism are more than just elements in social well being, since they are also indicators of lifestyle and of an individual's position in society – that is, they are positional goods. Weber (1968) argued that a specific style of life is expected from those who wish to belong to a particular social circle. Rojek (1985: 73) adds that while the composition of lifestyle is contingent on time and place, "One important dimension of it in all cases and at all times is the conspicuous consumption of commodities and leisure time." In this sense the lifestyle attached to a given leisure form is a symbolic expression of power. Belonging to the "right" club, wearing the "right" designer leisure clothes, and being seen in a fashionable resort contribute to defining your position in the status hierarchy, and indicate your power base (see Featherstone 1987). The epitome of this was Veblen's (1925) "leisure class" who used their leisure time to display their wealth and status in society. Similarly, youth subcultures are partly defined by their leisure, whether it be biking, drugs, alcohol, music or voluntary work. In this way leisure can be one of the weapons in inter-generational, conflicts. Or it can be part of the "rite of passage" to adulthood, a role that Mason (2001) ascribes to the Big OE – the Australian and New Zealanders' overseas experiences in Europe, which are usually a mix of work and tourism activities.

Culture and internationalization

Leisure helps both to shape culture and is culturally contingent. This is evident as much in the books that are read as in the sports that are played (whether individualistic or collective) both within and between countries. There has been a tendency to greater homogeneity in culture, linked to the growth of mass culture which is "part of the process of the development of common unifying cultural values and attitudes in the new and vast population of modern national units" (Theodorson and Theodorson 1969: 245). Perhaps the best know variant of this debate is the McDonaldization thesis (Ritzer 1998). In short this involves "an increase in efficiency, predictability, calculability, and control through the substitution of non-human for human technology" which "involves a wide range of irrationalities, especially dehumaniza-tion and homogenization" (p. vii). This rationalization process has a strongly internationalist dimension. Beyond this, the mass media also play a critical role in the creation of mass culture. There has, of course, been an internationalization of the mass media, whether in terms of broadcasting, films, print, the web or, increasingly, multimedia forms. This has also contributed to the internationalization of culture. The process is, of course, neither unilinear nor monolithic and many groups retain distinctive leisure interest even in the most developed countries. For example, in North West England there has been a tendency for Asian workers to be employed on night shift work. Aubrey et al. (1986: 133) comment that "the pattern of Asian recruitment and the hours which they worked appeared to set them apart in many ways from the normal leisure patterns of the native white community, and to main-tain or reinforce their cultural isolation." There are also groups such as the Amish in North America, whose religious values permeate their leisure behavior.

Tourism is a particularly potent agent of cultural change, especially of internationalization. Lanfant (1980: 34) argues that "we are dealing, in tourism, with an all-embracing social phenomenon characterized by the introduction of new systems of relationships in all sectors of activ-ity, bringing about structural changes at all levels of social life and increasingly affecting all regions of the world." In a later contribution, Lanfant (1989: 182–3) argues that EuroDisney represents an extreme example of this process:

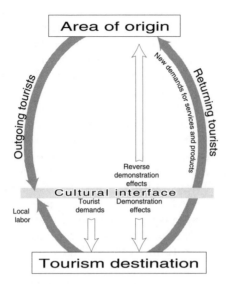

Figure 1.3   *Tourist circulation and cultural impacts*

This firm unites into one industrial whole the development of leisure parks, a cable communications network for press and television, the manufacture of pictures, models and all the apparatus essential to the creation of illusion. The new industry incorporates the most up-to-date scientific discoveries in communications, and is marshalling all the knowledge required to create a *planetary culture* of universal influence.

These arguments are given weight by the enormous growth that has occurred in international tourism: in 2000 there were an estimated 664 million tourist trips made, for all purposes, according to the World Tourism Organization (2000a). Each of these trips is potentially a cultural encounter, although their content varies enormously according to the motivations of the tourist (chapter 4) as well as the organization of the visit (chapter 5). But the conceptualization of the cultural impact of tourism can be extended beyond the immediate visit to take into account reverse cultural flows (figure 1.3). There is a cycle of cultural impacts even if the flows are asymmetrical. Golbey (1985: 131) argues that tourism produces "a wanderlust, not for other places but for other lives," in other words for new, more satisfying self images. MacCannell (1976) goes further and argues that one reaction to the harshness of modern, mass produced life has been the belief that "authentic" life is occurring elsewhere in the world. Holidays offer a transient opportunity to capture some of this "authenticity," at least for some groups of tourists (see chapter 4). It is hardly surprising, therefore, that these tourists seek to "repatriate" some aspects of this authenticity, although this inevitably further transforms what they have interpreted as the "authentic." This is evident in the growth of Spanish "*tapas*" cafes and Australian bars in Britain, or in the purchase of London Bridge for use as a tourist attraction in the USA. However, it is also present in the demand for lifestyles that accord more with idealized "authentic" rural life styles that have been observed on holidays to Tuscany or the Dordogne. This pervades home life and leisure activities in a variety of ways including household design (for example, "Tuscan" tiles) and attempts to recreate French or Italian country cooking in northern European homes. These cultural impacts also have reverberations through the life course for migration strategies (Williams and Hall 2000). For example, there is strong evidence that earlier tourism experiences influence international retirement migration decisions, such as the flows from the UK to France (Buller and Hoggart 1994) and Tuscany (King et al. 2000) which are informed by the search for a rural idyll that probably never existed. Tourism experiences also influence the flows of migrants – both working and retired – in search of the more relaxed lifestyles to be found in sunnier climates; for example, the Canadians moving to Florida or the Norwegians "wintering" in the Spanish *costas* (see Williams et al. 2000). All these different examples underline the ways in which tourism and leisure are intertwined, irrespective of whether or not this involves migration.

Production and Consumption: An Approach to Critical Issues

The previous discussion has highlighted not only the relations between tourism and leisure but also the need to situate these in context of wider social relationships. In part, this task requires that tourism geography bridges what has often been a significant distancing from the major debates in social science. In recent years, tourism geography has responded to the challenge of developing a more critical approach, and this is evident in the evolution of several distinctive approaches. In broad terms there has been a shift from largely inductive positivist (often behavioralist) or empiricist frameworks to approaches grounded in political economy or cultural interpretation. Despite this, tourism geography remains methodologically diverse, and research is often weakly rooted in theory. Box 1.1 sets out a brief summary of the salient characteristics of the three main approaches, but see also Hall and Page (1999) for a more detailed exposition of these.

Box 1.1   Approaches to tourism geography

Spatial models and behavioral research

Most positivist research has been inductive, aiming to generalize models of tourism structures and flows on the bases of detailed quantitative analyses. They focus on tourist travel, origin–destination flows, and the spatial structures of tourism destination areas (Pearce 1995). Evolutionary models have examined the development of tourism spaces through time, especially resorts, and the most widely known of these is Butler's (1980) resort life cycle model (see chapter 8). In recognition of the limitations of aggregate analyses of macrotourism flows and structures, tourism geographers have embraced behavioralism, aiming to understand the decision-making and (spatial) behavior of tourists. Thornton et al. (1997) provide an example of this approach and contrast the insights of data collected via questionnaires and time–space budgets.

The political economy of tourism

Political economy offers a more critical approach to tourism geography and broadly draws on structuralist theories. Britton (1991) set out a framework for this approach based on theories of capital accumulation, cultural capital and the representation of place. Much of the research in this field has been concerned with issues such as the commodification of culture and of place, and the particularities of tourism production and consumption in capitalist systems. Broad theories are usually explored through case studies which range from tourism dependency in less developed countries to urban and rural regeneration in developed economies (de Kadt 1979; Montanari and Williams 1995, Sindiga 1999). There has been particular interest in locating tourism in relation to the contested shift from Fordism to neo-Fordism, and this is explored in Ioannides and Debbage (1998).

Cultural interpretations

Tourism geographers have a longstanding interest in the notion of place, and in the way in which tourism is both shaped by and shapes places. In recent years, the experience of "seeing" or "the tourist gaze" (Urry 1990) has been influential; this assumes that the tourist gaze is constructed through signs and signifiers in the landscape, with tourists being collectors of such signs. Other approaches challenge the emphasis on the gaze and argue that tourism should be seen as an encounter between people, and between people and space (Crouch 1999). Moreover, their practises are embodied and tourism is experienced in multisensual ways. Cultural tourism geography also emphasizes that knowledge is fluid and incomplete; it shapes and is reshaped by practises which, in turn, inform our understanding of place (Crang 1999).

The approach adopted in this book is a study of critical issues in the production and consumption of tourism and leisure. We have already touched upon some of these aspects in the introduction and they are further elaborated in the first two parts. In terms of production there is a complex of industries involved in the supply of service and goods under distinctive conditions of temporality and spatiality (see chapter 5). The nature of production is distinctive in that the quality of labor at the point of service delivery is an essential part of the labor process. Tourism and leisure services (but not necessarily goods) also have to be delivered directly to consumers where they reside permanently, or temporarily, while on holiday. This poses particular requirements in terms of assembling the necessary labor force to fulfill this objective. Production is also distinctive in that tourism and leisure involve a high degree of self-provisioning. Partly in response to these conditions the industry tends to have a dualistic structure with large numbers of small, independently-owned firms operating alongside a few large transnational companies.

There are also distinctive features of the consumption of tourism. There is a degree of complimentarity/substitutability in the consumption of some tourism and leisure services; for example, cycling while in the home area or on holiday requires the same skills and experience, can use the same equipment, and may reinforce the motivation to cycle in the "other arena." In addition, the social construction of tourism and leisure is particularly well-developed and is linked to an exceptionally high level of market segmentation. Given that participation in tourism and leisure activities is conditioned by social structures as well as by life values, it is not surprising that both are highly segmented temporally and spatially. In other words, who you meet on a beach, at a dinner party, at a sports event, or at a night club is not random, because of the way participation is socially segmented. The social construction of tourism is, of course, continually evolving, and this can only be understood in context of changes in leisure. But the consumption of tourism is more than the end product of social structures and relationships, and of leisure practices, because it also contributes to the construction of lifestyles and to social differentiation.

The focus on production *and* consumption issues in this volume should not be taken to indicate that they can be considered as separate fields of inquiry, or that one is inevitably dominant in shaping tourism. This has been one of the central messages of the "cultural turn" in economic geography, namely that there is a need to examine their interplay (Gregson 1995). Consumers are not simply passive respondents or guilty fashion victims, rather they explore and experience sites of consumption (Jackson 1995). This is particularly apposite in tourism studies, where the cultural complexities of tourism experiences have been one challenge to the adoption of structuralist approaches. However, the cultural turn, with its focus on the inter-relationships between production and consumption provides exciting new challenges for tourism geography. This is recognised by Ateljevic (2000: 381) who has emphasized that we need to see tourism in terms of circuits:

> This approach, generally concerned with the broader analysis of culture, sees producers as "consumers" and consumers as "producers" who "feed off" each other in endless cycles. In this light the framework of tourism circuits has been forged in order to finally resolve an endless dilemma of whether tourism is driven by either production or consumption processes. More importantly, discussion revealed that geography lies at the heart of these processes, as tourism is inseparable from the spaces and places in which it is created, imagined, perceived and experienced.

While there is nothing new in the study of production and consumption features as such (for example, see Jansen-Verbeke and Dietvorst 1987), we believe that the first edition of this book did contribute to shaping approaches to the geography of leisure and tourism (discussed in Hall and Page 1999: 14). Drawing inspiration particularly from the work of Britton (1991) it sought to explore the particularities of the production and the consumption of tourism. Essentially, the second edition builds on this approach. As emphasized in the introduction, it remains committed to five main organizing principles: the need to consider tourism in context of leisure; the importance of building bridges to research in other social sciences; an emphasis on how circuits of production and consumption produce and reproduce particular types of tourism environments; adoption of a broad political economy framework; and a focus on the Developed Countries.

2

The International Dimension

Tourism and Globalization

The term globalization is widely used in tourism studies, suggesting somewhat imprecisely that there has been an intensification and a geographical widening of the linkages between places, leading to the internationalization of tourism and leisure "cultures," more global flows of tourists, and increased competition. In reality there are competing theories of globalization, and at least three main strands can be identified according to Held (2000: 3): globalism; traditionalism; and transformationalism.

- *Globalists* contend that massive economic, social, and political changes have eroded the power of the national state, ushering in the era of the "borderless world" (Ohmae 1990). This can be positively interpreted as a process that liberates tourism by removing constraints, or negatively as a process which makes more likely major environmental and other crises.
- *Traditionalists* argue that recent trends amount to no more than an intensification of long-established internationalization processes and that national states remain the leading regulators of economies where capital and economic activities remain mainly oriented to national markets. In the tourism context, this theory would argue that tourism activities have long reached the more distant parts of the globe even if the numbers involved are now at historically unprecedented levels. Moreover states – and in Europe, we would have to add, acting in association with the supra state of the European Union – remain the key regulators of tourism: through border controls, investments in infrastructure, or promotion activities.

- *Transformationalists* argue that globalization is creating new political, economic, and social conditions, which fundamentally transform the nature of states. They neither predict its demise nor its continuing supremacy but, rather, that "the social-spatial context of states is being altered and, along with it, the nature, form and operations of states" (Held 2000: 3).

These theoretical positions serve to remind us that globalization is a process to be explored rather than a simple mantra to be trotted out to explain the rapidly changing world of tourism and leisure. Despite this, there can be no doubt that there have been globalization processes in tourism, even if the full implications for the national state and the way lives are regulated remain highly contested. Cochrane and Pain (2000: 15–17) are helpful in this, arguing that globalization can be understood in terms of four main concepts:

- Stretched social relation. The existence of cultural, economic and political networks of connections across the world.
- Regionalization. Increased interconnection between states that border on each other.
- Intensification. Increased density of interaction across the globe which implies that the impacts of events are felt more strongly than before.
- Interpenetration. The extent to which apparently distant cultures and societies come face to face with each other at local level, creating increased diversity.

In addition, there is globalization of infrastructures, which is essential for the intensification of relationships: this may involve physical infrastructures such as satellites and cabling, the emergence of global markets, values and behavior which are deeply informed by the existence of relatively unrestricted markets, and bodies, such as the World Trade Organization, which seek to regulate these. Where does tourism fit into this picture? In many ways it is one of the most powerful exemplars of globalization, for the movement of people is fundamentally affected by the globalization of infrastructure: the ability to use the Internet for making bookings; the exponential growth in air transport; and the shift to free markets (notably in China and other East Asian countries in recent years) have all facilitated the growth of international tourism. Moreover, as we will demonstrate in the next chapter, these internationalization tendencies do merit the epithet globalization because they embody all four of the key features identified above: stretched social relations; regionalization; intensification; and interpenetration. Tourism relationships are increasing stretched across the world, as virtually the entire surface of the world (with minor exceptions such as North Korea) become tourist destinations. However, this occurs in parallel with most tourism flows remaining highly regionalized, that is in spatial proximity to a few major nodes of origin. There is also intensification as long-established trickles of visitors to even the most distant corners of the globe become transformed into large scale, even mass tourism flows: witness for example the experiences of Gambia, Thailand, or Bali. Finally, there is certainly interpenetration because one of the essential features of tourism is host–guest interactions (chapter 4), which potentially bring cultures face to face, even if the effects are moderated by the existence of tourism enclaves (chapter 8). But tourism is also affected by globalization in other ways. Not least, the globalization of the economy, which requires changes in business travel practises, that is in business tourism. The remainder of this chapter explores these various strands of globalization.

Tourism and Leisure: Internationalization and Globalization

There is strong evidence of globalization in tourism and leisure. This has been facilitated by the reduced length of the working week in most Developed Countries (World Tourism Organization 1983). This general tendency to uniformity is, of course, deceptive for as we have already noted in chapter 1, and investigate more fully in chapter 3, there are major differences in the distribution of leisure time between men and women, and among age cohorts and social classes. In addition, the commodification of leisure and tourism has facilitated the growth of mass leisure. Purchases of mass consumer goods, such as electronic sound and visual equipment, and PC- and Internet-based entertainment, facilitate the rapid global dispersal of new forms of leisure activities. This is reinforced by the role of the increasingly global media in the social construction of "desirable" life-styles.

The increased commodification of tourism services has to be seen in context of the expansion of world trade. Todaro's (1977: 271) comments on the implications of the internationalization of trade are relevant here: they have particular resonance for tourism, and apply to most of the Developed as well as the Developing Countries:

> international trade and finance must be understood in a much broader perspective than simply the inter-country flow of commodities and financial resources. By "opening" their economies and societies to world trade and commerce and by "looking outward" to the rest of the world, Third World countries invite not only the transfer of goods, services and

Table 2.1 *Domestic tourism: the share of all hotel and similar accommodation nights accounted for by domestic tourists*

	%
Austria	20.5
Denmark	50.3
France	69.0
Greece	22.3
Italy	61.7
Kenya	20.6
Morocco	17.7
Spain	33.4
Syria	52.6
Zaire	35.3

Source: World Tourism Organization (1989a: 61–3)

financial resources, but also the "developmental" or "anti-developmental" influences of the transfer of production technologies, consumption patterns, institutional and organisational arrangements, educational, health and social systems, and the more general values, ideals, and lifestyles of the developed nations of the world, both capitalist and socialist.

In this respect, tourism involves more than just the flows of people, or even economic transfers; it also implies transfers of consumption patterns, values, and lifestyles across international boundaries. In other words, it involves a high level of "interpenetration" (Cochrane and Pain 2000).

The internationalization of tourism is a process with long roots. It can be traced back to the earliest trading, to the pilgrimages of medieval times, and the Grand Tours of the aristocracy and the upper middle classes in the eighteenth and nineteenth centuries. However, mass international tourism is a product of the twentieth century, especially of the post-1945 period (see chapter 9), and in this sense there has been "intensification" (Cochrane and Pain 2000) as part of the process of globalization. In most countries, the vast majority of tourists are still domestic tourists but, as table 2.1 shows, there are several countries in which international tourists outnumber the domestic ones. These are mostly located in Western Europe, where international travel is facilitated by relatively high disposable incomes, political and social stability, and the relatively small geographical size of most states. More recent data for the European Union confirm the existence of two groups of Western European countries. First, there is a small group of countries where most of the national tourists take domestic holidays: these are the Southern European countries, France and (just) the UK. The highest proportion is recorded in Greece, where 89 percent of tourists went to domestic destinations in the late 1990s (TPR Associates 1999). In contrast, foreign holidays dominate the national markets of the other Western European countries, accounting for between 50 percent in Norway and 85 percent in Belgium. The Netherlands provides a good example of these internationalization trends (see box 2.1). Until comparatively recently, domestic tourism numbers exceeded outbound foreign tourism, but this has changed dramatically since, and the gulf between the two is predicted to increase further and sharply. While this provides strong testimony of "stretched social relations" and "interpenetration" (Cochrane and Pain 2000), the evidence of this particular study (Kroon 1995) places considerable emphasis on income growth and changes in social expectations as causes of these changes.

The growth of international tourism is striking. Whereas in 1948 there were only 14 million international tourists, in 1955 there were 46 million, in 1965 144 million, and in 1999 there were 664 million (World Tourism Organization 2000a). Such trends led Cosgrove and Jackson (1972: 42) to comment that "The pioneer fringe of international tourism ostentatiously flutters almost throughout the world." They were right then – and even more so in the 1990s – that there are very few regions, let alone countries, which have not been touched, in some way, by international tourism. However, this should not be taken to imply that global mass tourism has now arrived and that the populations of most countries are caught up in the whirl of international travel. Access to tourism remain socially filtered, even in the most prosperous of the Developed Countries.

International tourism is also characterized by distinctive spatial patterns. Mansfield (1990) provides an overview of spatial interaction within the "tourist space," and distinguishes between aggregated and disaggregated perspectives. The latter are subdivided into those that emphasize socio-demographic variables and behavioral segmentation. Here, we limit ourselves to some brief comments on the aggregate patterns (but see chapters 3 and 4 for a discussion of social and behavioral differences). Three main features can be noted: polarization, macroregionalization and European dominance. In a sense, these all bear testimony to the importance in tourism of what Cochrane and Pain (2000: 15) term "regionalization" as a central feature of globalization, namely "increased interconnection between states that border on each other."

- First, the international movements of tourists are highly *polarized*. Figure 2.1 shows the major international movements of visitors.

Box 2.1   The "internal" dynamics of tourism in the Netherlands

The Netherlands, in common with many other developed countries, has an S shaped tourism participation growth curve. At the time when statistics were first collected on a reliable and regular basis, the participation rate was 44 percent in 1969, before leveling off to some extent at around 70 percent in the early 1980s and then being predicted to grow more slowly to around 80 percent towards the middle of the twenty first century. There are, however, considerable differences between domestic and outbound foreign tourism. The numbers of domestic tourism trips have grown far more slowly and are even predicted to decline in the early decades of the twenty first century. In contrast, little change is anticipated in the absolute growth of outbound foreign tourism in the foreseeable future. These predictions are based on a number of assumptions but above all on what may be termed a number of "internal" factors, particularly income growth and the transformation of tourism from a luxury good to an "accepted" or more basic element of lifestyle and well being.

Source: Kroon (1995: 43–4)

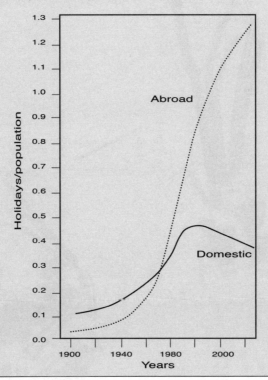

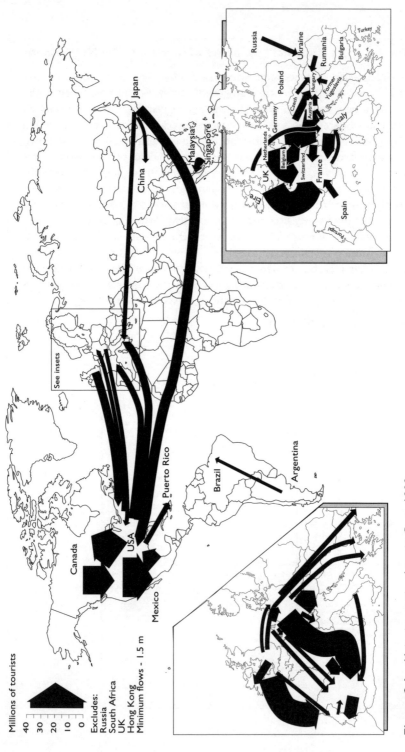

Figure 2.1 *Major international tourist flows, 1998*

Source: WTO (2000b)

These figures include international temporary labor migrants, business and holiday tourists, and are also based on two different types of sources: tourists at frontiers, and tourists in commercial accommodation. The national-level flows are not, therefore, strictly comparable, while additionally the UK is completely missing from the arrivals dataset. Despite these reservations, they provide a broad picture of the geographical pattern of international movement. As would be expected, the flows are primarily among the more developed countries (that is, intra- or inter-core; see also Jansen-Verbeke, 1995) or from these to less developed countries which offer relatively accessible holiday destinations (that is, core-periphery). Two of the three largest international flows are between the USA and Canada. There are also important trans-North Atlantic flows and large movements from Japan. There are parallels here with the notion that global trade and investment are dominated by the triad (Dicken 1998): Europe (centred on the EU), North America (the USA) and East Asia (Japan).

- Second, most international movements are *macro-regionalized* and are especially concentrated within Europe. There were two separate systems within Europe before 1989, centred on Western and Eastern Europe, but this has been modified to some extent by the collapse of state socialism in Eastern Europe (Williams and Balaz 2000a). Cartographic limitations mean that only the largest flows are shown on this map, and several other sub-systems of international movements are not so apparent. These include Japan and East Asia, the USA and the Caribbean, South Africa and southern Africa, and Europe and North Africa. For example, the relatively modest tourism flows into the Caribbean are highly dominated by the USA; it accounts for more than half the tourists in most of the Caribbean islands, while in the Bahamas this reaches 90 percent.
- Third, the *overall dominance of Europe continues but is in relative decline* (table 2.2a). International tourism expanded rapidly in Europe in the 1960s but its world share peaked in the early 1970s at 75 percent. Subsequently, this share had fallen back to 59 percent in 1999. The share of the Americas (especially the USA) has also fallen back, from 30 percent in 1950 to 18 percent in 1999, although it has been relatively stable since the 1970s. In contrast, there has been steady growth in tourism arrivals in Africa and spectacular growth in Asia/Pacific, although somewhat set back by the 1998 economic crisis in the region. This is underlined by the percentage change data for the 1980s and 1990s (table 2.2b). Africa and Asia have had far higher growth rates than the other world regions. In part, this reflects the "discovery" of these regions by the tour companies and tourists in the Developed Countries in the Northern

Table 2.2 *International tourism: global macro-regions*
(a)   Tourism arrivals by region – percentage distribution

	1950	1971	1989	1999
Europe	66	75	62	59
Americas	30	19	20	18
Africa	2	1	4	4
Asia/Pacific	1	3 ⎤	15	16
Middle East	1	2 ⎦		3

(b)   Tourism growth rates, 1980–89, 1990–99

	Total percentage change	
	1980–9	1990–9
Africa	+81.4	+79.3
Americas	+48.4	+79.3
Asia/Pacific	+102.4	+78.0
Europe	+28.8	+39.4
World	+41.7	+45.3

Sources: (a) World Tourism Organization, various reports and website (b) World Tourism Organization (1990: 11–12) and website.

hemisphere. However, it also reflects rising real incomes in some of the newly industrializing countries of Asia, and more especially Japan and Korea. In 1998, for example, there were 1.6 million Japanese tourists to China and 341,900 to Thailand, which also attracted 3 million tourists from both Singapore and Malaysia. Japanese tourism has been fueled by rising living standards, appreciation of the yen, and government promotion of foreign tourism as a gesture towards reduction of the balance of payments surplus. The scale of outbound tourism from Japan was depressed to some extent by the difficulties of the Japanese economy in the 1990s, but still continues to be significant on the world level. The overall stability in tourism flows is demonstrated by the rank order of the leading destination countries in 1999, and their respective positions in 1980 (figure 2.2). The top four ranked countries are the same at both dates and most of the other changes are relatively minor, with a few exceptions such as China and Russia that have opened to international markets in the intervening years. At present the East Asian countries still lag behind Europe and North America as sources

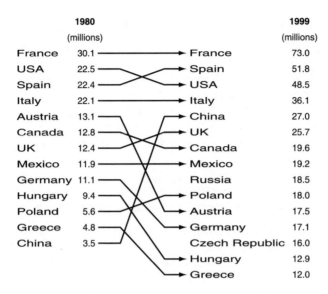

1980		1999
(millions)		(millions)
France	30.1	France	73.0
USA	22.5	Spain	51.8
Spain	22.4	USA	48.5
Italy	22.1	Italy	36.1
Austria	13.1	China	27.0
Canada	12.8	UK	25.7
UK	12.4	Canada	19.6
Mexico	11.9	Mexico	19.2
Germany	11.1	Russia	18.5
Hungary	9.4	Poland	18.0
Poland	5.6	Austria	17.5
Greece	4.8	Germany	17.1
China	3.5	Czech Republic	16.0
		Hungary	12.9
		Greece	12.0

Figure 2.2   *Rank order of leading tourism destinations, 1980–99*
Source: WTO (2000b) (note no equivalent data for Russia or Czech Republic in 1980)

of outbound tourism, but there is evidence that economic, socio-
demographic, price and regulatory changes are contributing to a
"catching up" process (box 2.2).

The Globalization of Business and Business Tourism

While most tourism is a form of leisure, it does have other important
functions such as visits to friends and relatives, as well as educational
or religious trips (see chapter 1). Tourism is also an adjunct to business relationships. If tourism is defined in terms of overnight stays,
then international business tourism has existed since the first emergence of international trading. Moreover, the more recent growth of
business tourism has paralleled the globalization of the world economy.
According to Palloix (1975), the internationalization of the world
economy has involved a historical sequence of distinctive forms of
mobility: from commodity capital (trade), to money capital (investment), through to productive capital (foreign direct investment as part
of a global strategy by multinationals). Each stage has generated new
forms and levels of international tourism. Trade required travel abroad
to buy, sell, and distribute products; portfolio investment required

---

Box 2.2   Demand determinants of East Asian tourism

- Aging populations with significant elements with discretionary income and leisure time.
- Rapid urbanization leading to a demand for more holidays to "escape" the pressures and pollution associated with urban life.
- Growth of a middle class with paid holidays and disposable income.
- Increased business travel reflecting the changing role of the "Pacific Rim" in the global economy, and the shifts within these economies to the service sector.
- Reduced real costs of mobility and exchange rate movements (with both positive and negative effects).
- Reduced controls on inbound and outbound international travel.

Although leisure time has increased significantly, this is still far lower than in Europe and North America. Whereas workers in Seoul and Bangkok had less than 10 days holiday on average in the early 1990s, 20–30 days holiday was common in major cities in the EU.

Source: Go (1997: 10–14)

---

travel for financial management purposes; and foreign direct investment demanded foreign travel to coordinate intra-company organization. International sub-contracting also generates foreign travel as part of the management of extended systems of production. However, this is put in perspective by data on the US which show that national business tourism in that country is overwhelmingly domestic.

In the late twentieth century, international business tourism has become a sophisticated industry. There are three constituent elements: incentive travel, conference tourism, and business travel. Their economic importance is underlined by two considerations. First, the per capita spending power of the business tourist is considerably higher than that of the leisure tourist, and the ratio between these has been estimated to be as high as three to one (Lawson 1982). Second, the sheer volume of international business tourism has reached an impressive level, with the World Tourism Organization (2000a) estimating that this now accounts for 18 percent of all international tourism.

Unfortunately, comprehensive statistics on business tourism are not available, although the World Tourism Organization collation of travel data provides information for some countries on the basis of tourist motivations in the late 1980s (figure 2.3). There is considerable variation in the importance of business tourism. Some countries in both the semi-periphery (Portugal) and the periphery (Seychelles) have

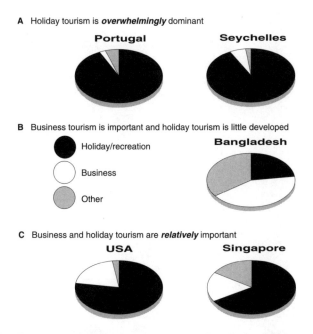

A Holiday tourism is *overwhelmingly* dominant

Portugal   **Seychelles**

B Business tourism is important and holiday tourism is little developed

Holiday/recreation   **Bangladesh**

Business

Other

C Business and holiday tourism are *relatively* important

USA   **Singapore**

Figure 2.3 *Tourist motivations: selected international examples, 1980s*

well-developed holiday tourism industries which account for more than 90 percent of international tourism. In the case of Portugal this makes a large absolute level of international business arrivals seem relatively unimportant. There are also some third world countries (such as Bangladesh) with very limited holiday tourism; as a result, even modest levels of business tourism become important in relative terms. Finally, there are countries in the Developed World (the USA) and among the Newly Industrializing Countries (Singapore) where both business and holiday tourism are relatively important.

Among the three main types of international business tourism, *incentive travel* is probably the least important and the least researched. Incentive travel is an employment perk used to reward or motivate employees. It is used by such diverse organizations as major sporting clubs, and large business corporations as well as magazines (which use holiday prize draws to boost their circulation). Above all, it relies on the socially-constructed nature of tourism and on the powers of the image-creating industry (Morgan and Pritchard 1998). The destinations may be relatively prosaic, perhaps a weekend on the golf courses of the Algarve or the beaches of Majorca for exhausted footballers or executives. Alternatively, it may involve "an individually tailored

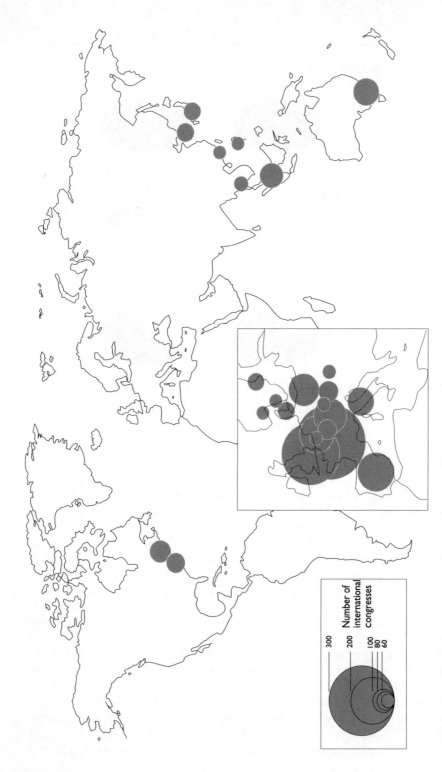

Figure 2.4 *World cities and international conferences, 1988*

fantasy which cannot be bought in an ordinary package" (*Financial Times* 2 September 1986). There is often an important gender dimension to these fantasy packages. They may be designed for the mostly female spouses of a largely male group of executives and represent a symbolic exchange for long hours spent at work and away from families. Whether the package is prosaic or fantastic, it is of considerable importance in economic terms. It has been estimated that one-third of the UK's top companies use tourism as a perk, and that the UK incentive travel industry was valued at £400 million, and that of the USA at over $2 billion even in the late 1980s (Smith 1990). Moreover, 80 percent of these incentive packages involve trips within Europe, so that their geographical distribution, as with tourism in general, is largely intra-core.

Conference tourism represents big business at both the national (see chapter 10) and international scales; the North American market alone was valued at around $45 billion in the late 1980s (Smith 1990).

> The Austrians like to claim that modern, organised conferences began with the Congress of Vienna in 1815, an influential affair which, like modern conventions, had a substantial social programme in addition to its working sessions. Perhaps it is more accurate though to look to the USA for the development of the modern convention industry. In North America, attending meetings has become something of a way of life. (Smith 1989: 61)

By the early 1980s, there were an estimated 14,000 international conferences (Law 1985a). These also have an overwhelmingly inter- and intra-core spatial distribution. Within Europe, the primary international conference centres are Paris, London, Madrid, Geneva, and Brussels (figure 2.4). Outside Europe the main venues are Sydney, Singapore, Washington, and New York. International conferences vary in size from brief meetings of a handful of individuals in an informal setting, to major assemblages of delegates and associated commercial exhibitors in large purpose-built conference centres. One of the largest international conferences ever held was the International Rotary meeting at the NEC centre in Birmingham, attended by 23,000 delegates. This is a highly competitive market and the competition is becoming more intense. Smith (1990: 211) writes:

> The last 20 years have seen considerable changes in the meetings industry, in itself a new phrase. . . . Now every sizeable town in the world sees itself as a meeting place, promotes its facilities for conferences and seminars, pays at least a little attention to the search for friends among meeting planners, welcomes their delegates, provides overt and covert inducements which can range from a free deckchair to a no-charge convention centre for 1,000 people for a week.

While there is a strong element of regionalization in the international conference market, this coexists with a growing tendency to globalization. For example, the American Law Association has held its conference in London, and there are increasing numbers of truly world conferences, such as the Rio "Earth Summit." In some market segments, therefore, Birmingham is in competition not only with Brussels and Barcelona, but also with Baltimore, Bangkok, and Bali. The requirements for success as an international conference centre are demanding: a high degree of accessibility, especially in terms of air travel; modern, well-equipped conference facilities; a large stock of high-quality accommodation; and an attractive tourism image which will attract not only the delegates but also their "accompanying persons."

International *business travel* has expanded considerably in recent years as a result of the globalization of the world economy. In 1989 the world business travel market had an estimated value in excess of \$320 billion (Petersen and Belchambers 1990). Its geographical distribution closely resembles that for trade in goods and services and therefore accords strongly with the core-periphery model of economic development. The most important elements are: macro-regionalization within the cores of the Americas and Europe, global linkages between the cores, and core-adjacent periphery movements. In addition, international business tourism is predicated by the internal organization of transnational companies themselves.

Transnational companies are involved in a global search to maintain capital accumulation. They seek out new international locations which offer access to markets, advantageous production costs, or the opportunity to secure strategic advantages over other transnationals. Given changes in technology and factor costs, large companies increasingly have tended to spread their operations across international boundaries. This often involves the spatial separation of different stages of production: in extreme form, headquarters are located in one continent, while production and regional management are located in others. Hymer (1975) is most closely associated with the conceptualization of this model (figure 2.5). The model has been criticized for ignoring the possible existence of production in all zones, and for the location of lower level management in the major metropolitan centre. However, if this fuller model is taken into account, then it can provide a simple framework for understanding the geographical distribution of international business travel. Not least, this new international division of labor is predicated on "enabling technologies" (Dicken 1986), which provide a "permissive environment" (Knox and Agnew 1989: 92) for decentralization while maintaining central coordination. The main "enabling technologies" are technological developments in transport and communications, and developments in company organizational methods.

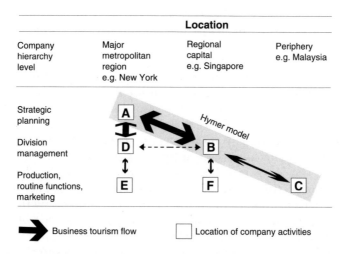

Figure 2.5 *The business tourism potential of the spatial organization of transnational companies*

Source: adapted from Hymer (1975)

The role of business travel in this model of spatial organization is somewhat ambivalent. Improved international travel was a precondition for the development of more sophisticated international divisions of labor. However, improvements in information technology (video-conferencing, faxes, satellite link-ups etc) are challenging the need for travel between company branches. This tendency does exist but, at the same time, there continues to be a need for face-to-face contacts. This can be understood in terms of the hierarchy of contacts in the structure of businesses (Goddard 1973). At the highest levels of company management, there is a need for a high intensity of face-to-face contacts in the process of strategic decision making. As you descend through management hierarchies, and as decision-making becomes more routine, the requirement for face-to-face contact diminishes. This is one of the principal reasons for the spatial concentration of company headquarters within national economic spaces, in metropoli such as New York, Tokyo, Milan, and Paris.

An important element of international business tourism involves the linking together of global headquarters cities. Indeed, Dicken (1986: 193) writes that the corporate headquarters of the global company "requires, above all, a strategic location on the global transport and communications network in order to keep in touch with its far flung empire." Regional headquarters have "to be accessible both to their corporate headquarters and also to the affiliates under their immediate control." Therefore, while some of the more routine international business travel may be replaced by new forms of information technology in the near future, business tourism is likely to become even more important as transnationals continue to extend their global reach.

In summary, business tourism strongly reflects the globalization of the world economy. The four defining features identified by Cochrane and Pain (2000) are strongly evident in the different forms of tourism but especially in the business travel associated with inter- and intra-firm business operations. There is the stretching of social relationships across space as economic transactions are globalized, for interpersonal relationships remain important in business practices. There is region-alization of business travel and conferences, directly reflecting the macro-regional structuring of the world economy around the triad. There is intensification as the result of the continuing growth of inter-national investment and trade at rates that far exceed that of produc-tion. And there is interpenetration as business travel brings diverse business cultures into contact. Moreover, these direct effects are mag-nified by the increasingly complex and multipurpose objectives of tourist trips, for the business traveler – and his or her accompanying persons in some instances – may also participate in leisure and other forms of tourism. This has particular implications for tourism as an agent of interpenetration.

Tourism and the Less Developed Countries

The Less Developed Countries are in process of being incorporated into the world economy, both as a consequence and a cause of global-ization. This is an uneven and contingent process and it does not nec-essarily follow a set sequence. Nevertheless, it is useful to conceptualize these economies as lying along a continuum, for which Hall (1986) pro-vides a working typology (table 2.3). There are four stages of incorpo-ration: none, weak, moderate, and strong. These stages are defined in terms of market articulation, the impact of the core on the periphery, and the impact of the periphery on the core. The form and level of tourism development in a third world country is partly dependent on the stage of incorporation because it requires certain infrastructures, social relationships and contacts with the potential countries of tourism origin. However, tourism is more than a "camp follower" in the process of development, for it also contributes to incorporation and, as noted earlier in this chapter, can even be the lead sector in this process.

In most respects, Hall's typology could be used to model the role of tourism incorporation. The greater the incorporation, then the greater the market articulation, and the greater the impact of the core on the periphery. This broadly accords with models of tourism development

Table 2.3   *The continuum of geographical incorporation*

| | The continuum of incorporation | | | |
	None	*Weak*	*Moderate*	*Strong*
Type of periphery	External arena	Contact periphery	Marginal periphery	Dependent periphery
Market articulation	None	Weak	Moderate	Strong
Impact of core on periphery	None	Strong	Stronger	Strongest
Impact of periphery on core	None	Low	Moderate	Significant

Source: Hall (1986: 392)

in the Third World. The main difference is that, with tourism, the impact of the periphery on the core remains limited even when there is strong incorporation of its tourism economy. This is because tourism flows – unlike those of industrial trade – remain highly asymmetrical; that is, from the developed countries to the less developed countries. However, at the same time, the fact that tourism moves people rather than goods between the First and the Third Worlds means that "There is no other international trading activity which involves such critical interplay among economic, political, environmental, and social elements as tourism" (Lea 1988: 2). Tourism is therefore one of the key processes of globalization which impact on the Less Developed Countries. This is evident in the extension of social relations across boundaries, macro-regionalization (as noted earlier in this chapter, in regards to what are in effect core-periphery relations between Japan, the USA and the EU and their adjoining regions), intensification with the growth of large volume tourism to the Third World, and interpenetration, especially evident in host–guest relationships.

In keeping with the overall focus of this book on the Developed Countries, this section provides only a brief overview of some of the critical issues in Third World tourism, although most of these themes will be developed in greater detail elsewhere in the text. Five major issues are considered here:

1. International tourism is characterized by asymmetrical power relationships, which are dominated by the more developed countries. This is symbolized by the nature of the unequal exchange which takes place: tourists from the Developed Countries demand high levels of services at prices below those which they are willing to

pay in their home countries. These are provided by indigenous labor sometimes working for indigenous enterprises but sometimes for multinational companies, often in local labor markets characterized by high unemployment, so that the latter are doubly disadvantaged in terms of unequal power relationships. Moreover, the national governments in the destination countries may prioritize the tourism sector as a means of generating "hard" (that is, convertible) foreign exchange (chapter 5), given the lack of alternative means of generating this in international markets. Therefore, they may be reluctant to intervene in the functioning of the system, and the levels of wages paid to tourism workers and the prices paid to sub-contractor firms. The increased competition inherent in globalization reinforces these tendencies.

2. The relationships between Third World countries and the tourists in the Developed World are mediated by intermediaries such as travel agencies, tour companies and airlines. Even more so than in the case of the semi-peripheral economies, such as Tunisia or Mexico, the Less Developed Countries lack the means of excluding the intermediaries from these relationships. This is partly related to their colonial backgrounds and the historic underdevelopment of indigenous capital. The result is not only structural dependence on external decision making but also a high level of income leakage. For example, it is estimated that in Gambia only 10 percent of gross earnings from tourism are retained by the local population (Cater 1987). This is reinforced by the enclave nature of many tourism developments, which limits the spatial and social dispersion of expenditure.

3. Tourism brings both positive and negative economic benefits to an economy (table 2.4). These centre on a number of relationships: its effects on other economic sectors (whether it stimulates or distorts these); the demand for and development of facilities and infrastructures which will affect the local populace (generating greater use of these, or overburdening their capacities); foreign exchange earnings (the net effect of leakage from total spending); GDP (growth versus external dependency); employment (dependent on the skills, wages, and temporality of jobs); and net government revenue (the balance between additional costs and revenues). Globalization theories remind us that these advantages and disadvantages have to be viewed in context of interdependencies between the core and the peripheral economies, or the host and destination tourism countries.

4. International tourism also has pronounced social and cultural effects. These are particularly pronounced because of the nature of tourism consumption: tourism experiences have to be enjoyed

Table 2.4 *The economic, social, and cultural impacts of international tourism*

Positive	Negative
Economic	
Agricultural stimulus	Distention of agricultural production
Create new markets for their products in the developed countries	Decline of certain products not in international demand
Stimulus to fishing	Decline of traditional fishing ports and beaches
Stimulus to manufacturing	Manufactured goods/imported
Creation of new tourism attractions such as beaches or swimming pools, which can be used by locals	Over-use of existing attractions
Funds new infrastructure: water, roads, power, and telephones	Saturates existing infrastructure
Earns foreign exchange	Leakage of foreign exchange income to intermediaries, and to imports
Increases government revenues from taxation	Increases government expenditure
Creates employment	In-migrants hold many key management jobs; seasonal nature of employment
Offers jobs requiring little training or previous skills	Condemns labor force to low-skilled jobs
External source of growth	Dependence
Social	
Modernization of society	Polarization of social structure and increases income inequalities
Modernization of the family, via new gender and intergenerational relationships	Disintegration of the family
Broadens social horizons and reduces prejudices among tourists	Social pathology, including prostitution, drugs use etc.
Cultural	
Development of indigenous culture	Disappearance of indigenous culture under the impact of commercialization
Greater protection of the natural environment	Destruction of the natural environment
Improves landscapes and architectural standards	Destroys landscapes and leads to non-integrated tourism complexes
Contributes to conservation of monuments and buildings	Degradation of monuments and buildings
Positive demonstration effects	Negative demonstration effects

Source: Elaboration on a classification developed in World Tourism Organization (1981: 9–13)

in situ and can not be deferred, so they necessarily involve a degree of host–guest interaction, whether this be with the indigenous population or in-migrant labor. The social effects centre on the contribution of tourism to the modernization of society, contradictions, and tensions in the family, and in gender and inter-generational relationships, a broadening of social horizons, and increased potential for social pathology. The cultural effects centre on interactions between the indigenous and the visitors' cultures, although we should note that host communities are only exposed to some aspects of the latter. Moreover, tourists' behavior may be significantly modified in tourism environments compared to when they are at home. The cultural effects of these host–guest interactions are evident in attitudes to the natural environment, the conservation of landscapes, the architectural influences on the built environment, and the demonstration effects on consumption and behavior.

5.   Tourism, given that it involves *in situ* experiences, also necessarily has impacts on the environment in the destinations. These are of course dependent on the scale and the form of tourism, and are very different for mass tourism organized around small enclaves compared to ecotourism which disperses small but significant numbers of tourists across a large geographical area. Again these impacts have to be seen in context of globalization and especially of interdependency, as places become increasingly linked by decisions taken elsewhere in the world, while the local also contributes to shaping the global. The environmental impacts of tourism in Thailand may be partly determined by decisions taken in the countries of tourism origin, but these impacts in turn shape the tourism industries and tourists in these countries.

The assessment of the economic, social, and cultural effects listed above has been left open-ended at this stage because of the difficulty of generalizing about the impact of tourism. This, in turn, is related to the multilinear nature of tourism (Cohen 1979b). Tourism can have organic growth rooted in an indigenous economy and society or it can be externally driven. This, together with variations in the volume, organization, and social character of the tourism inflows as well as the economic, social, and cultural character of the recipient areas, means that the impacts of tourism in the Less Developed Countries are highly contingent.

Finally, it can be observed that there has been a tendency within the tourism literature to treat tourism as a unique force for economic, social, and cultural change. While there are some unique features of tourism as an agent of change, de Kadt's (1979: 12) dictum that "tourism is not a unique devil" is worthy of note. There is a need to assess the opportunity costs of tourism, both in the sense of the diversion of resources from other sectors, and in the sense of evaluating what other economic strategies are open to a particular country or region. In the latter context, the "green revolution" in agriculture and rapid industrialization – even if achievable – have their own well-cataloged mixtures of positive and negative economic, social, and cultural impacts, which also require careful consideration (for example, see Knox and Agnew 1998). Therefore, while we advocate the need for stronger theorization of the critical issues in tourism, this needs to be linked to detailed empirical studies to tease out the complexities of consumption and production. In other words, globalization and other theories provide a framework for our studies of tourism rather than simple explanatory models to be applied in all or any circumstances.

Part II

Access to Tourism Consumption

3

Social Access to Tourism and Leisure

Socio-economic Change and Leisure Development

The links between levels of socioeconomic development and the growth in demand for tourism and leisure are relatively easy to describe in a general historical context, but more difficult to analyze in any detail. Most perspectives have focused on stage-type models, such as that by Maslow (1954) based on changing societal needs, to discuss increases in leisure demand. In this context, attention has been focused on using "lifestyle economics" (Mitchell 1983; Earl 1986), through the construction of "values and lifestyles" (VALS) typologies, to study changes in consumption. The original VALS typology, developed in North America (Mitchell 1983; Cooper et al. 1998), consists of nine types arranged hierarchically, as shown in figure 3.1 and table 3.1. However, for our purposes we need only be concerned with the broad categories; need driven; outer- and inner-directed; and integrated.

This model can be used in two basic ways; to explore the nature of demand in any particular society, or as a framework to examine broad changes over time. Within a developed, high-level economy, it is considered that there will be a hierarchy of VALS types and that these will range from need-driven individuals, concerned mainly with satisfying food and shelter needs, through to outer- and inner-directed individuals, while at the top of the system are the integrated types. In general terms, outer-directed individuals are mainly motivated by the search for esteem and status, as they are materialistic in nature. Those categorized as inner-directed are motivated by the desire for stimulating experiences, having little interest in displays of status. The bulk of people in Western societies tend to fall into the outer- and inner-directed groups. In the USA, for example, it has been estimated that

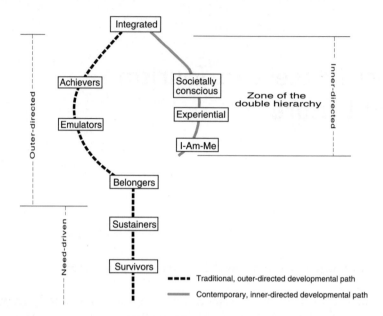

Figure 3.1   *The value and lifestyle hierarchy*

around 87 percent of the population fall within these two categories (Hartmann and Hennig 1989). Similarly, studies in the UK by MacNulty (1985) have examined such VALS types in terms of socio-economic groups. It was found that the needs-driven category is comprised mainly of groups of unskilled and skilled manual workers, together with the unemployed, while outer- and inner-directed covered those employed within professional, managerial, and clerical activities, with a small number of skilled manual workers. In general terms, it is the inner-directed types that are growing most rapidly in British society, accounting for an estimated 38 percent of the population in 1989, compared with 34 percent outer-directed and 28 percent needs-driven (MacNulty 1985).

In many developed western societies the inner-directed types, whom MacNulty terms "skilled consumers," have emerged relatively recently – in Britain, for example, from the 1960s onwards. The VALS model has been used in an evolutionary context in tracing the development of these different groups and their relationships with leisure patterns.

Gratton (1990) has provided a wide-ranging review of the model's usefulness in understanding tourism and leisure trends in Britain, while Hartmann and Hennig (1989) have applied it more specifically to outdoor recreation in the USA. In terms of the British case, it is

Table 3.1 *General characteristics of VALS groups*

A   *Need-driven groups*
- *Survivor lifestyle* – the most disadvantaged groups, who are removed from the mainstream of society.
- *Sustainer lifestyle* – a group who are struggling, but hopeful that circumstances will change

C   *Inner-directed groups*
- *I-am-me lifestyle* – very young, impulsive and confused, and fiercely individual
- *Experiential lifestyle* – youthful, seeking experience, orientated to inner growth, artistic
- *Societally conscious lifestyle* – a mission-orientated group, adopting environmental concerns. They are mature and successful
- *Self-directed lifestyle* – a group who see emotional rewards as important. They are not motivated by external views of them or by materialistic rewards

B   *Outer-directed groups*
- *Belongers lifestyle* – a conservative, comfortable and conventional group
- *Emulator lifestyle* – status conscious, competitive, ambitious, and often young
- *Achiever lifestyle* – middle-aged, prosperous and self-assured, the leaders of society

D   *Integrated: Combined outer- and inner-directed groups*

- *Integrated lifestyle* – this lifestyle group are mature, self-assured, and aware

Source: modified from Shih (1986) & Cooper et al. (1993)

possible to postulate the growth of these consumer groups over a period of 200 years. The broad changes in access to tourism and leisure in Britain, together with the estimated trends among consumers, are shown in figure 3.2. Before 1870–80 the outer-directed group represented an extremely small proportion of the population. During this period the group comprised the new industrial middle classes, together with the established aristocracy. Their access to leisure was very much routed towards the newly developing seaside resorts and, when the European political scene permitted, the wealthier still went on the "Grand Tour." Generally, they were concerned with using their access to leisure as a means of displaying their status, together with an element of conspicuous consumption (Gratton 1990). These trends in the

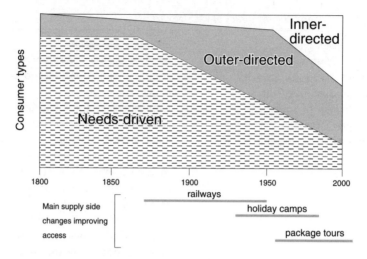

Figure 3.2 *Changes in consumer types and access to tourism in the UK, 1800–2000*

materialistic nature of leisure consumption intensified for a larger and more diverse range of people throughout the late nineteenth century and during the first part of the twentieth century (figure 3.2). By the early 1950s small numbers of inner-directed consumers could be identified, whose access to leisure was similar to the larger outer-directed group, but whose consumption patterns were very different. These individuals started to look for new holiday experiences, and by the 1970s activity and cultural holidays had become very important to them. As MacNulty (1985) and Gratton (1990) argue, these leisure activities require greater consumer skills than those characteristic of the outer-directed group. Krippendorf (1986) has termed these people "critical consumer tourists" who have a new consciousness of holiday travel and are more critical in their demand for tourist experiences.

In Britain, during the period after 1870, increased access to leisure and tourism was provided by improvements in overall real income, the growth of paid holidays for workers, and the provision of cheaper travel to seaside resorts by rail (Walvin 1978). Under such changes, a good many people moved from the needs-driven group into the outer-directed one, as the process of leisure access was achieved through the filtering down of activities from the controlling middle classes. Such access was also brought about by key institutional changes in the supply of holidays. Probably the two most important of these were the development during the 1930s of holiday camps (Burkhart and Medlik 1981), and the later introduction of overseas package holidays (see chapter 9).

The influence of the latter may be seen in the changing proportion of UK residents holidaying abroad, which increased from just 3.3 percent in 1947 to 30 percent 40 years later (Seaton 1992). In the late 1990s information from the UK *Family Expenditure Survey* (1999: 102) shows that "14% of all households recorded expenditure on package holidays abroad." Gratton (1990) argues that particular foreign destinations became a new source of conspicuous consumption for the more wealthy outer-directed consumers, that is, until some destinations became over-crowded, and the leading members of this consumer group then moved to newer, more distant locations.

New Forms of Tourism Consumption

There are other perspectives on the nature of socioeconomic change and tourism demand, and particularly important are those relating to the sociology of consumption (Urry 1990, 1992, 1995). Urry (1995: 129) sought to outline a sociology of consumption "concerned with the differential purchase, use and symbolic significance of mate-rial objects"; but more especially he was interested in the consumption of tourism – a significant feature of which is the ability to buy time and replace work with leisure activities. One over-arching framework for organizing these ideas can be found in the discussions of the shift from modernism to postmodernism and from Fordist to post-Fordist forms of production and consumption (for a discussion in a tourism context see Mowforth and Munt 1998; Ryan 1997; Sharpley 1994). Within the context of tourism, these shifts involve a move away from mass tourism through to post-Fordist forms of consumption, characterized by an emphasis on greater choice and plurality (table 3.2).

There are a number of different but overlapping strands in under-standing the importance of such shifts for tourism. Urry (1995) iden-tified two of these research strands, namely tourism consumption and societal change, and place and tourism consumption.

Post-Fordist forms of tourism consumption emphasize contrasting patterns which centre on enhanced tourist choice and the growth of new forms of tourism as suggested in table 3.2 (Featherstone 1991; Munt 1994; Urry 1995). Urry (1995: 148) argues that disorganized capital increasingly involves the dissolving of "tourism's specificity," when tourism as a form of consumption "starts to take over and organ-ise much contemporary social and cultural experience." The extension of this perspective Urry (1995: 148) has termed the "end of tourism" in that people become in essence tourists much of the time, "whether they are literally mobile or only experience simulated mobility." Of course, these changes are complex and difficult to disentangle, as well

Table 3.2   *The shift to post-Fordist consumption*

Post-Fordist consumption	Tourist examples
Consumers increasingly dominant and producers have to be much more consumer-oriented	Rejection of certain forms of mass tourism (holiday camps and cheaper packaged holidays) and increased diversity of preferences.
Greater volatility of consumer preferences	Fewer repeat visits and the proliferation of alternative sights and attractions.
Increased market segmentation	The multiplication of types of holiday and visitor attractions based on lifestyle research.
The growth of a consumers' movement	Much more information provided about alternative holidays and attractions through the media.
The development of many new products each of which has a shorter life	The rapid turnover of tourist sites and experiences because of rapid changes of fashion.
Increased preferences expressed for non-mass forms of production/ consumption	The growth of "green tourism" and of forms of refreshment and accommodation that are individually tailored to the consumer (such as country house hotels).
Consumption as less and less "functional" and increasingly aestheticized	The "de-differentiation" of tourism from leisure, culture, retailing, education, sport, hobbies.

Source: Urry (1995: 151)

as being of a relative nature. In this sense, the framework outlined in table 3.2 tells only of general trends and gives us little understanding about different types of tourism consumption. For example, while there is growing evidence in postmodern societies, such as the USA and the UK, that the edges of tourism and other forms of consumption are becoming increasingly blurred (Falk and Campbell, 1997; Gabriel and Lang 1995; Lury 1996), many other commentators have pointed to the persistence of "older" or Fordist forms. Sharpley (1994: 245) for example, has argued that recent experience in the UK, "demonstrates that the original Fordist-type basis of the package holiday remains as popular as ever." Morgan and Pritchard (1998) go further and, using the work of Roberts (1997), attempt to demonstrate that postmodern forms of consumption are not that clearly defined even in such areas as the youth market. They argue that differences in consumption are still linked with traditional predictor variables – social, ethnic, and gender groups. This is questionable, and while it may be difficult to uncover the detailed nature of post-Fordist consumption patterns, tourism and leisure are arguably defining shapers of our society, especially in the way space is constructed and used (Featherstone and Lash, 1999).

As we have shown, the nature of shifts in tourism consumption are complex and contested. Indeed, it is easier to examine the new geographies of tourism consumption than explore the detailed aspects of tourist demand that have produced them. The literature (Richards 1996; Sharpley 1994; Urry 1995) has identified a number of key changes associated with heritage tourism, new spaces of consumption linked to theme parks and shopping malls, and tourism based around environmental issues. It is the latter that has received greatest attention, with a number of authors recognizing new forms of tourism consumption (for example, Holden 2000). Krippendorf (1986) identified so-called "critical consumer tourists" who were leading the demand for environmentally sound holidays. Similarly, Gordon (1991) argued that many of these tourists came from the "inner-directed" lifestyle group, as identified earlier in this chapter. For these people, leisure pursuits are strongly motivated by: creativity, health, new experiences, human relations, and personal growth. As a consequence, environmental issues become an area of considerable importance and Gordon (1991: 10) believes "it is their growth. . . . Which has helped to ensure that business and politicians treat the environment as a matter of genuine concern" (see chapter 12). In a broad ranging perspective, Poon (1993) conceptualized these interests and forms of behavior as the "new tourist." Others (Cleverdon 1999; MacKay 1994) have taken more specific characteristics and identified "ecotourists," while Swarbrooke and Horner (1999) have suggested that there are different categories of "green tourists." In this instance, attitudes and commitment to environmental issues are conditioned by a whole range of lifestyle variables. For many other commentators examining the "new tourists," many of these forms of consumption are expressions of the new middle classes and their struggle for cultural acendancy (Mowforth and Munt 1998; Stauth and Turner 1988).

It seems evident that new forms of tourism consumption are being recognized and examined through a number of different lenses. As a consequence, definitions and the identification of clear trends are problematic, leading Mowforth and Munt (1998: 102) to claim that "there is no clear agreement on . . . definitions and conceptual and practical boundaries."

Despite such difficulties, some empirical studies have been attempted, with Wearing and Neil (1999) suggesting that ecotourists in the USA are characterized by higher than average incomes and levels of education. Similarly, work in North America (www.ecotourism.org.2001) has identified ecotourists as being slightly older and that most (82 percent) were college graduates. Research by Dinan (1999) in England has investigated the market for sustainable tourism and tentatively identified different forms of what she terms sustainable tourism behavior. She was able to discern two main types of tourist based on an index measure of sustainable behavior, namely: "unconcerned tourists" (48 percent of the sample) and "concerned tourists" (52 percent). The latter group were slightly older, better educated and generally supportive of the local environment and economy. They were more likely to be concerned with recycling and environmental issues in their home environments. The fact remains, however, that in this small-scale survey Dinan was unable to identify strong, clear socio-demographic differences between the two main tourist groups. This led her to contend that defining such behaviors is difficult, since they are dependent on time- and place-specific factors.

In recognizing these new forms of tourism, attention has focused on the nature of tourism consumption as well as to the notions of place commodification and the reproduction of place through new forms of cultural capital (Zukin 1990, 1991). This opens the way for a critical examination of the geographies of tourist consumption as well as to the notions of place commodification and the reproduction of place (Zukin 1990, 1991). At the heart of this debate is the recognition that cultural capital is both a means of personal distinction for the new middle classes (Mowforth and Munt 1998) as well as an attribute of place (Featherstone 1991; Richards 1996). The latter ideas are discussed further in chapter 8, while the remainder of this chapter explores variations in access to tourism and leisure.

Inequalities in Tourism and Leisure Access

Structural features and individual circumstances obviously condition people's ability to participate in tourism and leisure: these include the stage in the family life cycle, gender, cultural conditions, the amount of leisure time available, levels of disability, access to tourist areas, and disposable income.

Such structural features not only condition access but also represent considerable differences in the quality of experience. There is a world of difference between taking your holiday in Puerto Banus rather than in Torremolinos. From a sociological perspective Newman (1983: 102) comments that, "To rank the working classes as equal members of 'leisure society' is clearly absurd. Even their sole brief interlude from routinisation – the annual holiday – is subject to the grossest

Table 3.3 *Reasons given by EU citizens for not taking a holiday during 1997*

Country	Financial	Work related difficulties	Family and personal reasons	Health problems	Others	Not specified
Belgium	42.4	8.1	26.1	16.8	22.2	3.3
Denmark	38.9	17.5	23.9	21.0	13.2	1.7
Germany	49.0	12.6	26.8	24.0	5.0	1.5
Greece	58.2	33.4	21.8	12.6	7.5	0.2
Spain	51.8	27.2	23.2	12.0	9.5	0.9
France	53.3	19.2	20.2	14.1	11.3	0.0
Ireland	48.9	12.7	19.0	12.1	17.1	2.5
Italy	33.9	19.0	33.0	13.7	12.8	1.1
Luxembourg	29.1	12.5	27.8	19.1	19.2	4.6
Netherlands	47.6	10.2	15.1	15.5	18.6	0.8
Austria	42.3	20.5	27.6	16.6	6.0	2.3
Portugal	65.7	15.5	20.0	11.5	8.6	1.1
Finland	44.9	20.8	12.3	16.1	15.3	5.1
Sweden	35.8	15.5	17.7	17.4	23.8	2.2
UK	60.2	10.1	14.3	8.9	12.1	2.6
Average	49.3	17.0	23.5	15.5	10.5	1.4

Source: European Commission Directorate General XXIII (1998)

commercialisation. . . . In common with other facets of social existence, their leisure experience is stratified and no less alienated than that of family, life chances, or avenues for social participation." Such a perspective is particularly true of the underclass in many capitalist societies, especially the increasing numbers of long-term unemployed who may be regarded as "leisure or tourism poor." As we shall see later in this chapter, some governments have recognized the access problems faced by this group and intervened to reduce these.

Socio-economic influences on access to tourism and leisure have attracted most attention. For example, surveys by the European Commission Directorate General XXIII (1998) have shown strong correlations between GDP per capita and the proportion of people taking holidays. Furthermore, tourism is characterized by a positive income elasticity of demand. In other words, the demand for holidays rises proportionately more than increases in personal income. Such relationships were highlighted within the economies of the EU, where an estimated 53 percent of the population took at least one holiday, of four or more days, away from home (European Commission 1998).

A closer inspection of table 3.3 reveals that the EU average hides considerable variations, ranging from 35 percent of Portugal's

Table 3.4 *Social class, age, and regional influences on holidaymaking in the UK, 1998*

	Adult population[a] (%)	Adults taking no 4+ nights holiday (%)	Holidays in Britain[b] (%)	Holidays abroad[c] (%)
Socio-economic group				
AB (professional/managerial)	17	9	22	24
C1 (clerical/supervisory)	29	22	29	37
C2 (skilled manual)	22	21	22	21
DE (unskilled/pensioners etc.)	33	49	27	18
Region of residence				
North	5	6	5	5
Yorkshire and Humberside	9	8	11	9
North West	11	11	9	12
East Midlands	7	6	8	7
West Midlands	9	10	9	9
East Anglia	4	5	4	3
South East London	12	13	8	13
Rest of South East	19	17	21	22
South West	9	8	10	7
Wales	5	6	6	4
Scotland	9	9	9	8
Age				
16–24	13	16	8	14
25–34	20	20	17	22
35–44	18	14	20	20
45–54	16	13	17	20
55–64	12	11	14	13
65+	20	26	23	10

Regions of residence are the Registrar General's regions
[a] Based on the characteristics of the British resident adults who formed the basis of the sample survey
[b] Holidays of four+ nights
[c] Holidays of one+ nights
Source: British National Travel Survey

population who take a holiday, to around 75 percent of Danish people. These differences serve to highlight the whole issue of access to tourism and leisure, especially since some 46 percent of EU citizens did not take a holiday in 1997, this compares with only 40 percent in 1985 (Commission of the European Communities 1987). As the table shows, a variety of reasons appear to condition this access, although for the majority of countries economic constraints were particularly dominant. More specifically, we can recognize a group of countries within which economic constraints appear to have a major influence on holiday-taking, these are; Portugal, the UK, and Greece.

Within the EU survey, some 49 percent of manual workers stayed at home, compared with only 18 percent of those in professional occupations. The survey also showed that older people, those with large families, and those living in rural areas were less likely to take holidays away from home. For example, 66 percent of Europeans living in large towns went on holiday, compared with 45 percent living in villages, but this may simply be the restrictions imposed by agricultural work. Furthermore, such differences appear to be far greater in the less-developed economies, such as Italy, Spain, Greece, and Portugal, than in the more developed ones. Travis (1982) has shown that in Italy there is generally a low level of holiday-taking, but that there is also considerable divergence between different socio-economic groups.

In a developed economy such as the UK, there are variations in access to tourism and, more particularly, to certain forms of holiday tourism. The social class and geographical dimensions of such variations are partly shown in table 3.4. From these data, based on large-scale surveys at a national level, it can be seen that socio-economic factors do relate to the consumption of holidays. While those from social class groups D and E (including unskilled workers) account for 33 percent of the population, they make up 49 percent of adults not taking any holidays. Conversely, those in professional and managerial occupations (groups A and B) comprise 17 percent of the population, but only 9 percent of those not taking holidays. In addition, there are some regional variations, although these are slight, with the South East of England standing out as a region with a higher than average consumption of holidays. Such patterns obviously relate to levels of household income rather than distinctive cultural differences. More general discussions seem to suggest that these class influences are also responsible for quite "different attitudes and values towards tourism" (Seaton 1992: 108) that result in much higher priority being given to holiday-taking by the middle classes.

Table 3.4 suggests that inequalities in holiday-taking among socio-economic groups are as much to do with the type of holiday taken as with participation rates. For example, socio-economic groups A and B (professional and managerial employment) are much more likely to holiday abroad than are groups D and E (unskilled workers and pensioners); the latter only accounted for 18 percent of overseas holidays compared with 24 percent for the former group. This is despite the impact of cheaper overseas packages which, according to Thurot and Thurot (1983), have allowed holidaymakers from lower income groups to emulate those with higher incomes, thereby "democratising" foreign travel. The use of such packages is, in fact, linked to socio-economic factors, with higher-status consumers being associated with greater levels of independent travel, compared with the stronger use of organized packages by lower socio-economic groups (Seaton 1992). Such differences are becoming most readily identifiable with the growth of short-break holidays (trips of between one and three nights) which are very much the domain of socio-economic groups A and B. Short break holidays tend to be taken more evenly throughout the year than long holidays, especially in the Easter–May and September–October periods. Furthermore, they tend to be related to special events, exhibitions or interest holidays. It would seem, therefore, that financial constraints, timing, and the types of activities that are offered, limit access for certain socio-economic groups. Gratton (1990) goes further and suggests that the growth of short-break holidays is indicative of the demands from an increasing inner-directed group of consumers, since they involve more skilled consumption than conventional holidays.

Variations in holiday-taking are also strongly related to age and stage in the family life-cycle, which is clearly recognized by the way that many holiday companies strongly segment their product by age of tourist. Holidays tailored to meet the demands of young people, family groups and retired people figure prominently in the marketing of tour companies. As well as being offered and seeking different holiday products, inequalities also exist between different age groups, as shown in table 3.4. For example, in terms of the ages of people taking no holidays, the highest proportions are to be found in the 25–34 group and those over 65 years old. Similarly, the retired age group generates a large proportion of domestic holidays rather than foreign trips, 23 percent compared with 10 percent (table 3.4). The importance of stage in the family life-cycle is suggested in the middle-age groups, which have relatively high family incomes and high demand expectations. The 35–44 and 45–54 age groups each represent 18 and 16 percent of the population respectively, but account in total for 40 percent of the overseas holidays taken by UK residents.

While retired people are less likely to take a holiday than other adults, when they do have access to the holiday market they are equally likely to take two or more holidays. This select group of retired people take holidays more frequently than the rest of the adult population.

Socio-economic differences do, of course, play a part in accounting for such variations. This is indicated by the fact that almost two out of three retired people, formerly in professional or managerial jobs, take at least one long holiday per year, while only one in three of formerly unskilled workers do so. Of course, many retired people have moved to live in seaside areas and, in a sense, are trying to recreate a holiday-type experience all year round (Karn 1977; King et al. 2000). In a way these individuals have gained total access to a particular leisure environment, although the reality of the experience often fails to match expectations.

Leisure Patterns and Constraints on Leisure Participation

Some commentators have argued that because of institutional changes in tourism (including cheaper air travel, package tours, and holiday camps) access has been improved for large sectors of society (Pimlott 1976; Thurot and Thurot 1983). This view is, however, contested with Smith and Hughes (1999: 124) pointing out that "holiday experiences are diverse and non-travellers are not insubstantial." Similarly, Haukeland (1990: 177) argues that for many people "no real choice exists," as holidays were beyond any practical considerations. In contrast to these views on holiday taking, much of the literature suggests that there are far greater inequalities in access to certain types of leisure activities. Such ideas are discussed in this section, followed by the notion of the disadvantaged tourist.

The interest and concern over such issues has become sufficiently focused to spawn a new subfield of investigations on leisure constraints research (Jackson 1988; 1991 provide wide-ranging reviews). This work includes diverse studies, with attention being given to specific forms of leisure, levels of constraint, and variations in access by different subgroups in society. Thus, McGuire (1984) has focused on the elderly, Willits and Willits (1986) on adolescents, and Henderson (1990) on constraints to women's leisure. The picture that emerges is one of variable access, with constraints being related to socio-economic, gender, life-cycle, racial, and cultural features.

Initial work in both North America and the UK (Rapoport and Rapoport 1975; Kelly 1978) indicated that leisure behavior is strongly influenced by class, together with individual orientation and family–home–local relationships (Smith 1987). More specifically, early emphasis was given to the importance of family life-cycle, especially through the research of Young and Willmott (1973) who focused on the concept of the symmetrical family. From their studies of leisure in the London region, they argued that social class was far less of an influence on leisure behavior than were age, marriage, and gender. Their views were

---

Box 3.1   Main findings in gender differences of leisure activities in the UK

- Women were more likely than men to have leisure activities.
- Women appear to engage in fewer leisure activities than men.
- Women have a lower level of active participation in physical pursuits, apart from walking, dancing, and swimming.
- Women appear to attach greater importance to cultural and social pursuits in their leisure.

Source: modified from Smith (1987) and based on *General Household Survey* data

---

strongly colored by two underlying assumptions: one was the belief in a process of stratified diffusion whereby middle-class lifestyles were being adopted by the working classes; while the other was associated with the rise of the symmetrical family. As Smith (1987) demonstrates, however, such perspectives give a false reading of the nature of leisure patterns, especially concerning differences relating to gender and household structure. For example, the idea of gains from more shared family roles between men and women (the symmetrical family) have been offset by more females taking employment outside the home. While this may have reorientated some women away from purely home-based leisure activities, its more general impact has been to reduce the total amount of time that working-women with children have for leisure. Such reductions have an obvious impact on leisure access and, together with broader structural factors, act as a powerful constraint.

At the heart of these structural factors is the relationship between the family and leisure which in turn relates to gender differences. Smith (1987), using re-worked data from the General Household Survey, identified a number of key differences between male and female leisure, including the major inequalities of time (box 3.1). Similarly, earlier studies by Sillitoe (1969) and Talbot (1979) identified three main characteristics of womens' leisure: (i) its strong home-based nature, with more women likely to engage in crafts; (ii) the emphasis that women themselves place on family duties curtailing their leisure pursuits; and (iii) the very different leisure activities engaged in by men and women (box 3.1). Taken together, these factors condition and produce strong gender differences in many areas of leisure. In this respect, Aubrey et al. (1986: 133) write about women's leisure being vulnerable since "it is subordinate to the demands of men's and children's domestic and leisure needs. Women are unable to organise their time to reconcile 'normal' leisure with unorthodox schedules." More recent reflective

Box 3.2   Gender and leisure: conceptual themes

Gender and theory
- Differences in leisure patterns between men and women are more conceptual than biological.
- Gender theory is emerging as a foundation for better understanding women's leisure.
- The more roles undertaken by a woman, the more likely that individual is to have less personal leisure.

Continua of meanings
- Leisure has multiple and varied definitions for women when examined as "self" or "other" orientated.
- Paid-work is both an enhancement and a constraint to women's leisure.
- Leisure may be a context for the empowerment of women as well as a context of victimization and concomitant disempowerment of women.
- Leisure is an avenue for conformity to social roles as well as resistance to such roles.

Diversity
- Constraints to leisure may be more acute for women who are in non-dominant groups or women who exist on social and economic margins.

Source: Henderson (1996: 152)

reviews, as shown by Henderson (1996), have, in part, re-directed the debate concerning women and leisure, drawing attention to the relationships between leisure experiences and gender identity. More importantly, this work stresses the duality of many of the processes at work, and that women have a variety of leisure experiences (box 3.2).

Of course, access to leisure both for women and men is potentially improved by increased disposable income. This has been mainly examined by socio-economic class variables, although when using such measures we should be aware of work-leisure relationships. Evidence seems to suggest that occupational variables are important in conditioning leisure behavior, but that these appear to operate through a series of attitudinal relationships linking work patterns to leisure (Kelly 1982; Parker 1983). Spreitzer and Snyder (1987) have identified four basic perspectives on these relationships, including, spillover, compensation, segmentation, and joint determination (box 3.3). As yet, empirical work has not provided any clear fit between these work–leisure relationships and particular occupations, or socio-economic groups. However, the

---

Box 3.3   Main perspectives on work–leisure relationships

- *Spillover*: a basic continuity of attitudes, interests, and activities flowing from the work context to a person's leisure.
- *Compensation*: involvement in leisure activities that are the complete opposite of a person's work, thereby providing satisfaction not gained from work environment.
- *Segmentation*: work and leisure as autonomous spheres of experience; experiences in work and leisure are completely unrelated.
- *Joint determination*: work and leisure are reciprocally related: there is a two-way influence between these two spheres of experience.

Source: modified from Spreitzer and Snyder (1987)

---

limited evidence does suggest that compensation or segmentation, covering the case in which work and leisure are seen as autonomous spheres of experience, are more likely to be found in mass-production, manual occupations, where many jobs are repetitive. Conversely, in many professional occupations, there may be a strong tendency for attitudes and interests to flow from work to leisure, as described in the spillover relationship.

Specific attempts to relate social-class variables to constraints on leisure have also highlighted the complexity of assuming simple causal relationships. Work in the UK by Kay and Jackson (1991) has attempted to relate leisure constraints to different social areas: (i) inner-city environments that cover low-status, stable older communities; (ii) inner-city areas of a more transitional nature (dominated by bedsitters, higher proportions of young people and non-indigenous groups); (iii) local authority housing estates containing low-status occupants and having all the indications of relative deprivation; (iv) middle-class suburban areas dominated by younger families; and (v) high-status, prestigious areas characterized by a mature age structure. Survey work in each of these areas revealed a number of constraints affecting leisure participation, with money, time, family responsibilities, and work being the main ones cited (Kay and Jackson 1991). However, very few of the major constraints appeared to vary significantly between the different social areas. However, the largest proportions reporting that they experienced such constraints on leisure did come from the inner-city transitional area (80 percent of respondents), followed by the local authority estate (77 percent) and the middle-class suburban area (76 percent). Clearly, complex influences are at work, including not only income, family life cycle, gender, and location but also culture.

The impacts of working- and middle-class cultures on leisure patterns do have important constraining effects that operate through a range of variables. Wynne's (1990) study of leisure lifestyles on housing estates in northern England illustrates some of these effects, while more broadly-based studies (Bourdieu 1984) suggest that these cultural differences relate to status and occupation. Bourdieu (1984) argues that substantial, available capital, often related to industrial and commercial management jobs, is used mainly to pursue more commercial types of leisure interests, such as tastes for second homes, the use of sports clubs and the commercial theatre. In contrast, many of those in occupations related to higher education tend to have more cultural capital, which is used to pursue interests in art, classical music and opera. More specifically, Dimaggio and Useem (1978) put forward a model for understanding variations in the consumption of arts-based leisure, which is strongly related to social class differences and the notions of social control. This projects the idea that variations in cultural consumption reflect the appreciation of arts-based leisure activities by certain social groups as a method not only of identifying such classes, but also of excluding others. Access is controlled by: flows of information; expected norms of behavior; high costs of attending concerts; and the physical environment of opera and concert halls (Hughes 1987). In turn, such ideas take the discussion back to a consideration of the cultural relationship between work and leisure, which appears to be critical in understanding the use of leisure.

Leisure patterns and participation rates also seem to vary with ethnicity, although here the situation is again complicated by a range of socio-economic and life cycle influences. However, in many capitalist societies access to leisure by many racial minorities is limited by their position in the underclass. In extreme cases, such as South Africa under apartheid, such differences were clear to see; while on average 63 percent of Whites went on holiday in any one year, only 10.5 percent of urban Blacks and just 3.5 percent of other Blacks did (Ferrario 1988: 24). Much of the specific work examining race and leisure has been undertaken in North America, where a number of comparative studies exist (table 3.5). As Stamps and Stamps (1985) argue, while the literature highlights differences between the leisure activities of non-white and white Americans, it is far less clear in delineating the leisure patterns of middle and lower social class blacks. In their study of race and leisure activities, they found race not to be a conclusive variable, although there were differences in leisure participation between middle-class blacks and whites. Such variations may very well be the result of past experiences, in this case the rural origins of many urban blacks in North America who brought with them limited leisure experiences (Craig 1972). Thus, in Stamps and Stamps' (1985) sample,

Table 3.5 *Comparative studies of racial differences in leisure behavior in North America*

Authors	Methodology	Main findings
Meeker et al. (1973)	Historical analysis	Blacks, who are more group oriented, are more likely than whites to utilize urban recreational activities; while whites, who are more individualistic, are more likely to participate in wildlife recreation.
Cheek et al. (1976)	Sample of urban blacks and whites	Small differences between whites and central-city blacks and whites in outdoor recreation, with the exception that whites more than blacks are involved in various sports.
Washburne (1978)	Sample of low-income urban families	From a theoretical perspective, blacks should have limited accessibility to leisure because of poverty and discrimination; and that variations in leisure, based on race are due to ethnicity.
Kelly (1980)	Regionally stratified national sample of 4,029 individuals	White participation in winter sports, camping, waterskiing, and golf higher than black participation.
Edwards (1981)	Random sample of 819 households	Ethnicity a factor in leisure; however, ethnicity ceases to be a factor when blacks live in white areas — blacks living in black areas are more likely than blacks or whites living in white areas to participate in outdoor recreation and belong to recreational association.

some 40 percent of black respondents had been born and brought up in the rural South before moving into urban areas. For many, past limitations had affected current leisure activities and acted as a constraining background influence.

Obviously, a certain amount of leisure activity takes place away from the home environment. In the UK, for example, this is of the order of

30 percent in terms of total time spent on leisure (Gershuny and Jones 1987). Such out-of-home activities are affected by the availability and spatial distribution of leisure facilities, bringing distance into play as a constraining factor. Activities dependent on specific facilities can be termed "confined activities," where participation is only possible at some given purpose-built leisure resource (Veal 1987a). In these cases, constraints are caused not only by distance, but very often also by defined capacities within the leisure facilities. In these circumstances increased access involves both changes in the leisure attitudes of potential participants, and the increased provision of facilities. Policies for sport centre provision by local government, as well as efforts to develop more golf courses within the commercial sector, reflect the range of such needs. For example, in the latter case insufficient facilities in the UK mean that in most regions there are considerable waiting lists to join golf clubs, with the highest levels of constraint being in London and the South East of England, despite relatively large numbers of existing and planned golf developments. Evidence from work on spatial patterns of leisure behavior is that distance, travel time, and travel costs all constrain access.

Relationships vary depending on the size and nature of the leisure facility, as well as the type of consumers (Veal 1987b). As can be seen from figure 3.3, there is a marked decline in the rates of visiting, which is also strongly related to the type of leisure facility on offer, as well as the characteristics of the urban environment. Of course, not all leisure away from home takes place in confined activities. Many people also use a range of so-called "unconfined facilities," such as trips to the countryside, walking, and jogging. In relative terms, these may have fewer constraints, depending on where people live.

The Disadvantaged Tourist

It seems clear that within most capitalist economies there are relatively large proportions of people who, for a variety of reasons, do not take holidays. According to Haukeland (1990) these can be categorized as either "constrained" or "unconstrained," with the latter group deciding not to travel. It is the former group, as we shall see, that we can term the "disadvantaged" tourists. Within the constrained group, Haukeland identified two further sub-groups those whose social living conditions were either, "satisfactory" or "unsatisfactory." As table 3.4 shows, the largest and the most variable group of "disadvantaged" tourists are those constrained by costs, while the other group are limited by some form of disability. Haukeland's "constrained – unsatisfactory" group encompasses both of these.

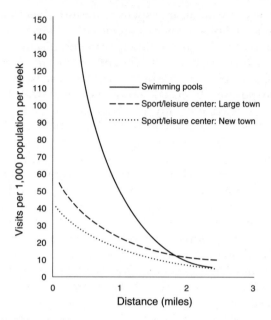

Figure 3.3   *The effect of distance on the use of sports centers in the UK*
Source: Veal (1987b)

Research by Hughes (1991) and Smith and Hughes (1999) has attempted to determine the meaning of holidays to those who are economically and socially disadvantaged. From a small sample of disadvantaged families, Smith and Hughes (1999: 132) concluded "that unlike many other leisure pursuits, the holiday does have a meaning for those without work." For these people the notion that "spectacle and excitement are everywhere and form part of our everyday lives" was clearly inappropriate, as their everyday environment was often "ordinary" and unappealing (1999: 132). A meaning of holiday was often a break from the routine and the focus was on a change of place. Other important motives arising from the survey concerned, "the strengthening and re-negotiation of family ties," alongside an improvement in physical and mental well-being (1999: 130). While these motives and meanings are common to many people, "the intensity and significance of the meaning" were seen as substantially different for these disadvantaged families, compared with the general tourist population (1999: 132).

In addition to these economically disadvantaged families, there are also constraints imposed by other factors producing social marginality, including viability, ethnicity, and gender. These have been researched to different degrees although in many cases all these constraining factors overlap with economic variables. There are obvious constraints imposed by illness and disability (table 3.3), although little is known about the effects on patterns of demand and the meaning of the holiday. For this group (see Butler and Bowlby, 1997 for a general discussion of disability and the use of public spaces; also *Disability View*, 1998) there are only very limited discussions on the access, meaning, and nature of holidaytaking. By contrast, work on women and holidays has exposed the problems of disadvantaged tourists. Deem (1996) found that for the latter the notion of a holiday was strongly identified with a change of place, while Davidson's (1996) study highlighted the need for a break from the routine. Both of which were important meanings that arose in the studies of disadvantaged families. Stephenson and Hughes (1995) have also identified the importance of the economic dimension in their research on holidays and the Afro-Caribbean community in the UK. They found that this sub group were characterized by "deprivation in social and economic terms" (1995: 434) and were less likely to take holidays compared to the rest of the UK population.

Improving Access to Leisure and Tourism: The Role of the State

Many researchers have identified the important role of leisure activities and free time for both the individual and society. Leisure, in all its forms, is part of the individual and collective needs of a society, complementing work, reinforcing group or family relationships, and providing for many a therapy or even a preventative medicine to the pressures of everyday living (Roberts 1981; see also chapter 4 for a discussion of tourist motivations). Such values have been increasingly recognized by many governments and labor organizations; while more recently they have also formed the basis of a series of international statements on the individual's right to rest, leisure, and holidays (World Tourist Organization 1983). The first of these formed part of the United Nations' "Universal Declaration of Human Rights," which emphasized that "everyone has the right to rest and leisure" (table 3.6). More specific statements on the rights to holidays have followed this 1948 declaration, as is shown in table 3.6: the so-called "Manila Declaration" supports the view that "Tourism is considered an activity essential to the life of nations because of its direct effects on social, cultural, educational and economic sectors of societies" (World Tourism Organization 1983).

Goals such as the provision of the right to holidays are usually encompassed by the term "social tourism" (Murphy 1985). This refers

Table 3.6 *International statements on the right to rest, leisure, and holidays*

Date	Organization	Statement	Basic principle(s)
1948	United Nations	Universal Declaration of Human Rights	Everyone has the right to rest and leisure, including reasonable limitations of working hours and periodic holidays with pay
1966	United Nations	International Covenant on Economic, Social, and Cultural Rights	The right to periodic holidays with pay, as well as public holidays
1980	World Tourism Organization	Manila Declaration	Tourism is considered an activity essential to the life of nations because of its direct effects on the social, cultural, educational, and economic sectors of societies. Its development can only be possible if people have access to creative rest and holidays
1982	World Tourism Organization	Acapulco Document	This stresses the essential nature of the right to holidays for all

Source: modified from World Tourism Organization (1983)

to the situation in which deprived, disadvantaged, or economically weak sections of society are provided with the means of taking a holiday. In one sense it highlights the increasing importance placed on tourism as a leisure activity and its duality in many societies, where it is perceived both as a luxury and as a basic right of each individual. A number of international organizations support the latter view, with the World Tourism Organization suggesting specific measures to encourage the development of holidays. These range from the encouragement of low-cost accommodation and cheap travel, through to incentives for producing package holidays adapted to the needs of all wage-earners (World Tourist Organization 1983: 41).

The effectiveness of these international declarations is of course mediated by the commitments of individual governments, very few of which operate any comprehensive form of social tourism. As Murphy (1985) points out, while the aim of social tourism is unitarian in philosophy, it is expressed in a variety of ways, either through government involvement or, more probably by some form of voluntary means.

At the most informal level, access to holidays has been improved through the activities of church organizations and youth movements, such as the YMCA, scouts and guides, which often provide subsidized holiday centers and summer camps. Similarly, labor and trade union organizations have sought to provide cheap holiday centers for their members, while in some countries (Germany and Japan) a number of companies make contributions towards the cost of their employees' holidays. Within this context, one of the earliest and most progressive social tourism schemes was in Switzerland, where the Swiss Travel Saving Fund (REKA) was established in 1939. Teuscher (1983) has shown how this scheme, and developments of a less formal nature in other European countries, came about largely in response to the increases in workers' holiday leave during the 1930s. In Switzerland, for example, access to holidays was greatly increased for many workers between 1910, when only 8 percent of factory employees were entitled to a holiday, and 1937, when the figure had risen to 66 percent. REKA itself was established as a cooperative by the tourism and transport industries, trade unions, employers and consumer cooperative associations, with the aim of improving real access to holidays for many of the country's lowest paid workers. Its initial areas of activity focused on providing a method of saving for holidays, and giving information on low cost holidays (Teuscher 1983). By the 1950s, however, REKA had widened its operations and had constructed its own holiday centers which, together with its leased apartments, provide more than 4,000 guest beds. Other countries provide similar, although less comprehensive, schemes. For example, Brazil has holiday camps run by workers' associations, while Israel has holiday chalets operated by both trades unions and employers (World Tourism Organization 1983; Annex III).

Government involvement in increasing access to holidays often assumes an indirect approach, usually through increasing statutory rights to paid holiday leave. This does widen access to tourism, as was witnessed in the UK after the passing of the 1938 Holidays with Pay Act, which proposed a minimum of three consecutive days of paid holiday. When the Act was fully implemented after 1945, it provided an important growth stimulus to British tourism. However, despite discussions in 1974 between the English Tourist Board and the Trades Union Congress, which established the "Social Tourism Study Group," no formal action has been taken in the UK to establish a social tourism scheme. In 1989 the problems of access to tourism were highlighted in the English Tourist Board's report *Tourism for All*, which stated that tourism should be available to all people irrespective of age and disability. It also sought to widen holiday opportunities for low income families. However, Stephenson and Hughes (1995) argue that it understated the needs of the economically disadvantaged. This contrasts with the situation in France, where central government and regional authorities have created the Villages-Vacances-Familiales in 1959; this scheme now provides subsidized serviced and self-catering accommodation for low income families in either villages or campsites.

If most governments have steered away from direct involvement in social tourism programmes they have, in contrast, been more likely to involve themselves in some type of general leisure policy. This has taken many forms, ranging from the subsidy of arts and cultural activities, through to establishing access to the countryside, putting into place policies for greater involvement in sport and, more recently, the development of leisure programmes for deprived sectors of society. In all of these cases, there are strong grounds for arguing that such "leisure policies" are far from being either politically or socially neutral. As Bramham et al. (1989: 17) point out, such issues are, "inherently connected to a wide range of political tensions and contrasts" and especially "to the ways in which these [policies] mediate existing socio-economic differences."

At the level of national governments, Bramham and Henry (1985) have shown how successive British governments have adopted the view that state intervention in leisure should be kept at arms length, and not intrude into the private lives of individuals. In contrast, Hantrais (1989) argues that the coming to power of a socialist government in France during the 1980s put leisure policies firmly on the political agenda. After appointing a Minister of "Free Time," the French government went on to proclaim a programme in which leisure was seen as both a public good as well as a citizen's right. During the early 1980s a number of urban leisure programmes were developed to provide better access for young people and also to prevent the private sector from gaining a monopoly over leisure services. Attempts were also made to solve problems of regional disparity in leisure provision, with central government promoting and part funding 300 new leisure centres in under-resourced smaller towns between 1982 and 1984 (Hantrais 1989). In addition, the socialist government also sought to decentralize culture by allocating 70 percent of the Ministry of Culture's budget to projects outside the Paris region. This latter fact also highlights the class and political conflict generated by what was seen as the paternalistic tradition of "cultural heritage" pursued by previous conservative governments in France (Hantrais 1989).

The notion of class divisions in leisure access has led many authors to conclude that most subsidies of leisure activities have been largely to the benefit of the middle classes, at the expense of the "leisure-poor"

(Bramham et al. 1989; Hughes 1987). Thus, many central governments have traditionally aided the arts, heritage, and cultural sectors, while leaving improvements in access to other leisure activities to local government. At this local level, it is possible to detect the development of distinct urban leisure policies directed at improving conditions for both young people and the unemployed. Within the British context, Glyptis (see Glyptis 1989; Glyptis and Riddington 1983) has examined the provision of sports facilities for the unemployed by local authorities, 64 percent of whom were operating such schemes by the mid-1980s. In many urban areas this service was based on the possibility that unemployment was not a temporary feature of economic adjustment and that, consequently, longer-term policies were needed. This, as Bramham et al. (1989) argue, raises the central question of whether, if work is no longer the main role of community organization, leisure could, and should, take its place. If this should be the case in many urban communities, then not only does the issue of social access need to be more seriously addressed, but such policies will also need to cover a much wider sector of the "leisure poor."

Increased sports facilities will cater for some needs, but such activities will not fit everyone's needs. Indeed, the provision of increased leisure access through local policies still appears to suffer from the same kinds of limitation that operate in the commercially driven market. This has been clearly highlighted by Dietvorst's (1989) research in Nijmegen, Holland which strongly suggests that class biases exist in the organization of local projects for the unemployed; these tend to reproduce the interests of the better-educated among those out of work. With this in mind, it has been argued that local leisure policies must be structured as a response to existing local ways of life, and aimed as widely as possible at the full range of "leisure poor" (Bramham et al. 1989: 296). Before this can happen, however, it may well be that we require much more understanding of, and agreement on, the whole notion of what constitutes leisure.

4

Tourist Motivation and Behavior

In Search of the Tourist

The previous chapter introduced a broad discussion concerning the patterns of tourism and leisure consumption, along with various constraining influences. By contrast, this chapter will focus in much greater depth on some of the more specific factors involved in tourist motivation and behavior and the relationships tourist engender with the socio-cultural environments of destination areas.

It is significant that some of the earliest sustained attempts to identify the tourist came not from academics but from official organizations interested in monitoring the growth of international tourism. In this context, the League of Nations in 1937 recommended that a tourist be defined as someone "who travels for a period of 24 hours or more in a country other than that in which he usually resides." Of course such simple definitions tell us little about tourist behavior and completely ignore the importance of domestic tourism. Broader, and at an international level, more meaningful definitions put forward by the World Tourism Organization (previously the International Union of Official Travel Organizations) have, through the UN Conference on International Travel and Tourism (1963), agreed the term "visitors." This covers two main categories: tourists – temporary visitors staying at least 24 hours, whose purpose could be defined as either leisure or business; and excursionists – temporary visitors staying less than 24 hours, including cruise ship travelers, but excluding travelers in transit. Such ideas have been greatly extended into the construction of more comprehensive and elaborate classifications that relate types of travelers with scale and purpose of journey (figure 4.1). Within this perspective

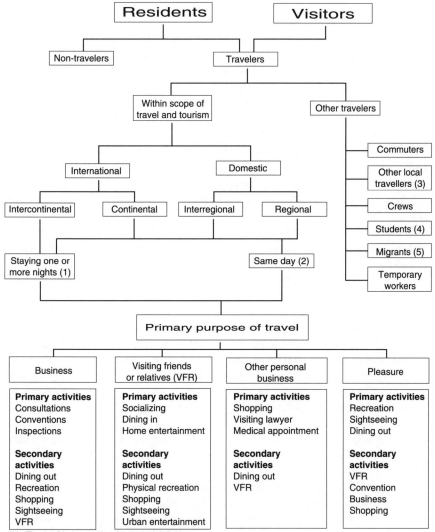

(1) "Tourists" in international technical definitions
(2) "Excursionists" in international technical definitions
(3) Travelers whose trips are shorter than those which qualify for travel and tourism, e.g. under 50 miles (80 km) from home
(4) Students traveling between home and school only – other travel of students is within scope of travel and tourism
(5) All persons moving to a new place of residence including all one way travelers such as emigrants, immigrants, refugees, domestic migrants and nomads

Figure 4.1   *A classification of travelers*

Source: Chadwick (1987)

many trips are multipurpose, involving a range of primary and secondary activities.

Such definitions are important when attempting comparative studies of international tourism. Their purpose is to provide an international standard, but not to explain or examine tourist behavior. Moreover, even as official definitions, such adopted standards still ignore the wide range of domestic tourists and, as a consequence, many countries have also developed their own official definitions for internal use. As a consequence, the definitions of a tourist and a visitor still vary between countries, despite the efforts of the World Tourism Organization and the United Nations (Theobald 1994). Moreover, even in highly developed economies problems persist, for as Theobold (1994: 11) explains, "in the United States there is no standard definition valid throughout the country."

Set against these official approaches are numerous attempts by academics to define the tourist and to conceptualize the process of tourist behavior. Some of the early attempts to produce broader definitions were similar to the official ones. Ogilvie (1933), for example, saw tourists as being someone on a temporary trip away from home who also spent money derived from their home area and not from the place being visited. Put simply, tourists were travelers and, equally important, consumers but not labor migrants (see chapter 1). Examinations of the tourist and tourist behavior did not, however, figure in early work by geographers and, instead, come primarily from sociological studies. The results of this research are a fairly close-knit set of typologies of tourists, based on their travel characteristics and motivations. As we shall see, such classifications also have important implications for the study of the impact of tourism on destination regions, a feature re-emphasized by geographers (Mathieson and Wall 1982; Murphy 1985).

Many of the typologies are based around identifying the significant traits of tourists and, in particular, their demands as consumers. Cohen (1972), in his early studies, draws attention to the fact that all tourists are seeking some element of novelty and strangeness while, at the same time, most also need to retain something familiar. How tourists combine the demands for novelty with familiarity can in turn be used to derive a typology. In this way Cohen recognized a range of possible demand combinations, from those where familiarity was given priority, through to those where novelty of experience was the most important factor. Such demands can be matched by a classification of tourists. Cohen's (1972) initial study recognized four main types, ranging from the organized mass tourist to the individual mass tourist, the explorer and the drifter (table 4.1). In addition, these groups were also differentiated along the lines of contact with the tourism industry, with mass tourists being termed "institutionalised" and the more individualistic tourists being regarded as non-institutionalised.

Cohen's tourist typology, and the more detailed variant developed by Smith (Smith, V. L. 1977) which identifies seven categories of tourist (table 4.1), focus on the relationships between tourists and their destinations; as such they have been termed "interactional typologies" (Murphy 1985: 5–6). In contrast, other studies have stressed the motivations that lie behind tourist travel, and have been described as "cognitive–normative models." In some cases, these approaches to identifying and classifying tourists have their roots in the commercial needs of the tourism industry, with typologies often being established for a specific client. We find, for example, that Plog's (1972) typology, which recognizes three main groups of tourists – the allocentric, midcentric and psychocentric was initially constructed to enable airline and travel companies to broaden their market. As shown in table 4.1, the basis of this typology is the idea of a norm or center around which more diverse patterns of tourist motivation can be recognized.

Typologies, such as the one devised by Plog, are based on asking tourists about their general "lifestyles" or value systems, often using perceptual information derived from interviews (Holman 1984; Lowyck et al. 1990). This psychographic research (Plog 1987) can be used to examine tourist motivations as well as attitudes to particular destinations and modes of travel. In terms of the latter, a tourist typology developed for American Express (1989) has categorized travelers into five distinct groups – adventurers, worriers, dreamers, economisers and indulgers – all of whom viewed their travel experiences in very different ways (table 4.1).

These tourist typologies, only a few of which have been presented here, are not without their problems, chief among which is that they are relatively static models based on fairly limited information (Lowyck et al. 1990). It is certainly the case that such perspectives assume that tourists belong to one type or another, and that there are no mechanisms for individuals to move between categories. Set against this, sociologists such as MacCannell (1976) have called for more detailed studies of how people experience tourist settings, so as to provide a better understanding of tourists. Perhaps of even greater importance in identifying different types of tourists is the need to learn more about how individuals change as tourists over time. This can be achieved by taking a biographical approach, as introduced in the concept of a tourist's travel career (Pearce 1982). This would involve longitudinal studies of changing patterns of tourist behavior which, at the present time, do not exist in sufficient detail or scale. Therefore, a number of critical issues remain to be researched, and we are left with nothing more than the generalities of the tourist typologies.

Table 4.1 The main typologies of tourists

	Experience	Demands	Destination impacts
Interactional models			
Cohen (1972): a theoretically derived approach not based on any empirical survey:			
Non-institutionalized traveler	Drifter	Search for exotic and strange environment	Little because of small numbers
	Explorer	Arrange own trip and try to get off the beaten track	Local facilities sufficient and contact with residents high
Institutionalized traveler	Individual mass tourist	Arrangements made through tourist agency to popular destinations	Growing commercialization and specialization as demand grows
	Organized mass tourist	Search for familiar, travel in the security of own "environmental bubble" and guided tour	Development of "artificial" facilities, growth of foreign investment, reduced local control
V. L. Smith (1977): a theoretical approach limited to empirical information:			
	Explorer	Quest for discovery and desire to interact with hosts	Easy to accommodate in terms of numbers, acceptance of local norms
	Elite	Tour of unusual places, using pre-arranged native facilities	Small in number and easily adapted into surrounding environments

Off-beat	Get away from the crowds	Minor, because willing to put up with simple accommodation and service
Unusual	Occasional side trips to explore more isolated area or undertake more risky activity	Temporary destinations can be simple, but support base needs to have full range of services
Incipient mass	Travel as individuals or small groups, seeking combination of amenities and authenticity	Numbers increasing as destination becomes popular, growing demand for services and facilities
Mass	Middle-class income and values leads to development of a "tourist bubble"	Tourism now a major industry, little interaction with local people beyond commercial links
Charter	Search for relaxation and good times in a new but familiar environment	Massive arrivals; to avoid complaints, hotels and facilities standardized to Western tastes

Cognitive–normative models
Plog (1972): based on original work for 16 airline and travel companies:

Allocentric	Adventuresome and individual exploration	Small in number, board with local residents
Mid-centric	Individual travel to areas with facilities and growing reputation	Increased commercialization of visitor–host relationship

Table 4.1 _continued_

	Experience	Demands	Destination impacts
	Psychocentric	Organized package holiday to "popular" destinations	Large-scale business, with facilities similar to visitors' home area
Cohen (1979a): a theoretically based approach:			
Modern pilgrimage	Existential	Leave world of everyday life and practicality to escape to "elective center" for spiritual sustenance	Few participants who are absorbed into community: little impact on local life
	Experimental	Quest for alternative lifestyle and to engage in authentic life of others	Assimilated into destination areas due to nature of demand and relatively small numbers
	Experiential	Look for meaning in life of others, enjoyment of authenticity	Some impact as destination provides accommodation and facilities to "show" local culture
Search for pleasure	Diversionary	Escape from boredom and routine of everyday existence, therapy which makes alienation endurable	Mass tourism with large demand for recreation and leisure facilities, large impact because of numbers and commercialization

American Express (1989): based on results from a classification of 6,500 respondents in the USA, UK, West German and Japan:

Recreational	Trip as entertainment, relaxation to restore physical and mental powers	Artificial pleasure environment created; major impact on local lifestyles
Adventurers	New experiences of different cultures and activities	Independent travelers affluent and better educated; limited impact
Worriers	Mainly domestic-based trips, limited travel	Older; less educated; limited impact
Dreamers	Attach great importance to meaning of travel and experiences; orientated towards relaxation	Modest income group rely on guidebook and stick to main tourist areas
Economists	Travel a routine outlet for relaxation rather than experience	Average income: mainly go to established tourist areas
Indulgers	High demand for travel, making above average trips	Generally stay in large hotel and resort complexes; willing to pay for better services

Despite their limitations, the tourist typology models remain useful for three main reasons. First, they highlight the broad diversity of tourists, their demands, and consumption. Second, they provide an insight into the motivations of tourists and their behavior. Finally, and most importantly, such perspectives provide a platform from which to explore the relationships between tourist consumption and the socio-cultural fabric of destination areas. The remainder of this chapter will focus on these latter two themes, after considering the nature of tourist image-making.

Tourists and Tourist Images

Tourists may vary in type as we have shown, but they are all influenced by images of destinations and activities. Furthermore, all tourists appear to be driven by a process of image-making which relates to a series of influences. Many commentators have argued that tourism is about creating a myth or, as Dubinsky (1994: 65) points out, "all tourism is about illusion." Taylor (1994: 2) goes further and argues that tourist image-making "is like dreaming . . . a period [of time] which is magical." The importance of image within tourism is such that the World Tourism Organization (1979, quoted in Cooper et al. 1993: 25) have established their own definitions. They suggest that the term embraces "the artificial imitation of the apparent form of an object; the ideas, conceptions held individually or collectively of a destination." The phrase "tourist destination image" has taken a wider currency within the tourism literature, although according to Jenkins (1999) its exact meaning and measurement is problematic. The significance of tourist images is also reflected in the literature concerned with the creation and marketing of place, as discussed in chapters 8 and 10.

Tourists possess different images relating to holiday-taking and destinations which, in part, are formed by past experiences of travel or induced by the promotion of particular destination areas through a variety of media. In this context, Murphy (1985: 25) concluded that image was "the sum of beliefs, ideas and impressions that a person has regarding a tourist destination." Of course, such image-making goes beyond destinations and, for many individuals, also concerns types of holiday. Such ideas strongly relate to attitudes and are also influenced by a range of self-images that the tourist holds (Shaw et al. 2000). For the tourist, such images are constructed around the notions of the "tourist gaze." Boorstin (1964: 7) was one of the earliest to recognize this, arguing that, "over time, via advertising and the media, the images generated of different gazes come to constitute a closed self-perpetuating system of illusion" (quoted in Morgan and Pritchard

(1998: 18)). The notion of the tourist gaze, which has been explored by Urry (1990: 2), "presupposes a system of social activities and signs which locate the particular tourist practices." In terms of image, the tourist gaze is constructed through signs and signifiers in the landscape, and tourists are collectors of such signs (see also chapter 8). Tourists may, therefore, be regarded as semioticians (Culler 1988; Dann 1996a; MacCannell 1976) and, increasingly, they are constructing the "gaze" around well-defined signs or markers. These are used to identify people, things, and places. According to Taylor (1994: 5) "becoming a tourist is to risk the failure of not feeling or perceiving whatever is expected." In order to lessen this risk of failure, tourists desire to view destinations in a "prescribed manner and so overcome anxiety" (Taylor 1994: 5). Urry (1992: 172) has clarified these ideas, noting that "the tourist gaze is a mix of different scopic drives by which things of significance in history/culture/nature/experience are identified, signified and totalised" (see also Hollinshead 1999).

The construction and focus of the tourist gaze is becoming more catholic, although a number of themes emerge from the literature. First, in terms of tourist image-making and the construction of the gaze, tourists are being increasingly drawn to destinations that have been popularized by literature, television, and film (Morgan and Pritchard 1998; Riley and Van Dorn 1992; Schofield 1996; see also Chapter 8). Second, research has explored the relationship between the tourist gaze, and the search for nostalgia and the heritage industry (Urry, 1990). This has been seen by most commentators as an important segment of postmodern tourism consumption, but in terms of tourist image it can also act as a form of social distinction (Munt 1994; Richards 1996). Such ideas embrace the general holiday process for as Gabriel and Lang (1995: 52) point out, "holiday destinations are not innocent or risk free; they are part of a process whereby meanings of social worth are established and elaborate hierarchies of social standing are sustained." Here we can clearly see the links between tourist image-making and motivation as discussed in the next section.

Tourist Motivation and Decision-making

The understanding of tourist motivation and decision-making processes is important for a number of reasons, but not least because it links to the impact on destination areas (Crompton 1979). In addition, there are strong economic considerations related to the promotion of tourism and tourism planning that are highly reliant on an understanding of tourist decision-making. For example, in terms of tourism marketing and promotion, it enables the identification of market

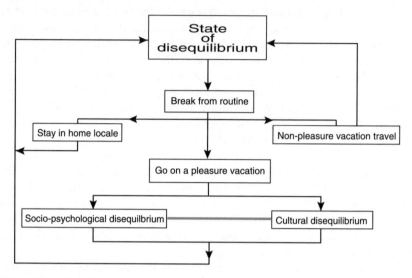

Figure 4.2   *Possible responses to personal disequilibrium*
Source: Crompton (1979)

segmentation and target marketing. The tourist travel market is extremely competitive, especially within the area of mass tourism, and the market is highly segmented. Similarly, the potential to control or strongly influence tourist decisions is important in tourism planning as, for example, in diverting tourists from sensitive areas.

Set against these practical reasons for understanding tourist decision-making, we should recognize at the outset that the question of measuring motivation is extremely problematic (Dann 1977), and little in the way of a common understanding has emerged (Jafari 1987). As Pearce (1993: 113) explains "tourist motivation is a hybrid concept," a view also expressed by Dann (1983). Pearce (1993: 114) goes on to argue that, "some of the novel features pertaining to tourist motivation are that tourists select a time and place for their behaviour often well in advance of the event." In this context researchers have stressed different combinations of factors; Thomas (1964) for example, listed 18 reasons, Gray (1970) discussed just two distinct motivations, "wanderlust" and "sunlust," Lundberg (1972) identified 20 factors, while Crompton (1979) recognized nine different motives.

From empirical studies of tourists, Crompton (1979) also conceptualized states of disequilibrium or homeostasis which could be rectified by taking a break away from the routine. As shown in figure 4.2, there are four main components of this process, starting with an initial state of disequilibrium, followed by the recognition of the need to break

> **Box 4.1   The dimensions of tourist motivation**
>
> *Push factors*
> Motivation per se why people decide to take a holiday:
>
> - desire for something different;
> - anomie in origin society;
> - ego-enhancement, usually associated with relative status deprivation: holidays offer temporary alleviation; and
> - peer pressure to take a holiday, especially among the middle classes.
>
> *Pull factors*
>
> Refer to destination "pull," why tourists decide to visit a particular resort destination

from routine behavior. The third component involves three behavioral alternatives, which range from leisure activities in the local area, to taking a holiday or travel to see friends and relatives, to traveling for business purposes. Finally, there is the recognition that particular motives obviously determine the nature and destination of the leisure trip. Such motives can either be classified as socio-psychological (push factors) or cultural (pull factors), as shown in more detail in box 4.1. These broad ideas have, to some extent, been confirmed through larger empirical studies; for example, by Schmidhauser (1989) in Switzerland who has shown that a single leisure trip cannot satisfy all the tourism motives of an individual.

The recognition of push and pull factors within tourist motivation forms a critical issue in much of the literature, although little attention has been directed at any cross-cultural comparisons. Dann (1977) has stressed the initial importance of push factors which determine the need for travel, while the pull factors tend to affect the choice of destination. The need for leisure travel is, according to Dann (1977), the consequence of anonymity and ego-enhancement. The first cause is somewhat similar to Crompton's disequilibrium in the sense that it identifies a socio-psychological need to move away from the home–work environment. In contrast, ego-enhancement relates to motives of relative status deprivation or prestige, including the need for people to impress their friends, which in itself can also lead to to disequilibrium or homeostasis (Mill and Morrison 1985).

The ideas of escaping from particular environments, as well as seeking personal rewards, have been explored in greater depth by Iso-Ahola (1984) and Mannell and Iso-Ahola (1987) who defined leisure travel in terms of "escaping" and "seeking" dimensions

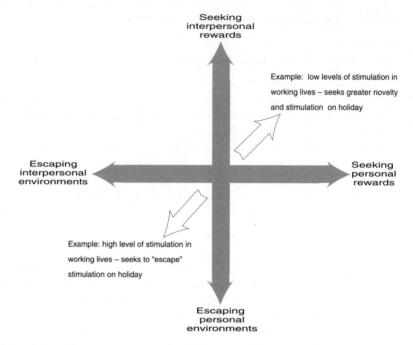

Figure 4.3   *The escaping and seeking dimensions of tourist travel*
Source: after Iso-Ahola (1984)

(figure 4.3). At one extreme they identify those individuals who have a high level of stimulation in their working lives and therefore seek to "escape" stimulation on holiday. In contrast, those with low levels of stimulation at work have a tendency to seek greater novelty and stimulation on holiday. But, of course, leisure preferences also depend to a great extent on personality traits, as well as lifestyle experiences. Furthermore, many of the authors writing on tourism motivation highlight the complexity of an individual's real motives, in that many have a hidden agenda (Krippendorf 1987a). The difficulties in uncovering such hidden agendas are formidable and involve both conceptual and measurement problems. Ryan (1997) has sought to advance progress by stressing the importance of "self" in motivation which relates to the notions of ego-enhancement as discussed by Iso Ahola (1984). However, Ryan also opens up a different dimension to this debate by arguing that the concept of "self" for a tourist may relate to the sum of places visited. In this context, "social interaction occurs within a place and the attributes of place subscribe connotations to the sense of self" (Ryan 1997: 30).

Table 4.2 *Holiday intentions: the reservations of commercial accommodation made by British holidaymakers*

	Percentage of holidaymakers	
Reservations made	Holidays in Britain	Holidays overseas
Before September 1987	6	5
September and October 1987	3	7
November and December 1987	10	9
January 1988	24	22
February 1988	12	9
March 1988	6	8
Total reservations before Easter 1988	59	64

Source: English Tourist Board (1990)

The decision-making process has been conceived in a variety of ways. Howard and Sheth (1969) drew attention to the influence of environmental variables, while the importance of imagery and marketing are explored by Crompton (1993). More significantly, Ryan (1997) has attempted to conceptualize the whole decision-making process in terms of a model of "the tourist experience." Leaving aside the variables that interact in this process model, it is possible to identify three key stages; the pre-trip planning stage, the actual holiday experience, and the recall and assessment of the experience.

As with other forms of consumption, there are particular stages in which tourists participate, such as the buying process. However, unlike other consumer purchases, the holiday has some very distinctive features. The tourist product is an experience rather than a good, and there is therefore no tangible return on the investment. It also involves, for many people, a relatively large expenditure and a high degree of planning. Finally, many tourists are not distance minimizers; for most, the travel element is an important part of the holiday product.

Buying a holiday is, for many families, a high-risk decision, and for this reason pre-purchase planning assumes a greater role (Gitelson and Crompton 1983). The degree of planning obviously varies between different types of tourists but, in the Northern Hemisphere, it is often in full-swing by January. The timing of this process can be illustrated by surveys of holidaying intentions (table 4.2) which show, for example, that 59 percent of British holidaymakers had already booked their holidays in Britain before Easter, while for holidays abroad the figure was 64 percent. In terms of tourists' search and pre-purchasing decision-making, we can therefore recognize three main types of buyer

Table 4.3   *Sources of information used by holidaymakers visiting Cornwall, England*

Source	Percentage of sample[a]
Previous visit	57.8
Personal recommendation	29.7
Tour operator's brochure	20.6
Tourist board guide	12.2
Local resort guide	11.8
Newspaper advertisement	6.3
Magazine advertisement	6.9
TV holiday program	6.7

Percentages do not sum to 100 as many respondents used more than one source
[a] Based on a sample of 902 holidaymakers
Source: Greenwood et al. (1989)

behavior. The first are "impulse buyers" who may be attracted by a "cut-price" holiday offered by travel agents – these individuals have very short planning horizons (Goodall 1988). A second group are "repeat buyers" who generally go back to the same resort ever year. The final group are the so-called "meticulous planners" who obtain specific and up-to-date information, and make detailed comparisons; as a consequence they tend to have fairly long planning horizons.

These search processes are obviously strongly influenced by the media and the images projected of various destination areas. Most individuals have a preferential image of their ideal holiday, clearly influenced by their motives. This, according to Goodall (1988: 3) "conditions their expectations setting an aspiration level or evaluative image, against which actual holiday opportunities are compared." The information and images of destination areas are provided by the media industry (formal sources), and informal recommendations from friends (Nolan 1976). In some destination areas, informal sources figure highly (table 4.3). It should be recognized, however, that most people use a combination of formal and informal sources to construct an image of each destination area. Clearly, the matching of preferential, evaluative and factual images will determine what type of holidaymaker goes to which type of destination, and how they travel there in terms of the type of holiday selected (that is, package or non-package tour).

Ryan's (1997; 1998) empirical studies of UK tourists have helped to pinpoint some dimensions of the "tourist experience." He has also drawn attention to the role of experience in the context of the travel career ladder, and found that for many tourists the "past experience is important in making decisions about holiday purchases" (Ryan 1998: 949). Similarly, more detailed, repeated studies of holiday-makers visiting Cornwall have confirmed such a view (table 4.3).

Tourist decision making has also been increasingly explored in terms of age and gender influences within the family structure. Particular attention has been focused on the role of children in the holidaymaking process (Thornton 1995; Thornton et al. 1997), in part reflecting related studies in consumer behavior. This work was based on Cornwall, using diary-based space–time budgets, and found that children influenced tourist parties either through their direct physical needs or their ability to negotiate with parents. Similarly, earlier work by Ryan (1992) had argued that children were an important catalyst in a family deciding to visit an attraction. The influence of children on decision-making has also been confirmed by Seaton and Tagg (1995) in a survey of UK families, using self-complete questionnaires. However, as Thornton et al. (1997) indicate, strong differences in methodologies have made it difficult to compare across these different surveys.

Gender differences have also been explored, with Ryan (1997: 35) raising the issue as to whether "females have different expectations of holidays when compared to males." In a study of lifecycle effects on holiday motivations he found mixed evidence. However, while there was little difference between the motivations of young males and females, latter stages in the lifecycle have highlighted greater variations. In this context, the influence of age has also been identified by Zalatan (1998) when exploring the involvement of wives in family holiday decisions. Ryan (1997) also draws attention to the complexity of the gender issue in tourist motivation and decision-taking, raising the question of whether there are specific male and female tourist experiences. The notions of sexual differences are being further explored in terms of the tourist motivations of gay tourists, with work focusing on the emergence of the gay consumer, including the development of related tourism products and destinations (Pritchard et al. 1998). Thus, Cliff and Forest (1999) have conducted empirical research on a sample of gay men and examined travel patterns outside the UK, showing that in many cases sexual behavior was an important holiday motivation – as also in the case of some heterosexual men.

Tourist Behavior: At the Scene of their Dreams

Patterns of tourist behavior have an important impact both on the structure of facilities within particular resorts and the relationships that tourists have with the host population. The tourist typologies explored at the start of this chapter obviously go some way to suggesting possible ranges of behavior, although they say little about the detailed leisure activities and patterns of consumption indulged in by holidaymakers.

According to Krippendorf (1987a: 32), having "arrived at the scene of their dreams," many tourists behave in much the same way as they do at home. For them the break with routine is a functional and spatial one, in that they do not have to work and are away from home. The holiday resort is an "exotic backdrop" (Krippendorf 1987: 32), against which they can play out the usual patterns of behavior. Such traits are common, however, only to the point of enjoying home comforts as, for many tourists, aggressive – almost colonialist – behavior becomes a norm while on holiday. Holidaymakers become totally self-oriented, having little regard for others, especially the host population. Such antisocial behavior, in its most extreme form, has become an increasing feature of many of the mass tourism resorts in the Mediterranean.

Approaches to the study of tourist behavior have focused on two main themes, namely, general tourist activities and more detailed analysis based on tourist time-budgets (Cooper 1981). Much of the published material falls into the former category and presents generalized lists of tourist pursuits derived from basic questionnaire surveys, usually of people on holiday (table 4.4). In the example taken from research in Cornwall, the emphasis for many visitors is on "sightseeing," with 85.5 percent rating it as very or fairly important; also significant were "strolling in the countryside" (84.8 percent) and "going to the beach" (82.9 percent). On the surface, such activities look passive and harmless, but closer inspection reveals the potential for problems. Thus, according to MacCannell (1976: 13), the focus of sightseeing is part of a systematic global scavenge for new experiences to be woven into a collective, touristic version of other peoples and other places. However, this touristic integration is nothing more than a catalogue of displaced forms as both modernization and tourism separate out objects from the societies and places that produced them. At a broader level, Krippendorf (1987a) draws attention to the contradiction between tourist motives (involving the desire for peace and something different) and actual tourist behavior, which for many holidaymakers tends to be focused in congested resorts.

One of the difficulties in interpreting tourist behavior from the data contained in table 4.4 is that activities are space and time contingent. Tourist time-budgets allow an insight into such variations, and the few studies undertaken using such techniques have revealed some significant variations. Thus, Pearce (1982) showed an increase in self-initiated activities (walking, reading, and admiring views) by holidaymakers after four or five days of being on holiday in Australian resorts that provided structured activities. Similarly, a diary-based

Table 4.4   *The importance of activities to holidaymakers in Cornwall, England*

Activity	Taken part in only – no rating (%)	Very important (%)	Fairly important (%)	Not very important (%)
Going to the beach	6.1	52.0	30.9	11.0
Walking around town	7.3	26.5	53.0	13.2
Strolling in the countryside	6.2	47.5	37.3	8.9
Climbing/hiking/rambling	3.5	29.0	24.3	43.3
Sightseeing coach	6.7	50.0	35.5	7.8
Shopping	7.7	21.6	47.9	22.8
Visiting pubs/bars	5.7	22.6	37.4	34.3
Visiting restaurants	5.7	26.2	43.3	24.8
Cinema/theater	2.4	9.2	25.9	62.5
Festivals/outdoor show	2.2	13.5	35.4	48.9
Historic buildings/country houses	5.6	34.5	43.4	16.4
Fun fair/amusement arcades	3.6	8.5	25.2	62.7
Dancing/disco	2.3	9.9	21.3	66.6
Museum/art galleries	3.4	22.6	50.1	24.0
Theme parks	4.2	16.9	44.0	35.0
Scenic railways	4.3	13.0	34.6	48.0
Miniature golf/putting	4.0	13.0	33.1	49.9
Other	6.1	59.1	22.7	12.2

Source: Greenwood et al. (1989)

study of a sample of visitors to the South Pacific island of Vanuatu found variations in activities even over a four-day period, although strong regular diurnal rhythms were also evident (Pearce 1988b). Also significant in the Vanuatu study was the strong spatial concentration of tourist activity in and around their hotels (figure 4.4).

Unfortunately, despite its importance, the consideration of spatial patterns of tourist behavior has received little attention. Indeed, one of the significant behavioral issues on which geographers are particularly qualified to comment has seen them remain largely silent. One of the few major contributions has been by Cooper (1981) who examined the space-time budgets of tourists on Jersey over a five-day period. This revealed that most tourists determined a hierarchy of sites on the basis of the facilities provided at each one, while over time there was a progressive filtering down this hierarchy of sites. The decision to visit the largest, most important sites first and then move down the hierarchy

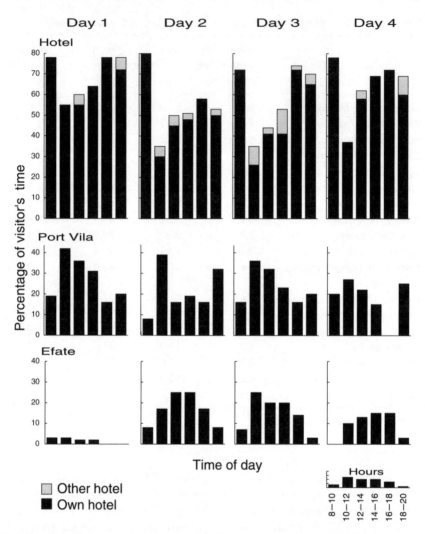

Figure 4.4 *The percentage of time spent by visitors in hotels and visiting resorts on Vanuata (South Pacific)*

Source: Pearce (1988b: 110)

suggests, first, that tourists reduce uncertainty at the expense of effort (Cooper 1981) and, second, that their time is discretionary.

It is worth stressing that such time budgets will obviously vary between different types of tourists (however we may define such differences). Thus, Cooper (1981) found variations between different tourists, as defined by social class, with the lower social groups tending to limit their visits to only the major sites. Work by Thornton (1995) has reactivated these debates by drawing attention to "activity sequences," "activity spaces," and "group relationships," as three key interrelated elements which help explain tourist behavior. In this context, "activity sequences" relate to the characteristics and timing of tourist activities, while "activity spaces" are the spatial coordinates of these activities, and the use of these spaces are determined by "group relationships." This research, based on the application of space–time budgets, has highlighted the importance of the measurement of tourist behavior, revealing a significant gap between tourists' preferences for, and perceptions of, how they utilize their time (Thornton 1995; Thornton et al. 1996).

Hosts and Guests: Perspectives on Tourist Cultures

Leaving aside economic considerations, in many societies tourists tend to be viewed in a negative way. Many studies have commented on the disdain in which tourists are held, and as MacCannell (1976: 9) explains, it "is intellectually chic nowadays to deride tourists." Even tourists dislike tourists, who are "reproached for being satisfied with superficial experiences of other peoples and other places" (MacCannell 1976: 10). Similarly, Krippendorf (1987a: 41) explains that whatever "the tourist does he does it wrong" by being the "rich tourist," the "uncultured tourist," the "exploiting tourist," the "polluting tourist" and so on. This critique of tourists is related to larger issues associated with the culture of tourism, and with the fact that many tourists want to have a deeper involvement with the society and culture they are visiting, but very often on their terms. Krippendorf (1987a) feels that the blame is too narrowly focused on the tourist, and that the negative effects of global tourism are its massiveness, which has much to do with the international institutions that control tourism. Whatever the rights and wrongs of the argument, the fact remains that tourists are mainly perceived in a negative fashion.

Much of the established literature holds that tourists bring with them positive and negative impacts, but the latter dominate host–guest relations. Such views are most extreme when tourists come into contact with marginal or peripheral economies and sensitive cultures. These perspectives stress the exploitative view of tourism which, in extremes, is perceived as a form of imperialism or the "prostitution" of developing economies. This is grounded in the idea that developing nations have few alternatives to tourism with which to earn foreign exchange. As host nations they have to sell their "beauty" which is then often desecrated by mass tourism. The analogies with prostitution come, it is

---

Box 4.2 The self-destruct theory of tourism development (based on Caribbean case studies)

There are four phases of development and decline:

Phase 1 Remote and exotic location offers rest and relaxation – provides an escape for rich tourists.

Phase 2 Tourism promotion attracts middle income tourists – come for rest and to imitate the rich. More hotels built, transforms original character away from an "escape paradise".

Phase 3 Area develops mass tourism, attracting a wide variety of tourists leading to social and environmental degradation.

Phase 4 As resort "sinks" under the weight of social and environmental problems tourists exit – leaving behind derelict tourism facilities. Most of the population cannot return to original way of life.

---

claimed, at a psychological level as developing nations are forced into a servile role in order to secure foreign exchange (Nash 1977). Another equally exploitative view is provided by the so-called "self-destruct" theory of tourism that postulates the rise and decline of resorts in a cyclical fashion (box 4.2). More recent reviews have recognized both the critical or cautionary perspectives on the impact of tourists, as well as the so-called advocacy perspective as shown in table 4.5 (Jafari 1989).

Perhaps more constructively, we can examine the sociocultural impact of tourists at three different levels, not all of which are necessarily negative. First, we can explore the nature of host–guest encounters. Second, we can follow through a functional view of those elements of the host society experiencing change due to tourism. Third, we can examine aspects of cultural change that are due to the influence of tourists (Lea 1988; Mathieson and Wall 1982; Sharpley 1994).

A generally held view is that the impact of tourism on a host community will vary according to the differences between the tourists and their hosts. Such differences may be measured in terms of race, culture, and social outlook, while the number of tourists is also significant. At this juncture we can turn back to the tourist typologies examined earlier in this chapter, especially those developed by Cohen and Smith, both of whom directed their identification of tourists toward an understanding of their potential impact on host communities (table 4.1). As can be seen from these typologies, the impact of tourism on host–guest relations becomes most prominent and critical under the influx of mass tourists to underdeveloped countries. Under such conditions, as Unesco (1976) indicates, relations between tourists and the host

Table 4.5 *The advocacy and cautionary perspectives of the impacts of tourism*

Economic	Sociocultural
Advocacy perspectives	
Is labor intensive	Broadens education
Generates foreign earnings	Promotes international peace
Can be built on existing infrastructure	Breaks down racial and cultural barriers
Can be development with local products and resources	Reinforces preservation of heritage and traditions
Spreads development	Enhances an appreciation of cultural traditions
Complements other economic activities	
Important multiplier effects	
Cautionary perspectives	
Causes local inflation	Generates stereotypes of the host and guest
High leakage of money from local economies	Leads to xenophobia
Highly seasonal and contributes to seasonality of employment	Results in social pollution
Very susceptible to change and economic fluctuations	Commodifies culture, and traditional ways of life
Results in unbalanced spatial development	Threatens traditional family life in host communities
Leads to extraneous dependency	Contributes to prostitution
Increases demonstration effects	Produces conflicts in the host community
Destroys resources and creates environmental pollution	

community tend to be characterized by four main features: the transitory nature of encounters between hosts and guests; temporal and spatial constraints on encounters; a lack of spontaneity in most encounters; and, finally, unequal or unbalanced relationships (box 4.3). The dimensions and complexities of these encounters have also been highlighted within specific case studies, such as the work of Karch and Dann (1996) in Barbados. This examined tourist–beachboy interactions and argued that such encounters typified much of the Third World's dependency on tourism.

At the root of these differences and their related problems is the fact that hosts and guests not only have diverse socio-cultural backgrounds but also very different perceptions. The tourist is living in what Jafari

---

Box 4.3   Features of mass tourism and host–guest relationships

Transitory nature of encounters
These are viewed differently by visitor and host. To the former they are fascinating and perhaps unique. To the host they may be just one of many superficial encounters experienced during the holiday season.

Temporal and spatial constraints
These influence the duration and geography of visitor–host encounters. Tourists want to "see" as much as possible of a culture in a short period of time, but they are also restricted very often in tourist enclaves.

Lack of spontaneity
Tourism turns traditional human relations into an area of economic activity; package tours, planned attractions, and cultural events become cash-generating activities.

Unequal and unbalanced relationships
This is especially so in developing countries: because of the wide disparities in wealth, hosts often feel inferior. Resentment at such differences may often make host community compensate by exploiting wealth of tourists.

Source: modified from UNESCO (1976)

(1989: 32) terms "non-ordinary time and place," while to the host it is ordinary life and home. Furthermore, these non-ordinary worlds are structured and conditioned by their respective cultures. The degree of contrasting values and conflict will obviously depend on levels of differences, together with the inherent flexibility of "each world" to adapt. As we have seen, the least flexible tourists are those involved via some form of mass tourism. While such contrasts have received considerable attention, far less interest has been directed at the receiving system, which is comprised of the host community and the host culture (Jafari 1989). Of particular importance in examining host–guest encounters is the structure of the community – its openness to other cultures and its traditions of hospitality. The main operating force within the community is the host culture, which structures community life and defines the degree of outside influence. As Jafari points out, some host communities are multicultural, which produces a far more complex response to tourists.

The non-ordinary world of the tourist is, in turn, structured by both the tourist culture and their residual culture. Despite the fact that tourists come from diverse social, ethnic, and cultural backgrounds, the "observable rituals, behaviours and pursuits . . . bind them into one collectivity" (Gottlieb 1982; Jafari 1989: 37; Krippendorf 1987a). In

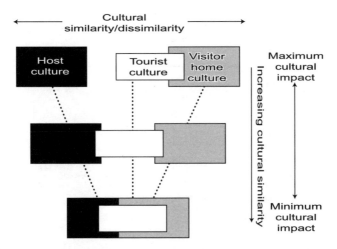

Figure 4.5 *Tourist cultures and cultural distance*
Source: modified from Williams (1998)

contrast, residual culture stresses the differences between tourists, since it denotes the "cultural-baggage" that tourists bring from their home cultures. Such residual culture shapes the behavior of tourists and can play an important role in the host community. The notion of cultural distance is also central to such interactions but, of course, as we have argued, this is complex and not merely based on a dictotomy between the culture of the host and the tourist. Such complexities arise because tourists come from a range of cultural backgrounds (even from within the same country) and tourist culture differs from the background culture of the tourist. We have in effect three potential different cultures, host, tourist, and background tourist culture as shown in figure 4.5. This illustrates in a somewhat basic way the impact of cultural distance, showing that in principle the greater the degree of cultural overlap the lower the impact of tourism on host cultures. Of course, there are other factors at work, in particular the effect of tourists, as discussed in the following section. The nature of host–guest relations is therefore conditioned by the complex interactions between these different elements of culture, together with the level and nature of tourism development (see also chapter 6 and figure 6.3).

The Sociocultural Impact of Tourists

The changes brought about by host–guest encounters are transmitted through both social and cultural impacts, the dimensions of which are

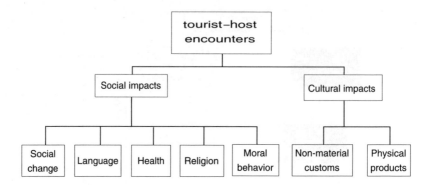

Figure 4.6   *The dimensions of tourist–host encounters*

indicated in figure 4.6. In reality, as Mathieson and Wall (1982) explain, it is extremely difficult to disentangle such sociocultural impacts, although for the sake of clarity we can examine some of the specific areas of change.

One of the simplest but most widely used frameworks for describing the effects of tourists on a host society is Doxey's (1976) so-called index of irritation. This represents the changing attitudes of the host population to tourism in terms of a linear sequence of increasing irritation as the number of tourists grows (figure 4.7). In this perspective host societies in tourist destinations pass through stages of euphoria, apathy, irritation, antagonism and loss in the face of tourism development. The progression through this sequence is determined both by the compatability of each group – which is related to culture, economic status, race, and nationality – as well as by the sheer numbers of tourists (Turner and Ash 1975). While Doxey's index is useful in exploring the reaction of residents to increasing tourism pressures, the approach does have some limitations. It is, for example, unidirectional and fails to address the situation where visitor management schemes may help to reduce tourist pressures or where the local community may become more involved in directing tourism growth. Alternative models, which offer greater degrees of flexibility, have been proposed by Bjorkland and Philbrick (1975) and Ap and Crompton (1993). Both are more dynamic in that they allow for varying sections of the local community to simultaneously hold different views. The work of Bjorklund and Philbrick perhaps holds the greatest potential in that their model encompasses both "active" and "passive" behavior as well as "negative" and "positive" attitudes all within a dynamic framework (figure 4.8). In this way it can place members of host communities with differing attitudes towards tourism.

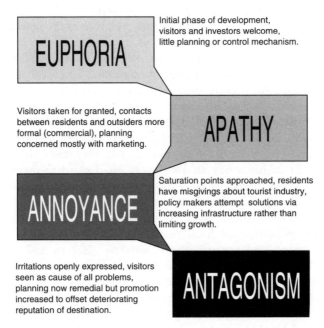

Levels of host irritation

EUPHORIA — Initial phase of development, visitors and investors welcome, little planning or control mechanism.

APATHY — Visitors taken for granted, contacts between residents and outsiders more formal (commercial), planning concerned mostly with marketing.

ANNOYANCE — Saturation points approached, residents have misgivings about tourist industry, policy makers attempt solutions via increasing infrastructure rather than limiting growth.

ANTAGONISM — Irritations openly expressed, visitors seen as cause of all problems, planning now remedial but promotion increased to offset deteriorating reputation of destination.

Figure 4.7 *Doxey's index of irritation*

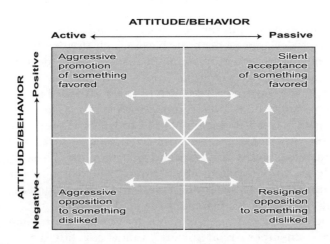

ATTITUDE/BEHAVIOR

Active ←——————————————→ Passive

ATTITUDE/BEHAVIOR — Positive / Negative

Aggressive promotion of something favored

Silent acceptance of something favored

Aggressive opposition to something disliked

Resigned opposition to something disliked

Figure 4.8 *Bjorklund and Philbrick's resident attitudinal and behavioral matrix toward tourism*

Source: modified from Page (1995)

Indeed, one of the most important factors in the growth of hostility to tourism relates to the physical presence of large numbers of tourists. This numerical impact is clearly relative to the size and spatial distribution of the host population, as is evidenced by some of the smaller island economies: the ratio of tourists to host population ranges from 15.4 per 100 in Samoa to almost 33 per 100 in the Maldives (Crandall 1987). Harrison (1992), among others, has stressed the impact of such numerical effects and measured them within the context of "tourist intensity rates" (TIR). This relates annual tourist arrivals with population size as a percentage and highlights the very high "TIRs" experienced by islands such as the Bahamas and Barbados. Dann (1996b) in his study of St. Lucia has linked numerical effects with tourist types, recognizing low-impact, long-staying tourists compared with the high-impact mass market.

A further underlying factor is the so-called "demonstration effect," which is the adoption by local residents, especially young people, of tourist behavior and consumption patterns (Rivers 1973; Sharpley 1994). Such a process can have some benefits if local people are encouraged to get a better education in order to improve their living standards. Much evidence, however, points to the social disbenefits as locals adopt the marks of affluence paraded by tourists, and live beyond their means (McElory and De Albuquerque 1986). As part of this adoption process, the host population often starts to demand more luxury items which tend to be imported goods, thereby generating an economic drain on the local economy (Clevedon 1979).

The adoption of foreign values also leads to what Jafari (1973) has described as a premature departure to modernization, producing rapid and disruptive changes in the host society. Under these circumstances social tension develops as the hosts become sub-divided between those adopting new values (usually young people and those deeply involved in the local tourism economy), as opposed to those retaining a traditional way of life. Such social dualism has been recorded by V. L. Smith (1977) in her study of Eskimo communities, and by Greenwood (1976) in rural Spain; while Lundberg's (1972) studies of Hawaii and Cowan's (1977) work on the Cook Islands detected societal disruptions in the form of increases in divorce rates and split families. These changes in family life are often brought about through increases in rural-urban (resort) migration, as individuals search for employment, and an increasing number of women enter the paid workforce.

The societal changes brought about by tourists are not always easy to isolate from other "modernizing" influences, but they appear to impact on a range of social elements (figure 4.6 and Pizam and Milman 1986; King et al. 1993). It is not the intention of this chapter to review all of these, but rather to identify certain key features. Indeed, in certain areas, such as language, only limited research on the impact of tourists has been undertaken (Mathieson and Wall 1982; White 1974). In contrast, considerable and growing attention has been directed toward the moral changes attributed to tourism, particularly the rise in crime (Chesney-Lind and Lind 1985; Nicholls 1976; Pizam 1982), gambling (Pizam and Pokela 1988), prostitution (Fish 1984; Graburn 1983) and most recently the spread of AIDS through sex tourism (Cohen 1988b; Ford and Eirowan 2000). For example, Sindiga (1999: 113) argues that a number of social problems including: "a high drop out rate from schools by male children, drug peddling, petty crimes, family disputes and prostitution have been blamed on tourism," along the coastal area of Kenya.

Given the difficulties in establishing tourism's role in changing the moral standards of host societies, it is not surprising that many of the early studies were empirically based and, at the same time, cautious over their findings. However, despite some methodological problems, Jud (1975) was able to present strong evidence of a positive relationship between tourism and crime in Mexico, while studies by McPeters and Stronge (1974) in Miami focused on the seasonality of crime. Within host societies in developing countries large differences between the incomes of hosts and guests, often highlighted in the demonstration effect, lead to increased frustration in the local community, which sometimes spills over as crimes against tourists (Chesney-Lind and Lind 1985). In turn, this frustration and friction is influenced by the volume of tourists, which obviously varies over the season. Thus, Rothman's (1978) study of resorts in Delaware showed massive seasonal changes in crime, which increased fivefold over a 12-month period.

Surveys among British tourists by the Consumer Association have revealed that the Caribbean tops the theft league, with tourists having a 1 in 14 chance of having their property stolen. Similarly high figures are recorded in the Gambia, while in Spain the risk falls to 1 in 30. As more tourists venture to an increasing number of destinations, crime does appear to be increasing, so some travel companies, such as Hogg Robinson and Tradewinds (a specialist long-haul company) even issue warnings of world trouble-spots (see also Pizam 1999). As the Tradewinds brochure puts it, "beauty seldom comes without a price," although of course the price is paid by both tourists and the local community. Not all crime is directed at the tourists; indeed, many research projects have found that increasingly local people are the victims (Rothman 1978). In some circumstances the tourists themselves behave in extremely anti-social and criminal ways: as witnessed in many

Spanish coastal resorts throughout the late 1980s and early 1990s, and as recorded earlier within the provincial nature parks of Canada (White et al. 1978).

In their early review of tourism and prostitution, Mathieson and Wall (1982: 149) suggested four main hypotheses that may be related. One was locational, in that tourism development often creates environments which attract prostitutes. The second was societal and related to the breaking of normal bonds of behavior by tourists when away from home – circumstances conducive to the expansion of prostitution. A third hypothesis is related to the employment offered by prostitution to women, and the opportunity to upgrade their economic status. Finally, they suggested that tourism may be a mere scapegoat for a general change in moral standards. They went on to conclude their review with the idea that there was a lack of firm evidence concerning connections between tourism and prostitution. More recent studies have confirmed such links and highlighted the articulation between the commercial sex industry and travel. Herold and van Kerkwijk (1992) have identified specific factors that have helped forge such links, including the travel media, which portrays tourist settings in exciting and romantic ways, where perhaps very different patterns of behavior may apply.

The dimensions of sex tourism are wide, incorporating both developed and developing economies, urban and coastal tourism, as well as organized and independent travel (Carter 2000; Ryan 2000). Much has been written on the sex tourism industry focused on parts of South-East Asia, especially in Thailand, the Philippines, and South Korea (primary areas), together with secondary areas throughout Indonesia (Seager and Olsen 1986; Truong 1990). The clients are normally men and the prostitutes are usually women in this particular division of labor. Tourists participating in this trade – either as individuals, small groups of friends or as employees offered a company bonus (often Japanese, as Blasing (1982) points out) – are sold holidays through sex-tour brochures. These thinly disguise the actual prostitution market by such images as "Thailand is a world full of extremes, and the possibilities are limitless. Anything goes in this exotic country – especially when it comes to girls" (Heyzer 1986: 53).

Attempts to quantify the scale of prostitution in places such as Thailand or the Philippines are difficult, considering the nature of the activity and its supposed illegality. The numbers of masseuses and prostitutes in Bangkok are estimated to be between 100,000 and 200,000 (Hall 1996), while other studies have recorded at least 977 establishments in the same city which are associated with prostitution (Heyzer 1986). The driving force behind such developments appears to be economic, since young female prostitutes can earn at least twice

> **Box 4.4   Main elements of culture that attract tourists**
>
> - Handicrafts
> - Traditions
> - History of a region   These tend to be ranked
> - Architecture   as most important by tourists
> - Local food
> - Art and music
> - "Ways of life"
> - Religion
> - Language
> - Dress – traditional costumes
>
> *Source*: modified from Ritchie and Zins (1978)

as much in the so-called hospitality industry as in other forms of employment. As Heyzer (1986) explains, although tourism increases the dividends of the prostitution trade it is not solely responsible for it. Certainly in Thailand the trade in female sexuality is supported by a complex network of ideological, economic, and political systems. Both Graburn (1983) and Heyzer (1986) have explored these systems, identifying three main reasons why Thai society sanctions this high level of prostitution. These revolve around employment discrimination against females in most formal sectors of employment, the economic crises facing many rural areas from where most prostitutes are drawn, and the breakdown of many marriages, which leaves women cut off from traditional society. In Thailand, however, there are noticeable changes in the tourist industry, with a decrease since 1987 in single male tourists (usually associated with the sex tourism industry) and an increase in family tourism. This, as Cohen (1988b) argues, is entirely due to the fear of contracting AIDS, and to the authorities placing greater stress on the cultural and natural attractions of the country.

Most cultures hold a fascination for tourists, who tend to be attracted by a number of overlapping cultural elements (box 4.4). Of particular importance to tourists are those forms of culture that are based around physical objects, the purchasing of local crafts, visiting cultural sites, and folk-culture as reflected in daily life or special festivals (Mathieson and Wall 1982: 159). There have been numerous anthropological studies on tourism and culture (see Jafari 1989), although two main areas of interest can be identified. The first follows the ideas already discussed on societal change, and concerns the processes of acculturation, which refers to the degree of cultural borrowing between two contact cultures (Nunez 1977). An alternative conceptual approach to this theme is through the concept of "cultural drift," as discussed by Collins (1978). Under the seasonal and intermittent contacts that characterize host–tourist relations, cultural drift assumes that changes in the host culture are at first temporary and then exploitive. Obviously, the degree to which acculturation or cultural drift occurs is strongly related to the patterns of host–tourist encounters, as discussed in the previous section.

The second group of studies relates to the marketing and commodification of culture as traditional ways of life become commercialized for tourist consumption (Cohen 1988c; de Kadt 1979). In some of the initial studies of the commoditization of culture by tourism, Greenwood (1977) observed, in the Spanish Basque town of Fuenterrabia, that local rituals lost all meaning when repeatedly staged for money. His more general conclusions were that local culture could easily be commodified, often without the consent of local people who would, in most cases, be exploited. The destruction of local cultural products, whether rituals or craftwork, leads to what MacCannell (1973) termed "staged authencity." In its most basic form it is associated with "airport art," cheap imitation products sold to tourists as local craftwork (Graburn 1967) or fake rituals that stress exotic local customs (Boorstin 1964). Furthermore, Cohen (1988c) suggests that in some instances a contrived cultural product may, over time, become recognized as authentic both by tourists and, more importantly, by local people. This emergent authenticity has been recorded by Cornet (1975) in the case of a supposed revival of an ancient Inca festival in Cuzco. This process is also frequently to be found at the heart of many revitalized local craft industries.

There are examples of the positive impacts of tourism on local cultures mainly through the revival of craft activities, and in many circumstances these can be strongly related to the concept of emergent authenticity. Within this context Graburn's (1976) study of the emergence of Eskimo soapstone carvings provides a ready example, as does Deitch's (1977) work on the art forms of Indians in south-west America. Similarly, Horner (1993) and Sindiga (1999) claim that there has been a revival of Kenyan art associated with the growth of tourism. But, of course, for each example of a more positive inter-play between tourism and culture, even though such impacts derive from the process of emergent authenticity, the literature contains many more cases of negative impacts (Mathieson and Wall 1982). Cohen (1988c) has argued that many of these studies and, indeed, Greenwood's early categorical assertion that commoditization removed all meaning from cultural products, are over-generalizations. He believes that even though events become tourist-orientated, they may still retain meanings for local people, and he argues that such impacts need to be submitted to more detailed empirical examinations, especially of a comparative nature. Such studies would make it possible to identify the conditions under which cultural meanings are preserved or emergent, as opposed to those environments under which tourism destroys culture. This debate takes us back to an assessment of tourism consumption and behavior, which in turn calls for a reworking of tourist typologies.

Part III

The Production of Tourism Services

5

The Tourism and Leisure Industries

The Tourism and Leisure Complex

Sinclair and Stabler (1997: 58) stress the difficulties of defining the tourism industry:

> It is a composite product involving transport, accommodation, catering, natural resources, entertainments and other facilities and services, such as shops and banks, travel agents and tour operators. Many businesses also serve other sectors and consumer demands, thus raising the question of the extent to which suppliers can be considered as primarily suppliers of tourism. The many components of the product, supplied by a variety of businesses operating in a number of markets, create problems in analysing tourism supply. It is therefore convenient to consider it as a collection of industries and markets.

This is the tourism production system. It includes tourism resources, infrastructures – both general and those specifically devoted to tourism – receptive facilities, entertainment and sports facilities, and tourism reception services (box 5.1). As would be expected, the definition of tourism is strongly contested. On the one hand, Smith (1998) argues that the tourism industry is an aggregate of all the businesses that directly provide goods or services to facilitate activities away from the home environment. Leiper (1990), however, argues that such a market-based definition does not constitute a definition of an industry. Wilson (1998) concurs, stating that an industry is defined as "a grouping of firms which operate similar processes and could produce technically identical products (or services) within a given planning horizon." Tourism fails this test, for tourism services are produced by

---

Box 5.1   Elements of the tourism industry

Tourism resources
- Natural resources
- Human resources

General and tourism infrastructure
- Means of communication and travel
- Social installations
- Basic installations
- Telecommunications

Receptive facilities
- Hotels, guest houses, towns, and villages
- Condominiums
- Complementary residences
- Residences for receptive personnel
- Food and beverage installations

Entertainment and sports facilities
- Recreational and cultural facilities
- Sports facilities

Tourism reception services
- Travel agencies
- Hotel and local promotional offices
- Information offices
- Car hire
- Guides, interpreters

Source: Sessa (1983)

This scheme is only indicative of the range of facilities and services that constitute the tourism industry. In practise, the tourism industry is temporally and spatially contingent.

---

organizations as diverse as airlines and guesthouses, while a variety of firms – including banks and railway companies – produce some tourism services. An alternative approach recognizes that there is a tourism related industry, in which "a considerable percentage of supply is generated by tourist demand" (Wilson 1998). It is, therefore, a composite industry, being an amalgam of industry sub-sectors, producing diverse products for which tourists constitute markets of varying importance.

This holistic definition is important as it colours the arguments surrounding the economic, social, and cultural impact of tourism. The costs of providing jobs in tourism, the income generated by tourism, and the seasonality effects of tourism have to be estimated for the complete tourism production system, not only for the most obvious tourism services such as accommodation. This also has implications for the analysis of ownership patterns in the tourism industry. While most property rights over the provision of commodified tourism services and goods is in various forms of private ownership within capitalist economies, the state as well as the voluntary sector plays an integral role in the development of the tourism related industry.

The leisure production complex differs in important ways from the tourism production complex, as would be expected given the definitions outlined in chapter 1. Tourism resources are also leisure resources. However, some leisure resources, such as lesser known beauty spots or networks of friends and neighbors, may predominantly serve the leisure needs of local populations. In terms of Sessa's scheme, the "general infrastructure" of an area is likely to serve the needs of both tourists and local residents, although international and inter-regional means of communications are utilized by tourism rather than for local leisure. "Receptive facilities" and "tourism reception services" are largely devoted to tourism although food and beverage installations, car hire firms and information services may also be elements in the consumption and production of local leisure. Entertainment and sports facilities are important to both tourism and leisure; while some of these may be shared – such as public swimming pools or squash courts – others are exclusive. Hotels and holiday villages may reserve facilities for the exclusive use of their guests, while some local facilities may be exclusive to membership groups that, by definition, exclude tourists. Finally, there is a range of home based leisure pursuits, such as gardening, which – again by definition – are excluded from tourism. This is to say that despite the fact that tourists and local residents may share the same spaces, the practices of tourism and leisure may be segregated within and between these. Alternatively, they can use the same facilities and spaces, and this may be competitive or complimentary. Tourist use of the local swimming pool may generate the marginal income that makes this facility financially viable, or significantly lowers costs and prices. But, at the same time, it may diminish the quality of experience it provides, so that in economic terms there is a trade off between marginal costs and benefits.

Commodification, Spatial Fixity, and Temporality

One important feature is a tendency to the *commodification* of tourism and leisure services. Leisure and tourism enterprises tend, over time, to bring into the market products or services which traditionally were provided outside the market (see Benington and White 1988: 17). Watson and Kopachevsky (1994) provide a more formal discussion of commodification, drawing mainly on Marxist writings. They argue that tourism should be understood as an extension of the more generalized commodification of modern life. And that it "is the process by which objects and activities come to be evaluated primarily in terms of their exchange value in the context of trade" rather than their actual use value (1994: 645). We can also note here MacCannell's (1976: 19) argument that there are also sign values embedded in modern commodities, and that they have to be culturally as well as economically interpreted. However, here we focus on the processes of commodification and the exchange values of tourism and leisure. Garden centres, for example, are selling more and more convenience and other products that were traditionally produced by the gardener at home. Larger numbers of guide books and leisure wear items are being produced for walkers and motorists. One notable aspect of this has been the commodification of place. Beaches or areas of countryside (such as Lands End in England or Nordkap in Norway) may be purchased by private capital and access to them may be commercialized. This gives rise to hotly contested property rights: evident for example in the Spanish state's *Ley de las Costas*, which seeks to maintain unrestricted access to the coast. Where it is not possible for capital to control access to a site – such as a historic city – it is still possible to commodify the experience of place, through the sale of tourist souvenirs, tour guide services, and the like.

The commodification process is significant in several ways. It can lead to restricted social access (predominantly by income) to leisure or tourism resources. Alternatively, it can generate increased flows of visitors so that the resulting economies of scale in production costs may lead to improved accessibility to the area by both public and private transport. Commodification can generate the income to help conserve an important site, such as the town of Williamsburg (USA), or it can lead to the construction of commercial facilities, as at Niagara Falls, which detract from the intrinsic value of the place for many visitors. Commodification, and in particular the introduction of private ownership into tourism and leisure services, also increases the potential for ownership of particular resources to pass into external control. This may involve ownership being acquired by large, diversified multinational corporations whose interests may not coincide with those of local communities. Box 5.2 illustrates some of the complex changes in commodification in the case of one of the former state socialist economies of Central and Eastern Europe.

Box 5.2   Commodification of tourism in the transition to the market economy in Slovakia

- Tourism under state socialism was shaped by an ideological legacy, rooted in the Marxist theory of production. Only the production of material goods, and services which directly supported this, could be considered a real and, or efficient form of production. As an "unproductive" and "inefficient" activity, the main role was "to regenerate the labour force." Extensive tourism facilities were owned by industrial companies, trades unions, and the state.

- After 1989 the tourism industry was subject to privatization, and there was a sharp decline in state-owned enterprises. For example, in 1997 state ownership in the tourism sector had been reduced to a residual 49 enterprises in Slovakia, while there were 1,275 private companies and 14,521 small personal businesses.

- As a result, market mechanism became the prime means of allocating access to tourism. The main "winners" were younger people, those living in larger cities, and the more educated, while the main losers were pensioners and employees who lost out as a result of the privatization of the tourism facilities of many industrial companies. In 1996, for example, holidays abroad were taken by 58 percent of managers but only by 16 percent of workers and 9 percent of pensioners.

- But there is also surprising continuity despite the commodification of tourism. For example, approximately one-quarter of all tourists stayed with friends and relatives both in the latter years of state socialism, and in the new market economy. The poorest members of society also continued to be heavily reliant on the residual state and company provision of tourism services. This reflects the mixed commodification of tourism which is evident in all market economies.

Source: Williams and Balaz (2000a, 2000b and 2001)

Tourism, and to a lesser extent leisure, is also characterized by *spatial fixity*. Urry (1990: 40) writes that "while the producers are to a significant extent spatially fixed, in that they have to provide particular services in particular places, consumers are increasingly mobile, able to consume tourist services on a global basis." There are of course exceptions; large transnationals can relocat capital in response to demand changes, while there is considerable scope to create new tourist attractions, given that these are socially constructed. But the vast majority of entrepreneurs are small scale and their businesses are characterized by spatial fixity in that they are associated with particular tourist attractions. As a result they are subject to the high degree of volatility in tastes in tourism and leisure, and are restricted in their ability to respond to this.

Temporal variations in demand exacerbate the difficulties associated with spatial fixity. While the demand for manufactured goods can also be temporal, producers can respond to this by accumulating stocks of (non-perishable) goods. However, the production capacity of a tourism service is "fixed by inelastic physical and geographical limits and by the impossibility for this kind of production to accumulate stocks of products" (Sessa 1983: 68). Producers usually respond to the temporally uneven nature of demand via differential pricing, and temporary labor contracting. Higher prices are charged at peak times when market demand will bear these. Lower prices will be charged in the off-periods in the hope of attracting deferred, unsatisfied peak period demand.

The tourism and leisure production systems are composed of very diverse elements, in terms of both ownership and scale. In tourism, in particular, the successful development of a service complex will depend on a partnership between public and private sectors and between small and large capitals.

A Question of Scale: Company Structures

The tourism and leisure industries tend to have highly polarized structures, being dominated by a few large businesses operating alongside a large number of small, independent businesses. For example, in the USA in the late 1980s there were only two national bookshop chains – Daltons and Walden Books – after a long series of mergers and acquisitions (Benington and White 1988: 14). In the American travel agency business there are some large corporate chains but 99 percent of businesses – as opposed to business – are small firms (Richter 1985). In the UK fast food industry, it is estimated that small independents accounted for 55 to 60 percent of fast food sales in 1987, despite the growing presence of corporate chains (Key Note 1988). However, fast foods also illustrate the trend to increasing scale and transnationalization in the leisure and tourism industries. In 1987 the world's four largest chains owned or franchised almost 28,000 outlets between them, and this number is continuing to increase. The increase in scale is, of course, linked to transnationalization: one of the driving forces behind internationalization is the drive to increase markets so as to achieve economies of scale.

Increasing scale is also evident in the tourism industry. By 1995 four international corporate chains owned or operated more than 1,000 hotels each, with Choice Hotels International in first place with

Table 5.1   *Major international hotel chains 1995*

Company	No. of hotels	No. of countries
1. Choice	3,431	38
2. Best Western	3,395	60
3. Accor	2,313	65
4. Holiday Inn	1,977	62
5. Forte	926	54
6. Marriot	903	27
7. Sheraton	419	63
8. Radisson	300	33
9. Club Med.	262	36
10. Hyatt	169	36
11. Hilton International	162	46
12. Inter-Continental	143	55

Only includes hotel chains with more than 50,000 rooms, at least 75 hotels and with a presence in at least 15 countries
Source: based on Economist Intelligence Unit (1995)

3,431 hotels (table 5.1). Their ownership was concentrated in the three main economic cores of the world economy: six were American owned (Choice, Best Western, Marriott, Sheraton, Hyatt, and Radisson), five were European (Holiday Inn, Forte, and Hilton International of the UK, Accor, and Club Meditérranée of France), and one was Japanese (Inter-Continental). The scale of hotel operations has been increasing. Between 1991 and 1995 the five largest international corporate groups added just over 200,000 rooms to their assets, an increase of 17 percent (Economist Intelligence Unit 1995). Similar trends are evident within individual countries. In the UK, for example, the first really large hotel group was formed only in 1970, following the merger of Trust Houses and Forte (Tarrant 1989). By the mid 1980s, however, corporate chains accounted for 13 percent of all hotels and 55 percent of all hotel rooms in the UK (Slattery and Roper 1988). This does not mean that the demise of the small independent hotel is imminent. While the large chains and hotels have access to economies of scale, the small inde-pendents can compete on the basis of costs (using low wage family or other labor), individuality or personalized service. The critical size appears to be the medium scale establishments with 25 to 60 bedrooms, which find it difficult to benefit from either individuality or economies of scale (Burkart and Medlik 1981: ch. 14).

Scale economies in the leisure and tourism sectors are not greatly different in character from those that operate in the service – and to a

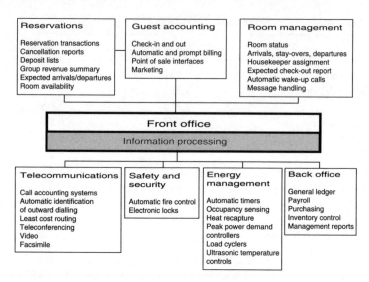

Figure 5.1 *The total hotel information system*
Source: Sheldon (1983: 270)

lesser extent the manufacturing – sector at large. There are economies of scale in production, relating to the purchase of inputs, the internal division of labor and specialization, and indivisibilities in the use of capital (Sinclair and Stabler 1997: 86–8). Aircraft provide an example of the latter: the more that the aircraft is used, then the more its fixed purchase costs can be spread over a larger number of trips, reducing their unit costs. The question is at what points do economies of scale become diseconomies of scale – perhaps because of the increased management costs of organizing larger, and perhaps more geographically dispersed, companies. However, new management techniques and technologies can counteract the onset of diseconomies of scale. The latter is illustrated by the application of information technology. Hotels have developed relatively sophisticated information technology systems that offer cost reductions and more effective management to help counter some of the managerial disadvantages of increased scale (figure 5.1). In air travel, computer reservation systems (CRS) have been a significant innovation, and these initially favored the largest carriers. The substantial capital costs involved in the development of these super CRS operations originally meant that only the largest airlines were able to participate. This eventual advantage was lost as other world airlines developed their own CRS networks. However, scale remains important as the costs of developing successively more sophisticated CRSs tend to preclude most of the smaller air carriers, while even the largest carriers are increasingly concentrated into international alliances.

There are also scale economies in marketing. There are minimum scales of operations necessary to justify national – or international – marketing whether for hotels, air transport, or travel agencies. Large hotels have also been able to capitalize on the advantages of "branding," that is offering a standard product of known quality and price in key locations. This allows them to maximize repeat business which is important given the lower costs of attracting return visitors compared to new customers. The process of branding is assisted by the homogenization of taste among regular travelers, so that there is a virtuous cycle of uniformity of demand, product standardization with reduced unit costs of production and minimum quality guarantees, enhanced customer satisfaction, and increased brand loyalty. However, successful branding requires close control and rationalization. Tarrant (1989: 188) writes that major hotel corporations have been ruthless in their rationalization programs: where refurbishment of individual hotels, in accordance with target goals of efficiency, is not possible, they are quickly disposed of.

In some sectors of the tourism and leisure industries there are minimum capital requirements for successful operation. Airline operations, for example, require large initial capital outlays in aircraft and supporting installations. Furthermore, maintaining competitiveness requires continuous programs of large scale re-investment, with high levels of risk in what is an increasingly competitive market. Small companies cannot hope to compete in these sectors, especially if there are large research and development costs involved. However, they can find niche markets, serving particular routes, which perhaps have insufficient capacity to attract the attention of the major corporations. More significantly, many tourism sub-sectors are dominated by small firms, and this usually reflects relatively low entry barriers in terms of capital, or knowledge: examples include souvenir retailing, small guest houses, cafes, and renting rooms.

In addition, other advantages accrue to large scale operations, such as internalization of linkages in vertically integrated operations, and diversification in the face of uncertain market conditions. For example, in the 1980s Grand Metropolitan's holdings included Berni Inn, Chef and Brewer, Express Foods, Eden Vale, Ski, Cinzano, Foster's lager in the UK, and hotels such as The Carlton in Cannes. This allowed them to reduce risk against all but the most generalized and internationalized of recessions. Increased scale also brings advantages in terms of market leadership that facilitates price setting, and excluding or making

---

Box 5.3   Strategic growth options available to tourism and leisure companies

- *Acquisitions of and mergers* with existing companies: characteristic of tour companies, airlines, and hotel corporations.
- *New investment* in green-field sites: e.g. Euro-Disney.
- *Franchising*: especially important in the fast food industry and, more recently hotel chains.
- *Intensification of production in situ*: via a reorganization of the labor process or addition of new capital.

Any one company may adopt one or more of these strategies, and these will be spatially and temporally contingent on regulations, market conditions and the supply of entrepreneurs.

---

it difficult for competitors to enter that market. For example, Cannon's purchase of the ABC cinema chain, when added to their existing holdings, gave them control of almost 40 percent of UK cinema screens in the mid 1980s (Benington and White 1988: 13).

There are a number of strategic options for a company that wishes to increase the scale of its operations and, in practice, it may adopt a combination of these (box 5.3). These include acquisitions and mergers, new investment sites, intensification of production, and franchising. The last of these is particularly characteristic of the leisure industries, notably fast food chains. The precise strategy chosen depends on both internal company structures (the availability of, or the potential to raise, capital), whether the product market is in the early or mature stages (hence whether existing establishments are available for take-over) and local contingencies (whether there are potential entrepreneurs and sufficient capital in particular areas to facilitate franchising).

While there are strong concentration tendencies in these industries, many sectors continue to be dominated by small firms. Individuality and personalized services are commodities that command a premium and that allow small establishments to survive in even the most competitive markets. In addition, there are some market segments which are too small – serving a small town or some highly specialized leisure or tourist interest group – to be attractive to large companies. Furthermore, small firms may be able to secure some of the scale advantages of the corporate chains by forming voluntary groups for marketing or purchasing purposes. One of the best known examples is the Best Western hotel group which has successfully developed branding even though the establishments remain in individual ownership.

Box 5.4   Foreign investment in tourism in Australia

	1986–7	1990–1
Foreign investment in tourism (AUS$m)	1,553	1,860
% share of all foreign investment in tourism	4	9
% from Japan	74	67

data for *planned* foreign investment
Source: Dwyer and Forsyth (1994)

Although foreign investment has grown in absolute and percentage share terms in this period, the peak level was much higher, at AUS$4997m in 1988–9. This illustrates both the increasing importance of tourism in international trade and the increased volatility that may be associated with this. Japan accounts for 25 percent of all foreign investment in Australia in this period, but for more than two-thirds of that in tourism. This reflects both the general importance of Japan as a source of investment in the Pacific Rim and the high levels of inbound tourism from that country.

Internationalization and Transnational Corporations

The growth of transnational companies is one particular aspect of the increasing concentration in the leisure and tourism industries. Some leisure products, such as films, sports wear, and video machines, are already highly internationalized. However, there is also growing internationalization of the production of leisure and tourism services. This is illustrated in the case of Australia in box 5.4.

Taylor and Thrift (1986: 6) suggest that there are at least three levels of transnational corporations: global corporations; multinational corporations; and "small" multinationals. These are differentiated by the extent to which their activities are internationalized, as opposed to remaining nationally based. All three are to be found in the tourism and leisure industries. For example, the ITT group, owners of the Sheraton hotels, are a diversified global corporation with a strong presence in 61 countries and most of the world's largest markets. The Trusthouse Forte group – which was broken up in the 1990s – was an example of a multinational corporation in the hotel sector; while one of the largest chains in the world, its operations were highly regionalized, being concentrated in Europe. An example of a "small" multinational is Journey's End Corporation of Canada which, in 1990, had 133 hotels but had only recently begun to operate outside its home country. In the hotel sector, there are few global transnationals and even the largest corporations tend to concentrate on particular regions. A survey in the late 1970s found that: UK transnationals were most active in Europe, Africa and the Caribbean; American transnationals were most active in Asia and Latin America; and Japanese transnationals were most evident in the Pacific Rim region.

There are a number of reasons for the growth of transnationals in tourism and leisure, some of which have already been considered in the earlier discussion of scale economies. The international market provides even greater potential for large companies to secure competitive advantages through scale economies and market dominance, although these have to be balanced against the increased costs of such operations. These tendencies are similar to those that have been observed in the manufacturing sector (see Dicken 1998). Furthermore, there are direct links between internationalization of different economic sectors; for example, international hotel chains have partly developed in response to the requirements of international business travel (see chapter 2), while some global manufacturing corporations, such as ITT, diversified into tourism.

In addition, there are a number of specific reasons for the internationalization of operations. Urry (1990: 48) refers to "an international division of tourist sites." For example, Spain, Austria, and the UK, respectively, specialize at the international level in beach, winter sports, and heritage-related holidays. This has two implications for internationalization: tourism companies wishing to diversify their portfolio of holiday products, or (tour companies) wishing to secure a larger share of their national market must, therefore, internationalize their activities. The role of the transnationals is not necessarily passive in this, in the sense of following consumer preferences. Instead, they are one of the agents that contribute to the social construction of tourism preferences through their advertising campaigns and facilitating roles. Another reason for the growth of transnational corporations is their strategic response to differential costs of production and the pressures, especially in the mass tourism market, to lower the costs of holidays: this leads international companies to seek out those destinations (such as Spain in the 1960s, and Gambia in the 1990s) with low production (especially labor) costs.

Air travel and hotel chains offer two classic but contrasting examples of transnationalization within the tourism industry. International airlines figure on the lists of the world's largest multinational companies. The need to develop comprehensive regional or global networks so as to attract clients and internalize the revenue from connecting flights, provides a strong logic for the growth of multinationals. Yet their operating environment is highly constrained. Wheatcroft (1990: 353) writes that "Air transport . . . has been shaped in the past by the combined forces of sovereignty, nationalism and protectionism." Many

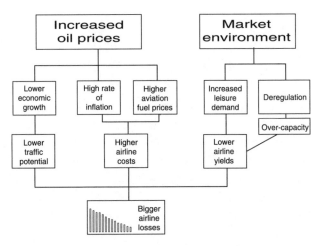

Figure 5.2   *International airline economics: patterns of change*
Source: Wheatcroft (1982: 72)

airlines have been heavily subsidized and protected for nationalistic, economic, and prestige reasons. However, the operating environment is changing (figure 5.2). On the market side, deregulation (especially in the USA, and more gradually in Europe) has exposed overcapacity in the industry. The growing proportion of leisure as opposed to business travelers is also pressurizing prices downwards. At the same time, periodic rises in oil prices have squeezed the operating margins of airlines. Privatization is also changing the competitive environment: more than 30 airlines were privatized during the 1980s, including market leaders such as British Airways and Japan Airways, and this provided these companies with greater scope for using financial markets to fund aggressive expansion programs.

The increased competition, consequent upon deregulation, has seen a major restructuring of the industry. This has been evident in a number of spectacular airline bankruptcies such as PanAm, which had been a market leader. The other notable response has been the attempt by some airlines to create mega carriers via a program of mergers and acquisition (Wheatcroft 1990): these would have the advantages of extensive route networks, and economies of scale in production (e.g. purchasing and maintenance of aircraft) and marketing. British Airways, for example, acquired British Caledonian in 1988 and has subsequently investigated alliances with both KLM of the Netherlands and United of the USA.

Hotels present a different picture of transnationalization:

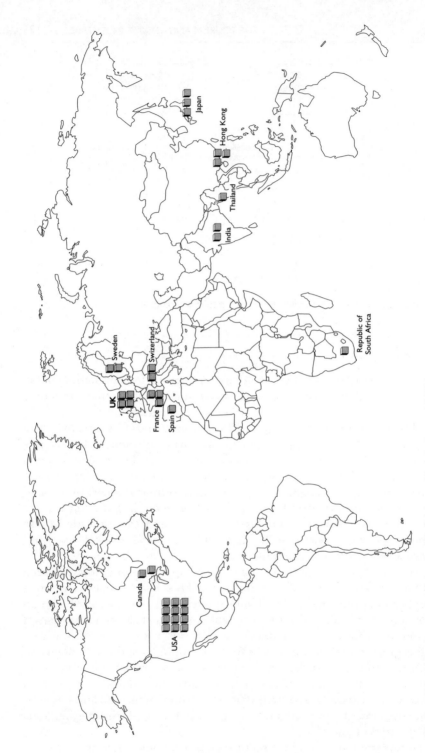

Figure 5.3 Headquarters of the world's 36 largest hotel chains, 1995

Before the Second World War, there were already a few small international hotel groups crossing national frontiers. They were prestigious,
family controlled, or personally owned groups of hotels associated, for
example, with the names of Ritz or Marquet. These enterprises bore
little or no resemblance to the major international hotel chains of today.
(Fenelon 1990: 97)

Among the major international hotel groups, Accor, Best Western,
Holiday Inn and Sheraton are the most internationalized, with each
having operations in more than 60 countries in 1995, but all the other
12 leading groups also operated in at least 25 countries (table 5.1). By
2000, the level of internationalization had increased further, with Bass
Hotels, Best Western International, Accor and Starwood Hotels emerging as clear leaders, with operations in more than 80 countries each
(Hotels 2000). These could form the bases for the emergence of mega
hotel chains with 100,000–350,000 rooms distributed globally, which
will "set the pace through their sheer weight in terms of investment,
global positioning, and management talent" (Go et al. 1990: 298). The
headquarters of the largest chains have traditionally been concentrated
in the USA and Europe (especially the UK and France). However, this
is gradually changing (figure 5.3). While one-third of the largest international corporations have their headquarters in the USA, and a further
one-third in Europe, there are also significant number of headquarters
in Asia. With a few exceptions, the operations of most of these companies tend to be regionalized. Most of their hotel rooms are in Europe
and North America, although this pattern is being modified by the
rapid expansion of hotel capacity in the Pacific Rim region. To some
extent, then, the emergence of truly global transnational companies in
the hotel sector is constrained by the highly regionalized pattern of
tourism flows (see chapter 2), but over time there is a tendency to
increased globalization in both of these.

Dunning and McQueen (1982) provide a systematic theoretical
framework for the analysis of multinationals in one tourism sector, the
hotel industry. Drawing on Dunning's wider research on the theory of
multinationals, they argue (1982: 19) that "the propensity of a firm to
engage in international production depends on three conditions being
satisfied": these they term ownership, location, and internalization.

First, firms have net ownership advantages in relation to other firms
that they compete against in any one market. These stem from the fact
that hotels sell experience goods (already familiar to the customer)
rather than search goods (which can be examined and compared to each
other and to advertisements). Hotels sell a package of on-site and off-
site services before, during, and after a stay at the hotel and these constitute the total experience of using that hotel chain. Ascher (1985: 37)

comments that, in practice, there is remarkable similarity in the range of services offered by the main hotel groups even though individual corporations have very diverse origins. There are, however, differences in the quality and the presentation of these services and this is the basis for branding. Branding ensures that the services provided or experienced in any one hotel owned by a chain match the client's expectations. The multinational hotel has an advantage over the domestic hotel in competing for the lucrative business provided by international travelers because they have the knowledge and the experience to provide a package of services tailored to demand. It is these proprietary rights over a differentiated product which create the ownership conditions for transnationalism in this sector.

The second main factor is that it must be profitable for the firm to combine its assets with the factor endowments located in foreign countries. In the case of hotels these locational advantages are based on market segmentation. Their appeal to the international traveler lies partly in being able to provide their particular "experience good" in most of the major international destinations that he or she is likely to visit. In other words, they have presence in the key locations for this market segment. There is therefore a compelling reason to be truly global, as business activity continues to globalize. In practise, very few hotel corporations have been fully able to capitalize on this "locational" factor. Instead, as observed earlier, most international hotel corporation have regionalized international markets. However, given that most business travelers operate in such regional rather than truly global fields – despite recent trends – this is consistent with securing locational advantages.

Finally, there are internalization advantages to be secured from expanding across international borders. Internalization is explained by Taylor and Thrift (1986: 7) as "a simple term that applies to a simple insight, namely that a whole series of transactions are internalised within the multinational corporation rather than taking place within the market, either to protect against or to exploit market failure." Examples of this are the ownership of hotels by tour companies or international airlines: for example, in the early 1990s Wagons Lits owned 314 Pullman International Hotels, while AIR Nipon airways owned 31 Ana Enterprises hotels (*Hotels* July 1991). In effect, these companies were creating strong intra-firm vertical and horizontal linkages. Buying and selling services from other firms in the same group offers a number of advantages: it reduces risk and market uncertainty, allows economies of scale and scope, and internalizes profits.

Taken together, these three aspects of ownership, location, and internalization provide a useful framework for the analysis of transnationals in the hotel sector (see Williams 1995). However, Dunning and

McQueen also highlight a particular feature of international hotel chains, namely, the use of sub-contracting. This is based on the division between ownership of the buildings required for the hotel, which represent a long-term investment in real estate, and the know how required to deliver a particular hotel experience. The latter requires a short-term return for a constantly changing service product. There is, therefore, a tendency for the separation of property ownership and hotel management. Increasingly, the large hotel corporations are specializing in providing management know how under contract to the owners of the hotel building. For example, Hilton International, prior to its take over by the Ladbroke group, owned 44 hotels, partially owned and operated 14 hotels, and operated another 33 hotels under management contracts (Laws 1991: 219–20).

Given the varied nature of the tourism and leisure industries it is not surprising that there is considerable diversity in the form of internationalization. This is evident in the examples provided here of just two sub-sectors, hotels and aviation. The next section examines a third and very distinctive form of transnationalism, the international tour company.

Packaging Paradise: The International Tour Companies

International tour companies play a critical role in the international tourism industry: they link millions of individual consumers, mostly in the more developed countries, with large numbers of individual enterprises in the travel industry, the accommodation sector and other tourism-related services. These enterprises are often located in countries that are less economically developed than those the tourists originate from. With the exception of the air travel industry, most such enterprises are relatively small scale.

Historically, the creation of package holidays is associated with Thomas Cook. Cook's first foreign holiday was arranged only in 1855 but within 10 years he had a thriving international business. By 1872 Cook was able to offer round-the-world holidays. Its main rival in the USA was American Express which, from the 1850s, offered financial and other services to travelers (Feldman 1989). Eventually other companies entered the market that was boosted by, as well as being integral to the development of mass tourism. From the 1950s, competition in the industry intensified, as inclusive air tours were developed for mass tourists. The industry has continued to expand and in the UK, for example, the number of package tours sold has increased from only 6 million in 1980 to 17 million in 1995 (Economist Intelligence Unit 1996; Fitch 1987).

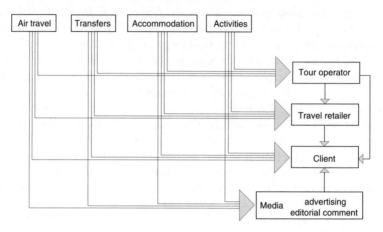

Figure 5.4 *Channels of travel distribution*
Source: Laws (1991: 41)

Foreign travel can be dominated by but is rarely monopolized by tour companies. Individuals can make their own direct arrangements with travel companies and hotels, or can purchase these services from travel agents (figure 5.4). The choice between making individual arrangements, as opposed to reliance on a tour company, will depend on personal knowledge, experience, and resources (including the time to make arrangements, or access to the Internet to facilitate these), the difficulty of making arrangements in particular countries, and the attractiveness of the holiday packages offered by the tour company. For example, in the UK 84 percent of outward tourists to Greece, compared to only 34 percent of those to France, used tour companies for their holidays (figure 5.5). This reflects ease of access, types of holiday experiences sought, and previous experiences. One notable trend has been the growth of package holidays, or inclusive tours, to long haul destinations, reflecting the globalization of tourism: between 1985 and 1995 the proportion of all inclusive tours accounted for by the long-haul segment increased from 6.7 percent to 12 percent.

In practise, therefore, there is considerable variation between countries with respect to the role played by tour companies. Their role is relatively strong in Northern Europe and Japan, and weaker in North America and Southern Europe. Germany has the world's largest tour operator industry, with 27 million inclusive holidays sold in 1996 compared to only 16.6 million in 1988 (Economist Intelligence Unit 1996). The UK has Europe's second largest outbound package tour market with about 17 million packages sold in 1995, while 1.6 million were sold in Sweden in the same year.

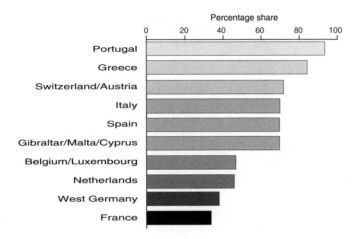

Figure 5.5 *The market share of inclusive tours in the main overseas holiday destinations of UK residents, 1985*

Source: Fitch (1987: 31)

Box 5.5   The economics of tour company operations

- *High productivity and low-cost products*: through generating high volumes of sales; e.g. Thomson (UK) sold over 3 million holidays per annum, during the late 1980s and most of the 1990s.
- *Largely undifferentiated products*: offer similar bundles of tourism services.
- *Efficient marketing systems*: allow tour company to market, and charge for, bundles of services in advance of their delivery.
- *Subcontracting system*: tour companies only own a limited proportion of travel and other facilities, which means they have very low capital outlays. However, some companies have their own charter airlines and hotels in order to internalize an important revenue element.
- *High risk*: due to reliance on relatively short season and impossibility of deferring demand.

The economics of tour company operations are based on five main elements as shown in box 5.5, and the high level of risk is particularly noteworthy. The system of sub-contracting is most open to variation for there have been differences as to whether some tour companies establish their own charter airlines in order to internalize one of the most important revenue elements from the sale of holiday packages. This is seen in the UK where Thomson own the Britannia charter

Table 5.2 *Assets of the five leading European tour operators, 1999*

	Packages (million)	Travel agencies	Planes	Ships	Beds	Hotels
Preussag (Germany)	13.5	3,469	60	4	80,738	164
Airtours (UK)	9.0	940	47	11	9,617	26
Thomson (UK)	7.0	862	41	4	4,000	13
C&N (Germany)	6.0	1,200	39	0	34,500	51
Kuoni (Switzerland)	4.0	150	3	0	100	2

Source: *Financial Times* (May 16, 2000)

airline, whose operations exceed those of many major scheduled European carriers. The other leading UK tour operators also own airlines: First Choice has Air 2000, Thomas Cook has JMC Airlines, and Airtours has Airtours International. The reverse pattern can also be observed with airlines owning tour companies. For example, Japan Airlines owns Japan Creative Tours, Swissair has a majority holding in Kuoni, the largest Swiss group, and Air France has a majority interest in Sotair, the French tour operator. However, most tour companies rely on sub-contracting, especially for services other than air travel. Typically contracts may be signed for a single season, or on a rolling basis over several seasons, with hotels, coach companies and providers of other hospitality and leisure services and products in the destinations. Alternatively, as Drexl and Agel (1987: 37) report occurs in Germany,

> the main operators also have direct involvement through the setting up of hotel management companies in some foreign hotels such as TUI with Iberotel (35 hotels) and RIU (17 hotels) in Spain. Similar structures exist for NUR with Royaltur and Aldiana Clubs. Mallorca, one of the main destinations in Spain for West German tourists, offers a number of TUI and NUR-exclusive beds (through its subsidiaries Iberotel and Royaltur) which is larger than the total accommodation capacity of Greece.

Tour operators in the UK are also increasingly moving to ownership of at least some hotels in their key destinations. There are, then, substantial economies of scale in production (including internalization of vertical linkages) and marketing of package holidays, as can be seen from the diverse assets of the leading European tour companies (table 5.2). This is linked of course to the concentration of ownership. In the USA, for example, in the mid 1970s there were over 1,000 tour operators but 3 percent of these handled 37 percent of customers

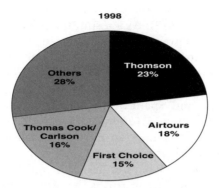

Figure 5.6   *The market shares of tour operators in the UK, 1998*

(Sheldon 1988: 53). While the main players remained constant, there was a high rate of instability in the industry as a whole with large numbers of births and deaths of firms. The UK tour industry has a similar structure. Hundreds of small operators offer specialist packages or operate on a regional basis, but 57 percent of the market was accounted for by just three companies in 1998: Thomson, Airtours, and Thomas Cook/Carlson (figure 5.6). There is a long standing tendency to concentration in the UK, where the three leading companies – Thomson, International Leisure Group, and Horizon – accounted for 60 percent of the British air tour market in 1987 (Fitch 1987: 29). Subsequently, Horizon has been taken over by Thomson and International Leisure Group has become insolvent. However, the leading European tour companies are German rather than British. Even in 1999, the German company Preussag sold 13.5 million packages and this was before it made a bid for the third-ranked European company, Thomson, in 2000.

Given the particular conditions in the international tourism market, tour companies have achieved strong positions in the air travel holiday industries of many developed countries. A number of important consequences follow from this. First, the economies of scale secured by the tour companies have allowed them to reduce significantly the cost of foreign holidays. This has been critical in the growth of mass international tourism (see chapter 9). Second, their success comes from "maximising load factors on the travel portion, and through volume buying to negotiate very low rates with the accommodation suppliers they use" (Laws 1991: 36). The large numbers of mostly small independent operators mean that supply conditions resemble those of perfect competition, whereas the concentration of ownership among tour companies mean that demand is delivered under oligopolistic conditions (that is where a small number of producers dominate the industry – see Sinclair and Stabler 1997: 68–9). As a result, the prices paid to local entrepreneurs tend to be depressed. It is hardly surprising, then, that UK tour companies – which are characterized by one of the highest levels of concentration in Europe – secure some of the lowest hotel prices in the destination countries. For example, in 39 out of 57 hotels surveyed in Portugal, Greece, and Spain in the late 1980s, the lowest price was offered by a British company (quoted in Urry 1990: 48).

Third, tour companies play an important role in the social construction of tourism. Their advertising and, above all, their brochures help shape the images of what are desirable and expected holidays in the mass market. One feature of this is the promotion of holiday types, such as "winter ski" or "summer sun," which are essentially placeless. The resorts are defined mainly in terms of their leisure attributes and are presented as devoid of nationality, culture, and local context. It follows from this, and from the internationalization of services and architectural styles in these "identikit" resorts, that virtually the only point of competition is price. This strengthens the bargaining power of the tour companies *vis-à-vis* the independent local operators and contributes to the depression of prices. While reinforcing the conditions for the further expansion of mass tourism, this also has a profound impact on the distribution of income from tourism.

Finally, the tour companies do not market all tour resorts equally. The search for economies of scale (in marketing, chartering air services, and sub-contracting to local hospitality outlets), as well as the availability of air links where they rely on scheduled flights, mean that they concentrate on a few resorts or regions. This has already been referred to in chapter 2 in the discussion of international tourist movements. As a result, particular resorts or tourist regions tend to become highly dependent on particular market segments. This makes them especially vulnerable to fluctuations in demand within those markets. This has been a particular problem in the Mediterranean region; for example, the Algarve receives 50 percent of its visitors from the historically volatile UK market. In some respects, therefore, the geography of tour company operations is also a geography of dependency relationships.

State Intervention, Government, and Governance

While tourism and leisure enterprises are mostly owned by private capital in capitalist societies, the state is usually involved in these sectors either through regulation or, in some instances, ownership. There are a number of reasons for state intervention and these change over time in response to national and international economic developments,

---

Box 5.6   Reasons for state interventionism in tourism and leisure

1. National economic goals such as balancing the current account.
2. Political legitimation, whereby the state "justifies" its existence through intervention.
3. Equity and social needs such as ensuring minimum provision of leisure and tourism access to citizens.
4. Where externalities and social investment (for example, from building a new road or water treatment plant) mean that the state has to intervene because there are insufficient returns to individual owners of capital.
5. Regulation and negative controls, such as protection of the landscape and environment (and perhaps the main tourist attraction) from the actions of private capital.
6. The use of tourism and leisure as instruments of urban and regional development.

---

changes in the tourism industry itself, as well as in government and governance. According to the OECD (1974: 3), there have been three main phases of tourism policies in the developed world since 1945. In the late 1940s and the early 1950s the emphasis was on dismantling health, customs, and other regulations that hindered international movements. Subsequently, in the 1950s governments became more involved in promoting tourism in response to its increased importance in international trade. Finally, in the 1970s and the 1980s, governments became more aware of the environmental, social, and regional implications of tourism development (see also Airey 1983). To this we should also add that in the 1980s and 1990s, the increased neo-liberal dominance of the policy arena has led to a "rolling back of the frontiers of the state" in tourism and leisure as in many other arenas of state intervention. There are six principal reasons for state interventionism in the tourism and leisure industries (box 5.6).

The prime attraction of tourism for national policy makers is *as an agent of economic development*. The high ratio of labor to capital in many sub-sectors, ease of entry into the market, and the rapidity of development – especially compared to most agricultural and manufacturing sectors – make tourism and leisure particularly attractive to national policy. The state may therefore intervene directly (for example, in developing the previously publicly owned *pousada* hotel chain in Portugal) or indirectly (via infrastructural investments or subsidies to private capital) in these industries. The global recession in manufacturing industries in the 1980s and the crisis of overproduction in agriculture has added to the attraction of tourism and leisure services as objects of economic development and diversification policies.

International tourism offers the added attraction of generating foreign exchange. International tourism trade is growing faster than merchandise trade, and accounts for more than a quarter of the value of internationally traded services. This can have a considerable impact on a country's balance of trade. In 1997, for example, tourism receipts in Western Europe were equivalent to 1.5 percent of GDP and 5.9 percent of exports, while in Australasia the equivalent figures were 2.5 percent and 14.5 percent (World Tourism Organization 1998). For these reasons, most governments have become involved in national tourism promotion in foreign markets. There may also be parallel promotion strategies to encourage nationals to take domestic rather than foreign holidays.

Cultural and sporting events can also become the focus of mega-events supported by the state. The Olympic Games and the World Cup, for example, can act as the focus of major events that not only generate tourism revenue but also attract world attention. This can raise the profile of a country, region, or city and enhance its international competitiveness. Barcelona (Carreras i Verdaguer 1995) and, more recently, Sydney provide shining examples of this phenomenon. This is particularly important in the competition between places for footloose international investments. Such investments – whether in financial services or electronics research – increasingly are informed by quality of life considerations, as much as by labor or transport costs. The development of quality tourism and leisure facilities – usually focused around a particular event – can therefore be a long-term investment in the future of a city or region. Hence, the keen competition to host events such as the Olympic Games or the World Cup, or to be designated the European Cultural City. There is also similar competition between localities within countries. Arts festivals and sporting events, for example, are hosted to enhance the reputation of an area as well as to improve the leisure facilities available to local populations.

Tourism can be used as an instrument of *political legitimation*. There are many examples of governments that have used tourism as a means of improving their international political image. Spain (under Franco), and more recently Israel and the Philippines, have all consciously used tourism in this manner. The reverse position can also be observed and states may prohibit outward bound tourism to particular countries as part of a package of sanctions against that regime. For example, for many years the USA banned travel to China and Cuba, and more recently to Libya (Gunn 1988: 62). The role of the state in providing leisure and tourism facilities (for example, in the form of national parks or publicly owned sports facilities) is also a form of legitimation of the role of the state to its citizens.

In capitalist economies, access to tourism and leisure services is allocated by market mechanisms, and thereby reflects the distribution of income and time resources in society, and so is inherently uneven. In most capitalist societies, the state intervenes in reallocating access in order to bring about greater equity if not equality (Gratton and Taylor 1988: 41). The motivation for this may be the need for the state to legitimize its own role, or it may be in response to sectional pressures exerted by political parties or interest groups. The state has, in practise, been particularly important in helping to provide free or low cost access to sports, arts, and cultural facilities in recent decades, and this has largely survived the neo-liberalist shift to reduced state intervention. In some countries (for example, Switzerland), the state also provides "social tourism" to disadvantaged social groups (see chapter 3).

Amin (1983: 142) writes that "the necessity of the capitalist state arises when the circulation (distribution, exchange and consumption) of commodities is impeded." This comes about in tourism and leisure when individual groups of capital can not guarantee their own long-term survival because they can not meet the general requirements of production, such as the need for investment in airports, roads, or training. There are positive externalities to be obtained by the tourism and leisure industries from such investments. However, these may not be profitable investments for individuals. Social investment by the state may therefore be required to undertake these key investments. Damette (1980) terms this the devalorization of capital.

Tourism and leisure services can be developed in such as way as to be harmful to local communities, to consumers, or to the long term interests of the industry itself. For example, a series of large hotels may be built to poor standards in a beauty spot. This would destroy the initial tourism and leisure resource, and provide substandard accommodation for the tourists. The extra traffic generated on the roads could also inconvenience the local community. Therefore, as with most building and with most consumer goods, the state has *intervened to regulate the production and delivery of tourism and leisure services and goods*. Regulations may be introduced to control the location, quality, and appearance of facilities, while health and safety regulations apply to their operation, and some attempt is made to regulate quality via consumer laws. In recent years, there has been increasing concern about the environmental impact of tourism and leisure and growing calls for more sustainable tourism provision (chapter 12). Increasingly, however, state interventions are being framed within partnerships of interested parties, rather than being autonomous policy interventions. This is part of the wider shift of emphasis from government to governance.

Tourism development tends to be unevenly distributed spatially both because of differential access and the uneven spread of attractions. While capital city and other forms of urban tourism are important, many major tourism regions tend to be less developed and more peripheral regions. Indeed, one of their attractions may be their relatively unspoilt nature. There are of course exceptions; for example, Florida, one of the primary poles of tourist attraction in the USA is also a relatively high income region, as in the Balearic Islands within Spain. However, the generalization does hold and for this reason, therefore, tourism frequently has been used as an *instrument of regional development policy*. This is more plausible in the more developed countries where even the poorest regions have basic infrastructural provision. However, tourism can also be the object of regional policy in less developed economies. For example, the 1975 master tourism plan for Malaysia attempted to decentralize tourism from the urban areas of the west by developing tourist regions and corridors on the east coast (Pearce 1989: 251).

The actual form of state intervention varies according to the political economy of a country. The most basic divide is that "institutional frameworks lead to compulsory planning in collective societies and to indicative planning in capitalist economies" (Gunn 1988). However, there are also more subtle differences in accordance with the organization of the state, and the division of responsibilities, resources, and powers between the local and the regional state. In the USA, for example, planning is mostly at the local level and involves physical planning measures such as land use zoning. In contrast, there is growing local state involvement with tourism in the UK as an instrument of economic policy. At times, the interest of the local state and the central state may conflict. For example, the national aim of expanding tourism to generate international earnings may conflict with the interests of local communities that wish to limit new developments in their areas. The actual role of the state is too complex to consider here in any detail, but Hall (2000, ch. 6) discusses seven main areas of public sector involvement in tourism (box 5.7).

A further level of complexity is added by the increasing involvement of supranational bodies in tourism policy. Prime among these is the European Union which, in 1985, established a policy framework that covered enhanced freedom of movement and protection for EC tourists, improved working conditions for workers in tourism, integrating tourism into the Common Transport Policy, safeguarding heritage, and using tourism as an instrument of regional policy (Williams and Shaw 1998b). This has been steadily expanded subsequently although most aspects of tourism and leisure policies (other than transborder mobility, consumer rights, competition, and environmental impacts) continue to remain the domains of national policies.

Box 5.7   Seven main forms of public sector involvement in tourism

- *Coordination*: to avoid duplication of effort, and ensure effective strategies.
- *Planning*: identifying goals for tourism, and the means and resources for achieving these.
- *Legislation and regulation*: industry-specific and general regulation affecting tourism practises.
- *Government as entrepreneur*: owning and operating tourist ventures.
- *Stimulation*: supporting and encouraging tourism development via financial measures, sponsoring research and innovation, and marketing/promotion.
- *Social tourism*: the extension of holidays to economically marginal groups.
- *Public interest protection*: arbitrating between competing interests, and acting as general interest protector.

Source: based on Hall (2000, chapter 6)

Finally, we consider briefly the importance of a governance perspective on tourism. Governance emphasizes that regulation is a continuous process of governing which is, above all, embedded in a wide set of practices (Painter and Goodwin 1995), and is far larger than the state and the agencies of formally elected local political institutions. The agents of governance are firms, management, employees, trade unions, national, regional and local states, and non-state institutions. These are the bodies that, in some way, manage or regulate tourism. Governance mechanisms are relatively weak in tourism with low levels of networking among firms, and between them and the public and voluntary sectors. There are also poorly developed systems of interest group representation (Greenwood 1993) and notoriously weak institutionalization. Governance regimes are not invariable in time or space. Instead they stem from the social relations that are constituted in, and constitute, particular places (Massey 1984). Some of these forms of governance are considered later in this book in the chapters on urban and rural tourism, and sustainability.

The Tourism Industry and International Trade

The importance of tourism in international trade has already been noted as one reason for state intervention in the sector. It has a high and positive income elasticity of demand, which has been translated into strong growth in the volume of international tourism and in the foreign exchange transfers generated by the industry. Between 1965 and 1987 the growth of tourism's foreign exchange earnings matched the overall growth of world exports. The significance of this is underlined by the realization that the growth of world trade itself has outstripped that of GDP since the 1950s (Knox and Agnew 1998). While this, in itself, is impressive, a disaggregation of temporal trends reveals a major shift in the composition of trade in recent years. Between 1985 and 1998, international tourism receipts increased at an annual average rate of 10.7 percent, although this fell back to only 2.8 percent in 1995–8, partly reflecting the economic crisis in East Asia and slower economic growth in Europe.

The growing economic significance of international tourism has also been emphasized by deindustrialization in the developed countries which means that, in effect, the relative weight of the service sector – including tourism – has increased in these economies. Ricardo's concept of comparative advantage provides an interesting theoretical perspective on specialization in tourism. This holds that an area should specialize in producing and exporting those products in which it has competitive or relative cost advantages compared to other countries. Initially, this would seem to rule out international tourism in the more developed countries of northern Europe. However, the application of this simple economic principle to tourism is inappropriate because of the nature of tourism attractions which are, to a large extent, socially constructed, and diverse. Market segmentation and product diversification mean that competition is not simply based on costs, except in the case of some mass tourism products (chapter 9). Moreover, even in the case of costs, a country or region can be competitive by specializing in a particular tourism product especially in the short term (Sinclair and Stabler 1997: 126).

In addition, the conditions of production of tourism services are distinctive. Tourism requires relatively low initial capital investment, especially if it is integrated with existing settlements and infrastructure. Obviously, the development of large-scale tourism will require significant capital investments (perhaps in a new airport, in attractions, or in new hotels) but even these are usually easier to facilitate than a major investment in manufacturing capacity. Generally, tourism requires lower per capita investment, lower technological and labor skills, and faces less protectionism in world markets than, say, manufacturing. Not surprisingly, for these reasons international tourism tends to be attractive to national states as instruments of economic policy.

It is easier to establish the importance of international tourism receipts and expenditures than to quantify them. Data for different countries for the same time period can be inconsistent because of differences in definitions and in data collection methods. There are two main methods for estimating tourism expenditures, and these are often used in conjunction:

> The direct method relies on information provided by tourists themselves and by financial institutions. The indirect method multiplies the number of tourist nights by an average of daily expenditures. These procedures involve errors in generating the net balance on "tourist" expenditures abroad (the balance on tourism) and fail to include the related transactions which owe their existence to tourism. (Baretje 1982: 59)

There are considerable problems in providing such estimates: poor reporting by financial institutions; incomplete records of tourist numbers and tourist nights; and inaccurate estimates of tourism spend levels. There is also a need to take into account net financial transfers related to tourism such as foreign investments, transport costs, imports of goods, remittances by migrant workers and so on. International tour companies add an additional layer of complexity to international tourism trade flows. For example, Bull (1990: 325) estimated that, on average, only 31 percent of the money spent on a British package holiday in Spain is received by that country, 50 percent is received by the UK tour company, and the remaining 19 percent is received by other UK businesses. The extent of these leakages from the destination countries is contingent on the nature of the tourism product, and the structure and organization of the tourism industry. Thus Sinclair and Stabler (1997: 141) report that the import content of food and drink in many less developed countries was in the range of 40 to 60 percent, although in Kenya it was only 35 percent for food and 10 percent for beverages.

These, and other related financial transactions, must be taken into account to calculate the net tourism balance, what Baretje (1982) terms "Tourism's External Account" or what Sessa (1983) calls the "Ideal Tourism Balance." The latter is summarized in table 5.3. Arguably, even this broader calculation is incomplete in that it is based on the market traded impacts, that is on individual costs rather than the full social and environmental costs of international tourism, such as traffic congestion or ecosystem degradation. Despite these shortcomings, the Ideal Tourism Balance is useful for analysing the economic importance of international tourism, although in practice it is difficult to obtain comparable international statistics for its measurement. Instead, we have to rely on the less complete – and usually narrower – estimates of receipts, and expenditure which are collated by the World Tourism Organization and by the OECD.

Table 5.3 *Idealized model of the national tourism balance*

Outflows	Sum	Inflows	Sum
Tourism expenditures (outlays of national citizens abroad)	–	Tourism receipts (expenditures of foreign tourists)	–
Imports of commodities (chiefly foodstuffs and instrumental goods)	–	Exports (goods, durables, or semi-durables, handicraft products)	–
Transportation (share of international travel by national citizens)	–	Transportation (share of international travel by non-nationals)	–
Tourism investment abroad	–	Inward tourism investment	–
Interest payments on foreign investments and refund of capital	–	Income from tourism investments made abroad	–
Remittances by foreign tourism workers	–	Remittances by national tourism workers residing abroad	–
Publicity, advertising, etc.	–	Publicity, advertising, etc.	–
DEBIT BALANCE = deficit		CREDIT BALANCE = surplus	
Total		Total	

Source: Sessa (1983: 136)

Earnings from international tourism have long been important to a number of economies. As early as 1966, it was estimated that $13.1 billion of the total $60 billion tourism spend was international (Cosgrove and Jackson 1972: 45). The importance of the international component has almost certainly increased substantially subsequently. In the following discussion some of the salient features of the international trade in tourism services are analyzed. There is a broad but imperfect association between the numbers of international tourists and the share of total tourism receipts accounted for by the major world regions. Africa (2.2 percent) and South Asia (1.0 percent) have relatively small shares of both, while 95 percent of receipts are accounted for by Europe, the Americas, and East Asia/Pacific. Both the Americas and Asia account for a larger share of receipts than of tourists, reflecting a relatively efficient income-extracting industry. In comparison, Europe has 7 percent more arrivals than receipts. This is partly due to the geography of the region, whereby prosperous states and major

Table 5.4 *International tourism receipts as a percentage of all exports: 1997 global regions*

	%
Asia Pacific	6.8
Developing Countries	9.0
Indian Ocean Countries	8.2
Mediterranean Countries	15.2
OECD (Developed) Countries	7.8

Source: World Tourism Organization (1999)

tourist destinations are in close spatial proximity. But it is also due to the institutionalization of mass tourism, in the sense of both deeply-instilled values and behavior, and a highly developed all-inclusive "package" holiday industry (chapter 9). Over time, as would be expected, the shares of receipts accounted for by both Europe and the Americas have declined; their respective shares in 1965 had been 62 percent and 29 percent (Cosgrove and Jackson 1972: 43). This reflects the globalization of tourism in the 1970s and 1980s as well as the specific rise of Japan as a major source of tourism expenditures.

A more detailed disaggregation of international tourism financial flows reveals a number of other features. The USA is the world leader in terms of total receipts (figure 5.7). However, with this exception, the main feature of the distribution is strong regionalization. European countries are dominant, particularly the UK, Italy, Spain, and France. The other two important macro regions are the Americas, largely driven by tourism from the USA, and East Asia, where Japanese tourism is the principal generator. The existence of dominant tourism relationships between a small number of core economic areas and adjacent peripheral economic areas has parallels with global industrial trade patterns (Knox and Agnew 1998). The growth of Japanese tourism also mirrors the growing significance of Japan in world industrial production. Between 1950 and 1981 Japan's share of world exports increased from 1.4 percent to 8.2 percent, and its share of world tourism trade has followed this trend, although at lower levels and somewhat laggardly.

A fuller understanding of the economic significance of tourism requires, however, that overall receipts are set against tourism expenditures, as some countries, notably the northern European ones, but, above all, Japan and Germany have large net outflows of tourism expenditures. As a result, the geographical distribution of the net balances on the tourism account (figure 5.8) reveal a contrasting pattern.

Figure 5.7 *International tourism receipts, 1998*

Source: WTO (2000b)

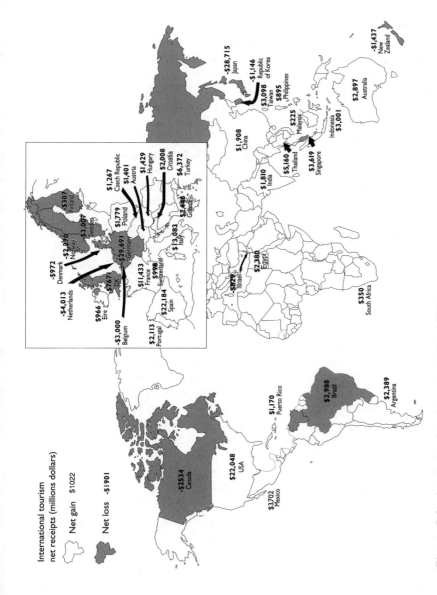

International tourism
net receipts (millions dollars)

Net gain $1022

Net loss   -$1901

-$1,437
New Zealand

-$28,715
Japan

-$1,146
Republic of Korea

-$3,098
Taiwan

$895
Philippines

$2,897
Australia

$225
Malaysia

Indonesia
$3,001

$1,908
China

$5,160
Thailand

$3,619
Singapore

$1,810
India

$2,360
Egypt

-$825
Israel

$350
South Africa

-$307
Finland

$3,007
Sweden

-$2,270
Norway

$1,267
Czech Republic

$1,401
Austria

$1,429
Hungary

$2,008
Croatia

$6,372
Turkey

$1,779
Poland

-$972
Denmark

$29,691
Germany

$2,486
Greece

$13,083
Italy

-$4,013
Netherlands

$7,676
UK

$11,433
France

$998
Switzerland

$966
Eire

-$3,000
Belgium

$22,184
Spain

$2,113
Portugal

$1,170
Puerto Rico

$3,988
Brazil

$2,389
Argentina

-$2534
Canada

$22,048
USA

$3702
Mexico

Figure 5.8 *International tourism net receipts, 1998*

Source: WTO (2000b)

Reflecting the north–south pattern of tourism, the less developed countries make a far stronger showing in terms of net receipts than of gross receipts. Europe also appears more polarized. Northern Europe mostly has large deficits, while Southern Europe records large surpluses. Another feature is the large surplus in the USA (a reversal of the position in the 1980s, partly due to the decline in the dollar exchange rate) and the large deficit in Japan. In some countries, notably Germany and Japan, these deficits partly offset large surpluses on the balances of trade. In the case of Spain, Italy, and France, tourism adds significantly to the current account.

The overall importance of tourism to these different economies is, of course, contingent on their economic structures, and is not simply related to the absolute size of the net balance. A deficit of $29 billion is relatively insignificant to Japan given its historic trade surpluses, while a small positive balance can be of major importance to a less developed economy. The significance of the net tourism balance is partly dependent on the absolute size of the economies as well as the extent to which they are diversified. For example, in Mexico the share of tourism earnings in total exports declined from 52 percent to 6 percent between 1954 and 1982, largely as a function of industrialization and increased oil exports rather than from any intrinsic change in tourism (Truett and Truett 1987). In summary, the overall position is one whereby tourism is a relatively large proportion of exports in the Mediterranean, but also to some extent the developing countries and Indian Ocean countries, compared to the OECD and Asia-Pacific countries (table 5.4). However, there are also considerable national variations, as for example in the contrasts between South and North Korea, or between Libya and Tunisia.

The pattern of commodity trade is mainly inter-core or intra-core trade, in that it centers on North America, Europe, and Japan. The industrial core economies have dominated international commodity trade, accounting for 60–70 percent of world exports and imports in every decade since 1950. In general, there has been an intensification of this long standing dominance at the expense of core–periphery trade, with the exception of the oil producing states. Tourism trade is different, however, in that some of the peripheral or semi-peripheral economies in the Caribbean or on the fringes of the Mediterranean have secured important shares of total international tourism trade. Moreover, this share has increased over time. Finally, there is broad similarity between trade in tourism and in commodities, in that both bring vulnerability to the less developed countries. Vulnerability can be interpreted as structural dependence (Gill and Law 1988, ch. 6) on external decision making.

6

Tourism and Entrepreneurship

**Tourism, Economic Development, and Entrepreneurial
Activity: A Neglected Issue**

The growth of the tourism industry and its potential for stimulating
economic development has formed an important focus in much of the
literature on tourism. However, despite considerable debate on the
subject (see, for example, Britton 1996; de Kadt 1979, 1992; Dicke
1995; Mathieson and Wall 1982; Williams and Shaw 1998a; Young
1973) there is still little agreement as to tourism's role in economic
development. The overall picture remains clouded, not only by the different assessments of what constitutes economic development (Pearce
1989: 6–10), but also because of tourism's sociocultural and environmental implications (Cooper and Wanhill 1997; Murphy 1985). Nelson
(1993: 4) goes further, claiming that the debate concerning tourism and
development is largely "a discordant and unreconciled set of thoughts."
In order to comprehend tourism's role in economic development, it
is necessary to reveal and understand underlying mechanisms. In
Britton's (1996: 155) view, this involves constructing a framework, "for
investigating the articulation of international tourism." In this framework, two main factors need to be examined. One concerns the commercial structure of the industry (especially the dominance of certain
activity components and ownership groups), while the second relates
to an understanding of the general organization of economic power
structures. Britton was very much concerned with tourism development
within the Third World, but his views nevertheless highlight the wider
geographical importance of commercial and organizational structures.
We would extend this perspective and argue that within the literature
on tourism's economic potential, relatively little attention has been paid

Plate 6.1   *Local entrepreneurs, petty trading and tourists in the Gambia. Such exchanges bring small-scale financial benefits to local people*

to the role of entrepreneurial activity and, in particular, to how tourism enterprises operate in different economies (Morrison et al. 1999; Shaw and Williams 1998a).

This chapter aims to explore the importance of entrepreneurship and to highlight its key position in understanding tourism's impact on economic development. Of necessity, our starting point needs to be a general one, reviewing briefly the study of tourism and economic development, before examining in more detail those studies that have considered entrepreneurial activity.

The general literature on tourism and economic development has focused broadly on two major themes: the economic cost–benefits of tourism, and the measurement of tourism's economic impact. Of course, in many cases these themes overlap, but for the purpose of clarity they will be given separate consideration, with the second theme being discussed in chapter 7. The first approach embraces a considerable range of studies drawn from a number of academic disciplines, although most are grounded in political economy perspectives of tourism and development. Early work was stimulated by the research of Young (1973), Bryden's (1973) study of the Caribbean, and various conferences on tourism's role in developing countries (see, for example, Shiviji 1973). The range of these early studies was such that Kassé (1973) was able to discuss the formulation of a theory of tourism development in under-developed countries. His emphasis was on attempting to understand how tourism could generate capital that, in turn, could be transferred to other economic sectors, as well as measuring the real costs of tourism development. In a geographical context, Bryden (1973) gave early recognition to the fact that tourism took different forms and, more importantly, that its impact was conditioned by the environment within which development took place. Similarly, van Doom (1979) has argued that tourism development can only be understood within the context of the developmental stages which particular countries have entered. More recently, Sindiga (1999) has explored the changing development paradigms of tourism within an African context and concludes that despite changing approaches, tourism development remains problematic.

Unfortunately, there is little consideration of the linkages between these two dimensions of development. Indeed, such an obvious analysis may well be too simplistic, as there is strong evidence that the size of the local economy is also an important consideration Thus, Latimer (1985) demonstrates how larger tourism economies, such as Kenya and Tunisia, have a wider range of entrepreneurial opportunities and locational options compared with some of the mini-economies of the Caribbean.

Within most of the literature, particular attention has been paid to the structure of the tourism industry in developing economies, especially the role played by transnational companies (UN Centre on Transnational Corporations 1982). In Kenya, for example, foreign equity participation accounts for almost 60 percent of hotel beds, with large transnational hotel groups such as Inter-Continental and Hilton International having major developments (Rosemary 1987). Foreign investment in hotels also varies geographically with 78 percent of hotels along the coast having some foreign capital compared with 67 percent in Nairobi (Sinclair et al. 1992). The implications of transnational activities for developing countries are considerable: a loss of control by the host country over its national tourist industry; leakage of foreign earnings (since only between 22 percent and 50 percent of the gross revenue remains in the destination country), and the development of tourist enclaves isolated from the host population (Freitag 1994; Lea 1988). In the Gambia, for example, the tourism industry is dominated by 17 large hotels together with a significant holiday village complex catering exclusively for international tourists (Thompson et al. 1995). Given this structure, it is hardly surprising that the Gambia suffers some of the greatest leakages and consequently has some of the weakest economic benefits (Gamble 1989). Some of these problems have been confirmed in surveys by the World Tourism Organization (1985), which covered 22 developing countries. This research enquired into the countries' attitudes towards transnational tourism, and found that most still considered that the disadvantages outweighed the benefits (table 6.1; see also chapters 2 and 5).

Reliance on international tourism as a strategy for the growth of developing economies has been criticized because it is often associated with a dependency upon external sources of capital and expertise (de Kadt 1979; for a regional view see Sindiga 1999). Such sources tend to be fickle in nature. Choices of tourist destinations are highly suscepti-ble to volatile fluctuations, particularly because of economic conditions in the tourists' country of origin or the perception of the situation and status of the holiday destination. There are also significant structural and geographical dimensions of tourism dependency, as shown in figure 6.1 (Britton 1996; Pearce 1989). In this perspective, the major tourist flows and controls emanate from the developed economies, while in the destination country small resort enclaves are created. As Freitag (1994) has shown in terms of the Dominican Republic, one of the character-istics of the resort enclave is its exclusiveness, with the management creating a totally controlled tourist environment (box 6.1). Such enclaves are operated by global capital and transnational organizations through a series of spatial networks, which unless they are strongly regulated by the local state, allow only limited economic benefits to accrue to the host communities (Shaw and Shaw 1999). It is through such spatial networks that transnational tourism organizations operate, and unless they are strongly regulated by governments, only limited economic benefits may accrue to the host communities. Such models of tourism development (figure 6.1) have also been couched in terms of core–periphery theory. Hills and Lundgren (1977) argue that there are powerful hierarchical dimensions in the spatial networks, and that these are explained by dependency theory (Britton 1996; see also chapter 2).

Table 6.1   *Perceptions of selected developing countries towards transnational tourism*

Assertion	True (%)	Partly True (%)	Untrue (%)
Transnational corporations (TNCs) have to some extent influenced the type of tourism activity attracted to developing countries	36	55	9
Lack of bargaining power is the main problem of developing countries in dealing with TNCs	50	41	9
Developing countries are insufficiently informed about the various transnational corporations and forms of their involvement in tourism development	50	27	23
TNCs appear at times reluctant to employ local managers and senior staff	59	32	9
The most significant benefit of TNC involvement is in speeding up the pace of tourism development	45	32	23
The most significant lasting contribution made by TNCs to the developing countries is the transfer of skills, product knowledge, technology, and product techniques	27	64	9
The working methods and training schemes of TNCs are not always adapted to the stage of development of the receiving country[a]	45	45	9

[a] Row adds to 99 due to rounding
Source: World Tourism Organization (1985)

Moreover, these hierarchical relationships are, according to Lundgren (1972), a clear expression of metropolitan hegemony, being a function of the technological and economic superiority of large urban areas in the developed economies (Pearce 1989: 93–4).

According to many observers, these geographical shifts in activity, and the concentration of tourism resources, also produce structural changes in developing economies. Winpenny (1982: 218), claims that "tourism displaces existing sectors of the economy and makes it more difficult for new ones to develop." Such sectoral changes operate via

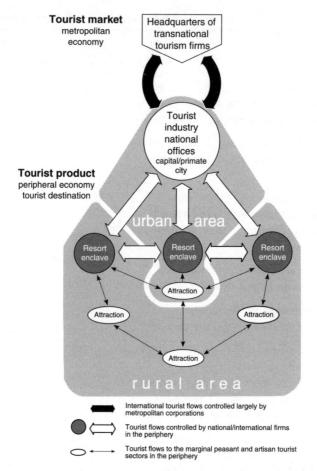

Figure 6.1   *The structural and geographical dimensions of tourism dependency*
Source: Britton (1981)

Box 6.1   Basic characteristics of resort enclaves

- Physically separated from local communities and settlements;
- minimum of economic and other structural linkages between the enclave and local settlements;
- strong dependency on foreign tourists, as reflected in exclusivity of the enclave; and
- strong economic differences between enclave and local communities.

Source: modified from Williams (1998: 76)

competition for labor, and sometimes land, against traditional agriculture (Bryden 1974). However, Latimer (1985) highlights two significant features of such views. First, much of this literature concerning tourism's development role dates from the peak years of international tourism in developing countries, 1960–74, when the pace of change was dramatic. Second, and more importantly, there seems little hard evidence that tourism has been the main cause of agricultural decline in many developing economies. While Brown (1974) noted a 7 percent decline in the number of agricultural workers in Jamaica between 1960 and 1972, Latimer (1985) has shown that the workforce in Jamaican hotels only rose from a ratio of one job per 50 agricultural workers in 1960, to two jobs per 50 by 1972. This increase only represented one year's net addition to the Jamaican workforce from school leavers. From his review of conditions Latimer (1985: 42), concluded that "from a strictly economic view, if projected benefits outweigh costs, tourism ranks with any other export choice." In contrast, Sindiga (1999: 34) claims that, "Tourism's contribution to the African economy appears to be frequently overestimated." Of course, such economic possibilities still do not negate the problems associated with the external control of capital and dependency.

These debates on levels of dependency are not limited to developing countries, although much of the early literature would have us believe that this is the case. More recent research has highlighted similar problems associated with the role of tourism in more mature economies. In Austria, for example, foreign tourists account for 75.4 percent of all tourism spend, while the equivalent proportion in Spain is 60 percent (Shaw and Williams 1998a: chapter 2). Within the Mediterranean countries, foreign investment is another dimension of the relationship between tourism and economic dependency, and in this there are at least superficial parallels with the developing countries. For example, in Greece the relative importance of foreign investment in tourism peaked at 66 percent in 1968 (Leontidou 1998). Most of this foreign capital went into hotel complexes in prime coastal locations, creating a phase of speculative development with all the related environmental and sociocultural problems of tourist enclaves.

The Role of Entrepreneurship in Tourism Development

Within the political economy approach discussed in the previous section, only scant attention has been paid to the role of entrepreneurs in the tourism industry. Beyond general discussions of the impact of transnational organizations, the literature is remarkably uninformative on the influence of small or even medium-sized businesses

(Harper 1984). However, as Mathieson and Wall (1982: 82) argue "there is little doubt that the tourist industry exhibits backward linkages and that external economies have emerged," yet few researchers have examined the relationship between such linkages and entrepreneurial activity. This situation is slowly being rectified as more recent studies have started to recognize the importance of local entrepreneurial activity (Dahles and Bras 1999; Shaw and Williams 1998a). In this context Din (1992) argues that by stressing the dominance of metropolitan control via transnational corporations, researchers have ignored the opportunities for local entrepreneurial activity. In a wider ranging discussion, Dahles and Bras (1999) argue that the position of entrepreneurial culture via tourism needs to be viewed within the context of structural power relationships.

One major exception is the work of Lundgren (1973), which examined the characteristics of tourism-based entrepreneurship associated with different forms of hotel development in the Caribbean. Lundgren suggested that a three-stage model of entrepreneurial development could be recognized, based on supply and demand linkages for food by hotels; this was illustrated by the example of an island economy. In stage one a new hotel has no links with its local hinterland, and supplies must be imported from overseas suppliers (figure 6.2). Much of the early hotel development in the Caribbean took the form of large metropolitan complexes which developed closely integrated systems with foreign suppliers. This was either because the local agricultural base could not meet the rapid increase in demand, or because the hotel was foreign-owned and had a policy of not using local produce.

The evidence from the developing economies of the Caribbean during the years of fastest tourist growth supports the dominance of such foreign supplies. In Barbados, for example, Gooding (1971) estimated that two-thirds of all food eaten by tourists was imported, with similar figures being recorded by Cazes (1972) for Jamaican hotels. During the early 1970s such high food imports were attributed to the failure of domestic agriculture in countries such as Jamaica (Brown 1974); although Latimer (1985) has argued against such one-sided views, preferring instead to talk about entrepreneurial response being patchy. Indeed, Lundgren (1973), in his study of Jamaica, had found that some large agricultural enterprises had arisen to supply produce, such as pineapples, to hotels over large areas, but that in general most produce came from nearby locations. Other studies have shown difficulties in local entrepreneurs responding to changes in demand, with Latimer (1985) quoting the example of a hotel manager in the Seychelles being unable to obtain locally grown mangoes because no marketing system existed. There is also evidence to support the argument that foreign-owned hotels framed a supply policy around the perceived

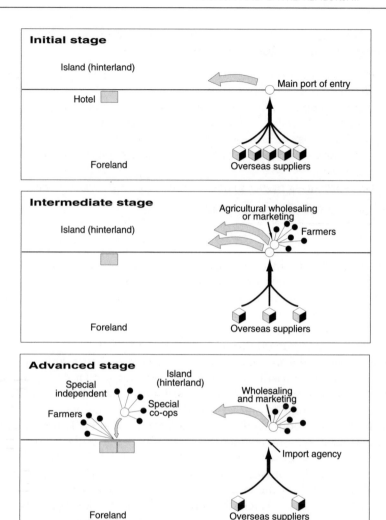

Figure 6.2 *Lundgren's model of entrepreneurial development and hotel linkages*
Source: Lundgren (1973)

demands of their guests and showed little interest in local suppliers. Belisle (1983) has examined food production in the Caribbean from this perspective and concluded that six main factors have influenced hotels' links with local entrepreneurs, as shown in box 6.2.

In Lundgren's model local entrepreneurs may develop links with the hotel sector and thereby a marketing channel is opened up between farmers and hotels (the intermediate stage in figure 6.2). The final or

---

Box 6.2   Main factors affecting linkages between local food production and hotels in the Caribbean

- Most tourists are conservative in their tastes, especially those from North America.
- Imported food may be cheaper than that locally produced.
- Hotels will pay more to ensure high quality and reliable supplies.
- Local food may be processed in unhygienic conditions.
- Hotel supply managers may be unaware of the possibilities of locally produced food.
- Local producers may not know how to contact the hotel trade.

Source: modified from Belisle (1983)

---

advanced stage of entrepreneurial activity sees further expansion of local wholesaling facilities, both in organizational and technological terms, with the latter involving more cold-storage capacity. Such changes stimulate agricultural development, improve food processing as well as marketing, and generally reduce the tourism industry's reliance on imported supplies (Mathieson and Wall 1982).

The stage model proposed by Lundgren serves to highlight backward linkages in tourism's demand for food, but similar changes could be explored for other external linkages. Unfortunately, such a progressive change through to the so-called advanced stage has rarely been identified in developing countries. From the limited evidence available, most developing countries seem to be in either the initial or the intermediate stages. Momsen's (1986) work on the small Caribbean islands of St. Lucia and Montserrat, for example, shows an improvement in the linkages between the hotel industry and local agriculture over the period 1971–83. In St. Lucia, 70 percent by value of the food consumed by tourists was imported in 1971, compared with 58 percent in 1983 (Momsen 1986: 17–18). Such a change highlights the fact that better linkages have been established. In the cases of St. Lucia and Montserrat, there has been careful government monitoring of local food production and, as Momsen (1986) suggests, tourist tastes in food have also changed. In the early 1970s very few hotels made a feature of local food, whereas by the mid-1980s most hotels served some Caribbean food to cater to changing tourist demand.

Clearly, strong linkages between the tourism industry and, in the case of developing countries, local agricultural systems are important if the benefits of tourism are to spread through the local economy. As Mathieson and Wall (1982: 82) argue, "Although it is attractive to think of a sequence of developmental stages, the exact pattern of

Table 6.2   *Tourist accommodation in St. Lucia and Montserrat, 1972–84*

Type	Number of rooms					
	St. Lucia			Montserrat		
	1971	1980	1984	1973	1980	1984
Hotels	555	1,043	1,080	101	106	100
Apartment-hotels	5	235	312	–	–	–
Apartments	–	–	65	–	25	20
Guesthouses	82	106	71	40	–	–
Villas	–	–	177	10	100	100
Total	642	1,384	1,705	151	231	220

Source: Momsen (1986)

entrepreneurial activity is likely to vary from place to place." Unfortunately, such geographical variations in the development of entrepreneurial activity, which can be conceptualized as local contingencies in their formation and operation, have been little researched. The exception has been the general recognition that linkages between tourism and local business depend on the types of suppliers and producers in operation, the historical development of tourism within the area (only vaguely conceptualized), and the type of tourist development under consideration.

Momsen's (1986) research touches on many of these factors, exploring as it does variations in visitor patterns and tourism development in St. Lucia and Montserrat. In the former island, hotel investment was predominantly British-based (68 percent of hotel rooms were in British-owned hotels in 1971) and most tourists came from Europe. Montserrat, in contrast, had few European or package tour visitors, while most tourists were from the USA and tended to stay twice as long as the average visitor to St. Lucia (just over two weeks compared with 6.8 nights). The pattern of development has produced very different tourist accommodation structures (table 6.2), with villas being more important in Montserrat. These different patterns have influenced the level of entrepreneurial development within local agriculture, with the type of tourist and the structure of hotel development both being important. Indeed, Lundgren (1973) has suggested that the speed of hotel growth is also significant in generating local entrepreneurial activity; with gradual development allowing time for a succession of infrastructural improvements, and creating a gradual increase in demand for local food. The experience of the Caribbean has not followed this pathway, since most growth was rapid and over a short time period (see chapter 9). Many developing countries fall into the second type of development, the so-called metropolitan hotel model. In this case, growth is rapid, creating an instant demand for large amounts of food products. Local entrepreneurs are unable to respond and most food is imported, giving rise to the initial stage of tourism linkages described in figure 6.2. Variations around this metropolitan model are to be found throughout the developing world. In Kenya, for example, the national economy is large enough to allow high backward linkages between the tourism industry and local agriculture (Summary 1987). However, as Rajothe (1983) points out, although these linkages are strong, they are mainly forged between large hotels and large-scale agricultural producers, thereby excluding small-scale farmers. Similar examples exist in the Caribbean where there are problems of gaining stable supplies from local agriculture. In St. Lucia for example, one of the largest hotels, Club St. Lucia, provides over 2,000 meals per day, but finds it uneconomical to use local supplies, which are only available for 3 months of the year (Pattullo 1996).

To date, the limited work on entrepreneurial activity has focused on the linkages between hotel development and local agricultural systems in developing countries. This is not surprising, given the focus of the early debates on tourism's impact on agriculture. However, there are two other aspects worthy of consideration. First, we should recognize that there are a range of backward linkages within tourism, and that their utilization depends on entrepreneurial activity. Second, there are also important entrepreneurial issues in the tourist accommodation sector itself, many of which have been neglected in the discussions of tourism in developing countries.

In the case of other backward linkages, Bond and Ladman (1982) have shown that in Mexico strong linkages could exist with the construction industry, while demand for handicrafts can create linkages back to small factories and cottage industries (table 6.3). In addition, external economies can also result from general infrastructural improvements in local transportation networks. While the creation of tourist enclaves (box 6.1) hinders the establishment of local linkages and limits the wider economic impact of tourism, most evidence suggests that such enclaves tend to break down over time. At this point something of a dichotomy emerges in the literature on tourism development. Many commentators believe that tourism plays its major role during the early stages of a country's economic growth because in the later stages industrialization becomes more widespread (Bond and Ladman 1982; Lea 1988; Mathieson and Wall 1982). However, as we have seen, it is precisely in the early phases that the tourism industry

Table 6.3 *The estimated distribution of tourist expenditure and potential backward link-ages in Mexico*

Type of expenditure	Percentage spend	Potential backward linkages
Food	34	Local agriculture
Hotels/holiday accommodation industries	24	Local construction
Merchandise	14	Small factories and cottage industries
Transportation	14	Local workers in transport
Entertainment and shows	13	Local agents
Other expenses	1	
	100	

Source: modified from Bond and Ladman (1982)

tends not to be embedded in the local economy. One way of counter-acting such a shortcoming is for governments in developing economies to examine carefully the forms of tourist growth being proposed, as well as attempting to work more closely with the transnational hotel groups.

In much of the literature there has been a strong tendency to view all transnational development as potentially harmful. Such a perspective is oversimplistic, as was made clear by the UN Centre on Trans-national Corporations (1982: 59). This organization argued that "allegations of high import content of transnational-associated hotels have more to do with the 'product' which they may produce, that is, luxury or first class hotel accommodation, than with any specific prac-tices of transnational corporations *per se*." The same report went on to highlight how transnational hotels can act as channels of knowledge through their staff training programmes: these not only provide for better hotel staff, but such skills may also gradually spread to other sectors of the tourism industry. For example, in some hotel corpora-tions, efforts are also being made to improve the management skills of the local workforce, with the ITT Sheraton Corporation launching an MBA course for executives in the Asian region (Go and Pine 1995). Field studies undertaken by the UN project found that, in most coun-tries, the transfer of skill was an important factor in the creation and development of an indigenous hotel sector, with many senior managers having been trained previously by transnational hotels. This process is essential if locally-owned hotels are to both develop and compete

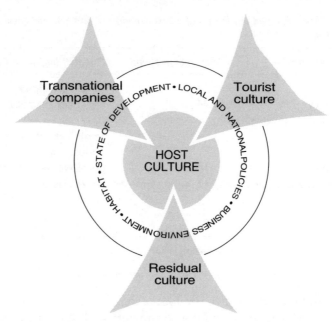

Figure 6.3   *Operational forces impacting on host cultures*
Source: modified from Jafari (1989)

successfully with foreign-based ones. It is also a factor that conditions the future pattern of the growth of tourism in developing economies, and serves to highlight yet another important dimension of entrepreneurial activity.

Tourist entrepreneurs also have another important role which is to act – either directly or indirectly – as brokers within the host community. This particular role is obviously conditioned by whether they are drawn from the local community or, if large transnational hotels are dominant, come from outside. According to Jafari (1989), these entrepreneurs operate according to a tourism business culture, and yet they may also be members of the local social system. Given this dual pattern of behavior between the ordinary and non-ordinary worlds, they can act as brokers between the hosts and guests (figure 6.3). In the context of developing economies Smith (1994: 172) suggests that ownership "of a successful business is ego-enhancing and confers the privilege . . . to create employment." In this perspective the sociocultural impact can be largely determined and shaped by the nature and characteristics of the entrepreneurs themselves. The final section of this chapter is directed at considering the social and economic features of "the captains of tourism."

Table 6.4 *State intervention taken to improve training standards in holiday accommo-dation in selected developing countries*

Country	Measures
Brazil	Establishment of school for hotel management in State of Rio Grande do Norte
Ivory Coast	Emphasis on training of hotel managers and proprietors; organization of handicraft cooperatives and groups
Jamaica	Attitudinal and skill training programme for hotel workers started in 1982
Philippines	Foreign language courses (German, Japanese, French), mobile training program focused on rural communities
Thailand	The establishment of a Hotel and Tourism Training Institute

Source: modified from World Tourism Organization (1985)

The Nature and Characteristics of Tourism Entrepreneurs

A considerable part of the analysis of the tourism industry is set within aggregate studies of supply and demand. As was shown in chapter 5, the industry itself is a complex network of operations that functions, in many cases, within a framework of some form of state intervention. While this, and the general trends in the role of large-scale enterprises, are well known, very little has been written on the nature of the entrepreneurs themselves. Indeed, it is safe to say that our knowledge is patchy about the operating characteristics of tourism firms in developing countries, beyond the transnationals and related businesses (United Nations 1982; World Tourism Organization 1985). Within the developing countries, the emphasis has been firmly placed on providing increased training either by the action of transnationals, as we saw from the previous section, or through direct state involvement in training programmes. These range from courses aimed at employees to broader ones that also cover the needs of the managers and proprietors of hotels, in the case of countries such as the Ivory Coast (table 6.4). From official statistics, however, it is difficult to gauge the detailed characteristics of tourism businesses or the dynamics of firm formation. Furthermore, given the dominance in many countries of small, owner-managed tourism businesses (according to Stallinbrass 1980, close to 90 percent of hotels in the UK fall into these categories) it is surprising how little attention has been paid to small tourism businesses. This neglect is all the more conspicuous given that this segment of the service sector has been identified as a key growth point in the European economy (Commission of the European Communities 1987).

Linked with these businesses has been the growing awareness of local cultural systems in mediating economic processes such as restructuring. Within developing countries, Jafari (1989) has highlighted the importance of a tourism business culture while, more generally, Cooke (1983) and Massey (1983; 1984) have stressed the role of local cultural systems in economic development.

As was discussed in the previous part of this chapter, such concepts are especially appropriate to understanding the development of tourism. It is not surprising that sociologists have begun to investigate the ways in which cultural features interact with economic changes in tourism (Bagguley 1987; Urry 1987). Such work has not only focused on "changes in the cultural practices of tourism and leisure" (Bagguley 1987: 4), but has also highlighted those pertaining to entrepreneurship.

There are growing numbers of studies on firm formation and entrepreneurial skills in tourism research where the importance of entrepreneurship is finally being given more recognition (Ateljevic and Doorne 2000; Dahles and Bras 1999; Morrison et al. 1999). Yet, in both traditional tourist regions and in newer areas of tourist development there is a strong need to understand the potential of the local business culture to respond to change. Studies in the UK have identified very diverse business motivations within the dynamics of the hotel industry, and in a case study of Scarborough it was observed that only 33 percent of hotel owners had any previous experience in tourism (Stallinbrass 1980). Brown's (1987) research on hoteliers in south-east Dorset confirmed this pattern, showing that few owners had any relevant experience or qualifications, and that two-thirds had extremely low turnovers (less than £22,000 in 1985). Two other important features emerge from these studies. The first is that many of the owner-managers had non-economic motives for entering the business. Second, the sources of business capital used to establish firms were extremely varied. Both of these highlight the need to re-evaluate critically many of the conventional economic models (especially those based on multipliers) used in the analysis of the tourism sector .

Within this context, Goffee and Scase's (1983) work on entrepreneurship provides one important lead concerning non-economic decision-making. Their work has drawn attention to the importance of capital structures in understanding general managerial and entrepreneurial skills. As shown in table 6.5, they suggest that four main types of firm characteristics can be identified, ranging from the highly marginalized self-employed category through to owner-director companies, where management and ownership are clearly separated. The few studies of hotel businesses that have been undertaken suggest that

Table 6.5 *Organizational structures and entrepreneurial characteristics*

Category	Entrepreneurial characteristics
Self-employed	Use of family labor, little market stability, low levels of capital investment, tendency towards weakly developed management skills
Small employer	Use of family and non-family labor; less economically marginalized but shares other characteristics of self-employed group
Owner-controllers	Use of non-family labor, higher levels of capital investment, often formal system of management control but no separation of ownership and control
Owner-directors	Separation of ownership and management functions, highest levels of capital investment

Source: modified from Goffee and Scase (1983)

many in the UK would fall into either the first or second groups described in table 6.5 (Shaw and Williams 1987).

Research in South West England has focused more closely on the operating characteristics of tourism businesses, as well as widening the range of empirical information in the debate (Shaw et al. 1987; Williams et al. 1989a, b). This research was based on detailed firm-level studies and, unlike previous surveys, it covered most major sectors in the tourism industry, including accommodation (serviced and non-serviced), attractions, retailing, and catering. For our purposes we need only consider the accommodation sector to examine the main findings, which highlight three significant characteristics of entrepreneurship in what is a substantial sector of the tourism industry.

The first concerns the levels of experience and expertise of the entrepreneurs, or their social routes to entrepreneurship (Williams et al. 1989b). As shown in table 6.6, the dominant route to entrepreneurship is as an ex-employee without any directly relevant job experience. As ex-employees have no obvious access to either management skills or capital, this group may well be expected to encounter the greatest obstacles to entrepreneurship. However, within the Cornwall study this was shown to be the most important route in all sub-sectors of the tourism industry. The accommodation sector would seem to be the one with the lowest entrance barriers, which of course supports the notion that the minimum requirement is the provision of bed and breakfast services from the family home. In this most basic case, investment in personal consumption (the home) is used to underwrite the costs of

Table 6.6 *Characteristics of businesses within Cornwall's holiday accommodation sectors (% of respondents)*

	Hotels and guesthouses	Self-catering
Ownership		
Individual	85.6	79.7
Group	6.0	4.1
Limited company	2.4	8.1
PLC	1.2	0.0
Partner	4.8	8.1
Total	$\overline{100}$	$\overline{100}$
Age of owner		
20–30	8.6	2.8
31–40	27.2	15.2
41–50	32.1	28.4
51–60	17.3	37.5
61+	13.6	18.1
Non-response	1.2	0.0
Total	$\overline{100}$	$\overline{100}$
Birthplace (first five regions)		
Cornwall	16.9	33.8
South West	8.4	9.5
South East	34.9	25.7
Midlands	7.2	8.1
North West	7.2	12.2
Main previous occupations (only top five listed)		
Professional	27.3	23.5
Farming		17.6
Secretarial/clerical	16.9	
Retailing	13.0	13.2
Tourist industry	10.4	11.8
Principal sources of capital		
Personal savings	37.1	37.8
Family savings	15.7	18.0
Bank loan	21.4	19.7
Personal savings and bank loan	11.3	9.8

Source: modified from Shaw and Williams (1987) and Shaw et al. (1987)

producing accommodation services. It should be stressed, however, that in the Cornish research most establishments surveyed were considerably larger than this, with 60 percent having five or more bedrooms available.

The second factor to emerge from the survey concerned sources of business capital. Personal and family savings were the main source of capital, and were found to have been used by more than 50 percent of the entrepreneurs in the Cornwall study (table 6.6). This, and other research (Williams et al. 1989b), highlights the strong links between sources of capital and the age of the entrepreneur with, for example, older people relying more on personal capital. Given the dominance of ex-employees among the tourism entrepreneurs, the reliance on personal or family savings at first appears rather surprising. However, the results are not at odds with research on other economic sectors (Lloyd and Mason 1984), and merely serve to stress the small amounts of capital that are initially required.

The third major element identified relates to business motivations. This is typically a complex combination of motives, aspirations, and constraints, although in the Cornwall study it was measured simply by responses to the question of why people established their firms. Significantly, in this particular region, economic motives were matched by the importance given to non-economic reasons, such as "wanted to live in Cornwall." Such locational and environmental factors were especially important in the accommodation sectors, where they accounted for almost 33 percent of all responses. Related to this desire for a "better way of life" was the fact that a large proportion of entrepreneurs (over 80 percent) who ran hotels were in-migrants. Indeed, further analysis revealed that many of these had originally come to Cornwall on holiday and had then decided at some time to try their hand in the tourism industry. This has led to the suggestion that such tourism entrepreneurship can be seen as a form of consumption rather than production (Williams et al. 1989b). Related studies of family-based businesses operating within rural tourism have also highlighted the strong motivational elements associated with lifestyle and family-related goals (Getz and Carlsen 2000). This research, based in Australia, identified two distinct motivational types, namely; "family first" and "business first," although 50 percent of the sample had no formal business goals.

All these contingencies and features relating to entrepreneurial characteristics obviously have an impact on the economic health of the tourism industry and of particular local economies. Unfortunately, we have only a few such studies, and it is therefore not possible to examine how such factors vary in their geographical impact. There has been a tendency in both developed and developing countries to overconcentrate research on the role of large national and transnational firms, at the specific expense of smaller businesses. It seems obvious, however, that future research on tourism and economic development will need to examine more closely the relationships between the nature of entrepreneurship, the structural characteristics of the tourism industry, and its overall impact on economic change. Certainly on a wider scale, the performance of local entrepreneurs holds the key to strengthening and spreading the benefits from tourism in many developed and developing areas.

7

Tourism Employment and Labor Markets

Employment in Tourism and Leisure

The tourism and leisure industries constitute a diverse set of economic sub-sectors, including accommodation services, catering, entertainment, sport and other leisure activities, and travel and transport (see chapter 5). There are difficulties in locating the boundaries between leisure and tourism and their shared boundaries *vis-à-vis* other sectors. These are particularly acute when trying to disentangle the employment generated by tourism and leisure; many if not most leisure facilities and restaurants are used by both locals and tourists, and there is no simple way to distinguish between these two distinct segments. Indeed, in most official statistics, accommodation services are usually the only official category that is virtually exclusively dedicated to tourism; but even in this instance, the bar, restaurant, and other facilities in the hotels may also be used by local residents.

An indication of the complexity of tourism is given in Sessa's (1983) classification of tourism occupations (box 7.1). The list includes construction, maintenance, agricultural suppliers, transport, commercial services such as recreation and retailing, receptive services, and administration. Some are more obviously tourism-dependent than others. The difficulty lies in knowing what proportion of agricultural or construction employment is dependent on tourism. In the absence of official statistics, researchers usually rely on multiplier estimates.

In its simplest form, a multiplier is "calculated by dividing a unit of exogenous expenditure (coming from outside the economy) going to savings or being spent on imports to the economy: in the case of tourism, therefore, it measures the economic impact on the economy, having taken into account savings (reducing the immediate impacts)

Box 7.1   Principal tourism-related jobs

- Construction of basic infrastructures (e.g. roads, airports, sewage systems, and cultural facilities).
- Maintenance of basic infrastructures.
- Agricultural and other primary activities.
- Agroprocessing.
- Transport.
- Commercial and complementary services (e.g. banks, insurance, retailing, sports, and cultural services).
- Construction of receptive installations – the tourism superstructure (e.g. accommodation, restaurants, bars, and tourist sports installations).
- Operation of receptive services.
- Tourism welcoming services.
- Public administration.

Source: Sessa (1983: 102–3)

Sessa's list is based on direct and indirect linkages to tourism; for example, employment in hotels or in agriculture as a result of purchases by hotels. It excludes "induced" employment generated by the household expenditures of tourism employees.

and leakages to external firms" (Lundgren et al. 1995: 139–48). This is only the starting point for the calculation and decisions have to be taken as to the length of time that the "rounds" of impacts are measured over, as well as the sectors taken into account. Box 7.2 summarizes evidence on employment multipliers for Ireland. There are, however, a number of reservations to note about the use of multipliers.

First, estimating multipliers requires detailed survey work or statistical estimations. In practise, therefore, there is a tendency for most employment multipliers to be derivative, relying on a small number of original multipliers based on primary data. There are, of course, inherent difficulties in this for the multiplier effects depend on the size, structure, and diversity of the economy in question. Geographical scale is clearly important and, in general, the larger the area of analysis the smaller the leakage effect and the larger the multiplier.

Second, the reliance on multipliers is an attempt to counterbalance the error of underestimating the importance of the tourism industry. However, their widespread use in tourism can lead to the contrasting error of overestimation. There is a tendency to compare multiplier estimates of tourism employment to official statistics of employment in other sectors, such as electronics or car manufacture. But all

Box 7.2   Employment multipliers, Ireland, 1995

Source	Direct	Direct + Indirect	Direct + indirect + induced	Government interacting
(a) 1995 Employment weighted-average multipliers, per IR£m				
International	26.80	39.69	46.79	59.70
Fares	14.39	22.47	27.98	40.52
Domestic	22.12	36.31		
(b) 1995 Tourism employment impacts, number of jobs				
International	36,850	54,574	64,336	82,088
Fares	4,346	6,786	8,450	12,237
Domestic	13,829	22,701	22,701	22,701
Total	55,025	84,061	95,487	117,026
(c) The 1995 contribution of tourism to total employment %				
International	3.0	4.4	5.2	6.7
Fares	0.4	0.5	0.7	1.0
Domestic	1.1	1.8	1.8	1.8
Total	4.5	6.8	7.7	9.5

Source: Henry and Deane (1997)

In this example, four types of multipliers are calculated: direct (directly resulting from tourism expenditures), indirect (purchases by firms selling directly to tourists), induced (expenditures by employees working in firms selling directly or indirectly to tourists) and government expenditures and revenues linked to tourism. The authors also distinguish between the impacts of expenditures or domestic tourism, international tourism and fares. International tourism has the largest direct effects, and this is intensified by the induced and government interacting effects. This is because the expenditures on foreign tourism present a net gain to the economy – it represents a form of "invisible exports" which generates additional income over and above that already within the system. As a result it is estimated that all tourism contributes 9.5 percent of total employment in Ireland, with international tourism accounting for 6.7 percent.

economic activities have multiplier effects, and the real comparison is to be made between these. The error of overestimating jobs in tourism is also to be seen in the global estimates of employment provided by the World Tourism Organization for 1980. As the report acknowledges, "The primary data are highly aggregated, which makes it difficult to obtain those most directly related to characteristic tourism activities. They include employment in shops, hotels, restaurants and cafeterias,

and sometimes in other services" (1984: 81). According to these estimates, the lowest proportion of total employment in tourism is
8 percent in South Asia and the highest is 20 percent in the Americas.
These figures are considerable overestimates but they are the only ones
available at the global scale. The figures for individual countries are
often no more reliable than the global estimates. For example, Johnson
and Thomas' (1990) review of UK estimates found that these varied
between 1.1 million and 1.7 million jobs (see also Williams and Shaw
1988). Moreover, Champion and Townsend (1990) consider that there
is generally a tendency to overestimate tourism employment in the UK
through inclusion of leisure jobs attributable to day visitors.

Third, Sinclair and Stabler (1997: 142) remind us that the multiplier
does not take into account wider welfare and distributional questions.
Thus hotels and small guest houses could have identical multipliers,
but one might produce high levels of profit and high incomes for a small
group of workers, while the other might spread the benefits more
widely and equitably.

> Each type of tourist expenditure is associated with different distribu-
> tional repercussions and although the aggregate welfare gains may be
> significant, there may be adverse effects on particular individuals and
> groups, notably those who do not use the land used in the service sector.
> (Sinclair and Stabler 1997: 142)

Fourth, multipliers also assume that there is spare capacity in an economy. Otherwise, the response to an increase in tourism expenditure
may be higher prices and wages, rather than expansion of output and
employment.

Another problem is the prevalence of the informal economy in
tourism and leisure. There are important issues here. The divide between leisure and work is itself blurred. When, for example, does silk
screen printing for relatives and friends become work rather than
leisure? Or when does operating a steam train steam cease to be a hobby
and become a job? Bishop and Hoggett (1989) provide some guidance
in unravelling the complexity of the informal economy. They differentiate three sites in which goods and services are informally produced,
exchanged, and consumed: entirely within the household, outside of
households but within the community, and outside of the household
and the community. They also differentiate between two types of
exchange relationships and, therefore, two different forms of production and consumption: where production is a means to an end (commonly to earn income), and where it is intrinsically valuable to the
producer (such as running a hotel situated in a beautiful location, or
working in a ski centre to support a personal passion for skiing). On

Box 7.3   Tourism and the informal economy

1.   An unregulated economy based on outworking and cottage industry. Goods are produced for exchange outside of the community but in an unregulated way. Examples include cooks working at home to supply prepared foods to restaurants or unregistered bed and breakfast services. The "black economy" is one version of this but produces mainly for the local community.

2.   A communal economy in which goods and services are circulated within the economy and an informal local network, largely through direct exchange unmediated by money. This is often based on a leisure interest such as knitting or carpentry. It also tends to be a system of mutual aid, although it can provide a stepping stone to self-employment or to a cottage industry.

3.   The household economy which involves the production and consumption of goods within the home itself. This is linked to Gershuny and Miles' (1983) idea of the "self-service" economy. Bishop and Hoggett (1989: 160) argue that "The huge expansion in the production of leisure equipment has meant that more and more people have the means to 'do' leisure rather than consume leisure services provided by others." This also applies, via mobile homes and caravans, to tourism.

Source: after Bishop and Hoggett (1989)

this basis they identify three distinctive forms of informal economic systems, and we can apply these to tourism and leisure (box 7.3).

As the above analysis makes clear, there are considerable difficulties in estimating employment in tourism and in leisure. However, there is little disagreement that the overall importance of tourism and leisure employment is increasing in most national economies. In a way this is part of the wider process of the tertiarization of employment, especially in the more developed economies. For example, in the USA between 1977–86 all net permanent new jobs – some 17 million – were in services and construction (Champion and Townsend 1990). While employment nationally increased by 20.4 percent, employment in hotels and retailing increased by more than 29 percent. The growth of tourism jobs in the UK was even more marked, since between 1981 and 1989 total employment increased 2.6 percent, while that in hotels and catering grew by 17.3 percent. When the broader group of leisure industries in the UK is considered, it becomes clear that there have been diverse trends within the tourism sector. Between 1960 and 1983 employment in cinemas and theaters fell by 18 percent reflecting the

Table 7.1   *Employment in the leading world hotels: global regions, 1993*

Region	Full-time equivalent Employees per 100 rooms	Total sales per employee ($)
Middle East	91.9	39,231
Africa	155.9	19,109
Asia	147.5	21,870
North Africa	103.7	45,086
Australia	39.4	45,700
North America	41.5	40,201
Latin America	96.4	22,141
Europe	59.0	52,438

Source: based on Economist Intelligence Unit (1995: 31–3)

growth of home-based leisure. This is in contrast to a growth of 36 percent in all leisure services, with employment gains in excess of 50 percent in sports and recreation, betting and gambling, pubs and clubs (Gratton and Taylor 1987). The restructuring of employment also has a strong gender dimension. This, along with other labor-market changes, forms the subject of the next section, which focuses mainly on tourism.

Estimates of employment are usually more reliable when they focus on a single sector, or a sub-sector. For example, the Economist Intelligence Unit (1995) provides an overview of employment in the leading world hotels which shows up significant differences between world regions (table 7.1). In particular, there are considerable differences in labor productivity. This is a concept that can be measured in different ways, but here we consider the number of full time equivalent employees per 1,000 rooms and the total sales per employee. Between two and four times as many workers are employed per room in Africa and Asia as in Australasia, Europe, and North America. This reflects differences in labor costs, levels of service provision, and investment in technology, all of which are interrelated. Not surprisingly, the sales per employee follow a broadly similar pattern, with much higher turnover per employee in the developed countries. This is not a direct indicator of profit levels, of course, as it does not take into account labor costs, land and building costs, or marketing and other outlays. However, it is indicative of different levels of competition and the greater pressure to reduce labor costs in the high wage developed countries – as well as, increasingly, in many parts of Asia. In the next section, we consider the issues of labor market flexibility which are at the heart of the organization of the tourism industry.

Table 7.2   *Employment ratios in tourism in Portugal, 1994: by accommodation type*

	Number of jobs per bed 1994
Hotels	
5-star	0.41
4-star	0.27
3-star	0.20
2-star	0.15
1-star	0.16
Pensões	
4-star	0.20
3-star	0.13
2-star	0.14
1-star	0.13
Total	0.19

Source: Direcsão do Turismo (1996)

Labor-force Composition: Flexibility and Internal–External Labor Markets

The debate about tourism and leisure employment is peppered with references to the quality of the jobs that are generated. A not uncommon stereotype is that the tourism employee is "uneducated, unmotivated, untrained, unskilled and unproductive" (quoted in Pizam 1982: 5). In response to this, one leading industry figure, the Chairman of the English Tourist Board, declared that there are many who believe that "a job in the tourist industry is in some way less than one in a manufacturing industry" (quoted in *Financial Times* July 16, 1986). In reality, of course, employment in tourism and leisure is as heterogeneous as the different sub-sectors which together constitute the tourism industry complex. Furthermore, there is considerable diversity in employment within a particular segment, such as accommodation: the numbers of jobs per tourist, the gender and migrant composition of those jobs, their seasonality, pay, and conditions differ considerably between, say, small guest houses or pensions, and five star hotels. This is illustrated by Portugal (table 7.2), where there are 0.41 and 0.27 jobs per bed in four or five star hotels, but 0.2 jobs or less in other hotels and small guest houses (*pensões*). In reality, these differences are even greater given considerable underemployment or part-time employment of family in many smaller accommodation establishments. Another bias inherent in most measures of skills is that they concentrate on "technical" aspects, that is the physical and manipulative skills involved while ignoring the interpersonal and communication skills (including foreign languages) that are critical to "front-line" tourism jobs in many countries (Baum 1996).

While the stereotypes outlined above are oversimplifications, there are several distinctive features of the tourism and leisure labor markets. These are related to the nature of these services, the role of labor in the delivery of the services, and the temporal and spatial organization of the industry. One of the central features is the weight of labor in the overall costs of producing tourism and leisure services. For example, Pine (1987) has estimated that wages represent 20–30 percent of the pre-tax sales of multiple restaurant chains such as Pizza Express and Berni Inn. Moreover, compared to manufacturing, the scope for substituting capital for labor in the production of services is limited. This is held by Bell (1974) to be one of the key reasons for the emergence of what he terms "post industrial society."

This is not to say that capital cannot be substituted for labor in tourism production. Bagguley (1987) argues that in the UK there have been two technological revolutions within catering in recent decades. The first was the introduction of automatic dishwashers in the 1950s and 1960s, which led to a reduction in the number of kitchen assistants' jobs. The second revolution was the introduction of sophisticated methods of pre-preparing foods, such as cook-chill technology and microwaves in the 1970s and 1980s. This led to a de-skilling of kitchen work and an increase in the numbers of kitchen assistants at the expense of chefs. Linked to this, there has been rapid growth of fast food outlets based on both new technology and new work practices which have allowed companies such as McDonalds to reduce their labor costs significantly.

Technological change is also modifying the face of other segments of the tourism industry. For example, the travel agency industry is being revolutionized by the introduction of new forms of computer reservations systems. These allow for more sophisticated searches of available holiday options, combined with online booking and ticket issuing, which facilitate increased labor productivity. As a result, there are reductions in customer–employee ratios and the displacement of jobs from the high street to centralized booking centers. This tendency will be reinforced by the growth of tour operators' direct sales to individual customers via the Internet. The productivity gains from such technological advances can be substantial, and are not only limited to recent Internet developments in electronic retailing. In the UK, for example, Portland Holidays were able to increase the number of holidays sold per employee by 21 percent in 1985 largely through the introduction of an advanced booking system (*Financial Times*, January 8, 1987).

Despite some instances of significant changes in the capital:labor ratio, the potential for substitution in tourism and leisure services tends to be limited compared to, say, agriculture or manufacturing. In the face of this constraint, employers' attempts to reduce labor costs have firmly focused on labor market strategies. There is, of course, no universal pattern in this, for labor market strategies are specific to the particularities of individual labor markets. For example, Sessa (1983: 106) estimates that in the developed countries a 1,000 bed medium category hotel would employ approximately one person per five beds. In contrast, in less developed countries, where labor was relatively and absolutely cheaper, the ratio was more likely to be one employee per bed. More generally, labor market strategies will depend on prevailing regulation, work cultures, and organization, labor and capital costs, and these are all temporally and spatially contingent.

One of the most common strategies, observable in a number of countries, is the formation of dual labor markets within companies. These can be characterized as core and peripheral workers. Atkinson (1984) is largely responsible for the formalization of the concepts of core and peripheral workers, although there are strong links with Doeringer and Piore's (1971) concept of the internal labor market. Atkinson suggested that core workers were full time, permanent employees who received job security and high earnings in return for performing a wide range of tasks that cut across traditional skill demarcation lines. He considers that these workers are functionally flexible – that is they will be able and willing to move between different tasks. Characteristically these are managerial and professional staff whose skills are in short supply in the external labor market; employers are therefore keen to retain their services.

Several groups of peripheral workers are grouped around these core employees (figure 7.1). There is a secondary labor market made up of full time employees but whose jobs are less secure, lack career prospects, and are often semi-skilled. They have a high rate of labor turnover so that their employment offers numerical flexibility to employers. In addition, there are also several other groups of numerically flexible employees, including part time workers, temporary workers (on short-term contracts), training scheme placements, and homeworking. All of these categories offer a high degree of numerical flexibility to employers. They can be hired and laid-off as the volume of demand rises and falls. Another strategy available to employers is distancing, whereby certain labor tasks are sub-contracted to other firms (with lower production costs) rather than performed in-house.

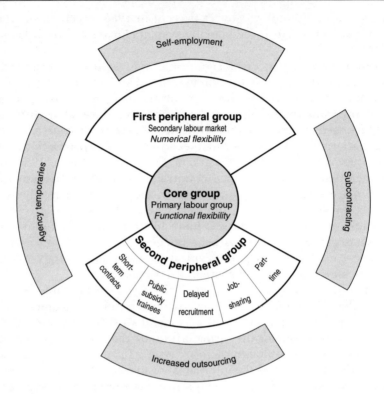

Figure 7.1   *Functional and numerical flexibility*
Source: Atkinson (1984)

Atkinson's treatise was largely written as an analysis of the reorganization of modern manufacturing. The empirical evidence for the
existence and the growth of the core–periphery structuring of labor in
manufacturing is, at best, mixed (Allen 1988). There is, however, considerable evidence of such structuring in the tourism and leisure labor
markets. Moreover, this is a long established form of internal labor
market organization in these industries (Bagguley 1987, 1990; Urry
1990). This stems from the particular nature of the demand for tourism
and leisure services. The temporal variation in demand is far greater
than is experienced in most branches of manufacturing. The rhythm
of demand varies between seasons, between working days and week-
ends/public holidays, and at different times of the day. This applies as
much to leisure and recreation as to tourism. The result is that tourism
and leisure services have to be delivered to customers in clusters in both
time and space.

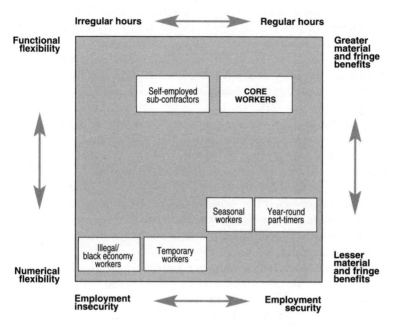

Figure 7.2   *Core and peripheral workers in tourism and leisure*

The response to this spatial and temporal rhythm, and to the weight of labor costs in production, has been the growth of a number of forms of numerical and functional flexibility in tourism and leisure employment (figure 7.2). *Temporary contracts* to cope with seasonal variations in demand have been a classic feature of employment in tourism. Some tourist industries – such as in capital cities or locations with an attractive climate all year round – do not have a marked seasonal variation in demand. In Portugal for example, there is a 30 percent employment shift between summer and winter in the highly seasonal Algarve, a 7 percent employment shift in Lisbon which has year round cultural and business tourism, and only a 2 percent shift in Madeira with its equable year-round climate for leisure tourism (Lewis and Williams 1998).

Most localities have a single peak season, flanked by shoulder seasons. The out of season period may be one of reduced activity or total closure. Employers respond to the build up of demand by employing labor on seasonal contracts, which tend to become shorter as the peak of the season is approached. These employees clearly constitute peripheral workers. If the enterprise closes during the off-season, then they may be the only employees even in the peak period. However, if low level activity is maintained through the winter, then a group of core workers may be maintained on permanent year-round contracts. Often, the difference in labor demands between the peak-season and the off season surpass the capacity of the local labor market to meet these, so that many seasonal workers may be in-migrants. As a result, seasonal workers may be provided with accommodation by their employers, which further weakens their bargaining position with respect to pay and conditions.

The impact of seasonal contracts on local labour markets depends largely on whether the workers are local or in-migrants. If they are seasonal migrants, then the off-season unemployment is effectively "exported" at the end of the peak or shoulder season. If the labor force is local, then potentially there may be high levels of unemployment during the off season. This, however, is contingent on the structure of the local economy; seasonal work in tourism can be complimentary to seasonality in other local labor markets such as fishing or farming. In the Alps, for example, winter tourism is complementary to the requirements of agriculture, while summer tourism may conflict with these. Seasonality need not be construed negatively and Ball (1988) for example found that more than half the seasonal workers he surveyed in tourist resorts in Wales could be classed as "involuntarily seasonal." These are workers who either prefer seasonal tourism job because it fits with other life style or working priorities, or who find sufficient recompense for the temporality in the occupational communities that can be found among seasonal workers. Lee-Ross (1999: 240) considers that occupational communities "exhibit a fusion of work and non-work life, with members having work-based friends, interests and hobbies."

Part time employment is a common response to the uneven distribution of work during the week or the day. Some staff may be on part-time contracts to work only at weekends or other times when demand peaks within the week. These workers are characteristically peripheral employees, who may work alongside core employees such as full-time supervisors, chefs, and head waiters. The key to their employment is that the temporal fluctuations in demand are mostly predictable and therefore allow regular employment, albeit on a part-time basis. Depending on the nature of the tourist or leisure industry, such jobs may be year round or seasonal. If the hours of part-time work are fixed and regular, then the tourism job can be combined with other part-time work, whether in tourism, in other paid jobs or in the household. Part-time jobs are more likely than full time jobs to be staffed by locals.

The tourism and leisure industries mostly provide a labor-intensive service at the point of contact with the customer. While demand is rhythmical and largely predictable, there are isolated peaks such as public holidays, a large group booking at a sports centre or a restaurant, or simply an inexplicable rush at the bar one cold and wet Monday evening. These isolated demand peaks can only be met effectively via *temporary increases in labor* at the point of contact. This can be achieved in one of two ways. Either via functional flexibility and the diversion of core workers from other tasks in the enterprise, or via numerical flexibility and the temporary hiring of labor. In practice, most small firms have a pool of friends and family that they can draw on to meet such peaks in demand. Firms will also have a reserve of part-time workers or "regular casuals" who can be drafted in to work a particular weekend or evening. The nature of such peripheral employment makes it likely that these workers will be local. Higher than average payments may be necessary to compensate for the social inconvenience of such unpredictable work.

Many segments of the tourism industry are dominated by *self-employment* or small family firms. This applies equally well to farm accommodation as to a shop in a capital city selling souvenirs. The individuals, and their families, provide another response to fluctuations in demand, that is self-exploitation. Rhythmic fluctuation in demand will be met by a willingness to work very long hours. The small-hotel owner will be up early to cook guests' breakfasts and will still be working late at night to prepare food for the next day or to welcome late arrivals.

Initially, it seems surprising that such large numbers of workers are willing to tolerate the rhythmical and the unpredictable variation in tourism and leisure work. To some extent it may not be a function of choice but a response to a constraint, the lack of alternative jobs in local labor markets. However, there is also a need to look at the total material and psychic income received. The material benefits include wages, accommodation, and tips, while the psychic income may include the opportunity to live in an attractive environment either seasonally or permanently. Chalet "girls" (a term which reflects the gender division of labor), ski instructors, the traditional Butlins' redcoats (British holiday camp entertainers) and the owners of businesses in attractive areas all fit into this model. In addition, Marshall (1986) argues that enterprises such as restaurants are able to retain the loyalty of their peripheral workers despite low wages because these are only one part of the total reward system. Customers were often friends, the employees spent some of their free time at the restaurant and, in general, the symbolic boundaries between work and leisure were weak. This is the notion of occupational communities referred to earlier (Lee-Ross 1999).

The core–periphery thesis provides an appealingly simple conceptualization of employment in tourism and leisure. However, Urry (1990) stresses the need for caution in applying this model of employment to these sectors. First, he argues that the simple core–periphery

---

Box 7.4   Structural features of strong and weak internal labor markets

Strong
- Specified hiring standards
- Single port of entry
- High skill specificity
- Continuous on-the-job training
- Fixed criteria for promotion and transfer
- Strong workplace customs
- Pay differentials remain fixed over time

Weak
- Unspecified hiring standards
- Multiple ports of entry
- Low skill specificity
- No on-the-job training
- No fixed criteria for promotion and transfer
- Weak workplace customs
- Pay differentials vary over time

Source: Simms et al. (1988: 6)

---

divide does not exist. There do seem to be core and peripheral workers, but the former are not always functionally flexible. Kitchen staff and receptionists in hotels, for example, are often functionally inflexible. However, there is evidence of growing pressure on hotels to move to greater functional flexibility. For instance, the Reo Stakis group which has 33 hotels in the UK ceased to recognize trade unions in the 1980s and introduced the new grade of multi-skilled hotel employee. Second, Urry argues that in hotels and catering, the peripheral workers on temporary contracts often do exactly the same jobs as the core staff. This is because temporary workers are taken on to replicate the work done by core staff in order to meet fluctuations in demand.

Urry's second point is important, and it may therefore be useful to consider the alternative conceptualization offered by Simms et al. (1988), which suggests that there is a continuum from strong to weak internal labor markets (box 7.4). Weak internal labor markets are relatively open to external labor markets. The authors' empirical work confirms that tourism is characterized by a weak internal labor market. They found high levels of on-the-job training, small numbers of promotions and transfers, and ad hoc management practices. This all fits convincingly with the model of a weak labor market. Such firms fulfill their labor requirements via greater openness to external labor markets: there is recruitment from outside the company, and there is a high degree of turnover with low levels of training. This is in marked contrast to those sectors where firms provide lengthy formal and informal training, and there are clear career ladders.

There is little empirical testing of the various theories concerning employment flexibility in tourism. However, we can note two important studies here. First, Lockwood and Guerrier (1989) have examined employment practices in major UK hotels, and found little evidence of functional flexibility – management have either been unable or unwilling to require greater mobility between tasks from their workforces. Their study did, however, confirm that numerical flexibility was a relatively widespread practice, although the fact that the wages and benefits of part time workers were not significantly different to those of full time "core" workers casts doubt on the core–peripheral worker model. As conditions may be different in small or medium sized hotels, and in other tourism sectors, the form and the extent of flexible labor practises in tourism remains open to question. In a second study, Krakover (1999) examined seasonal employment in Israel. He found that in general there was evidence of employers using seasonal employment contracts to adjust to temporal variations in demand. However, he also found that they did not fully synchronize employment and demand: instead there tended to be some surplus of labor in the low season, and some labor shortages in the high season. He suggests there are two reasons for this. First, reflecting on the views of Riley (1991), he considers that this may be due to relatively low labor costs, and relatively high training costs. But, in addition, he considers the importance of geographical differences in labor markets. There is much better seasonal adjustment of the seasonal demand and supply for labor in larger labor markets such as Tel-Aviv, rather than in smaller economic areas, due to the availability of potential workers in the external labor market.

The discussion of employment flexibility inevitably raises the question of whether tourism in capitalist economies displays tendencies to shift from Fordist to neo-Fordist modes of production, and this question is addressed in Ioannides and Debbage (1998). They concluded that "In a sector as amorphous as the travel industry, with so many permeable boundaries and so many diverse linkage arrangements to exploit, a polyglot of coexisting multiple incarnations has evolved, displaying varying traits of flexibility" (1998: 108). Some elements display pre-Fordist characteristics, especially many of the smaller hospitality establishments, but also souvenir shops and craft workshops; these are characteristically small and produce customized goods, largely relying on in-house production. Other elements display Fordist characteristics of mass consumption and mass production; sectorally this is most evident in international hotel chains and airlines, while the principal geographical manifestation is in the large-scale mass tourism resorts. Yet other elements display neo-Fordist characteristics of more flexible and fragmented production, characterized by increased vertical disintegration and sub-contracting, and greater individuation of consumption; examples of the former are to be found in the outsourcing of laundry and food preparation by, respectively, hotels and restaurants. But whether this represents new forms of mass consumption or a distinctive neo-Fordism is a moot point that we return to in chapter 9.

The Social Construction of Labor Markets: Gender and Flexibility

In different ways, the work of both Atkinson (1984) and Simms et al. (1988) draw attention to the social composition of external labor markets. This is particularly important for those industries, such as tourism and leisure, that have weak internal labor markets. Two features of the social construction of external labor markets are considered here; questions of race and ethnicity in relation to international migration (in the following section), and the gender division of labor.

In broad terms, women are more likely than men to be peripheral rather than core workers, to be in part-time jobs and to receive lower wages (Bagguley 1990). While these stereotypes are largely true, it should be emphasized that the gender division of labor is socially constructed and changes over time and space (Beechey 1987; Dex 1985). There is strong occupational segregation in the tourism industry in most societies (Doherty and Stead 1998), and women tend to undertake tasks such as serving meals, working in kitchens and making beds which replicate some of the roles ascribed to them in the household division of labor. These jobs are not, of course, inherently gender-specific. Instead, the gender division of labor is socially constructed. Women workers carry into the work place their subordinate status in society at large. The work of women is often regarded as inferior or unskilled, simply because it is undertaken by women; in short, the definitions of skills may be no more than a social classification based on gender. The same argument applies to part-time jobs. This is exacerbated by the informal nature (and weak internal organization) of much tourism employment and the consequent lack of formal methods of recruitment and promotion (Jordan 1997). Some jobs in hotels and catering are socially constructed as part-time jobs because they are seen to be women's jobs either because of the type of work involved, or because they are seen to fit in with the (ascribed) role of women as carers in the household.

The social expectation that women have "dual careers," in which they combine paid jobs and domestic responsibilities, contributes to occupational segregation. Taking responsibility for child-rearing or caring for elderly relatives may mean that women are either unavailable for full-time work, or can only take jobs with fixed hours which are compatible with their domestic roles. This may exclude them from certain managerial or supervisory posts. Single women are not necessarily constrained in the same way but do suffer from the general social construction of what constitutes suitable work for women as well as outright discrimination in some instances. This brief analysis of women's roles in the labor force serves to remind us that weak internal labor markets are not simply the outcome of management strategies. Instead, they reflect the way in which managers have used the social construction of women's work as one element in the structuring of the internal labor markets in tourism. The tourism industry does not just provide jobs for women; the very existence of a pool of women, and of the social possibility of paying them lower wages or employing them on temporary or part time contracts, helped to shape the formation of the core–periphery divide in the labor force.

Burrell et al. (1997) provide one of the few detailed comparative studies of the gendering of tourism employment (table 7.3). While women, in general, were structurally disadvantaged in the hospitality labor force, there were also significant national differences reflecting cultural and political differences in institutions and practices. There was strong occupational evidence in all four countries that they examined. This was both horizontal (between sectors) with most housekeeping jobs being taken by women and most kitchen jobs by men, and vertical (between different levels of the employment hierarchy). Women not only formed a minority of managers and supervisors but they also held significantly smaller proportions of these jobs than they did of all hospitality jobs. The authors relate these differences less to formal training opportunities in the industry, than to general societal disadvantages for women with "dual" roles in the face of limited maternity leave arrangements, general managerial attitudes, and ineffective implementation of sex equality legislation.

Migration, Labor Market Segmentation, and Informal Labor Markets

The migrant and ethnic composition of the external labor market also impinges upon the organization of the internal labor market. As

Table 7.3 *Gendered employment in the hospitality sector: European comparisons, 1997*

	France	Spain	Italy	UK
Women's share (%) of hospitality jobs	50	41	46	63
Women as % of all employment in*:				
a) Housekeeping	97	99	74	92
b) Kitchen work	11	50	33	13
c) Management/supervision	39	37	24	54
Training for women compared to men	Some disadvantage	Neutral	Neutral	Neutral
Maternity legislation	6 weeks paid + up to 3 years unpaid	16 weeks paid + up to 3 years unpaid	20 weeks paid, and 6 months on min. of 30%	90% for 6 weeks and reduced rate for 12 weeks is common, followed by 22 weeks unpaid
% Employees with at least reasonable knowledge of employment law*	33	29	37	37

* Survey data

Source: Based on Burrell (et al. 1997)

Table 7.4 *The economic and cultural impacts of different forms of labor migration*

Migration system	On the tourism area		On the migrants' area of origin	
	Economic	Cultural	Economic	Cultural
Daily commuter	Limited	None	Major	None
Seasonal migrant	Limited	Limited	Major	Limited
Permanent in-migrant	Major	Limited/major	Limited	None
International migrant	Limited	Major	Limited	Major

tourism, in particular, involves the delivery of services to groups of consumers in particular times and places, there is a need to guarantee the availability of labor to fulfill this task. This may be provided by local residents, if tourism is relatively limited in scale and attractive as a source of employment. Alternatively, it may require labor to commute from the surrounding area. However, the demand for labor may exceed the supply available in a particular labour market catchment area, thereby requiring in-migration. This may be seasonal or permanent depending on the nature of the demand. In Portugal, for example, Cavaco (1980) shows that there are two main streams of migrant workers in the Algarve. The first is from villages, which lie beyond daily commuting distance, in the hinterland of the Algarve coast. The second is drawn from the poorer villages of the other regions of Portugal. Such migration has significant economic implications. On the one hand, it may denude the regions of origin of some of the most innovative and energetic members of the community. However, it also potentially facilitates the transfer of remittances from one of the more developed to the less developed regions of the country. Depending on the scale of the demand for labor, and conditions in the national labor market, the migration may be at the international rather than the intra-national scale, as discussed below.

Each of these strategies for sourcing labor potentially has different economic and cultural impacts both for the tourism area, and for the migrants' home areas (table 7.4). Daily commuters have limited cultural impact and considerable economic impact on their home areas. The same applies to seasonal labor although they may have a greater cultural impact on their home areas and the tourist areas. Permanent in-migrants have a considerable economic and some cultural impact on the tourist area. Finally, temporary international migrants have a major cultural impact on their home and the tourist areas.

International migration is clearly important in tourism and leisure labor markets and merits further discussion. While there has only been limited research on international migration in these industries, there has been more widespread research on the role of international migration in the economies of the more developed countries. Worldwide, there may be as many as 30 million international labor migrants and in countries such as Luxembourg and Switzerland they constitute as much as one-third of the total labor force. The main streams originate from relatively poorer countries and their destinations are North America, and the more prosperous European, Asian, and Middle Eastern countries. Clout et al. (1989), writing on Europe, stress that "Very roughly, we may say that 1 in 10 workers in the EC are cross-national migrants and about 1 in 10 of the workers in the main Mediterranean sending countries . . . earns his living in industrial Europe." Subsequently, King (1995) estimated that foreign workers account for between 10 and 40 percent of employment in the hotel, catering, and distributive trades sector in Luxembourg, Switzerland, and Germany. Their motives were mostly economic although some were driven by political and human rights conditions in their home countries. As King (1995: 184) reports, they operate in highly segmented labor markets, where recruitment is organized along nationality and ethnic lines:

> In both Spain and Italy, chambermaids and cleaners from the Philippines and some Latin American countries are widespread in hotels and apartment complexes. Hotels in big cities in Italy, especially Rome, employ kitchen and portering staff from many Third World countries such as Somalia, Eritrea, India and Morocco. Street-hawkers, a highly visible component of the street scene and beach life of Mediterranean tourist resorts, are mainly from Senegal and other West African countries. They migrate via kinship and tribal networks which they maintain abroad in order both to preserve their culture and facilitate access to housing and jobs.

International migrants fill critical labor shortages in many developed countries. King (1995) suggests that there is a three fold hierarchy of transnational migration relating to tourism (box 7.5). However, most of the migrants – who tend to be unskilled – occupy poorly paid, insecure, unpleasant, and/or boring jobs (Castles et al. 1984). Tourism and leisure often figure among the potential employers. The weak organization of internal labor markets in these industries means there are relatively weak barriers to entry. At the same time, the role of international migration in maintaining both flexibility and low wages in external labor markets may encourage the perpetuation of weak internal markets. Many such migrants occupy peripheral jobs, and if they are illegal

Box 7.5   Occupational hierarchy among international migrant workers in tourism

1. Highly skilled migration of managers and marketing personnel both within companies and on behalf of companies/national tourism bodies.
2. Agency representatives e.g. tour company resort representatives and guides.
3. Unskilled or semi-skilled labor e.g. working in kitchens, cleaning, or making up beds.

Source: King (1995)

migrants or do not have work permits, then this may reinforce their insecurity. The tourist migrant worker constitutes one particular type of such flexible, relatively low cost migrant labor (box 7.6). The importance of this reserve army of low cost, unorganized workers is immense and underpins the tourist industries of many areas, including several of the world's major city regions such as London, Paris, Sydney, and New York.

However, it would be wrong to assume that international migrants are permanently condemned to subordinate positions in the tourism and leisure industries. Böhning (1972) argues that there are four stages in international migration: the first stage mainly involves short stay young, male workers; the second stage sees the involvement of more older and married male migrants; in the third stage more families are involved and the duration of migration increases; finally, the migrant community "matures" and becomes "self-feeding" through generating its own demand for services. Migrants may develop businesses such as shops, restaurants, and travel agencies to provide specialist goods and services to their own communities. Peneff (1981), for example, records such experiences among Algerians in France while Anderson and Higgs (1976) record a similar process among the Portuguese communities in Canada. Migrants may also, or alternatively, be able to, market their ethnic distinctiveness. Examples include Chinese restaurants and shops in London or Vancouver, and Indonesian restaurants in the Netherlands. This is both part of the wider internationalization of culture and supported by this specific process.

International migration to work – in among others the tourist and leisure industries – within the more developed countries also has consequences for the migrants' home countries. They usually remit a high proportion of their savings; King (1986: 24) estimates that about 20 percent is common among Southern European migrants. This

Box 7.6   Tourist-migrant workers

Social and economic changes have led to an increase since 1945 in the number of, usually young, people, who travel abroad for a substantial time period for cultural and educational reasons. They often combine study, tourism and casual work, and can be considered to be "tourist workers." This takes many forms, including the "gap year" between school and higher education, or between the end of formal education and work. This has become a common practise in many countries. Mason (2001), for example, suggests that the "overseas experience" in New Zealand has become a form of "rite of passage" from youth to adulthood. While predominantly driven by consumption goals, this form of tourist-migrant experience can also be seen as a form of investment in human capital. The life skills gained in traveling overseas and contact with other cultures may enhance employment prospects when they return home to start or resume their careers.

Some individuals, however, become tourist-migrant workers on a more permanent basis; their motives are a mixture of the economic and tourism. They are attracted to particular tourism destinations because of their tourism product, and they work in order to support their visit. Examples include ski instructors and beach life guards. They may travel around destinations following the ebbing and waning of the tourist seasons.

Both forms of tourist-migrant workers provide a source of flexible and relatively low cost labor to the tourism industry, because concerns for wages and working conditions are counterbalanced by lifestyle and consumption goals.

represents a significant international transfer of resources in many cases, and makes a major contribution to the current account in several countries.

Temporary emigrants eventually return to their home countries. Most studies of returnees have found that their first priority is to invest in better housing conditions for their families. Only a small proportion of emigrants establish businesses on their return, but those that do invest most frequently in restaurants, hotels, or other commercial establishments (Lewis and Williams 1986; Unger 1986). King (1986: 21) comments that "going to Germany seems to convert peasants into petty traders." There are several case studies of return migrants' diversification into the tourism and leisure industries. First, King et al. (1984) showed that most tourism enterprises in Amantea in Calabria had been established by return migrants: they had small amounts of capital available for investment at a time when the local tourism industry was expanding rapidly. Second, Mendonsa (1983) demonstrated that return migrants in Nazaré in Portugal had higher incomes than non-migrants, because they used their accumulated capital to purchase houses and rooms to rent to tourists. Third, Kenna (1993) identified the key role played by return migrants in developing the tourism industry in Anafi in the Cyclades; they had access to capital, some foreign language skills, and used local networks to secure both supplies and political favors. Interestingly, they were able to combine the advantages of both insiders and outsiders, and used these identities in changing form in the many roles required of entrepreneurs.

Tourism therefore potentially provides jobs and income for the workers of less developed countries in one of two ways: in the home countries, providing services for tourists; or as international migrants working in tourism and leisure industries abroad. However, these two models have contrasting economic and cultural implications. The relationship between tourism and labor markets is, therefore, necessarily complex. Furthermore, while the concept of internal and external labor markets is useful for analysing these industries, it is important to remember that both of these labor markets (external – generalized migration; internal – intra-company transfers within transnational corporations) stretch across international boundaries with diverse economic and cultural effects.

Part IV

Tourism Environments

8

Tourism and Leisure Environments

Typologies of Tourism and Leisure Environments

Much of the discussion so far has focused on the functional processes operating within the broad areas of tourism and leisure. We have examined not only the structure of these industries but also the nature of consumption patterns and their social consequences (chapters 3 and 4). It should also be recognized that tourism and leisure take place in a diverse range of environments, although most have in common one or all of the following elements: a landscape to observe and enjoy; activities to participate in; and experiences to anticipate or remember. Attempts to classify or to come to terms with the nature and characteristics of these different environments (Gunn 1980) have been fragmented along a number of thematic lines. Lew (1987), in a wide-ranging review of the literature on tourist attractions, has attempted to overcome such fragmentation, and has identified three broad approaches towards developing typologies that encompass ideographic, organizational, and cognitive perspectives. The first and perhaps most important of these frameworks, that based on the ideographic approach, focuses on the concrete uniqueness of "environment" and, as such, stresses the differences between nature-orientated and human-orientated attractions (Perry 1975). In contrast, typologies based on organizational perspectives focus on the spatial characteristics of size and scale (Gunn 1980), carrying capacity, and the temporal nature of attractions (Lew 1987: 359). Finally, cognitive approaches stress classifications relating to tourist perceptions and experiences. These can either be at very general levels, as suggested by Pearce (1982) who defined a tourist environment as any place that fostered the feeling of being a tourist, or through such feelings of "outsiderness"

Plate 8.1   *The selling of mining heritage in Colorado, USA. Worked out mines provide a focus for heritage-tourism*

and "insiderness" as discussed by Relph (1976) from a humanistic perspective.

Each of these three main bases of classification reveals important characteristics of tourism and leisure environments, which in turn can contribute to understanding of developments and their impacts. In all three cases, Lew (1987) attempted to provide composite typologies based on past studies, and by using different classificatory criteria. In the ideographic approach (table 8.1), we can recognize a range of environments, from natural through to those comprising the nature–human interface and purely human-orientated ones. Within each of these, attractions can also be arranged according to their general environment characteristics, specific features and levels of inclusivity (table 8.1). Using such a framework, it is possible to classify the whole range of tourism and leisure environments in any one of nine major categories. For example, "general environments" are, as Lew (1987: 557) explains, "broad in scope and often large in scale," requiring little or no tourist involvement for them to exist. In contrast, "specific environments" tend to be smaller and often have clear links with tourism and leisure. "Inclusive environments" are the main attractions drawing tourists to a particular destination, with the inclusivity deriving from the fact that tourists are completely involved in the leisure experience. Clearly, the

Table 8.1 *An ideographic typology of tourist and leisure environments*

Nature	Nature–human interface	Human
General environments		
Panoramas	Observational	Settlement infrastructure
Mountains	Rural/agriculture	Utility types
Sea coast	Scientific gardens	Settlement morphology
Plain	Animals (zoos)	Settlement functions
Arid	Plants	Commerce
Island	Rocks and	Retail
	archaeology	Finance
		Institutions
		Government
		Education and science
		Religion
		People
		Way of life
		Ethnicity
Specific features		
Landmarks	Leisure nature	Tourist infrastructure
Geological	Trails	Forms of access
Biological	Parks	To and from a destination
Flora	Beach	Destination tour routes
Fauna	Urban	Information and receptivity
Hydrological	Other	Basic needs
	Resorts	Accommodation
		Meals
Inclusive environments		
Ecological	Participatory	Leisure superstructure
Climate	Mountain activities	Recreation entertainment
Sanctuaries	Summer	Performances
National parks	Winter	Sporting events
Nature reserves	Water activities	Amusements
	Other outdoor	Culture, history, and art
	activities	Museums and monuments
		Performances
		Festivals
		Cuisine

Source: Lew (1987)

nature of tourist involvement varies considerably between the different environmental types, although leisure superstructures intrude into a range of tourism and leisure settings. These overlaps lead to consideration of the two additional composite typologies derived by Lew (1987). The organizational one stresses scale and levels of participation, while the cognitive one focuses on activities, attraction, characteristics, and tourist experiences.

In addition to such broad-based typologies, there have also been attempts to develop specific classifications of resorts and resort development. Most of these are based on structural and spatial variations relating to a limited set of examples drawn from particular local or regional environments. However, despite such backgrounds, they all tend to have five main features in common: the resource being developed; the context of development; its spatial organization; the way in which development occurs; and the characteristics of the developer (Pearce 1987c, 1995). As shown in table 8.2, these typologies range from those concerned specifically with forms of coastal developments (Barbaza 1970; Peck and Lepie 1977), Alpine environments (Préau 1970) and broader-based classifications of resort development processes (Gormsen 1981; Miossec 1976; Oppermann 1992, 1993; Pearce 1978). Barbaza's (1970) typology, based on surveys of the Mediterranean and Black Sea coasts, identified three main types of development, while Peck and Lepie's (1977) work relates to small coastal resorts in North Carolina. Studies of Alpine environments have identified two main types of resort development which are characterized in Préau's work (1968, 1970) as the so-called Chamonix and Les Belleville models (table 8.2), This approach has subsequently been extended by Pearce (1978, 1987c, 1995), who attempted to recognize development processes that could be applied to a range of environments, using the concepts of integrated and catalytic types of resort growth (table 8.2). In both cases, single promoters are involved, although within the catalytic type the process of development also becomes strongly related to a number of secondary developers. According to Pearce (1987c), both processes produce differing resorts, with catalytic developments usually being grafted on to existing settlements (see also chapter 9).

Of greater significance than Pearce's attempts to produce a general typology of resorts are the resort models presented by Miossec (1976) and Gormsen (1981). These stress a far greater number of variables, as well as being grounded in a wider range of case studies. Miossec's (1976) model stresses the spatial dynamics of tourism development through a consideration of four main elements: resorts; transportation; tourist behavior; and the attitudes of tourist brokers in the local community (see also chapter 6). Within this framework, Miossec highlights

Table 8.2 *Main typologies of tourist resort developments*

Environment	Author(s)	Major findings
Coastal	Barbaza (1970)	Three main types of development; spontaneous resorts (e.g. Côte d'Azur, Costa Brava), planned and localized development (e.g. Black Sea littoral of Romania and Bulgaria), extensive planned developments (e.g. Languedoc, Roussillon coast of France)
	Peck and Lepie (1977)	Three main criteria identified with which to assess development; i.e. speed of development, power basis in terms of local/non-local control, and impact of development on host communities
Alpine	Préau (1968, 1970)	Stresses three factors; state of local community at onset of development, rhythm of development, and characteristics of site. Identifies two types: (i) *Chamonix* model – outside influences are only gradual and complementary; (ii) *Les Belleville* model – development conceived by outside promoters based on technical and constructional criteria for ski development
Mixed	Pearce (1978, 1987c)	Recognition of two main development processes: (i) integrated development involving a single promoter, e.g. ski resorts such as La Plagne (France); (ii) catalytic development – initial activities of a single promoter act as a catalyst for other complementary developments, e.g. ski resort of Vars

the relationships between phases of tourism development and changes in each of the four main elements. The model postulates that resort areas pass through four major phases of development. Phase one sees the establishment of a pioneer resort based on very limited transport networks, and used by tourists with global perceptions of tourism opportunities. This is followed in the next phase by a multiplication of resorts, increased transport linkages and a greater tourist awareness of the place. By phase three there exists the beginnings of a resort hierarchy and some resorts begin to specialize, while excursion circuits also develop, as does host–guest segregation. Finally, in phase four, the resort hierarchy is complete, as is the specialization of functions. Resorts become saturated under conditions of full mass tourism, which also sees the development of maximum transport connectivity. The significance of this approach lies not in its sophistication, for the model is somewhat basic in format, but rather in its attempt to draw together such a range of variables within a spatial framework (Pearce 1987c, 1995).

In contrast, Gormsen (1981) has presented a spatial-evolutionary model that describes seaside resort development at an international level. The model specifically focuses on three factors; the nature of holiday accommodation, levels of local and non-local participation in tourism development, and the social structure of tourists. The model is rooted in the historical evolution of European tourism and recognizes four major types of resort regions, which Gormsen terms "tourism peripheries." Periphery one covers Channel and Baltic coast resorts; periphery two, Mediterranean Europe; the third periphery includes the North African coast; and the fourth periphery covers more distant resorts in West Africa, the Caribbean, South America and the Pacific. Each periphery passes through a sequence, the early stages of which are characterized by external developers, elite tourists and mainly hotel accommodation. Later development stages show more local involvement, a greater diversity of holiday accommodation and a wide range of social classes using the resorts. Such a development sequence has been reached in periphery one since the 1960s, while periphery four is still within the early stages of the model. As Pearce (1995) points out, this model corresponds broadly with the earlier work of Lundgren (1972) and Britton (1980) who also, in a less formalized fashion, stressed the structural characteristics of resort development.

Like most of the other researchers who have attempted to provide some form of resort environment model, Gormsen (1981) based his work on one specific region, in his case Western Europe. However, we could use his ideas within very different regional contexts, which would obviously change the nature of the resort peripheries. For example, if the model is switched to focus on North America (periphery one) then the Caribbean would shift out of periphery four and into periphery three. Such re-positioning draws attention to two main factors concerning such models. The first is that most models are fairly specific and should only be taken out of their environmental context with great care. Second, none of the models are really general enough to provide what Pearce (1987c: 19) terms a "comprehensive, all-embracing model

Table 8.3 *A typology of the regional implications of tourism developments*

| | Locational bias | | Selective regions | | | |
| | | | Capital | | | |
Type of tourism	Core	Periphery	City	Urban	Rural	Coastal
International cultural	*		*			
Industrial heritage		*		*	?	
International conference and exhibitions	*		*			
Conference	*	*	*	*		*
Exhibition	*	*	*	*	*	?
Business general	*			*		
"Events"	*	*	*	*	*	*
Mass holiday (summer)		*			*	*
Mass holiday (winter)		*			*	
Short break (summer)	*				*	*
Short break (winter)	*		*	*		

Source: Williams and Shaw (1990)

of tourism." Indeed, one would question whether such a model could even be derived or be at all worthwhile, given the complex and dynamic nature of tourism environments.

Finally, it is important to recognize that there are many different forms of tourism, and that each has distinctive regional implications which do not necessarily conform to any simple centre–periphery model. For example, two of the most polarized forms of tourism are international conferences and exhibition activities, and mass winter holiday tourism, but they have very different regional implications. Thus, mass winter tourism is essentially located in the more peripheral regions of those states in, or bordering on, the Alps in Europe or the major mountain changes of North America. In contrast, international conference tourism, as well as international cultural tourism, is essentially a capital or major city activity (see chapter 10). Table 8.3 attempts to summarize some of the most salient regional features of these different forms of tourism.

Such activities also have different implications in terms of their contributions to centre–periphery patterns of regional development. Mass summer tourism is more likely than short-break tourism to favor peripheral regions, if only because of the accessibility and time constraints on the latter type of holiday. The typology in table 8.3 is somewhat tentative, and further research is still required to establish the precise regional implications of these different forms of tourism. There is also a need to establish a stronger temporal dimension to the typology, which is the seasonality characteristics of each of the main products. Such clarifications could aid considerably in the refinement of tourism models, and must surely form a critical issue in the geography of tourism.

Resort Cycles and Changes in Tourism Environments

Tourism environments tend to be extremely dynamic, influenced as they are by the changing tastes of holidaymakers and the often fickle nature of the tourist industry. The notion of lifecycle change in tourist destination areas has already been touched upon at several points within this book (see also Pearce 1995: chapter 1). Moreover, various authors have sought to conceptualize these changes, drawing on the general ideas surrounding the product lifecycle. One of the earliest such attempts was that made by Butler (1980), who popularized the idea of a resort lifecycle to explain the growth and decline of resorts. Butler (1980) suggested a six-stage cycle of the evolution of tourism destination areas, expressed in terms of changes in the numbers of visitors over time (see figure 8.1a):

- *Exploration*: small numbers of visitors attracted by natural beauty or cultural characteristics – numbers are limited and few tourist facilities exist.
- *Involvement*: limited involvement by local residents to provide some facilities for tourists – recognizable tourist seasons and market areas begin to emerge.
- *Development*: large numbers of tourists arrive, control passes to external organizations and there is increased tension between locals and tourists.
- *Consolidation*: tourism has become a major – if not the main – part of the local economy, although rates of visitor growth have started to level off and some older facilities are seen as second-rate.
- *Stagnation*: peak numbers of tourists have been reached, although the resort is no longer considered fashionable and turnover of business properties tends to be high.
- *Decline*: attractiveness continues to decline, visitors are lost to other resorts, and the resort becomes more dependent on day visitors and weekend recreationalists from a limited geographical area while long-term decline will continue unless action is taken to rejuvenate the area.

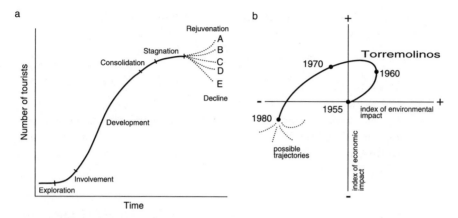

Figure 8.1   *Resort lifecycle models*
Sources: (a) Butler (1980); (b) Wolfe (1983)

This is not the only lifecycle model of changes in tourist destination areas, since Wolfe (1983) offers a similar approach that more explicitly takes environmental changes into account (figure 8.1b). In this respect, it provides some linkages with the more general evolutionary model proposed by Miossec, discussed earlier. Wolfe's perspective is that, in the early stages, tourism can have positive economic and environmental effects. However, with increasing numbers of tourists, the balance of environmental effects tends to become negative. Finally, the economic benefits may also become negative due to the leakage of revenue to organizations outside the local economy and rising operational costs within the resort. This pessimistic trajectory is known as the Ellis curve.

The model proposed by Butler has attracted criticism, particularly for failing to take into account changes in the demand and supply sides. Cooper (1990) points out that the lifecycle concept is extremely dependent on supply side factors, such as the rate of development, tourist access, government policy, and competing resort areas, as well as demand factors. Similarly, Debbage (1990) argues that Butler's model has focused on the internal dynamics of specific resorts, thereby ignoring both the structure of the tourism industry and the competition from other resorts. He therefore draws on Markusen's (1985) theoretical work on the profit cycle as "it allows the exigencies of industrial organisation and oligopoly to be explicitly introduced in a discussion of the cyclical theory of resort development" (Debbage 1990: 520–1). In some resorts, large companies may exercise oligopolitistic powers in order to

---

Box 8.1   Conceptual problems and measurement definitions relating to the resort cycle

- the area/unit of analysis;
- the relevant market area;
- the shape of the curve;
- the resort's stage in the lifecycle;
- the unit of measurement (i.e., numbers of tourists, visitors, overnight stays, and spend); and
- the relevant time-frame.

---

protect market shares and profit levels in the latter part of the resort cycle. However, this may lead to a long-term loss of competitiveness and innovation. These arguments are backed by Debbage through a case study of the oligopolistic powers of Resorts International in Paradise Island (Bahamas).

The exact shape of the Butler curve has also been criticized, as has the notion that all resorts have to pass sequentially through the six different stages of the lifecycle. Identification of such stages and of specific turning points between each stage is also problematic, with both Haywood (1986) and Cooper (1990) providing critiques of the difficulties of operationalizing the model. Prideaux (2000), in a general review of destination lifecycle models, identifies a number of specific problems: the ability of any one model to explain tourism development (Bianchi 1994; Choy 1992; Prosser 1995); conceptual limitations (Getz 1992; Haywood 1986); conceptual difficulties of the product life cycle (Hart et al. 1984); application to planning (Haywood 1986); a lack of empirical evidence (Choy 1992); the overall shape and stages of the curve (Cooper 1992), and the application of its later stages to resort restructuring (Agarwal 1997). Perspectives taken by economic geographers have stressed the need for more rigorous analysis of the supply and demand sides of the model, as well as arguing that "theoretical analysis has taken more of a back seat" (Gordon and Goodall 2000: 299). Haywood (1986), for example, suggests that there are six major conceptual and measurement decisions relating to operationalizing the resort cycle as shown in box 8.1. He argues that until such issues are fully resolved, the model's applicability to strategy and forecasting is questionable.

It should also be stressed that all these definitional problems are relevant to geographical research on resorts. Thus, the definition of the resort area touches on questions of spatial diffusion as well as the nature of functional areas. For example, when does tourism growth in an area adjoining an established resort represent the early stages of a new, quite different cycle of resort development as opposed to the rejuvenation of the existing area? The definition of the temporal framework is also problematic. In this respect, does a downturn in the tourism curve represent a temporary fluctuation or a long-term shift into the decline stage of the model? Another criticism is that the resort cycle model assumes a false universalism, and that this is maintained only by failing to take into account differences in the competitive positions or resources of different resorts.

Despite these criticisms, the resort model has been tested in a variety of situations, although with varying degrees of success. Meyer-Arendt (1987) has, for example, attempted to correlate resort morphology and environmental impacts with stages of tourism development in the Gulf of Mexico. He argues that the model provides a useful conceptual framework within which to study various forms of land-use intensification and environmental improvement or degradation. However, he rightly concludes that the resort cycle model is culturally and politically specific and, for example, seems inappropriate for application to developing countries. As with all such models – and we saw examples of this in the earlier part of this chapter – there is a danger in using them as anything other than descriptive devices that are relevant to the development of resorts in particular places and time periods. Newly emerging resorts face very different markets and trading conditions to those experienced by older resorts in earlier time periods. Furthermore, the model seeks to describe a process of change but, as Massey (1984) has shown, in economic geography process and structure are strongly linked. For example, previous rounds of investment have created a set of structures in particular resorts. In turn, these subsequently condition the possibilities for further investments within these resorts or perhaps in new areas. The view that the model is too deterministic is underlined by van Duijn's (1983) work on the product cycle. He argues that decline is not predictable, because the cycle can be predicted in one of three ways: substitution of a new product; extension of the lifecycle by updating the product; or changes in technology, which make a product more competitive. All three possibilities could apply to a tourism resort.

Other workers, notably Haywood (1986), have attempted to shift the resort model away from its relatively deterministic stance. Having recognized that the original model as expressed by Butler is destination specific, Haywood attempts to present a range of possible resort cycles for different types of destination areas. These include evolutionary curves for purpose-built resort complexes, through to those representing resorts strongly conditioned by external events. In this way, a certain degree of flexibility is introduced to the model, although these new perspectives still suffer from many of the criticisms directed at the original work. Perhaps a potentially more valuable contribution is made by Haywood (1986), through his introduction to viewing resort development via the process of natural selection. Such perspectives have been applied to forms of institutional change, particularly retailing (Alchain 1950), but these ideas remain undeveloped within tourism research. Haywood views the tourist destination area as the "organism" fighting for survival, and in doing so he draws attention to three significant points. The first is that, according to the theory of natural selection, whenever there is strong competition, specialization confers advantages on those resorts that focus on particular forms of tourism. Second, the theory draws attention to the fact that environmental changes establish new conditions that in turn influence resort survival. This also raises a third point, namely, that highly specialized resorts adapted to one specific set of environmental conditions tend to be less capable of adjusting to sudden changes in tourist demand, compared to less specialized areas. In this respect, resort areas directed at narrow market segments would tend to have much shorter lifecycles than those resorts aimed at more broadly based markets.

Such perspectives therefore give a more realistic as well as a flexible approach to the study of resort development, and open the way for more empirically based studies to examine these notions. The limited evidence that we have from studies of resorts suggests that, in addition to levels of specialization, size also plays an important part. In England, for example, on average the country's six largest resorts draw one million or more staying visitors per annum, and have sufficient market volume to organize their own programmes of regeneration (Shaw and Williams 1997). By contrast, the 60 or so smaller resorts, which have lost at least one-half of their market since 1970, have far less scope for arresting decline and shifting their lifecycle curve.

The Falsification of Place and Time in Leisure Environments

As we explained in Chapter 4, a great deal of leisure consumption, especially that related to tourism, is about myths and fantasies. The creation of unreal images is essential for many tourists seeking to escape the blandness of home and work routines. Early tourists, with large amounts of time and money, sought such differences in the romantic authenticity of the "Grand Tour," through an examination of ancient cultures (Towner 1996). Indeed, the present-day equivalents of this group still search for holiday experiences that bring them into contact with "original" cultures and societies untouched by the modern world. In contrast, we can also represent a very different set of tourist environments which have deliberately set out to attract visitors by falsifying both place and time. Such developments have increased dramatically over the past 30 years, and have attracted growing attention from a diverse range of academics. Urry (1990: 104) views these tourist sites within a threefold dichotomous classification based on whether sites are authentic or unauthentic, historical or modern, and whether they are subject to the romantic or collective tourist gaze. Thus, many theme parks may be classified as unauthentic, modern and the object of the "collective gaze."

For Urry (1990), the growth of this form of leisure setting is bound up with the rise of postmodernism, which in turn involves the dissolution of boundaries "not only between high and low cultures, but also between different cultural forms" (Urry, 1990: 82; see also chapter 3). At this point, we are less interested in overall causal processes then in the characteristics of the resultant environments. Indeed, we can recognize a number of different tourism products associated with the process of falsification; ranging from the semi-tropical artificial environments of Center Parc type developments found in England, Holland, and northern Germany (Shaw and Williams 1991b), to large theme parks and shopping/leisure malls, and developments associated with the so-called heritage industry (Hewison 1987).

Much has been written about the rise of the heritage industry, as well as its associated problems of historical falsification and cultural commodification. The debate has been brought sharply into focus in countries such as the UK and the USA due to the increased economic importance of heritage-based tourism. Much of this is based around the redefined idea of a museum which, according to Lumley (1988: 2), is not used in the "narrow sense of a particular building or institution, but as a potent social metaphor and as a means whereby societies represent their relationships to their own history and to that of other cultures." In basic economic terms, the shift is towards the open-air museum and the commercialization of the past. Morton (1988) sees this as part of increased competition within the leisure sector: the greater the success of shopping malls and theme parks, the greater has been the pressure on museums to mount expensive, innovative displays.

Inevitably, such trends in heritage development have raised some strong criticisms from commentators who view the whole process as one whereby the tourist industry produces a history-making business. Lumley (1988) has summarized the concern over these trends under three broad headings: the commercialization of history, the pursuit of realism, and the impact of the media. The first two echo the earlier and broader debates discussed in chapter 4, regarding tourism's impact on culture, although Lumley singles out developments in the UK as being driven by the cultural marketplace, with the museum addressing the "consumer" rather than the "citizen." It is perhaps the third element,

Table 8.4 *Main types of heritage environments*

Attractions	Characteristics
Natural history and science	Nature reserves and trails; zoos, aquariums, wildlife parks and rare breeds; technology centers; scientific museums; geomorphological or geological sites (caves, gorges, cliffs, or waterfalls)
Agricultural and industrial	Working farms and farming museums; quarries and mines; factories; breweries and distilleries; museums of industry
Transport	Transport museums; working steam railways; canals and docks; preserved ships; aircraft and aviation displays
Sociocultural	Historic sites; museums of rural or industrial life; museums of costume
Built	Stately homes; religious buildings
Military	Castles, battlefields, naval dockyards, and military museums
Landscape	Historic town- and villagescapes; national parks; heritage coastlines and seascapes
Arts based	Galleries; theaters or concert halls and their performances; art festivals
Associations with historic figures	Homes or working places of writers, artists, composers, politicians, military leaders, or leaders of popular culture

Source: Adapted from Prentice (1994) and Williams (1998)

the impact of the media, that adds a new dimension to the debate, since its influence has given rise to a new generation of multimedia museums. According to Hollinshead (1997: 180) "the media are inclined to confuse history and lore" by mixing fiction with fact. Of particular significance is the impact of film and television, the latter in particular becoming a "veritable history machine" spewing out "pseudo-historical events in dramatic form." This commodification or, as some would argue, falsification, of the past has spawned important tourism environments supported by both private and public investments (Shaw 1992). This growth in the heritage industry has significantly affected the scale, diversity and extent of heritage-based, leisure environments. Prentice (1994), among others, has provided a typology of such heritage attractions, identifying nine main environments (table 8.4).

While heritage centers have received substantial comment from historians and industrial archaeologists concerning the commodification of history, geographers have been relatively neglectful of those tourist sites involved in the falsification of both place and time. Of particular importance is the development of theme parks, the main aim of which is to create a wonderland, although Hollinshead (1997) argues that attractions such as Disney World are only an extension of what is happening in the construction of heritage sites. The visitor is immersed in a fantasy which provides "entertainment and excitement, with reassuringly clean and attractive surroundings' (Smith 1980: 46). Walt Disney is credited with the original notion of the theme park, with the creation of Disneyland (California), which opened in 1955. Originally, this contained just 18 attractions in five theme areas, but its success was immediate, attracting 3.8 million visitors during its first year. It was followed in 1963 by Walt Disney World in Florida, based on the "Magic Kingdom," which essentially duplicated the successful formula of the original Disneyland. This has now been extended into Europe, with the opening of Euro-Disney in 1992 near Paris. Disneyland, Paris, includes five themed "lands" containing 40 different attractions and includes 6 hotels, alongside 50 shops and 50 restaurants. The USA has approximately 450 theme parks which grossed a total revenue of $9.1 billion in 1999 from 309 million visitors (www.iaapa.org/media/f-stats.htm).

In the case of all the "Disneylands" and similar, if somewhat smaller, theme parks, the main focus of the theming tends to be geographical. Disneyland, for example, has Bear Country (the Rocky Mountains), Frontierland (the Mississippi and the Wild West), New Orleans Square, Main Street USA (typical small town America), and Adventureland (Africa and the Pacific) (Smith 1980: 51). This re-packaging of geographical areas onto one tourist site, together with numerous funfair rides, appears to provide an important element in the success of the theme park. Interestingly, the diffusion of such ideas to Europe has proved relatively easy using the same formula, a strong testament to the universality of theme parks. The globalization of the theme park has been a significant process in the late twentieth century, which shows few signs of slowing down. Loverseed (1994) has explored the continual growth of the theme park in North America, while Jones (1994) has charted their development in Japan. He shows that the opening of Tokyo-Disney in 1983 sparked a major expansion of similar types of developments, with 25 being opened between 1983 and 1991. The formula is based on fantasy, adventure, history, and different cultures, which has even involved the reproduction of Medieval German towns and Nordic villages within the Japanese landscape.

There appear to be at least two major reasons for the appeal of theme parks. The first, and most easy to identify, is associated with the fact that they offer the visitor a safe, controlled, and clean recreational environment. Second, they present an easy to comprehend view of very different geographical environments that can be readily labeled and consumed by visitors. As Urry (1990: 146) argues, the "scenes are in a sense more real than the original, hyper-real in other words," or in the words of Eco (1986: 44), "Disneyland tells us that faked nature corresponds much more to our daydream demands." Fjellman (1992) reinforces this view that visitors to Disney World are in hyper-reality where "illusion is no longer possible because reality itself is no longer possible" (Hollinshead 1997: 191).

The ideas of the theme park have also been developed in other leisure environments, especially the newer shopping malls that combine retail and leisure elements (Falk and Campbell 1997; Jansen-Verbeke 1990). Many of these have now been built, although much of the early literature has focused on the largest development to date; the West Edmonton Mall in Canada, which has over 800 shops, and 10 percent of its floorspace given over to leisure facilities. It has been planned to break away from the image of "elsewhereness" in an attempt to create both a shopping experience and to attract tourists (Goss 1993; Jackson 1991). This has been achieved through falsifying place "creating an appropriately entitled but spatially restricted Fantasyland" (Butler 1991: 291). Within the West Edmonton Mall, as in Disneyland, the focus is on geographical places, although in the shopping mall the emphasis is on "selling an ambience of foreignness rather than specific locations" (Butler 1991: 291; see also Hopkins 1990). The visitor can be in France, England, Asia, or West Coast America – all within Fantasyland (table 8.5). In the UK similar, if smaller, examples of the West Edmonton exist at the Metro Centre, Gateshead and Meadowhall near Sheffield, both of which are themed (Chaney 1990). More recent and larger malls have extended these ideas with the Trafford Park shopping centre in Manchester claiming that the "centres theming will allow you to breakfast in New York, lunch in Paris and have dinner in Egypt, Morocco or Italy" (*Trafford Centre Guide* 1999). In the context of the East Centre Mall in Helsinki, Lehtonen and Mäenpää (1997: 147) suggest that a trip to the mall is like going "somewhere else, where the real world is constantly challenged by the possible world." They further argue that the life of the mall from the perspective of the consumer is dominated by an "oscillation between what is and what could be." This notion of "real" and imagined worlds is at the heart of much of tourism and leisure environments.

The concept of the themed environment is, to a considerable extent, based around the use of "place," with the ideas reaching out into the development of World Fairs (Hall 1997; Ley and Olds 1988) and

Table 8.5   *The falsification of place in West Edmonton Mall, Canada*

Place	Representations in the mall
Europe	
England	Crown jewels
France	Versailles fountains
Italy	Roman room (theme room), Caesar's statue
North America	
Canada	Via Rial (theme room)
United States	Las Vegas (Caesar's Palace bingo), New Orleans (Bourbon Street), Miami (Water Park), California (Pebble Beach mini golf), Grand Canyon (rafting), Hollywood (theme room), truck room (theme room)
Asia	
China	Ming vases, rickshaws
Japan	Pagoda
Middle East	Arabian Room (theme room)
Oceania	Polynesia (theme room)
Ocean	Dolphin show, aquaria, submarines, *Santa Maria*

Source: Butler (1991)

Garden Festivals (Holden 1989). Thus, the 1988 Expo fair in Brisbane was organized around a number of different national displays, with over 50 themed environments based on different national stereotypes, such as the British pub, the German beer garden and South Sea Island dancing (Urry 1990: 152). These fairs, shopping malls, and theme parks represent a very different perspective on tourism, making it possible to experience the world's geography in a representative fashion (Harvey 1989).

Theming the Landscape

The importance of "themed" attractions from the tourist's perspective is that they are both locationally and perceptually convenient. The latter operates through a system of labeling, often using highly recognizable symbols or features to inform the visitor that what they are viewing is "old England" or "small town America." In this context,

Boorstin (1964: 7) explained that within advertising and the media, "the images generated of different gazes come to constitute a closed self-perpetuating system of illusion." This notion of the tourist gaze (see chapter 4), which has been developed by Urry (1990: 2), "presupposes a system of social activities and signs which locate the particular tourist practices." The tourist gaze is constructed through signs and signifiers in the landscape, with tourists being avid collectors of such signs. Moreover, these markers identify people, things, and places. Therefore, the tourist gaze "is a mix of different scopic drives by which things of significance in history/culture/nature/experience are identified, signified and totalised" (Urry 1992: 172; also see Hollinshead 1999).

Such signs and signifiers are constructed in a variety of ways, but increasingly as Boorstin (1964) observed, the media – literature, music, film, and television – are responsible for creating the impressions and images people have of places. The concept of image-making is at the heart of the tourism industry and media links are increasingly being used by tourist destinations to attract visitors (Morgan and Pritchard 1998). In this respect, places are labeled and sold to tourists on the basis of single themes acquired through history, novels, or television (Pocock 1992). We can recognize attempts to theme and market images of England and Wales in this way, as shown in figure 8.2. Under such theming, the Yorkshire Dales become "Emmerdale Farm Country" from a popular and long-running television "soap opera," while parts of East Anglia can be marketed as "Hereward the Wake Country," seeking links with Anglo-Saxon history. There is no doubt that writers have established various tourist places, for it is often possible to trace the origins of the popular image of a destination directly to specific literature (Newby 1981). This has been through the use of places as a setting for a novel or more directly by the production of travel guides (Selwyn 1996).

In terms of the construction of the tourist gaze, visitors are becoming increasingly drawn to places that have been popularized by literature, television, and film. Literary places are often the "fusion of the real worlds in which writers lived with the worlds portrayed as novel" (Herbert 1995: 33). Television and film are increasingly responsible for developing many of the most unlikely places into tourist destinations. For example, *The Full Monty* has helped popularize Sheffield while *Trainspotting* has formed another strand in Glasgow's tourist image. Many of these links between film and tourism have been formalized in the UK through the British Tourist Authorities "Movie Map." According to Tetley (1999: 1) "sites with media-related links are assiduously promoted and often have inordinate appeal for international as well as domestic tourists."

Figure 8.2 *A tourist image of England and Wales*
Source: modified from The Guardian (November 11, 1990)

The idea of constructing tourism environments is obviously nothing new, for some of the older traditional seaside resorts quickly acquired funfairs and piers to sell tourism or associated themselves with railway companies which advertised their attractions (Morgan 1999). What is new, however, is the scale, nature, and diversity of these concepts. The ideas of theming – which may involve falsification of both "place" and "time" – are strongly commercial forces within the tourism and leisure industries. Moreover, such ideas, and their associated developments, cut across much of the more traditional typologies of "tourist environments." The theme park, shopping mall, and heritage center are as likely to be found in rural areas as in urban ones, while the destination popularized by television or film can be anywhere. This also means that it is increasingly difficult to talk exclusively about tourist environments or tourist resorts, since tourism touches almost every type of place.

9

Mass Tourism

The Origins of Mass Tourism and Leisure

As noted in chapter 1, there are several definitions of leisure, but most of these incorporate notions of free time, function (non-work), and experience (the pleasure or satisfaction derived from an activity). There has been an increase in the free time available in modern societies (Shivers 1981), and this has opened up the possibility of mass leisure. There are, however, criticisms of this simplistic argument; Kando (1975: 43) for example, states that "the oft heralded leisure boom and the growth of a multibillion dollar leisure market are merely more mass consumption" as opposed to genuine leisure. An increase in free time is not necessarily translated into leisure; instead, it may be translated into "dual work," whether in the "black" economy or in household production such as cooking, gardening, or do-it-yourself activities (Rojek 1985). Despite these definitional difficulties, there is clear empirical evidence of an increase in both free time and the enjoyment of leisure activities in most developed countries.

Some of the most spectacular growth in leisure in the twentieth century has been in tourism. In the developed countries, there is a widespread perception that tourism is an essential feature of modern life. "'Not to go away' is like not possessing a car or a 'nice' house. It is a positional good or a marker of status in modern societies and is also thought to be necessary to health" (Urry 1990: 4). Tourism has become mass tourism in such countries. Mass tourism is now deeply-embedded in the organization of life in the more developed world. Over time the focus of these holidays – whether in terms of what Urry terms the tourism gaze, practises or embodied experiences (see chapter 1) – has changed: winter sports have been added to coastal holidays, and

Plate 9.1 *Mass tourism in the Costa del Sol (Spain) epitomizes elements of spatial polarization*

Plate 9.2 *Mass tourism in Sitges (Spain), the crowded beach is largely deserted in winter*

mass tourism has become increasingly internationalized. As we saw in chapter 8, new attractions have been added such as industrial heritage and theme parks. In spite of this diversity, mass tourism has a character and impact which is different to most other forms of more selective tourism. This stems from it being a form of mass-consumption. It is also potentially an agent of profound economic and cultural change.

The origins of mass leisure lie in the reorganization of production in the Developed Countries during the nineteenth and the twentieth centuries. This was driven by the logic of capital accumulation although not in any simplistic way; technology (for example, innovations in household equipment, or in travel) has played a partly autonomous role, while there has also been a continuous struggle between capital and labor over the distribution of the material and non-material rewards of production, including free time. Increased free time was not an automatic by-product of economic development for the working classes; rather it was one of the contested areas in the struggle between organized labor and the owners of capital. Even so, the experience of leisure, and the ability to enjoy leisure, remains strongly socially differentiated (de Grazia 1984). The employed and the unemployed, men and women, different income groups and different age groups all have differential access to leisure (chapter 3).

The modern growth of mass leisure is less impressive when seen in longer historical perspective. Wilensky (1960) estimated that the skilled urban worker of the mid-twentieth century had only just regained the leisure he/she would have enjoyed in the thirteenth century in Europe. Leisure – conceived as a rest from work – was well established in the medieval period when approximately one in three days was a holiday of some kind. In Europe these conditions were decisively lost during industrialization and urbanization in the eighteenth and nineteenth centuries. It was only in the twentieth century that the moral and legal right to leisure time was re-established in the developed world.

Shivers (1981) has traced the growth of mass leisure in the USA, where there has been a marked decline in the hours of work; the average factory worker worked for 35 hours a week in 1980 compared to 60 hours a week in the 1920s. This trend is reflected in all the core regions of the world economy, at least in the formal economy if not the informal economy. The World Tourism Organization (1984) estimated that between 1960 and 1980 the proportion of countries in which the average working week exceeded 40 hours fell from 75 percent to 56 percent. There has also been an increase in those who are excluded from the formal economy; for example, there are more retired and early retired people able to enjoy leisure. Legislation has also excluded children from workplaces, at least in the developed countries. The position is different in many less developed countries and they will not necessarily follow the same line of development as the developed countries.

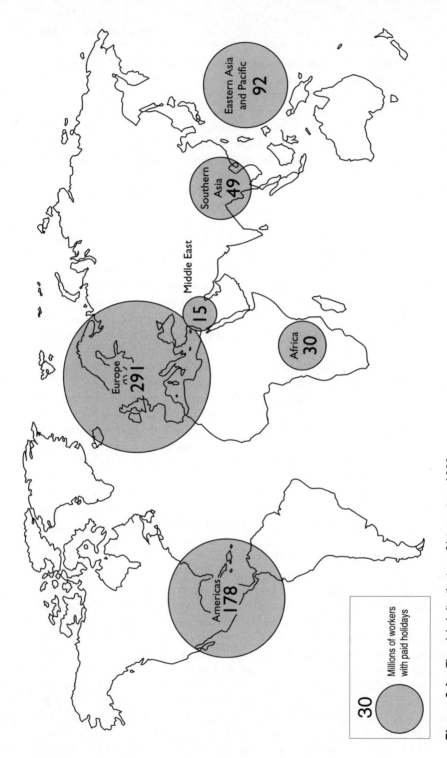

Figure 9.1 *The global distribution of leisure time, 1982*

Source: WTO (1984)

Table 9.1   *The structure of free time*

Distribution of free time	Potential for		
	Local leisure	*Short-breaks*	*Long holidays*
Daily	✓		
Weekly	✓	✓	
Annually/lifetime	✓	✓	✓

One form of mass leisure is mass tourism. The emergence of mass tourism was conditional not only on the growth of leisure time but also on the structure of free time and the economics of the tourism industry. Free time is distributed within days, weeks, years, and lifetimes (table 9.1). Changes in the length of the working day necessarily have only a limited impact on tourism. This is also true of the length of the working week; whether or not Saturday and Sunday were free days did not directly affect traditional long-stay holidays, although it has been an important precondition for the growth of short-break holidays. Instead, the distribution of free time within the year, and especially of paid holidays, was critical in the growth of mass tourism in the twentieth century. The World Tourism Organization estimated in 1982 that there were 645 million workers globally who received paid holidays from work. Their global distribution was, of course very uneven (figure 9.1). The lifetime distribution of free time has also been an important influence on mass tourism. The ageing of the population and the growth of older active groups with disposable income has added significantly to the demand for tourism. For example, Perez (1987) estimates that in Europe the proportion of tourism demand coming from the 65+ group increased from 15 percent to 25 percent between the mid 1960s and the mid 1980s.

Sessa (1983) summarizes the mega social trends that underlie the increase in mass tourism: demographic transition; social progress; international peace; broader tourism consciousness; and higher incomes. The aging of the population, combined with changes in income and income distribution, and in welfare and social redistribution, have provided the means for extensification and intensification of the demand for tourism. That demand is also fueled by the image makers who effectively create tourist attractions; the image makers are a diverse group and includes designers of hotels and attractions, as well as media and travel writers. Together they generate what Krippendorf (1987a: 10) terms "the promises of the paradise sellers."

The economics of the tourism industry are also important in the emergence of mass tourism. These were discussed in chapter 5 and only the most salient points are repeated here. Changes in transport technology – by air and by land – have speeded up travel and reduced costs. This has encouraged an increase in demand which, in turn, has led to scale economies and further cost reductions. There has also been the growth of tour companies able to sell large numbers of all-inclusive package holidays at relatively low costs. As a result, there has been a "virtuous circle" – at least in economic terms – of falling real costs, rising demand, and scale economies.

The "virtuous circle" of mass tourism in the Developed Countries has had five main phases. In the *first phase* mass tourism emerged in the USA in the 1920s and the 1930s. The two critical condition were the spread of paid holidays and the extension of car ownership. By the outbreak of World War One, there were already an estimated 2 million cars in the USA compared to only 132,000 in the UK (Burkart and Medlik 1981: 28). The growth of motel chains also provided the necessary accommodation infrastructure for the emerging tourism industry. The destinations of most tourists were coastal areas, spa resorts such as Yellow Springs and Saratoga Springs, and "the great American outdoors." Later, artificial attractions became popular. Places such as Coney Island became national attractions as well as recreation areas for nearby cities, in this case New York (Gunn 1988: 111). Comparable living standards in Canada and the development of an integrated transport system also meant that the two countries became locked together in the world's first significant international tourism market (Cosgrove and Jackson 1972). There was some working class tourism in Europe at this time but it was less universal, reliant on public transport and more directed at the coastal areas.

In the *second phase*, in the 1950s, domestic mass tourism emerged in Europe, fueled by the same preconditions as had existed earlier in the USA – enhanced leisure time and accessibility – and by the post World War Two economic boom. Public transport was still important although car ownership was becoming more widespread. The coast was the main destination although rural tourism was also important in some countries, particularly those where there were significant numbers of recent rural–urban migrants.

In the *third phase*, the late 1950s and the 1960s, mass tourism took on another dimension, becoming increasingly internationalized (see Burkart and Medlik 1981). Between 1950 and 1998 the number of international tourists increased sharply (figure 9.2). The USA and Canada led the way for, in addition to travel between these two countries, Europe was the main destination of North American international

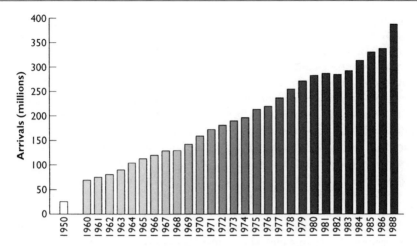

Figure 9.2   *The growth of international tourism, 1950–1998*
Source: WTO (2000b)

tourists. Cosgrove and Jackson (1972: 74) wrote that "traditionally the Grand Tour of Europe occupied at least half the time spent by Americans travelling abroad."

In the *fourth phase* there was an Europeanization of international tourism from the 1960s. According to the World Tourism Organization, globally there were 457 million international tourists in 1990 and Europe was the destination of 62 percent of these, with most movements being within the continent. This remarkable figure is, however, deceptive being conditioned by the nature of national boundaries. Even relatively short trips – by North American standards – become international trips in Europe (see chapter 2).

The growth of mass tourism has been facilitated by the easing of travel regulations and by the growth of the international air travel industry. The financial, legal, and practical barriers to foreign travel within Europe have been significantly reduced, as they have globally. The development of all-inclusive tours by air was critical in this and made Western Europe an integrated macro-region for mass tourism. Between 1965 and 1970 alone, the number of air package holidays sold in the UK increased from one to two million (Burkart and Medlik 1981: 32). Mass car ownership in Western Europe was also an important precondition of mass international travel, replicating the North American experience of 40 years earlier.

In the *fifth phase*, in the late twentieth century, there was globalization of the tourism industry. The two main nodes have been linked.
There had been a strong flow of tourists from the USA to Europe
throughout the twentieth century. However, the level of trans-Atlantic
movement in *both* directions soared from the 1970s as keen competition, and later liberalization of air traffic, reduced the real cost of travel.
At the same time, there was genuine globalization as more and more
countries became locked into international travel: tourists from Japan,
Europe, North America, and Australia/New Zealand have become
increasingly internationalized. Japan is particularly notable in this
respect but is also being joined by other economically dynamic Asian
economies (see chapter 2). At the same time, the range of destinations
of mass tourism has increased, and now encompasses virtually all countries in the developed and many of those in the developing world; in
short there are strong globalization tendencies.

Mass Tourism as a Form of Mass Consumption

Mass tourism is a distinctive form of tourism. This stems from its character as a form of Fordist mass consumption. Urry (1990: 14) summarizes the features of mass consumption as:

> purchase of commodities produced under conditions of mass produc-
> tion; a high and growing rate of expenditure on consumer products; indi-
> vidual producers tending to dominate particular industrial markets;
> producer rather than consumer as dominant; commodities little differ-
> entiated from each other by fashion, season, and specific market seg-
> ments; relatively limited market choice – what there is tends to reflect
> producer interests, either publicly or privately owned.

Both domestic and international mass tourism would seem to fit this
model of mass consumption, given the characteristics shown in box 9.1.
   The nature of mass tourism as a form of mass consumption also gives
rise to a number of features which have important economic and social
implications. Some of the latter have been explored in chapter 4. Mass
tourism tends to be highly *spatially polarized*. This is partly related to
how the tourist gaze is constructed. Urry (1990: 47) argues that "The
contemporary tourist gaze is increasingly signposted. There are markers
which distinguish the things and places worthy of our gaze. Such signposting identifies a relatively small number of tourist nodes." In the
latter half of the twentieth century the tourist image creators in North
America and Europe mainly promoted beach and ski holidays, and, to a
lesser extent, "rural idylls" such as National Parks and wilderness areas,

> **Box 9.1   The main characteristics of mass tourism**
>
> - The sheer volume means that the tourism product has to be offered under conditions of mass production.
> - There is a growing level of expenditure on consumer goods associated with tourism, e.g. surf boards for the beach holiday and skis and skiing accessories for the winter holiday.
> - A few producers dominate particular markets, e.g. Best Western in the global hotel sector, and travel companies such as Preussag and Airtours in the world of package holidays in Europe.
> - Producers take the lead in developing new tourism attractions, whether opening up new mass destinations such as Thailand, the Gambia, and Turkey, or in designing new theme parks such as Euro-Disney.
> - By and large, mass tourism products are little differentiated, e.g. the Mediterranean beach holiday offers much the same mix of architecture, facilities, food and drink and entertainment, whether it is located in Turkey, Greece, or Spain.
> - While individual travelers can assemble infinite combinations of elements to construct a holiday experience, those who use organized holidays face very limited choice.

as the rightful objects of the tourist gaze (see chapter 8). There is some flexibility in the way such attractions are promoted and presented, and even in the definition of what constitutes a desirable beach, ski, or rural environment. However, there are constraints on the supply of these types of environments, even if capital and technology can vary this at the margin: for example, opening up new high altitude ski areas through advanced transport systems, or transporting sand to construct beach areas. As a result, most tourists are necessarily concentrated into a small number of areas, which are further narrowed down by the system of signposting which, within Europe for example, ranks a Mediterranean beach holiday higher than a North Sea beach experience. This results in the strong channeling of tourists to a small number of areas. In addition, the economies of scale in developing airports and other infrastructure, and in providing charter flights, holiday accommodation, entertainment, and services are also conducive to the spatial concentration of mass tourists. Agglomeration economies thereafter reinforce the development of other complementary tourism services. The results are evident in Spain, which is the foremost destination for Mediterranean tourism in Europe: there are 47 bed places per sq km in the Balearic islands, one of the prime poles of attraction, compared to less than 2 per sq km in the country as a whole (Alvarez 1988). Eventually, diseconomies of scale arising from spatial polarization may lead to the decline of particular resorts. The most obvious manifestation of this spatial polarization is tourism urbanization. Mullins (1991: 326) writes that "Tourist cities represent a new and extraordinary form of urbanisation because they are cities built solely for consumption. Whereas Western urbanisation emerged in the nineteenth century generally for reasons of production and commerce, tourist cities evolved during the last twentieth century as sites for consumption." The development of such "tourist cities" or resorts, contains an inherent contradiction, in that the associated growth in tourist volume may lead to an ultimate decline in the quality of the tourism experience. Given shifts in tourist preferences, and the increasing maturity of some of the resort's tourism products, this can lead to stagnation or decline (see the discussion of the Butler resort cycle in chapter 8). However, the decline of individual resorts is not synonymous with decline in the generic type of tourism attraction: thus individual Spanish or Italian resorts may stagnate, but new mass tourism resorts may spring up along the coasts of Greece or Turkey (Williams 2001).

Mass tourist destinations also tend to have *segmented markets* despite an overall tendency to product homogeneity. This is determined by both spatial (mainly national) differences in the construction of the tourist gaze and by the economics of mass tourism. As minimizing costs is a paramount objective – in contrast to elite tourism – there is a well-established historical tendency for there to be high levels of tourist mobility between adjoining places (Williams and Zelinsky 1970): in other words, for tourism flows to be determined by transport costs and spatial proximity. Before the advent of low cost international travel, such flows were regionally organized. Thus, in the UK in the early twentieth century, Southend developed as a resort for East London, Blackpool as a resort for industrial Lancashire, and Skegness as a resort for the East Midlands. The same spatial proximity factors were replicated in mass international tourism. Germans constitute two thirds of the tourists in Austria (Zimmermann 1998), while Japanese tourists are dominant in South East Asia, and North Americans in Mexico (table 9.2). Of course, mass tourism can not be reduced to a simplistic distance minimization spatial model. For example, the fact that 50 percent of the tourists in the Algarve come from the UK (Lewis and Williams 1998) is to be explained not by distance but by two factors. First, by historical tourism links, and the way that the Algarve has been marketed in the UK. And second, by the fact that British tour companies have established sufficient business volume to secure significant cost reductions in organized holidays in this destination. Similarly, the relatively large volumes of British tourism to Florida, despite the apparent barrier of distance, is to be explained by marketing, a lack of

Table 9.2 *Segmentation and dependency in selected major tourism markets, 1998*

Destination country	Major source of tourists	Percentage of all foreign tourists/visitors
Bahamas	USA	81[b]
Botswana	South Africa	52[b]
Canada	USA	79
Czech Republic	Germany	40[a]
Cyprus	UK	46
France	Germany	21
Korea, Republic of	Japan	46[a]
Malta	UK	40
Martinique	France	80
Mexico	USA	94
New Zealand	Australia	34[a]
Pakistan	UK	25
Paraguay	Argentina	32
Portugal	Spain	51
Thailand	Japan	13
Tunisia	Germany	19

a = visitors, not tourists
b = 1997
Source: World Tourism Organization (2000b)

language barriers, and – above all – by reductions in transport costs as a result of fierce Trans-Atlantic competition in air travel.

In conclusion, three points can be made. First, there is evidence of market segmentation. Second, the level of market segmentation is scale specific; it tends to increase in inverse relationship to scale. While table 9.2 displays a high degree of market segmentation in selected national markets, this increases further in particular, regions, or resorts, and especially in individual hotels. The latter may be owned by, or have sub-contracted all their bed spaces to, particular foreign tour companies. Third, the geography of market segmentation is only partly explained by spatial proximity. Not only is globalization challenging the established macro-regional organization of tourism flows (chapter 2) but many such flows are path dependent in that they build on historical and cultural links between places.

There are a number of economic relationships inherent in the *dependency* on particular market segments. Destinations are already vulnerable to external influence, whether political (Richter 1983) or economic, but market segmentation exaggerates these effects. This is most marked with respect to international tourism where small changes in one or two markets can have major impacts on individual resorts. For example, fears of terrorism have led to dramatic fluctuations in the numbers of American visitors to Europe, particularly in cities such as London, Paris, Rome, and Athens. Within Europe, domestic political turmoil can easily deter international visitors. It took Portugal four years to recover the tourist numbers lost following the 1974 military coup. More dramatically, the nationalist conflicts in Yugoslavia in the 1990s effectively eliminated a well-established international tourist industry. Less extreme, but also significant, is the dependency on economic conditions in external markets, whether exchange rate fluctuations or recession. The Algarve, for example, with its high degree of dependency is highly susceptible to changing levels of prosperity in the UK market (Lewis and Williams 1998). The numbers of American tourists in the international market have also fluctuated from year to year as the value of the dollar has risen and fallen dramatically in value since fixed international exchange rates were abandoned in the early 1970s. The position is exacerbated by the role of the international tour companies. They only own a small proportion of the facilities they use in particular countries, instead preferring to lease these on short or medium term contracts. It is therefore relatively easy for them to shift their holiday packages between different resorts or countries in response to changes in costs or fashion. Within Europe, the creation of the Euro-zone will, in effect, serve to eliminate or reduce the risk, uncertainty, and potential volatility associated with exchange rate movements.

Mass tourism involves the movement of large numbers of tourists which therefore means that the market is being extended to medium and lower income groups, with the latter having relatively little surplus income. High gross income is yielded from relatively low expenditure per capita by large numbers of tourists. Mass tourists are seeking more and more exotic (if comfortably packaged) holiday destinations. Given that income is constrained in the mass market (demand is relatively price inelastic), there is a need to cut costs, so that these can only be provided in standardized forms with relatively minimal levels of services and facilities. In addition, the construction of the tourism gaze is related to the nature of tourism motivation. Krippendorf (1987a: 29) writes "Where the journey leads is not so important, the main thing is to get away from the routine, to switch off, change the scene. To this extent travel destinations are altogether interchangeable." This means there is intense competition between largely undifferentiated tourism products that have been constructed along the lines of "identikit resorts." Given they have similar combinations of attractions (in terms of beaches, types of hotels, and entertainment), *their main point of competition is price*. There is, therefore, strong downward pressure on price levels – both for the tour companies and for the local operators (Guitart 1982). This is confirmed by Truett and Truett (1987) who estimated the tourism demand functions for Spain, Greece, and Mexico; the quantity of tourism services demanded was highly elastic with respect to both income and price.

Mass tourism is necessarily highly seasonal. Tourists are purchasing access not only to particular places but also to particular (seasonal) environments or "space–time" packages. There are two principal reasons for this: "there is an institutionalized and a natural *seasonality* which both affect tourism" (Hartmann 1986: 25). First, the main objects of the mass tourist gaze – snow or sunny beaches – are temporal attractions. While snow exists in high mountain ranges all year round and some coastal areas are warm or hot all year, there are usually seasons in which conditions are optimum. Investments in, say, snowmaking equipment or indoor leisure facilities can modify but not fundamentally change this – at least at present. Only a few destinations are able to develop year round tourism. Florida provides winter sun for North Americans and cheap summer sunshine for Europeans. Some resorts in the Alps and the North American mountains have a double seasonal peak; skiing in winter and driving/walking through scenic mountains in the summer. However, most mass tourist resorts typically have an attraction which is single-season specific and characteristically of short duration. Seasonality is underlined by a second factor, namely the institutional nature of free time. In the developed world paid holidays tend to be seasonally specific. There is a season – usually the summer – in which it is expected that long holidays will be taken. Companies' work programmes and school vacations are both organized around this assumption. This is reflected in the temporal concentration of holiday-taking: in Italy, Belgium, and Portugal more than 70 percent of main holidays are taken in July or August (Romeril 1989: 207). Baron (1975) emphasizes that seasonality has a number of effects but, especially, reducing holiday enjoyment because of overcrowding and under-utilization of fixed capital in hotels and other facilities out-of-season. This has implications in terms of employment (see chapter 7), and in the economics of the tourism firms, which have to secure their profits through exploitation of their capital assets over a very limited proportion of the year.

Temporal polarization effectively reinforces spatial polarization. Mass tourism is already concentrated in space, and time adds another dimension to this: the dual concentration of tourists in time and space gives rise to tourism saturation, arguably a potent threat to the environment as well as to the inherent attraction of the tourism product. Again this is socially constructed because of how free time is organized in modern societies, combined with the prevalent signifiers of how and where holidays should be spent. Hence, the shoulder season may provide favorable holiday conditions (with some of the climatic, vegetation, or other attributes of the peak season), without the congestion costs of the main season. Yet, most mass tourists (and especially those constrained by school holidays) are temporally excluded from the destination in the shoulder and off-season. Hotels and tour companies respond to polarization by charging higher prices in the peak season, not because costs are higher but because the market will bear these at this time of the year (when demand outstrips or equals the capacity of the destination). In the off season, when tourist volumes are lower, and unit costs are higher, prices actually fall. This only has a limited effect in displacing tourist demand from the peak season because of institutional constraints on free time, reinforced by cultural habits of taking holidays at particular times of the year. Tourists have to bear the direct higher costs of this, but firms face the longer-term challenge of maintaining economic viability in the face of temporal and spatial polarization. Other industries also face peaks in demand – for example, for turkeys or Christmas cards in December – but they are at least able to distribute some of the production costs across the year as a whole. In contrast, the temporal and spatial fixity of tourism means that tourism experiences can not be deferred.

Mass tourism by assembling large numbers of tourists in small areas creates intense *environmental pressures*. There are the urbanization pressures of air, water, and terrestrial pollution that are associated with any population concentration. However, these are accentuated by the temporal polarization of mass tourism. Infrastructures are required to cope with the throughput of a large volume of consumers in a short period of time, yet they will be under-utilized during much of the remainder of the year. Therefore, the per capita (per tourist) costs of infrastructure provision can be formidable, and often lag behind need. In addition, tourism pressures are different from those of "normal" urbanization in that they bring particularly acute pressures to bear on very limited zones, which are often very ecologically sensitive, such as mountain slopes or coasts. The relaxation of many of the norms of conventional social behavior may also affect tourist behavior, leading to increased noise or litter pollution. Attempts have been made to relate the environmental impact of tourism to the carrying capacity of an area for environmentally sound development. But "while the theory may be easy to conceptualize, the practical reality leaves much to be desired" (Romeril 1989: 205). However, there is an alternative and more positive view of seasonality. Hartmann (1986: 31–2). argues that "dead seasons are the only chance for a social and ecological environment to recover fully." As would be expected, the environmental pressures and costs of mass tourism are temporally and spatially variable, and here we simply note how they can be exacerbated by concentration in particular spaces and times. This is not to say that they are more or less harmful that the effects of other more geographically and temporally diffused tourism, but this is a theme that we return to in chapter 12.

MacCannell (1973, 1976) sees the tourist as searching for an "authenticity" that he/she can not find in everyday life. However, the arrival of mass tourism, compared to other smaller volume forms of tourism, in an area does necessarily pose different types of challenges to the lives of local people. Some mass tourism resorts are developed on green field sites, but others are integrated into existing settlements: as evident for example, in the difference between the resorts on the southern and the northern coast of Tenerife. The latter introduce large inflows of tourists who may have different languages and cultural values, added to which they have lifestyle expectations which differ from those of local residents. They also have expectations in terms of their cultural images of the destination. Part of the tourism experience may be to experience elements of the imagined local culture, whether this be bullfights, street festivals, or particular types of music and dancing: these are the embodiment of the tourism experience as well as the fulfilment of the desired tourist gaze. Local communities can respond by organizing tourism spaces on the basis of "*staged authenticity*," as was discussed in chapter 4. Arguably, mass tourists – because of the scale of the demand exerted – are especially likely to experience culture via formidable social and commercial filters, as these tourist experiences are commodified, replicated, and increasingly externally controlled. Therefore, *staged authenticity* could be seen as an inevitable consequence of the logic of mass consumption and the requirements of capital accumulation. Temporal and spatial polarization mean that the demand for exceeds the supply of authentic cultural events, while increased numbers of folk events have to be staged in order to extract more money from the tourists. This is not fertile territory for authenticity – a problematic concept in any case. But the effects of mass tourism may extend beyond distorting local cultural practices and spectacles. One of the features of mass tourism is the demand for familiar comforts, and this may result in the creation in the tourist resort of "a small monotonous world that everywhere shows us our own image" so that "the pursuit of the exotic and diverse ends in uniformity" (Turner and Ash 1975: 292).

The characteristics of mass tourism discussed here are, of course, only tendencies and their precise form is highly variable (Smith 1998; see also Urry 1990: 57–60). The degree of spatial polarization, market segmentation, dependency and control, price depression, seasonal polarization, environmental pollution, and cultural sterility is contingent on local and national conditions. These and other dimensions of mass tourism are explored in the case studies presented in the following section.

Mass Tourism: Contrasting Case Studies

There are many different forms of mass tourism, but the most common are sunshine/seaside tourism and winter sports tourism. In the USA, "the great recreational outdoors" is also an object of mass tourism, as are different forms of rural tourism in Europe. However, as the effects are less polarized and there is a separate chapter (11) on rural tourism, this latter topic is deferred until later. Other forms of mass tourism – such as sex tourism in Thailand, and cultural tourism in New York, Paris, and London – are also excluded here but the latter is discussed in chapter 10. Mega events, such as the Olympic Games and the World Cup are also forms of mass tourism, where the temporal and spatial effects are extremely concentrated temporally and spatially. Mega events are, however, a very distinctive form of tourism, and the remainder of this chapter concentrates instead on the two archetypal mass tourism products.

While coastal resorts had been popular in the earlier period of elite tourism, only in the late nineteenth century and early twentieth century did they become the focus of mass tourism. There were several reasons for this including: the growth of paid holidays; the arrival of mass transport via the railways; and the desire to escape the harsh living conditions of urban-industrial capitalism. The attraction was sea and sand and the contrast to home provided by the absence of industry. In the early twentieth century, the arrival of mass car ownership modified this pattern. In North America, improved accessibility reinforced the attraction of "the great outdoors." In Europe, while it boosted rural tourism, it mainly led to a dispersion of tourism along the coast rather than away from the coast. Cosgrove and Jackson (1972: 39) summarize the changing spatial dynamics arising from the spread of car ownership: this "enabled the coastline to be utilised more in accordance with its linear resource base than by the point pattern of exploitation associated with the railway-based resorts." In Europe this incipient domestic coastal mass tourism reached a peak in the 1950s. Rising real incomes and transport improvements led to a massive increase in seasonal tourist movements to the coast.

As was discussed earlier in this chapter, there were further changes from the 1960s in mass coastal tourism in Europe. Internationalization was facilitated by changes in the technology and the costs of air transport, in the construction of the tourist gaze (the signposts now pointed to the Mediterranean), and in the falling real costs of foreign holidays at a time of rising real incomes. International coastal mass tourism has subsequently developed into a major industry. Europe is the principal focus of this although by no means the only one. The beaches of Australia, Mexico, the Caribbean, and Malaysia, among others, have also been attractive to mass tourists from many countries. However, the Mediterranean represents the most highly developed form of mass coastal tourism. The tourist flows are essentially from the North of Europe to the Mediterranean countries, especially Italy and Spain.

Mediterranean tourism growth has been underpinned by the development of all-inclusive tour holidays, or package tours. While these were popularized by Thomas Cook in the nineteenth century, the first package holiday by air – from the UK to Corsica – was only launched in 1950. Thereafter, growth was so rapid that by 1970 the volume of charter traffic within Europe surpassed the volume of scheduled traffic (Pearce 1987a: 183). Urry (1995: 143) comments that "Mobility depends upon the development of trust in professional experts who have developed systems of mass travel and transport which limit the risk involved." This reduction in risk probably represents one of the two main contributions of tour companies. The second is their role in reducing the costs of tourism (see chapter 7). The comparative cost advantages of package holidays stem from selling a bundle of services – air and ground transport, hotel, insurance etc – and from the use of charter aircraft. Reduced levels of service and comfort on these flights, combined with high and more predictable passenger loads, give them significant cost advantages over scheduled flights.

Pearce (1987a, b) has analyzed the origins and destinations of air package holidays in Europe, showing that Spain is the main destination of these flights. The UK–Spain and the Germany–Spain routes alone accounted for 35 percent of all intra-European package flights in the early 1980s. Over time the pattern has changed, with countries such as Greece and Portugal becoming more important while the Spanish share has fallen. Data for total tourism flows, as opposed to package holiday flows, show the enduring attraction of the Mediterranean region, especially Spain (figure 9.3). France is the other major tourist destination within Europe, followed by Italy.

Such data only present the overall picture, and further disaggregation reveals more complex and more polarized relationships between destinations and origins. Thus, Pearce (1987b) has shown that there is a high degree of regional segmentation. In Spain, for example, the British constitute relatively large segments of the tourism markets of Malaga, Gerona, Alicante, and Menorca. Similarly, Mallorca and Gran Canaria are particularly important for the German mass market. Within national markets there is further segmentation. Particular tour companies tend to specialize in serving particular resort areas, and again

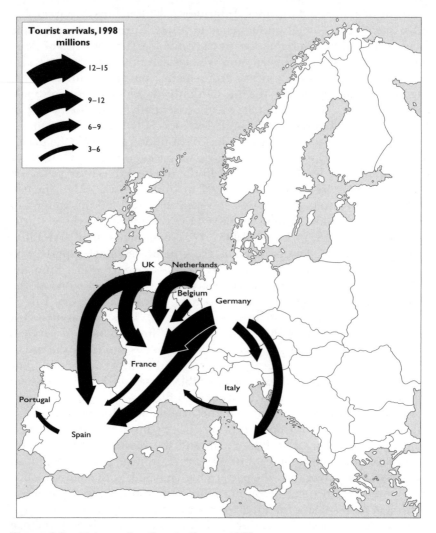

Figure 9.3   *Major tourism flows in Europe, 1998*
Source: WTO (2000)

economies of scale tend to dictate this. Thomson, one of the two largest providers in the UK market, provides a classic example. Figure 9.4 shows the major Mediterranean resort areas in which Thomson delivered more than 30 percent of all UK package holiday tourists in 1987. It was particularly strong in Spain, Italy, and Greece. Furthermore, this high degree of market control gives the major European tour

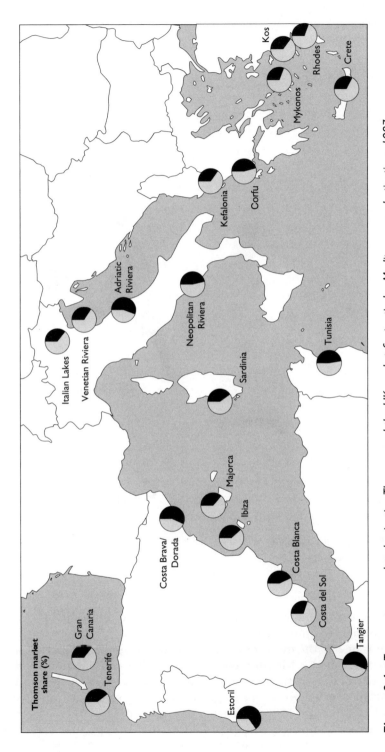

Figure 9.4 *Tour company market domination: Thomson and the UK market for particular Mediterranean destinations, 1987*

Source: Monopolies and Mergers Commission (1989)

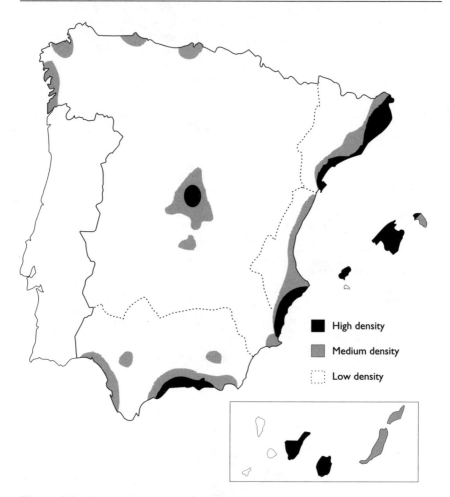

Figure 9.5   *Spatial polarization of tourism in Spain*
Source: Alvarez (1988: 72)

companies considerable influence over the place imaging of these resorts in their main markets, and their price levels.

Spain is one of the most important examples of international coastal mass tourism in the Mediterranean region. The combination of the social construction of the tourist gaze and the economics of the industry result in a very high degree of polarization of tourism within Spain (figure 9.5). Alvarez (1988) estimates that four-fifths of the country's tourists are concentrated within provinces that occupy just one-fifth of the land area of the country. Domestic tourism is more evenly distributed spatially than is foreign tourism. Thus, national tourism predominates in 41 of the country's 50 provinces, accounting for up to 90 percent of all tourists. In contrast, some regions – notably the Balearic Islands (87 percent) and the Canary Islands (82 percent) – are dominated by foreign tourists (Valenzuela 1998: 52).

Variations in the tourism attraction (especially climate) and in the organization of the industry result in considerable regional differences in the degree of temporal polarization. This influences occupancy rates, which vary from 21 percent in Gerona to 62 percent in the Canaries, and costs/rates of profit. There are also differences in the economic structures of the regions. Tourism in Catalonia is located in a more developed region with GDP per capita levels above the EU average. There is, therefore, less of a cultural divide between the local populace and the tourists, a large proportion of whom are from adjoining regions in France. In contrast, tourism in the Balearic and Canary Islands was located in what were some of Spain's and Europe's poorest regions. Tourism has had a far more profound effect in these regions, culturally, economically, and environmentally. Another important difference between the regions is the strength and organization of local capital. Whereas there were well-developed sources of capital in Catalonia, these were relatively weak in the Islands where, consequently, external capital played a more important role. As the islands are also more dependent on package tours than the mainland (where individual car-borne travelers are an important market segment), they tend to be more dependent on particular markets (Valenzuela 1998).

The Economist Intelligence Unit (1988) estimates there is strong leakage of income from tourism in the Balearic Islands. Furthermore, "Hotel profit margins have been steadily cut as pressure from the tour operators has risen" (1988: 26). There is also a high degree of dependence on the British and German markets, which accounted for 80 percent of all foreign tourists in the 1980s. In addition, UK tourists (6,476 pesetas per day in the late 1980s) are relatively low spenders compared to German (7,175) and Swiss (more than 9,000) tourists. The overall assessment of this report is that there has been over-development to cope with mass tourism, and the result has been poor quality, a loss of amenity and neglect of the traditional economy. Llinas (1991: 20) comments that "Tourism has consumed the landscape of Majorca as industry has consumed the reserves of coal or of minerals of the old Europe." Spain therefore provides an example of the diversity which exists within mass tourism and indeed the regions can be conceptualized as lying at different ends of a continuum of mass tourism characteristics as shown in figure 9.6.

Early mass tourism in the USA occurred in the north east region, where there was a combination of major population centers and

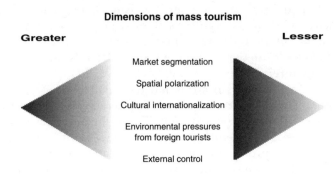

Figure 9.6   *Mass tourism in Spain: regional contrasts*

relatively cool coastal summer temperatures. For example, the linking of Atlantic City to Philadelphia by railway assured the development of the former as a middle class resort. Winter sunshine resorts in Florida and California also emerged by the end of the nineteenth century. The detailed forms of the new tourist destinations revealed the role of human agency, even if within structural constraints. In Florida, for example, Henry Flaglet built a series of luxury hotels down the east coast, including the Royal Palm in Miami (Lavery and van Doren 1990), and this helped shape the image, market, and popularity of this resort.

Mass tourism reached the take-off stage in the USA in the early part of the twentieth century. The post World War One economic boom boosted leisure and tourism, while growth in car ownership rates, the commercial bus network, and motels provided the means for increased mobility. This boom in mass tourism continued in the post World War Two period, fostered by further growth in incomes, leisure time, and individual mobility. "The society has truly reached a period of travel democratisation, the flowering of mass travel," according to Lavery and van Doren (1990: 30–1). Figure 9.7 shows the distribution of all major resorts in the USA by the mid-1980s, with the most notable clusters being in the North East, Southern California/Las Vegas, and Florida. The top performing resort hotels – measured by sales per room in leading resort hotels – were mostly clustered in Florida and Hawaii (table 9.3). Despite these healthy financial returns in some of the principal resorts, some of the older destinations have suffered declining markets since the 1950s, due to domestic and international competition. The more successful resorts not only offer quality products but are also well attuned to particular market segments, for example sport-based resorts (especially tennis, watersports, golf, and casinos), or adult education and conference provision.

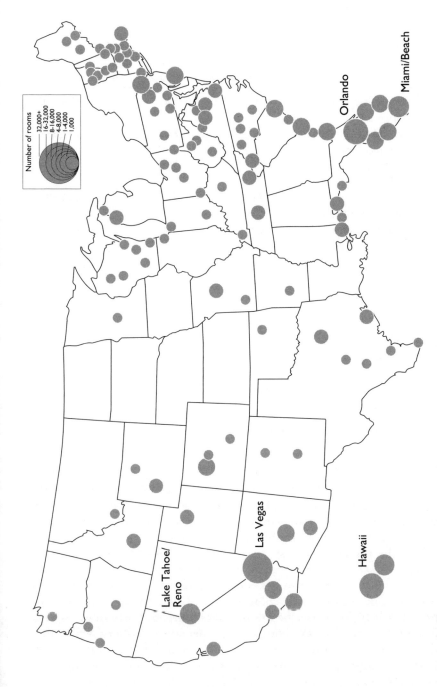

Figure 9.7 *The number of hotel rooms in major US resorts, 1985–6*

Source: Lavery and van Doren (1990)

Table 9.3 *The top ten performing US resort hotels, 1987*

Resort	Number of guest rooms	Average occupancy (%)	Sales per room ($)
1. Turnberry Isle (Miami Beach)	118	56	154,966
2. Holiday Isle and marina (Islamorado, Florida)	71	84	141,831
3. Hotel Hana (Mani, Hawaii)	61	70	139,344
4. Caneel Bay (St. John, Virgin Islands)	171	77	118,591
5. Kona Village Resort (Kailua-Kona, Hawaii)	100	76	117,880
6. Pier House (Key West, Florida)	120	87	112,500
7. Holekulam Hotel (Honolulu, Hawaii)	456	83	109,649
8. Boulders Resort (Carefree, Arizona)	120	75	109,525
9. Ilakas Hotel (Honolulu, Hawaii)	798	83	102,632
10. Trump Plaza Hotel (Atlantic City)	586	91	99,555

Source: Lodging Hospitality, August 1988

Mass winter sports tourism shares many features in common with mass beach tourism. The first point to emphasize is that this originated in Europe. Traditionally, the Alps had been an area of summer tourism, and the attractions were climbing, walking and viewing the scenery, related to the romantic tourist gaze. The first major expansion was in the nineteenth century. Writers and other image creators re-imaged the Alps as a highly desirable tourist destination, while the railroads and the role of tour companies such as Thomas Cook, made them an economically feasible objective of middle class tourism. Early in the twentieth century, the first ski course was opened at Arlberg while the staging of the first winter Olympics at Chamonix in 1924 was a major catalyst to winter sports tourism expansion. However, mass international winter tourism only developed in the 1950s and 1960s (Barker 1982). The necessary conditions were similar to international mass coastal tourism: the reconstruction of the tourist gaze, rising real

Box 9.2 The contingent nature of mass tourism: standardization and differentiation

Although there is a tendency to uniformity in the consumption and production of mass tourism, there is also differentiation. This can be either *generic* (beach and ski resorts) or place specific. Some of the principal influences on both standardization and differentiation are set out below.

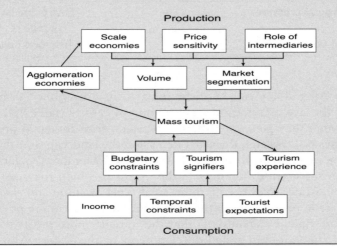

disposable incomes and car ownership levels, and falling real costs allied to increased tour company activity. This facilitated the expansion of numbers based on the geographical and social widening of markets. By the 1990s, there were 3 million tourist bed spaces in the Alps, approximately 12,000 ski lifts, and 40,000 recognized ski slopes (Zimmermann 1995: 20). As with coastal tourism, the industry is characterized by a high degree of spatial polarization, external control and environmental pressures. There is also a high degree of temporal polarization although some resorts have developed a significant summer season based on warm-weather pursuits or developing means to transport tourists to high altitude skiing areas.

The character of the mass winter tourism resorts is as variable as that of the summer coastal resorts; as with all mass resorts, there are twin pressures for standardization and differentiation (box 9.2). Winter tourism resorts can also be arranged along economic, social, and cultural continua. Barker (1982), for example, compares the resorts of the Eastern and Western Alps. The former have been developed at lower altitudes and are more integrated with the economic and cultural lives of the indigenous communities than are the high altitude resorts of the

Table 9.4   *The continuum of characteristics in Alpine resorts*

Low altitude	High altitude
Integrated settlement _____	New settlement
Local capital _____	External capital
Local labor _____	External labor
Cultural exchanges _____	Cultural islands
Environmental pressures _____	Environmental pressures
Temporal polarization _____	Temporal polarization

western Alps. They can be dichotomized, in a simplified fashion, as lying at the two extremes of a continuum of resorts (table 9.4).

Although they generate different types of environmental pressures, both types can threaten the ecosystems and the landscapes of their surrounding regions. Both are also characterized by temporal polarization, although there are differences in the extent to which they can attract summer visitors. Neither of these ideal types is static and the tourist resorts are in process of continual change. One of the more pessimistic aspects of Barker's analysis is that the initially more positive experiences of the more integrated developments of the eastern Alps can be temporary. She writes (1982: 409) that after the initial stages "the intensity and the volume of tourism in peak season, however, result in an over-commitment of financial resources to tourist accommodations and infrastructure as well as in congestion, suburban-like sprawl, pollution, and loss of traditional ways of life." The benefits and "dangers" of tourism were addressed more fully in the Krippendorf report (box 9.3).

Europe is the principal winter skiing focus, with some 24 million skiers in the late 1980s (see figure 9.8), dominated by the German, French, and Austrian markets (Travel and Tourism Analyst 1999). There are concerns that this market is becoming static (box 9.4). There are also important mass winter tourism markets in North America (12 million skiers) and Japan (also 12 million). One survey estimated that, in the USA alone, there were approximately 52 million skier and snowboarder visits in 1999–2000 with the Rocky Mountains accounting for 34.7 percent (Travel and Tourism Analyst 2000). The American resorts are highly seasonal and, on average, operated for only 117 days during the year. There are however important regional variations (table 9.5) and differences of scale; for example, the average number of beds per ski resort is only 123 in the Mid West compared to 3,812 in the Central Rockies. There are also seasonal differences with Western Canada managing 136 days of operation compared to only 101 in the

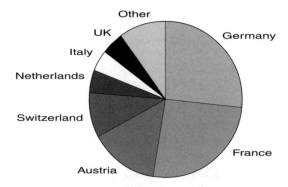

Figure 9.8   *The European ski holiday market, 1997–8: market shares*
Source: Travel and Tourism Analyst No 2 (1999)

Box 9.3   The Krippendorf Report on mountain tourism

Possible benefits:

1. Reduce or prevent depopulation.
2. Create employment.
3. Generate revenue for the state.
4. Help finance infrastructure.
5. Improve facilities.
6. Help to support agriculture and countryside management.
7. Help maintain the character and customs of mountain areas and people.

Possible dangers:

1. Can lead to a fragile mono-structural economy.
2. Un-coordinated tourism development can undermine the rural economy, leading to underutilization of capacity.
3. Takes over valuable cultivable land.
4. Can damage biodiversity and the quality of the landscape.
5. Can lead to over-dependence on foreign investment and external decision making
6. Can undermine the authenticity of local culture.
7. Tourism can generate social tensions and accentuate disparities of wealth.

Source: Krippendorf (1987b) as summarized in Gilg (1998)

Table 9.5 *North American ski resorts: regional contrasts, 1989–90*

Resort area	Features of average resorts			
	Gross fixed assets ($)	No. of beds at base	Number of skier visits (000s)	Average revenue per skier visit ($)
New England	19,586	1,453	271	24.74
East	10,308	529	158	23.64
MidWest	2,895	123	69	18.57
Central Rockies	23,339	3,812	358	24.18
Northern Rockies	11,302	886	181	22.82
California and Nevada	20,229	437	282	32.00
Pacific Northwest	10,676	146	185	16.62
Western Canada	16,789	840	231	24.81

Source: Goeldner et al. (1991)

Box 9.4   Challenges for mass Alpine winter tourism

Social and cultural changes are challenging the assumption of continued growth in Alpine tourism because of:

* Socio-demographic changes.
   The aging of the population reduces the potential market of (young) skiers.
   Increased numbers of young single households who favor long distance travel.
* Fragmentation of the tourism market and growth of diversified short break holidays at the expense of long holidays:
   Increased experience of traveling.
   Search for freedom and adventure.
   Increased body consciousness and environmental awareness.
* The need to enhance the quality of the environment in response to existing poor management in some areas, and the growth of environmentally-informed tourism demand.

Source: Zimmermann (1995: 22–23)

East region. This contributes to considerable variations in the economic efficiency of the resorts. The revenue extracted per skier visit ranges between $16.62 in the Pacific Northwest to almost double this, at $32.00, in California and Nevada.

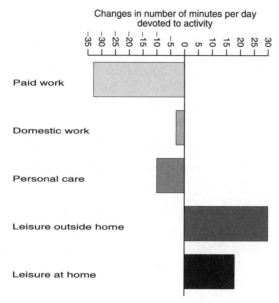

Changes in number of minutes per day
devoted to activity

Paid work

Domestic work

Personal care

Leisure outside home

Leisure at home

Figure 9.9 *Broad activity changes in Great Britain, 1961–84*
Source: Gershuny and Jones (1987: 20)

Changes in Tourism and Leisure: The End of Mass Tourism?

Mass tourism is one form of mass leisure. The amount of leisure time available in developed countries increased steadily during the twentieth century. Gershuny and Jones (1987) traced the major changes in the UK, 1961–84 (figure 9.9): the amount of time taken by paid work has decreased, domestic work has been largely static, personal care has declined and leisure, both in and out of the home, has increased. As would be expected, access to leisure time and activities is socially differentiated, especially in terms of class, income/unemployment, age, and gender. In general, while the leisure patterns of men and women have converged, the former remain relatively privileged (see chapter 3).

As well as an increase in overall leisure time, there have also been changes in leisure practices. Even at a fairly crude level of measurement, Gershuny and Jones' (1987) quantitative analysis of UK trends, for example, found that the amount of time devoted to walking and sports had increased, while passive leisure (listening to music, watching TV etc) had decreased. "Going for a drive," or excursions per se as a form of leisure had also declined in importance, leading the authors to conclude that "domesticating the means of production of transport services, seems to have robbed travel (or at least, local travel) of something of its previous romance."

Roberts (1989) provides a more general analysis of changes in leisure in the UK, and identifies three important trends. Arguably, these apply equally to other developed countries. First, there is greater *home centeredness* as a result of long-term privatization of leisure. This is linked to the decline of community, greater individual mobility, and the expansion of the leisure market in sound and vision equipment, computers and technology. Second, there is greater *out-of-home recreation* as sports participation, visits to historic sites and theme parks, tourism, and second homes become more important. This is linked to a growing preference for active rather than passive leisure. Third, *connoisseur leisure* is on the increase with more specialist minority interests spawning specialist magazines and shops, although these usually require relatively high disposable incomes.

These trends all affect tourism. Home centerdness leads to a greater preference for self-catering holidays, as well as challenging the very notion of tourism as traveling away from home. Out-of-home recreation interests lead to a demand for more active recreation while on holiday, and connoisseur leisure creates a demand for specialized holidays. Another important feature was noted by Tyrell (1982), the blurring of the distinction between work, education, and leisure. For example, educational courses are followed as a form of leisure, while some forms of domestic tasks such as gardening or do-it-yourself building and renovation at home have a dual function as work and leisure. Given these social changes, the continued growth of disposable income among those in work, and further developments in the supply side of the tourism industry (for example, globalization, new high technology theme parks, and a surge of interest in heritage tourism), it is not surprising that there have been changes in mass tourism. Some commentators have even predicted the end of mass tourism.

Let us consider the arguments about the demise of mass tourism more carefully. In mass tourism, the tourist gaze is focused on the extraordinary as a reaction to the harshness of life in the urban–industrial localities where most of the working and lower middle classes live. The extraordinary takes many forms but, in the case of mass tourism, has mainly been presented in terms of beach and winter sports holidays. However, the conditions of mass tourism have been changing and there is now the challenge of what Urry (1990) terms postmodernism. One of the essential characteristics of the mass tourism experience has been its discreteness as a set of practises and experiences – such as swimming, sunbathing, skiing, and eating different (foreign) foods. These could only be experienced or practiced in specific times and places, which were differentiated from the localities where people spent their "everyday" working lives. However, postmodernism has led to the

dissolving of the boundaries between high and low culture, and between different cultural forms such as art, architecture, shopping, and
tourism. New technologies also allow greater scope for creating or
recreating environments, such as leisure pools with beaches and wave
effects, and artificial ski slopes. As a result, spatial and temporal barriers between tourism and non-tourism have become blurred. In terms
of the tourist gaze, Urry (1990: 102) writes that this has become indis-
tinguishable from other social and cultural practices:

> Pleasure was associated with being away from the place in which one
> worked and from the boring and monotonous pain of work, especially of
> industrial production. Now, however, such a division is much less clear-
> cut. Pleasures can be enjoyed in very many places, not at all concentrated
> at the seaside. There has been a proliferation of objects on which to gaze,
> including the media. What now is tourism and what is more generally
> culture is relatively unclear. Pleasures and pain are everywhere, not
> spatially concentrated in particular sites.

Urry uses this argument to provide an insight into the decline of traditional British seaside resorts. These are no longer perceived as being
extraordinary; they can not compete in terms of the quality and costs of
accommodation available elsewhere, and their products can look old-
fashioned or aged in comparison to say the facilities available at theme
parks, or Centre Parcs holiday villages. There are also new attractions in
the forms of heritage museums and other centers of recreation, so that
almost everywhere has become "a center of spectacle" (see chapter 8).
While domestic seaside resorts in Northern Europe – such as Blackpool
or Scheveningen – have suffered from this trend, there are also signs of
decline in some destinations in the Mediterranean, especially in Spain
(Valenzuela 1998; Marchena Gómez and Vera Rebollo 1995). Many
Mediterranean resorts have become familiar to the mass tourist, while
their "different" food and drink is replicated in high street restaurants
and bars throughout the length of the UK, so that they cease to be
"centers of spectacle" or the embodiment of certain (gastronomic in this
case) tourism experiences. The resulting trends away from mass packaged holidays are conceptualized by Urry (1995) in terms of reflecting
a broader shift to post-Fordist consumption (table 3.2).

While Urry's thesis has attracted considerable interest, Ritzer
(1998: 137) provides an alternative perspective, the McDonaldization
thesis which:

> leads to the view that people often travel to other locales in order to expe-
> rience much of what they experience in their everyday lives. That is, they
> want, their tourist experiences to be about as McDonaldized as their
> day-to-day lives.

Ritzer (1998: 137–9) further asserts that people demand four qualities from a holiday. First, it should be highly predictable: "The last thing most of today's tourists want to experience is an unpalatable meal, a wild animal or a rat-infested hotel room." Second, it should be highly efficient as are their everyday lives – "they want the most vacation for the money." Third, it should be highly calculable in terms of costs. And fourth, it should be highly controlled, in terms of routines and the behavior of the hosts. For all these reasons, Ritzer concludes that there is strong continuing demand for package holidays, with their standardization and predictability. Moreover, he further argues that tours have only become more flexible in terms of the freedom they allow tourists precisely because the McDonaldization of society means that there is less need for the McDonaldization of the package tour. Tourists no longer have to be provided with standardized meals, for example, because when they now leave their hotels they are likely to find international fast food outlets and restaurants in the vicinity. Perhaps his most telling comment (1998: 149) appears in the conclusion, when he argues that:

> Both the McDisneyised tourist and the post-tourist exist, but neither gets at the truth of tourism. What exist are concepts that allow us to understand things about tourism that we might not have understood before. We are left with a pastiche of insights, some from a modern, others from a postmodern, perspective.

We tend to concur with Ritzer about the importance of understanding the coexistence of different forms of tourism, even if there is increasing evidence of post-Fordist consumption. However, while these tendencies are acknowledged, this should not be confused with the notion that mass tourism is in terminal decline. There are three main reasons for this.

First, although some segments of the market are saturated, there is still scope for a *social and geographical extension of mass tourism.* Large parts of the populations of less developed countries have yet to enjoy any holiday tourism, while many workers in the newly industrialized countries have disposable income for holidays but rarely take these for cultural reasons. There is strong potential for the growth of new forms of mass tourism from Central and Eastern Europe, and it is significant that the first charter flight from Moscow to the Costa del Sol was inaugurated in 1994 (Marchena Gómez 1995: 115). In the developed countries, second and third holidays are spreading from the middle classes to the working classes, or at least to those with disposable income. There is, therefore, likely to be a continued increase in mass tourism.

Second, some of the debate about tourism has confused *generic changes with changes in individual resorts*. In particular, a decline in inbound tourism to Spain in the early 1990s was sometimes interpreted as heralding a major shift in tourism preferences, but this has subsequently been seen as a short term blip in an otherwise continuing growth trend. Individuals resorts in the Costa del Sol and elsewhere may have faced stagnation or decline. But this has to be interpreted in terms of the resort life cycle (Butler 1980) and the maturing of tourism products created by investments in the 1960s and 1970s. Moreover, tourists will seek out new venues and new kinds of objects to gaze upon, and the fact that so many mass resorts compete on the basis of price means there is a high degree of substitutability between them (Knowles and Curtis 1999). This will mean that resorts will grow and decline more rapidly, and their cultural content and built form will also change. But this itself is not the harbinger of the end of mass tourism.

Third, there is some evidence of changes in mass tourism products. Reflecting social and cultural shifts, and changes in tourist preferences, package holidays have become more flexible, offering greater choice in terms of accommodation (more self-catering options), travel (business class offered as an alternative to economy class) and activities (more sporting and other events to participate in). However, greater differentiation reflects a change in the form of mass tourism rather than its replacement with postmodernist tourism. Similar trends have been observed in the manufacturing sector, for example, where Hudson (1997) comments that if Fordism is being transformed then this is into new forms of high volume production rather than post-Fordism. In a similar vein, it can be argued that what is being observed in the developed countries is *a shift from mass tourism to high volume tourism production*. In some ways this is different from the model of mass tourism that has dominated the late twentieth century. But it is also true that many of the essential features of mass tourism – spatial and temporal polarization, dependency and external control, and intense environmental pressures – are likely to remain little changed.

Therefore, while the emergence of new forms of tourism need to be recognized, this has to be seen as growing alongside mass tourism that continues not only to be a highly significant tourism form, but one which is still increasing at least in absolute terms. There are new tourism spaces that are very much the domain of postmodernist tourism, or neo-Fordist tourism consumption, but equally there are tourism spaces (the large resorts) that are organized along essentially Fordist lines of mass production and consumption.

10

Urban Tourism

The Dimensions of Urban Tourism and Leisure

Urban areas of all types act as tourism destinations attracting domestic and international visitors, including holidaymakers, as well as those on business and conference trips. This is not surprising as towns and cities offer a wide range of attractions, which tend to be highly concentrated spatially. Moreover, tourism in these environments is an extremely diverse phenomena in at least three different ways. The first concerns the very heterogeneous nature of urban areas, distinguished as they are by size, location, function, and age. The other two dimensions are associated with the sheer variety of facilities offered, that is, their multifunctional nature, together with the fact that such facilities are very rarely solely produced for, or consumed by, tourists but by a whole range of users (Ashworth and Tunbridge 1990: 52). Such users, and the facilities to supply their needs, define a range of different "types of city," In this context we can talk about the "tourist city," the "shopping city," the "culture city" and the "historic city," all of which may exist within a particular urban area (Burtenshaw et al. 1991: 165; see also figure 10.2). Moreover, at the city level others have argued that tourist cities exist in a number of different guises, most notably; resort cities, tourist–historic cities and so-called reconstructed cities (Fainstein and Judd 1999).

For most commentators, it is this very diversity that has led to urban tourism being difficult to describe (Law 1985b: 2). Consequently, until relatively recently, it has been misunderstood as a social, economic, and geographical force, and much underestimated in its importance (Ashworth 1989; Blank and Petkovich 1987: 165; Vandermey 1984: 123). Such criticisms have however become less relevant since the late 1980s,

Plate 10.1   *Harbor Place, Baltimore, one of the key visitor attractions developed along the city's re-claimed waterfront*

Plate 10.2   *Visitor pressure in Venice, showing a small part of the large number of tourists who crowd into the historic core*

Table 10.1 *Types of tourism cities in the USA*

Type	Characteristics	Examples
Cities with high-amenity sites	Well endowed with good tourism resources, e.g. scenery, climate	Phoenix, San Francisco, Miami
Speciality tourism cities	Socially-made or historical attractions, with complexity of tourism attractions	Las Vegas, Orlando, Boston
Hinterland metropolitan areas	Have locational advantages, and an important part of tourism based upon their trade center	Louisville, Sioux Falls, Wichita

Source: Blank (1996)

since increasing political and academic attention has been focused on the significance of urban tourism as a spur to economic and environmental regeneration. This interest has been reflected in a growing number of texts concerned with; the impact of tourism on urban regeneration (Law 1993), the general scope of urban tourism (Page 1995), specific assessments of the performance of cities within the tourism market (van den Berg et al. 1995) alongside attempts to analyze the market for urban tourism (Mazanec 1997). The latter two perspectives have been distinctly European and, by comparison, the analysis of detailed tourism trends within North American cities have been relatively neglected. Exceptions are the review by Blank (1996) which attempts a classification of US cities based on their perceived tourism experiences (see table 10.1) and the work of Judd and Fainstein (1999). The latter focuses on the ways in which cities compete for tourists but, as the editors explain, "the chapters in this volume permit only an impressionistic account of the economic impact of tourism on cities" (Fainstein and Judd 1999: 272). As a result of this increased attention, our overall knowledge of urban tourism has risen considerably, but detailed analysis remains, at best, patchy.

Urban tourism is also characterized by the fact that cities very often exist within distinctive spatial networks, that function at two different levels. One of these, as Ashworth and Tunbridge (1990: 51–2) point out, sees urban areas operating regardless of their regional and national contexts, with particular cities forming parts of important tourism circuits. At a West European level, Paris, London, and Rome may operate as part of an international tourism network. At a national level, within the UK, the overseas visitor circuit encompasses London (which accounts for almost 59 percent of all overseas visitors to the UK), Edinburgh, Bath, Stratford, and York, all of which are linked by strong historical and cultural factors. At a second spatial level, the tourism activities of cities, especially from the viewpoint of domestic tourists and local visitors, exist within a strong regional framework. In this context, cities act as important focal points for a region's tourism industry (again, London accounts for almost 15 percent of domestic tourism trips). Once again, this apparent dichotomy of spatial functions highlights the complex nature of urban tourism, together with the difficulties in isolating how facilities are perceived and used by different types of visitors.

One way to consider the different dimensions of tourism in cities is to view the urban environment itself as a "leisure product," which also has many common elements with the idea of an urban tourism product (Jansen-Verbeke 1986: 85–8). Both, for example, are based on the spatial concentration of a variety of facilities, together with characteristic environmental features. As shown in figure 10.1, these dimensions can be identified in terms of an "activity place," which defines the supply of facilities, and an overall "leisure setting," thus covering both physical as well as sociocultural facilities. In this perspective, three main elements, or levels of facilities, may be recognized; primary elements covering major tourist attractions, which in turn are supported by retail and catering facilities (secondary elements), and a general tourism infrastructure (conditional elements).

While such an approach allows a systematic consideration of the supply side of urban tourism, it is not without difficulties. For example, in many cities the so-called secondary elements of shops and restaurants may well be the main attractions for certain groups of visitors. Similarly, as we shall see in the following part of this chapter, the importance of the "leisure product" in an urban setting is also open to debate when discussing the factors that act as motives for sightseeing tourism (Jansen-Verbeke 1986: 87).

The supply-side elements identified in figure 10.1 tend to have distinctive geographies within urban areas, a fact recognized by the numerous attempts to provide a spatial model of the so-called tourist city (see Ashworth and Tunbridge 1990; Pearce 1995). These attempts range from studies that have placed tourism and leisure facilities within the overall framework of classical concentric landuse models (Yokeno 1968), through to those that have sought to define a "recreational business district" (Stansfield and Rickert 1970), or a "central tourist district" (Burtenshaw et al. 1991) by extending the concepts of the CBD. In many other cases, the spatial models have been based on specific

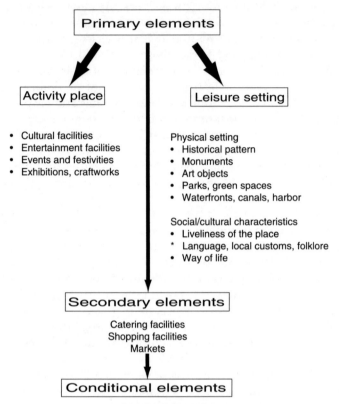

Figure 10.1 *Urban tourism and leisure settings*
Source: Jansen-Verbeke (1986)

supply-side variables, especially the locational distribution of hotels and other forms of tourist accommodation (Gutiérrez 1977; Knoll 1988; Pearce 1987c; Vetter 1985). In some cases these studies take an evolutionary approach that shows the early development of hotel locations in certain cities, and the spatial development of such groupings. Drawing on a range of studies, Ashworth (1989) has suggested that six types of hotel locations can be recognized within cities, and that these are controlled by such factors as land values, accessibility, environmental amenity, historical inertia and, in the postwar period, planning controls. Box 10.1 shows the six main types of locational clusters resulting from these factors, to which may be added a seventh category that describes those hotels located close to major tourist attractions. The

---

Box 10.1   Main types of hotel clusters found in urban areas

1. Traditional market/city gate locations in historic centers
2. Major tourist attraction locations
3. Railway station/road approach locations
4. Main access road locations outside of central areas
5. Medium sized hotels in favorable environmental locations
6. Large modern hotels in the zone in transition
7. Large modern hotels in the urban periphery on motorway or airport interchanges

Source: modified from Ashworth (1989)

---

different factors affecting hotel locations vary geographically and over time. Thus, in North America and Australasia, higher rates of car ownership have produced more motels located along major highways; a factor stressed by Mayo's (1974) findings of the influences determining American motorists' choice of motel and by Pearce (1995). In major cities such as London, a primary determinant of hotel location in the postwar period was planning control, as many local authorities in the city restricted hotel development to preserve residential landuse (Eversley 1977; Horwath and Horwath Ltd 1986). However, as Bull and Church (1996) have shown, although there was a rapid increase in London's hotel stock during the early 1970s, the locational pattern has remained very similar through to the present day.

Of course there are many other tourism facilities found within cities which also have recognizable spatial distributions, one of the most numerous of which are catering and specialized tourism-orientated retailers. Once again, distinctive forms of urban development are influential. Smith (1983) has highlighted some of the different spatial associations and emphasized the marked linear distributional pattern of catering establishments in many Canadian cities. Work in Paris by Bonnain-Moerdyk (1975) has also served to show how restaurants have moved as geographical changes in commercial activities and entertainment areas have occurred.

A further very diverse group of functions relating to tourism are those concerned with retailing. Both tourists and visitors to urban areas use all manner of shops but, more specifically, they also contribute to the formation of distinctive clusters of both tourist- and leisure-related retailers. The former term covers a more narrowly defined area of activity, while leisure-based retailing is just as likely to be used by local residents. Indeed, some observers have recently argued that a growing number of shopping trips are leisure-based, a fact reflected in the growth of specialized shopping centers (Ashworth and Tunbridge 1990). Increasingly, such trends have been recognized by developers, resulting in early redeveloped leisure-retail complexes such as Covent Garden in London, and the Forum in Paris. In both cases, the retail environment is strongly biased towards leisure activities, and in the case of Covent Garden at least 33 percent of all visitors are tourists (Wood 1981). There have been few detailed studies of tourist and leisure-based retailing, although interest is growing (Jansen-Verbeke 1990; Kuhn 1979; Shaw et al. 2000). Obviously, leisure retailing is not a new phenomenon, as Jansen-Verbeke (1990) argues that as long as cities have existed the pattern of going to town has included a leisure experience. What has changed, however, is the range of leisure-retail environments now available, as many city authorities and developers have constructed new centers. Some of these are in-town, as at Covent Garden in London or at the festival marketplace in Baltimore (see, for example, figure 10.7), while others occupy out-of-town/edge-of-town locations. In both cases we can speak of theme park shopping centers, as discussed in chapter 8, which cater for a leisure-based experience and are directed at the middle class. Such centers range in scale from the very large West Edmonton Mall in Canada, which combines distinctive leisure-based components (10 percent of floor-space), 800 shops and a "Fantasyland" Hotel, to the Metro-Centre in the UK, through to smaller so-called "free-time" shopping centers in Germany (Howard 1990). Such developments blur the distinctions between so-called primary and secondary leisure products, as tourists become increasingly attracted to these stage-managed shopping experiences.

It is clear from the discussion so far that tourism facilities have distinctive and diverse spatial distributions within urban areas. Moreover, when taken together with major attractions and cultural facilities, such activities provide fundamental components in the character of urban environments. As Pearce (1987c: 189) argues, the geography of urban tourist attractions and related facilities are best considered via networks of "nodes, clusters of nodes, and [the] routes linking them." In New York, for example, Broadway and Fifth Avenue have dominated the city as its major thoroughfare since the early twentieth century (Jakle 1985: 268–9). In terms of tourist demand, such an urban geography is often described by the many tourist circuits that feature in guides to particular cities. Where these are formalized through organized bus or coach tours, geographers have been able to map such circuits (Burnet and Valeix 1967). The critical nodes within these spatial circuits are viewing points which allow visitors to gain a general perspective of the city. Such tourist nodes and pathways can also be defined by the location of major tourist attractions and functional districts, enabling the tourist city to be geographically identified.

The Tourist in the City

All tourists and visitors approach cities with definite expectations of their sights and attractions (Jakle 1985: 246). Such expectations are formed not only by a variety of social experiences and information sources which produce distinct images of urban areas, but they also vary with type of visitor. Within the somewhat limited literature on visitor activity in urban areas, two main perspectives can be identified. One concerns types of users and visitor motivation, while the other, with an even smaller research base, examines visitor behavior within the city.

In terms of identifying visitor types and their motivations, problems center on devising a meaningful classification of visitors. Jansen-Verbeke (1986: 88) notes, for example, that urban tourists can be distinguished "from other visitors by two criteria, 'their place of residence', situated outside the urban hinterland, and 'their motives for visiting'." Within this particular view, tourists are identified by length of travel, being people drawn from outside the city region. This is a somewhat simplistic, if practical, approach that is very often used in surveys of urban visitor behavior undertaken by municipal authorities (Blank and Petkovich 1987). It is usually dependent on discovering visitor motivations through questionnaire methods. For this reason, much work to date is still fragmented along the lines of individual city case studies. In North America some cities have received detailed attention over a number of years (Blank 1996; Blank and Petkovich 1979), while in Europe, Jansen-Verbeke (1986) has researched Dutch towns, Ashworth and Tunbridge (1990) Norwich, Buckley and Witt (1985) Glasgow, Law (2000) Manchester and beyond these published results lies a wealth of local authority sponsored reports (for UK examples see Shaw et al. 1990 on Plymouth; ETB 1984 on Chester). One significant exception is the work of Wöber (1997) reporting the data collected by the Federation of European Cities' Tourism Offices (FECTO, see also Tourism on http//tourmis.wu.ed/db-ts/bsp_ehtml#F1), which has reported the main purpose of visit for 35 European cities. This indicates that, for these cities, only 27 percent of visitors came on holiday trips compared with 46 percent for business reasons.

Most of these studies, together with nationally based surveys, provide general information on the purpose of visit. In large British towns (those with populations over 100,000), short- and long-stay holidaymakers account for around 44 percent of all bed-nights, those

Table 10.2   *Types of trips to selected US cities*

Purpose	Percentage of trips		
	Orlando	Indianapolis	Portland
Visit friends and relatives	18	38	29
Business/conference	12	30	30
Outdoor recreation	6	3	3
Entertainment/sightseeing	53	8	13
Personal reasons	5	13	17
Shopping	1	0	3
Others	5	8	5

Source: Bureau of Transportation Statistics (1979), Blank and Petkovich (1987)

visiting friends and relatives 24 percent, with business and conference tourism a further 20 percent (English Tourist Board 1981). Table 10.2 shows similar tourist-based information for selected US cities and highlights the variation in tourist usage of different urban areas. Obviously, tourists are only one set of urban visitors (figure 10.2). Indeed, much of the detailed research at the individual city level has attempted to focus on the different motivations of tourists and other urban visitors. In Holland, Jansen-Verbeke (1986) has shown that the obvious motivational differences between tourists and day visitors (drawn from the local area) concern the priority given to "having a day out" and "sightseeing" by tourists, compared with "shopping" and "visiting restaurants" by day visitors (table 10.3). Some, but not all, of these differences have been borne out in British cities. For example, in Chester, 21 percent of day visitors, compared with only 4 percent of the tourists, came because of the shops, although detailed comparisons are difficult because of differing methodologies (English Tourist Board 1984: 13).

To date, much of our knowledge of urban tourism has come from the study of tourist facilities and their locational distributions. However, as was emphasized in the previous section, many of the components of the "tourist city" can only be fully understood through more detailed research on visitor behavior. Two important research questions follow. How closely do visitor motivations match their actual use of facilities? And how do visitors use the various nodes and routeways that seemingly make up the "central tourist district?"

Neither of these critical issues has been pursued closely in the research literature. Ashworth and de Haan (1986) have undertaken limited work on Norwich, comparing the motivations of visitors with their actual use of facilities in the city, while Jansen-Verbeke (1986) has

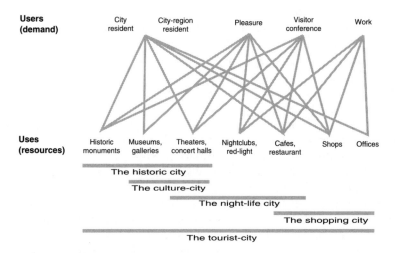

Figure 10.2 *Functional areas in the "tourist city"*
Source: Burtenshaw et al. (1991)

Table 10.3 *Main reasons given by tourist and day visitors for visiting city centers: Dutch cities, 1985*

	Percentage responses	
Reasons	Tourists	Day visitors
A day out	29.3	3.0
Shopping	13.6	30.0
Professional purposes	12.7	6.2
Visit family/friends	10.4	1.8
Sightseeing	9.1	0.5
Visit restaurant/pub/bar	6.9	14.3
Walking around	3.2	3.4
Visit market	2.9	5.0
Daily purchases	2.7	12.3
Visit museum	1.1	2.0

Sample sizes: 375 tourists and 762 day visitors
Source: modified from Jansen Verbeke (1986)

examined visitor activity patterns in three Dutch towns. The main points to emerge from these studies are that the vast majority of trips are of a multifunctional nature and that visitors who are attracted to one particular facility in a city invariably make use of many others. In Norwich, for example, while 18.9 percent of holidaymakers came primarily to visit the castle and cathedral, 35 percent also used the city's restaurants and department stores (Ashworth and Tunbridge 1990: 121–3). Studies in North America of Minneapolis-St. Paul have shown that people visiting friends and relatives in the city also generate large volumes of retail sales (Blank and Petkovich 1987: 166). One of the most detailed studies of visitor behavior is that by Tuynte and Dietvorst (1988) who have examined visitor linkages between museums in Nijmegen (Holland) and the town's other facilities. From this research a number of key functional linkages were identified, including a "museum and shops" combination which covered 26 percent of the visitors, and a "museum–general sightseeing" cluster encompassing 22 percent of visitors.

These functional linkages also produce particular spatial patterns, although geographers have rarely considered the activity space of urban tourists. Notable exceptions are Murphy (1980), working on Victoria in Canada, and Chadefaud (1981), who has presented detailed maps of Lourdes (France) showing the activity space of both organized groups of tourists and those traveling independently. The former had much more concentrated zones of activity compared with the relatively dispersed patterns of independent tourists. In both these studies pedestrian flows were the prime source of information and, to a large extent, functional linkages had to be inferred. A more detailed and accurate method of examining the activity space of tourists is to ask visitors which urban facilities they used and in what order. In this way functional linkages can be placed in a spatial framework. Such a study has been undertaken in Plymouth (Shaw et al. 1990). Visitors to the city were asked which tourist attractions they had visited before shopping in the central retail area, and which they intended to use after shopping. Some of the results from this survey (of over 4,000 visitors) are shown in figure 10.3, which highlights the strong linkages between historic part of Plymouth (the Barbican), the Hoe (a major tourist area) and the central retail area.

The information presented for Plymouth provides details of the routeways and nodes that comprise the city's "central tourist district," which in this case is relatively concentrated. In much larger urban tourist environments, such as London, the action space – and hence the routeways and nodes – of tourists are obviously more complicated, given the large diversity of competing and complimentary attractions (figure 10.4). In London the information is based purely on the main sites visited by overseas tourists and therefore does not give the same detailed linkages as the Plymouth study, although in both cases we can obtain impressions of the spatial complexity of tourist behavior. Of course, such routeways are constantly changing in response to the construction of new attractions. For example, despite its adverse publicity,

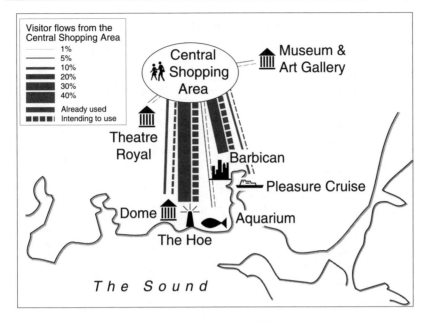

Figure 10.3   *Visitor movements within Plymouth, 1992*

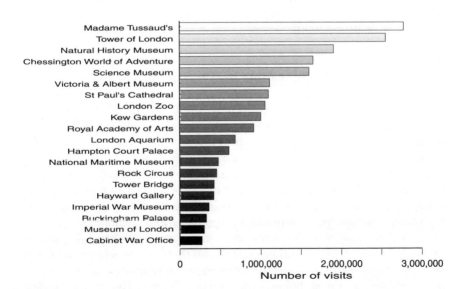

Figure 10.4   *Major visitor attractions in London (paying attractions), 1998*
Source: ETB (1999)

Table 10.4 *Visitor nights in European cities*

City	Millions of visitors
London	85.7
Paris	26.4
Rome	11.9
Dublin	11.2
Barcelona	7.8
Berlin	7.2
Madrid	7.1
Milan	5.3
Athens	5.0
Vienna	6.6
Munich	6.0
Amsterdam	3.6
Prague	3.5
Brussels	2.9
Copenhagen	3.2

Source: Wöber 1997

the Millennium Dome had attracted large numbers of visitors (6.5 million paying visitors by the end of 2000) and so has the Tate Modern Art Gallery (2.7 million free visitors in the first five months after its opening in 2000).

Tourism, Urban Regeneration, and Place Marketing

Tourism in large and historic cities is not a new trend; for example, Paris, London, Rome, and New York all have longstanding tourism industries. Unfortunately, it is difficult to document the scale and importance of urban tourism in a comparative context, since few statistics exist; those that do suggest that, at an international level, European cities are dominant. Within Europe, as table 10.4 shows, it is the capital cities that tend to dominate as in the case of London and Paris. Of course, these figures represent large variations in reasons for traveling and importantly the ratio of domestic to international visitors. However, an analysis of tour operators and their city brochures revealed that there are 19 classic tourism destinations marketed across six or more countries. These being: Amsterdam, Athens, Barcelona, Berlin, Budapest, Dublin, Florence, Istanbul, Lisbon, London, Madrid, Moscow, Paris, Prague, Rome, St. Petersburg, Stockholm, Venice and

Vienna (van den Berg et al. 1995). While tourism was traditionally recognized in historic towns, within large cities and industrial centers the significance of tourism had been neglected until the 1980s; since then it has been perceived as having important roles in economic and environmental improvements (see Law 1992, 1996, 2000). The issue of tourism's role in urban regeneration has had strong international dimensions (Falk 1987) concerning the transfer of ideas, and even stronger political ideological connotations in countries such as the UK. The ideas behind using tourism as a spur to economic and environmental regeneration were initially explored within North America, as Law (1996) demonstrates. During the late 1970s increasing numbers of US cities were experiencing decline of their central cores, sapping the strength of their economic base. Political and business interests combined to shape a new set of policies aimed at office development, tourism and gentrification (Fainstein 1983), although tourism was seen as the prime motivator of change (Judd and Collins 1979). Tourism was selected because it was a growth industry, provided jobs and could lead to environmental improvements. Judd (1999: 36) argues that in US cities the redevelopment of their physical infrastructure "has approached, in scale, the restructuring of downtown economies and land use wrought by the massive urban renewal projects of the 1950s and 1960s." For example, between 1976 and 1986 some 250 convention centers and arts facilities were constructed within North American cities. In 1970 the US had 6.7 m sq ft of conference space, but in the rush to expand elements of urban tourism this figure had risen to 18 m sq ft by 1990 (Judd 1999). At the heart of this strategy is the idea that visitors will be attracted to the city, generating income and jobs. Furthermore, as tourism develops, new facilities will help create a better urban environment, some of the benefits of which will be passed on to local residents, and there will be a general improvement in the image of the city to would-be investors (Law 2000, and see figure 10.5).

An important example of the initiation of this tourism-based strategy is the city of Baltimore which commissioned a plan for revitalizing its run-down inner harbor area in 1964. The overall plan was based on people having direct access to the shoreline and so the first step was to return this area to public ownership, with the city buying land, clearing derelict sites and laying out a waterside park. As the plan developed, tourism took a more prominent role, especially with the completion of the Convention Center in 1979 and the Harborplace festival shopping center in 1980 (figure 10.6). In addition, a World Trade Center was completed in 1977, together with a science museum and 12 new hotels opened between 1984 and 1987 (Law 1985b: 21).

These developments in Baltimore have certainly been successful in improving economically and environmentally a part of the downtown

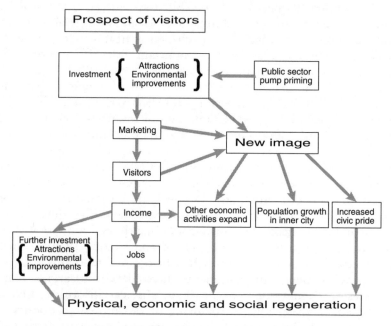

Figure 10.5 *The processes of tourism-based urban regeneration*
Source: Law (1992)

area, as well as developing a significant tourism and convention trade. Limited data are available on the scale of change, although survey data in the early 1980s showed that the volume of visitors increased from 2.25 million in 1980 to 6.8 million by 1985. Over the same time period, visitor expenditure grew from $125 million to $400 million, and a fifth of all visitors came from outside the region (Law 1985a: 24). In addition, the Baltimore Office of Promotion and Tourism estimated that, in 1981, tourism accounted for 16,000 jobs, a figure that increased to 20,000 by 1988.

The apparent success of Baltimore appears to have been based on two critical factors. The first was that the city was in receipt of large Federal Government grants, gaining more money under the Urban Development Action Grant (UDAG) scheme than any other US city. This was particularly significant for some of the large-scale projects; for example, the inner city hotel development was stimulated in 1981 by a $10 million UDAG (Law 1985b: 18–21). The use of Federal funds alongside private capital was a significant feature of Baltimore's regeneration efforts, as was the case in many other American cities (see Ehrlich and Dreier 1999 for details of Boston). The second factor was

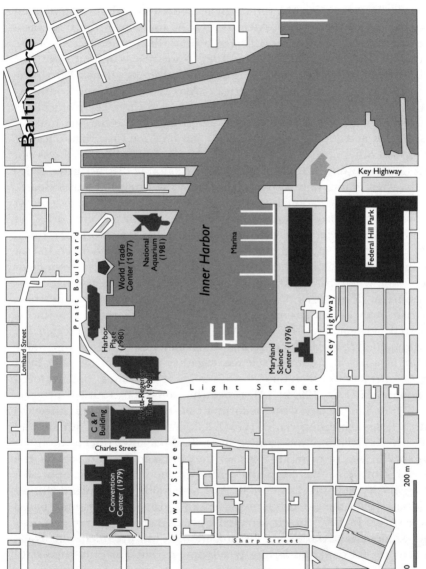

Figure 10.6 *Major visitor-related developments in Baltimore*

strong and stable political leadership which was able to carry through long-term, ambitious plans.

We have dwelt on the Baltimore case because it has been used as a template by other cities, especially in the UK where the British Government and agencies like the English Tourist Board have stimulated the take-up of these ideas. As in the USA, tourism in the UK was a growth industry during the 1980s at a time when other sectors of the economy were stagnant. During 1985 tourism's economic role was promoted in three key reports, The Banks Report (Banks 1985), the Confederation of British Industries (1985) report and, most influentially, the Young Report (1985). These stressed three key elements of tourism; its labor-intensive nature, its strong local economic multiplier effects and the low capital cost of job creation (less than one-half of that in other economic sectors). Such promotional material was not lost on city authorities suffering massive economic restructuring, especially when grants were also available from the English Tourist Board.

The focus of national authorities such as the English Tourist Board was on using tourism to revitalize the inner city areas of depressed industrial environments (English Tourist Board 1981). Local city authorities responded quickly and enthusiastically, so much so that by the mid-1980s a number of cities had started either to introduce or to strengthen tourism. As can be seen from table 10.5, a wide range of tourism developments was initiated, with conference and business tourism providing a strong component (Law 1987), together with industrial heritage sites. In 1982, Manchester, for example, created the Castlefield Urban Heritage Park, which included using an old warehouse as a new museum of science, together with other purpose-built visitor attractions (including the Granada TV studios) and restored Roman sites (Law 1991b: 14). Since the mid-1980s tourism projects proliferated in the city, with the former Central Station being converted into a large exhibition center (GMEX); significantly a "Tourism and Leisure Association" was formed in 1980. This latter organization has the specific aim of bringing together the public and private sectors, the marriage of which has formed a central theme in the state's approach to inner-city renewal (Law 1988). As Law (2000: 122) explains during "the late 1990s the city center experienced a growing renaissance based on leisure." In 1997 the city created a broad marketing strategy under the Manchester Marketing Organization. This provided one component for tourism and leisure developments but was only successful because the city had other important organizations working to improve its visitor attractions and urban environment. In this context, Manchester reveals the importance of the conjunction of a number of key elements. These include an effective and well-funded marketing organization, a means of obtaining and directing public–private investment

Table 10.5 *Tourism developments and estimated economic impacts in UK cities during the 1980s*

City	Population	Visitor characteristics	Economic impact
Birmingham	1 million	91% business and conference tourism (1 million + visitors)	£170 million (1983) 34,000 jobs (1985)
Glasgow	765,000	Mixed, day visitors and 40% overseas tourists	£57.6 million (1982) 5,000 jobs (1982)
Liverpool	510,000	Mixed, many day visitors	£58 million (1982) 10,000 jobs[a] (1982)
Bradford	460,000	Specialized trips and packages (30,000+); 500,000 visits to National Museum of Photography	£4.5 million
Nottingham	271,000	Mixed, but 58% business tourism in hotels	£16 million (1980)
Cardiff	200,000	Mixed market, mainly day visitors (439,000)	

[a] Impact figures based on Merseyside data
Source: Law (1985c)

– in this case the Greater Manchester Development Corporation. This was instrumental in promoting and directing an enterprise culture within the city and, although it closed in 1996, many of its functions have been continued by the government regeneration agency – English Partnerships (Law 2000). Another critical factor in Manchester's development was a "vision" for change and expansion. The important catalyst for this was the city's bid for the 2000 Olympics which, while it failed, nevertheless was critical in attracting schemes to the city. The importance of "vision" and leadership, so prominent in the early development of Baltimore's Harborside area, have been highlighted by van den Berg and Braun (1999) who outline a theoretical framework combining vision, strategy, and organization. They argue that these call "for skilled, entrepreneurial management" which in turn implies "that cities need to invest more in their human resources (van den Berg and Braun 1999: 98).

Much of the development of "new" forms of urban tourism appears to be associated with the emergence of city marketing. Certainly, since the 1980s the importance of effective marketing strategies to promote the post-industrial city has been stressed in a range of studies (for a general review see Ward 1998, and van den Berg and Braun 1999; Short and Kim 1999). Ward (1998) draws attention to the early leads given by Boston and New York during the late 1970s, and the launch of the "I Love New York" campaign has been credited with playing a crucial role in the regeneration of the city (Holcomb 1990, 1999). Certainly, most cities have created new marketing organizations and many have attempted to develop key slogans to attract visitors (Bramwell and Rawding 1994, 1996 and for a discussion of US cities see Short and Kim 1999). Within the UK Glasgow has led the way with its "Glasgow's Miles Better" campaign launched in early 1983. Backed by initial funding of £50,000 per annum the campaign was strongly targeted in London during 1984 and within a short time it had caught the public's imagination (Ward 1998). Perhaps one of the most significant and distinctive blends of image creation has been by Bradford in industrial Yorkshire. Bradford was quick to market itself for special interest holidays and to develop short-break holiday packages, based on: cultural tourism (the Bronte sisters), an industrial heritage tour, television themes and the National Museum of Photography, Film and Television (Buckley and Witt 1985; Davidson and Maitland 1997).

Investigations into the objectives of such marketing efforts by Bramwell and Rawding (1994) have highlighted a common set of ideas associated with stimulating urban regeneration, deriving economic benefits and environmental gains, and improving the city's image. All of which fit with the processes presented in figure 10.5. However, a closer examination of five British industrial cities reveals interesting variations around these common objectives in terms of what the marketing organizations see as their primary goal (table 10.6). For example, Stoke on Trent had the unusual objective of using marketing to "boost sales in the shops attached to the city's ceramic factories, thereby providing direct benefit to this traditional manufacturing industry" (Bramwell and Rawding 1994: 430).

The importance of what Kotler et al. (1993) termed strategic place marketing is clear in a broad spectrum of urban development strategies, although the terminology often appears ambiguous. In this context, Corsico (1994) suggests that urban marketing is used as a metaphor for the city as a market, as a commodity and as an enterprise. Within work on urban tourism, all three are relevant and encountered, although most emphasis is given to the first two.

The commitment to tourism as a means to regenerate urban areas was reaffirmed in 1989 with the English Tourist Board's launch of their five year "Vision for Cities" campaign. This formalized links with central government's "Action for Cities" program, as well as

Table 10.6   *Primary objectives of marketing operations in selected British cities*

City	Primary objective
Birmingham	Stimulating urban regeneration
Bradford	A tool for inward investment
Manchester	Establish as international capital of the "North"
Sheffield	New image based on sport and leisure
Stoke	Increase retail sales

Source: Bramwell and Rawding (1994)

Box 10.2   Key elements in the English Tourist Board's "Vision for Cities"

(a) Bring together partnerships of key public and private personalities.

(b) Prepare an agreed comprehensive development framework.

(c) Bring forward key development projects within the agreed frame work.

(d) Undertake a concerted and coordinated action program of environmental and infrastructure improvements.

---

introducing four key elements for urban tourism development (box 10.2). As in the earlier case of Baltimore (which figured prominently in the campaign's launch), great emphasis was given to the partnership of public and private enterprise. The process was focused on five inner city areas in Cleveland (North East England), the Black Country (Midlands), Sheffield, Manchester, and London, which were to act as models to inspire other urban areas. In addition, a number of Tourism Development Action Programmes (TDAPs) were established, which are partnerships between national agencies (tourist boards) local authorities and the private sector with the purpose of promoting tourism development. The aim of the programme was to "dispel the myth that tourism is a fringe activity and by the early 1990s . . . to see private and public sector investment in tourism and leisure projects rise to £3–4 million" (English Tourist Board 1989: 2).

At this stage it is worthwhile reiterating the perceived benefits of tourism to urban regeneration in order to get a clear picture of what the various government-led initiatives are attempting to achieve. In basic terms the potential benefits of inner city tourism developments are threefold. The first, and the most important in the policy documents, concerns economic benefits, especially the creation of new jobs. For example, within the five year ETB programme, the desired target was to create 250,000 new jobs. Second, there are physical and environmental improvements to the inner-city area. In the promotional material for the "Vision for Cities" campaign, the role of tourism was to create a "positive image" (English Tourist Board 1989: 2), while in physical terms "views, squares, streetscapes and waterfronts should be preserved and opened-up" for visitors (Collinge 1989: 2). Such a view recognizes, in policy terms, the main elements of what geographers have termed the "central tourism district," which in many of the industrialized cities, such as Manchester, corresponds to parts of the inner city. The third and final benefit is that tourism developments can bring improvements and better access to the leisure facilities for local residents. This is based on the presumption that most of these developments are multifunctional, incorporating new hotels, tourist attractions and conference facilities, together with retail and leisure components.

During the late 1990s, there was a shift in the funding of major tourism projects in the UK as the Millennium Commission became a leading player. The Commission was established under the 1993 National Lottery Act with the role of assisting communities to mark the millennium. Waycott (1999) claims it represents the largest single, non-government investment ever made in community schemes, many of which are associated with attractions, accounting for £4 billion of investment (including match funding). It is the large capital projects that are mostly associated with tourism, including the problematic Millennium Dome. Table 10.7 shows the full extent of these larger projects within British cities. These have in many instances added significantly to the reshaping of many traditional urban cores. What is uncertain is how many of these attractions will survive in what is becoming an increasingly congested and competitive market.

Tourism has been seen by policy-makers at all levels as a major catalyst for urban regeneration. Within the UK, central government has established a number of new actions and agencies including a national strategy alongside the creation of Regional Development Agencies (Church et al. 2000). However, what is not clear is tourism's ability to meet such ideals. The final section of this chapter will examine these issues within the context of the three major benefits supposedly offered by urban tourism schemes.

Hallmark Events and the City as Spectacle

According to Short and Kim (1999: 131) the Millennium Games held in Sydney "mark the culmination of a gradual shift in identity from imperial outpost of the British Empire to Australia's global city." Whether the 2000 Olympics were such a definable watershed may be

Table 10.7 *Millennium funded projects in British cities*

City	Projects	Millennium Commission grant	Total cost
Bristol	AT BRISTOL		
	Regenerating a derelict site with Science World, Wildscreen World	41 m	97 m
Kingston Upon Hull	THE DEEP		
	World Ocean Discovery Centre	18 m	36 m
Edinburgh	DYNAMIC EARTH		
	The story of the earth through state-of-the-art interactives	15 m	33 m
Doncaster	EARTH CENTRE		
	World center for environmental research and sustainable technology	50 m	100 m
Glasgow	GLASGOW SCIENCE CENTRE		
	National science center with interactive exhibits	35 m	85 m
Glasgow	HAMPDEN PARK STADIUM		
	Scotland's National Stadium and Museum of Football	23 m	46 m
Newcastle	INTERNATIONAL CENTRE FOR LIFE		
	High tech science-based visitor center with research facilities	28 m	58 m
Salford	LOWRY CENTRE		
	Lowry Gallery, Children's Hands-on, Virtual reality center	15 m	96 m
Rotherham	MAGNA		
	Conversion of steel mill to attraction focusing on British industry	18 m	37 m
Manchester	MANCHESTER MILLENNIUM QUARTER		
	Urbis Visitor Attraction, Cathedral visitor center, public squares	20 m	41 m
Birmingham	MILLENNIUM POINT, Birmingham		
	Discovery center, IMAX, shops and conference facilities	50 m	113 m
Cardiff	MILLENNIUM STADIUM		
	75,000 seater stadium venue, Rugby experience museum	46 m	126 m
Liverpool	NATIONAL DISCOVERY PARK, unsure future	20 m	120 m

Table 10.7   *continued*

City	Projects	Millennium Commission grant	Total cost
Leicester	NATIONAL SPACE CENTRE		
	An education and leisure facility based on space science	23 m	46 m
Norwich	NORFOLK AND NORWICH MILLENNIUM PROJECT		
	Millennium Library, multi-media auditorium TIC	30 m	60 m
Belfast	ODYSSEY PROJECT		
	Mix of entertainment, education, and sporting activities, IMAX	45 m	91 m
Sheffield	REMAKING THE HEART OF THE CITY		
	Art Gallery, Winter Garden and public spaces	21 m	42 m
Portsmouth	RENAISSANCE OF PORTSMOUTH HARBOUR		
	Creating an international maritime leisure complex	38 m	100 m
Cardiff	WALES MILLENNIUM CENTRE		
	International showcase of Welsh culture, opera, dance	37 m	70 m
	MILLENNIUM PROJECTS		
London	BRITISH MUSEUM GREAT COURT	30 m	94 m
London	MILLENIUM DOME	398 m	798 m
London	TATE GALLERY	50 m	130 m

Source: modified from Waycott, 1999

open to debate, but such statements illustrate the significance of so called hallmark events. Within the tourism literature these have been defined by Ritchie (1984: 2) as, "events of limited duration developed primarily to enhance the awareness, appeal and profitability of a tourist destination." Hallmark tourism encompasses a range of sporting events, fairs, festivals, and expositions. These can be classified in a number of ways including scale, ranging from major international events, through to national, regional, and local activities (Hall 1989, 1992). As Ley and Olds (1988) and Weiler and Hall (1992) show, such events are not new, but originated in the mid-nineteenth century as celebrations of industrialization, as in London's Great Exhibition of 1851.

It is not our intention to explore the changing nature of hallmark events, but rather to briefly discuss their role in shaping distinctive forms of contemporary urban tourism. Weiler and Hall (1992: 1) argue that "Hallmark events are the image builders of modern tourism," although it is a form of tourism that we know relatively little about. There is a clear economic element, although hosting major events like the Football World Cup or the Olympics can be highly speculative. For example, the 1996 Atlanta Olympics generated some £645 m but cost £557.9 m, while it is estimated that the Sydney Olympics should lead to a $7.3 billion injection of money into the city economy (Weiler and Hall 1992; Hall 1997; Waitt 1999). There are also obvious environmental and community impacts, which are often more difficult to examine. However, all indicators point to both economic and social impacts being unevenly distributed through urban communities, and sometimes being of limited input. Moreover, the nature of host–guest interactions and the role of community involvement certainly in large-scale events has been somewhat ignored in the literature. Obviously, such events can be viewed from a variety of perspectives. Increasingly, urban geographers are examining these mega events from the perspective of the "entrepreneurial city" with its emphasis on the role of enterprise, governance (a shift from the management of public services to the promotion of economic competitiveness), and links with image-making (Cockrane et al. 1996; Short and Kim 1999). Linked to this are those studies that develop the notions of image and place within the context of how the city is transformed into a product in order to produce "cultural capital" (Waitt 1999). We would argue that while both perspectives are significant, they fail to fully inform about how hallmark events impact on the urban tourist. Harvey (1989) and Waitt (1999) argue that the Olympic Games as spectacle is the ultimate tourist attraction and certainly these events are capable of generating very large numbers of urban visitors. These type of mega events also serve to condition forms of tourist behavior – increasing postmodern notions of tourism as play.

Finally, it should be recognized that large-scale events have taken on a new significance for the urban economy. The globalization of capital has served to increase the competition between cities in their attempts to attract tourism investment and jobs. These processes have also increased the scale and importance of place-marketing as previously discussed. In this, the city becomes identified, at least for a time, with a particular spectacle, in Sydney's case, the Olympics. However, as MacAloon (1984: 275; quoted in Waitt 1999) suggests, "spectacle takes the "realities" of life and defuses them by converting them to be played with like toys." The notion of play and revelry have been strongly identified in those few studies that have researched tourist behavior in hallmark events. In their study, Getz and Cheyne (1997: 152) conclude, "events are leisure opportunities in which play and the feeling of 'flow' (a state of optimal arousal) are facilitated." This emphasis on spectacle and play is becoming increasingly dominant in forms of urban tourism, and appear to have important influences on general patterns of visitor behavior. Such events also bring to the city very different expectations in both economic and cultural contexts. One critical issue is how far such impacts spread within the urban area and how long they last. Roche (1996: 329) argues that these hallmark or mega-events for research purposes need to be regarded as "essentially complex and multi-dimensional" requiring interdisciplinary study.

Selling the City: Who Benefits?

The restructuring of inner cities around the development of new tourism and leisure facilities raises questions over the wisdom of such projects. In effect, we can recognize two central issues or areas of debate. One concerns sustainability, and addresses the economic question of whether urban tourism projects can lead to sustained economic growth. The second debate is primarily social and concerns the distribution of who benefits from these developments. In addition, both of these overlapping debates are strongly linked by the significant geographical issue of how these socioeconomic and environmental benefits spread out spatially within the urban area.

Underlying these debates is the problem of how to combine public and private funding, since each tends to have a very different set of goals. Some of the most obvious differences are highlighted by the financial incompatibility of many schemes. Private-sector investment often aims to develop national and international conference facilities, festival marketplaces and international hotels, with seemingly little regard for the leisure needs of local people. Similarly, public and private interest have created land-use conflicts as new tourism schemes have commodified recreational land and created facilities for non-local residents (Spink 1989).

Such perspectives assume that all policy-making surrounding urban tourism projects is led by the demands of private investment. Clearly, this is not always the case since there are a number of possible outcomes from mixed public and private tourism ventures (box 10.3). However, what appears to be happening is a shift towards urban tourism and leisure schemes becoming more institutionalized as they

---

Box 10.3   Possible outcomes of private/public funded inner city tourism projects

1. Private success, and public success
    (Optimal outcome)
    *may be positive benefits for local residents
2. Private success and public failure
    * no real benefits to local residents
3. Private failure and public failure
    (most unlikely outcome)

---

become strongly linked with economic and political policy. In a review of the structuring of leisure policies in Dutch cities, Mommaas and van der Poel (1989) identify the increasing dominance of private invest-ment as dating from the 1980s. From this period, urban leisure policy changed from being local authority driven and funded (often linked in the 1970s to the needs of the unemployed), to a situation in which public and private partnerships developed to service the "pleasures of the well-to-do" rather than reintegrating disadvantaged groups (Mommaas and van der Poel 1989: 263). The thrust of the new policy, as illustrated by the building of the World Trade Center in Rotterdam, was to attract a larger share of the middle-class job market. Such trends, which are also clearly identifiable in British cities, relate to the institu-tionalized nature of capital accumulation as central government has reduced financial support to, but increased the costs of, local author-ities. The outcome has been that urban areas have increasingly been forced to compete with each other to attract new investment. As we have previously discussed, a positive image, which can be secured through quality tourism and leisure facilities, has become a major factor dominating leisure policy-making. Holcomb (1999: 69) claims that the "local state and business elites collude to remake a city in which their special interests are paramount." The creation and performance of partnership schemes have not been fully assessed, although limited evi-dence suggests that they are complex and require constant monitoring (Augustyn and Knowles 2000).

The selling of urban areas through such image creation has led some observers to question the whole *raison d'être* of tourism and leisure developments. Bramham et al. (1989: 4) ask "is the city a product to be sold on the tourism market," or "is a city a place to live, where people can express themselves?" From this perspective the new initiatives in urban tourism are seen as divisive, as they target the affluent members of society who have lifestyles based on sophisticated commodity

Table 10.8 *Estimates of job creation by selected inner-city tourism developments*

	Types of development		
Jobs created	Museum/shop	Hotel	Marina
On site	460	80	14
Off site	285	6	26
	745	86	40

Source: Vaughan (1990)

aesthetics and conspicuous patterns of consumption. Such patterns of development ignore or at best neutralize local ways of life merely by reproducing the leisure interests of the wealthy (Bramham et al. 1989: 296).

Running counter to these arguments are those which claim that tourism brings prosperity and jobs to inner-city areas, as well as high-profile environmental improvements. Evidence to support all these claims is often sadly lacking since, as Law (1992) emphasizes, few studies have assessed the impact of tourism. In Baltimore, for example, where the processes have had longest to run, Sawicki (1989) argues that many of the new jobs associated with retailing represent a geographical shift in employment within the CBD. Others have pointed to the creation of a "tourist enclave" around Baltimore's Harborplace, protecting visitors from seeing the "other" part of the city (Judd 1999). The creation of new opportunities for local businesses was somewhat limited. Indeed, the evidence from long-established tourism cities in the UK, such as Bath, suggests that while tourism has strong multipliers, there is also considerable leakage from the local economy (Bath City Council 1987). Other studies of specific inner-city projects show that job creation varies greatly between different projects, with hotels creating few off-site jobs compared with museums, retail developments and marinas (table 10.8). Furthermore, as Vaughan (1990: 24) argues, while tourism may not be providing the highest paid or skilled jobs, it is "providing jobs relevant to many of the [skills of] unemployed resident of the inner city." This somewhat negative approach is the pragmatic one accepted by many policymakers.

More recent studies of the economic impact of tourism on urban areas has been produced for selected UK cities. In the case of Birmingham, for example, in 1998 the tourism sector, including the business and conference market, supported an estimated 27,350 jobs (box 10.4).

Table 10.9 *Average expenditure patterns of conference delegates*

	Percentage of expenditure	
Items	European cities	US cities
Accommodation	44.8	43.5
Meals in hotels	7.7	10.7
Meals out	14.8	16.0
Entertainment	13.4	5.1
Shopping	14.6	9.8
Local tours/transport	4.7	6.8
Other	0.0	8.1

Source: modified from Lawson (1982)

Box 10.4   Tourism impacts on the Birmingham economy

* Birmingham receives around 22 million visitors a year.
* Most of these are day visitors enjoying sightseeing, shopping, eating out, and business.
* The overnight markets are predominantly through business tourism and visiting friends and relatives.
* £760 million was spent through tourists' visits to Birmingham in 1996/97.
* This supported 19,550 direct jobs, 7,800 indirect jobs – 27,350 jobs in total – dependent on the tourism industry in the city.
* In 1998 the National Exhibition Centre received 3.5 million visits to events and exhibitions.

Source: www.birminghameconomy.org.uk (2001)

Even if the numbers and quality of jobs are debatable, supporters of inner city tourism point to its role in helping refurbish the urban environment. Once again hard evidence is scant. However, Sawicki (1989) agrees that tourism schemes in Baltimore brought rapid improvements to the immediate inner harbor area, although there was little evidence that such environmental upgrading had spread to other parts of the inner city. Set against these limitations, however, is the fact that tourism schemes tend to produce a rapid change in the physical environment, albeit in relatively small areas.

Finally, we can return to the critical issue of whether tourism offers a viable and sustainable industry for depressed urban economies. Law

(1991b, 2000) has highlighted two features relating to such issues; one concerns the types of visitors, while the other examines trends in visitor numbers. In the case of Manchester, day visitors were dominant, representing 75 percent of all visitors. Furthermore, of those visiting from an overnight stay, only half were staying in hotels, with the rest visiting friends and relatives. Day visitors bring less economic benefits than staying tourists, as illustrated in a survey of Plymouth in Devon, where the average spend by a day visitor was £17.3 compared with £22.5 by staying tourists (Shaw et al. 1990). However, as table 10.5 showed, not all urban tourism projects are based on leisure visits, as an increasing number of cities are competing in the business, conference, and exhibition market (see chapter 2). This is an important, growing market (Exhibition Industries Federation 1990) but it is also extremely competitive. In the USA, major conference meetings have increased from just under 843,000 in 1981 to well over 1 million by 1987; while in the UK it has been estimated that there were some 700,000 conferences (including smaller ones) in 1990 (Law 1992). Unlike leisure visits, business and conference tourism generates income around hotels and, as table 10.9 shows, meals out, together with shopping. More importantly, on average, visitors to conferences spend between two and two and a half times per day more than the typical tourist (Law 1992; Smith 1989). Church et al. (2000: 329) conclude that the questioning of urban tourism's role "is a geographically uneven discourse" that involves debates over benefits, the negative externalities of tourism growth and the search for more holistic strategies.

The other issue to emerge from the reviews of urban tourism is that tourist demand is extremely variable, and highly dependent on offering new products. In other words, the implementation of an urban tourism policy is not a one-off investment. Tourist attractions and infrastructure must be constantly updated, a fact which also applies just as strongly to the conference and exhibition market. Tourism therefore can only be a viable economic policy if city authorities recognize the need for such long-term strategies. Failure to realize this, or indeed the very dynamic nature of tourist demand, could leave some cities in a similar position to many of the older coastal resorts – short on visitors and with few new jobs.

11

Rural Tourism

Tourism, Leisure, and Rural Areas

Rural areas play an important role in tourism and leisure within the developed world. For example, it is estimated that in 1990 three quarters of the population of England visited the countryside at least once (Countryside Commission 1991). Similarly, Cordell et al. (1980) consider that much of rural America has appeal to drivers and walkers. One of the defining features of rural areas is the different ways in which they are socially constructed as arenas for tourism and leisure; as idylls offering escape from the pressures of modern urban-industrial society, as untamed wildernesses which can rekindle the human spirit, or simply as large reserves of open areas suitable for space-intensive recreational pursuits. In at least some of these perspectives, rural areas are defined through their relationships to urban areas. Not least, Raymond Williams (1975), in his seminal work *The Country and the City*, argues that the country has come to be defined in terms of qualities which are absent from urban life. In short, the notions of urbanity and rurality are cultural definitions. This is an important starting point as we come to consider the production and consumption of rural tourism in this chapter.

The previous argument can be extended to rural recreation and tourism. There is nothing that is inherent in any part of the countryside that makes it a recreational resource. Patmore (1983: 122) writes that "there is no sharp discontinuity between urban and rural resources for recreation, but rather a complete continuum from local park to remote mountain peak." He rightly emphasizes the substitutability of some locales for recreation, although not necessarily for tourism. We can extend to this recognition that the location of places on this

---

Box 11.1   Rural tourism as a distinctive form of tourism production and consumption?

There are three key issues to address in considering the distinctiveness of rural tourism.

1. "Rural tourism" is a highly diverse product, ranging from farm tourism, which is deeply embedded, in "traditional" countryside workplaces and settlements, and hotels and facilities which are located in the countryside because land is cheap or offers a location alongside a major road, rather than because of the inherent characteristics of the rural area itself.

2. The definition of "the rural" is fraught with difficulties. Urry (1995) offers three possible non-chaotic definitions:

    • Areas where agricultural production is dominant.
    • Areas with particular social relationships, engendered by the ownership and control of the agricultural means of production.
    • Areas of low population density where, consequently, there are difficulties in providing collective consumption.

Tourism will have different social relationships in each of these types.

3. What is the meaning of "the rural" to the participants in rural tourism? Is it a permissive space for space-extensive activities, is it simply the site of particular non-embedded activities such as theme parks, or is it a series of places with deeply attached socially-constructed values?

---

continuum are culturally defined and or socially constructed. In this, tourism in rural areas does not differ from urban or mass tourism. However, there is an additional argument to take into account: "the countryside" has its own special appeal over and above the physical attributes that are considered by Patmore. That is to say, the countryside is socially defined as a premier area of leisure and tourism in modern societies; visiting the countryside is a socially-valued end in its own right, and can be a significant positional good. Box 11.1 provides some reflections on the extent to which rural tourism is distinctive.

While rural areas are highly esteemed as locales for leisure and tourism, their use is heavily contingent. The main contingencies are social access (reflecting free time, disposable income, and mobility) and the politics of countryside ownership and rights. The latter is nationally varied, with vast differences in the legal and customary rights to access rural land for leisure and tourism purposes. The remainder of this section considers the first of these contingencies – social access –

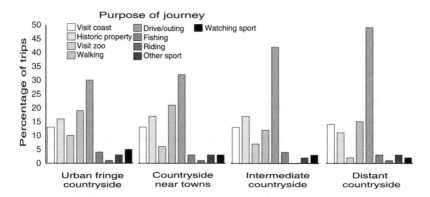

Figure 11.1 *Visitor activities in the urban fringe and countryside*
Source: Sidaway and Duffield (1984: 792)

as it pertains to the twentieth-century traditions of rural tourism and recreation in the Developed Countries. Three concepts are critical here: the rural opportunity continuum, accessibility, and time–space budgets.

There is a *rural opportunity continuum* in the countryside as the location of a wide range of outdoor leisure and tourist activities, although over time the composition of these has changed. The Countryside Commission surveys for the UK in 1977 and 1984 (reported in Harrison 1991), for example, emphasized just how quickly the use of rural areas may change. Drives, outings, and picnics were the most popular activities in 1977, followed by walks over two miles. By 1984 walks had been significantly overtaken in popularity by visiting unspoilt countryside and by visiting historic buildings. While many of these pursuits can be followed in the same spaces, where they may be complementary or conflicting, there is also a tendency for them to be segregated within the countryside. Different areas provide settings for different types of leisure activities, and there are overlap and discrete areas on the continuum. The most rugged mountain areas may be the reserve of mountaineers, but a country park near a city is likely to be an arena for varied rural leisure pursuits.

Spatial variation in the use of the countryside is also a question of *accessibility*. In the simplest terms, Clawson and Knetsch (1966: 36–8) consider that there are three types of rural recreation zones. There are accessible user-oriented areas, resource based areas with relatively scarce but often inaccessible physical attributes, and intermediate areas between these two types. Sidaway and Duffield (1984) explored some of the variations in how activities differ in relation to the location of rural sites (figure 11.1). Many types of outdoor recreational activities are of similar relative importance in all rural zones, but others significantly vary with distance from the city. In the urban fringe, visiting zoos or watching sport are relatively important; in the countryside near the towns, walking and visiting historic settlements are relatively important; in the intermediate and distant countryside, driving or outings are particularly important.

The rural opportunity spectrum does not in itself explain the varied use of different parts of the countryside. Access depends on more than simple distance, and expressed demand is not the same as latent demand, let alone need. Accessibility is necessarily socially conditioned in market economies. It depends on access to transport, either public or private. Research in the UK by the Countryside Commission (1991) confirms the socioeconomic basis of leisure use of the countryside. Frequent users tend to be young professional households with one or two cars; occasional users tend to be clerical and skilled manual households with one car; and rare users tend to be low income, unskilled, unemployed, elderly or ethnic minority households without a car. There is, then, social inclusion and exclusion in rural tourism and leisure, as there is in general well being and power in market societies (see chapter 3). This is not simply a question of household car ownership, for there are transport poor individuals in both high and low income households. The accessibility of children and of disabled persons may be constrained by lack of access to a car. In one car households, one spouse will inevitably have inferior access to transport. There is, therefore, a strong social filter on individual access to the countryside. This is not to say that the use of the countryside can be predicted from socioeconomic characteristics, for culturally-infused preferences are also important in this. Some preferred activities demand either urban or rural arenas, while others can be undertaken in both; and in the latter case, cultural values may influence whether individuals go walking in, or lunch in, the countryside as opposed to the city.

Another social filter on countryside recreation and tourism stems from the interaction between spatial distance and the *space–time budget constraints* of particular types of activities. The enjoyment of some types of rural activities requires relative large blocks of time; examples include long distance walking, or touring around remoter rural areas. Others, such as a picnic in a country park require hours rather than days. As a result, there are distinctive daily, weekly, and annual rhythms to recreation and tourism in different parts of the countryside. This can be represented in terms of a simple idealized model relating available leisure time to travel time (figure 11.2). During the working day, leisure time is limited to a few hours at best, so that most recreation for urban residents will be located within the city. If a full day is available, then the nearby countryside comes within his or her range for

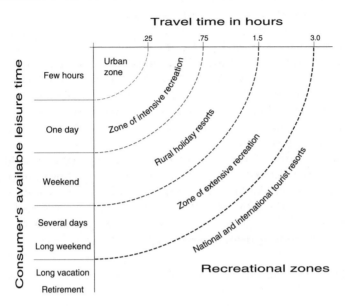

Figure 11.2 *Leisure time, travel, and recreational zones*
Source: Pigram (1983: 35)

recreation. If a weekend is available, then short-break rural tourism is feasible. Finally, if a long holiday is available, longer distance travel to remoter areas becomes possible. This is, of course, only a model of potentialities and there is no automatic conversion of leisure time into particular activities in particular rural zones. This is because of the intervening social filter of accessibility, and cultural values, as well as of competing leisure and tourism opportunities, interests, and perceptions. In this sense, a rural opportunity continuum of complex overlapping spaces provides a more realistic approximation of reality than a time–space model.

The Changing Social Construction of Rural Tourism and Recreation

The social construction of rurality can be illustrated by white Americans' relationship with "the West," and the changing role ascribed to the American national parks. The early white settlers feared the rugged and mountainous west as areas that were beyond human control (Hartmann and Hennig 1989). However, in the mid and late nineteenth century, the "wilderness" of the frontier areas came to be seen as a public good, for they were considered to offer restorative and psychological benefits, counteracting the stresses of urban-industrial life. This contributed to the national parks movement. The first national park, Yellowstone, was declared in 1872, followed soon after by the Adirondacks. At present, there are about 40 national parks in the USA, mostly in the West and Far West of the country. This symbolizes the social reconstruction of the remoter areas of the West from dangerous and feared areas to some of the most highly valued jewels in the national environmental heritage.

The white settlers' version of history is highly partial. The idea that they discovered the wilderness of the West ignores both the presence of the native North Americans and their relationships with these areas. The National Parks movement to establish preserved areas of wilderness was at odds with the native Americans' own social construction of these areas. Standing Bear wrote that:

> we did not think of the great open plains, the beautiful rolling hills and winding streams . . . as wild. Only to the white man was nature a wilderness . . . to us it was tame. Earth was bountiful and we were surrounded with the blessings of the Great Mystery. Not until the hairy man from the east came and with brutal frenzy heaped injustices upon us and the families we loved was it wild for us. (Standing Bear 1989; quoted in Katz and Kirby 1991)

In the early years of the national parks, considerable emphasis was placed on promotion: attracting visitors to the relatively little known, and – at that time – remote and spectacular wilderness areas. This was seen to be instrumental in building up support for the parks in order to counteract those hostile economic and political interests who were fundamentally opposed to their establishment. This opposition included the settlers who had been encouraged by government to develop these areas but now saw large parts of the resources of the west being "locked away" within national park boundaries; for them, new and impenetrable frontiers were being constructed within the frontier regions. Their opposition however would be drowned out by the demands emanating from a rapidly changing American society. By the end of the nineteenth century there was an expanding American middle class with available leisure time and disposable income. The railways, and later the automobile, made the national parks far more accessible to them. Places such as the Rocky Mountains national park rapidly grew in popularity; "once experienced, the cool, dry climate of Colorado's mountains became addictive for Americans seeking refuge from the hot summers of the East and Midwest" (Buchholtz 1983: 117). By 1915 wilderness was to be cherished rather than conquered. In a way, then, this illustrates how changes in time–space budgets and accessibility extended the rural opportunity continuum.

After 1945 the growth of population, disposable incomes, and free time, individual mobility and accessibility contributed to a further social reconstruction of the national parks. They became far more firmly embedded in the rural opportunity continuum for leisure. They were seen as national playgrounds and the park authorities responded by expanding the facilities offered to visitors. By the 1960s the social climate of opinion was again in transition as public concern mounted over the exploitation of the wilderness. As Buchholtz (1983: 212) writes "Observers wondered whether park planners had curried too much favour with concrete and Cadillacs." The emphasis shifted to preserving and, if necessary, recreating the natural. Public access to the most congested places was reduced, and the 1964 Wilderness Act set aside large expanses to be preserved in their "primitive" state. These roadless areas within the national parks, mostly in the West (figure 11.3), were to be visited but not remained in. In effect, this was an attempt to relocate the parks on the rural opportunity continuum. However, in no way has this reduced the attractiveness of the national parks and visitor numbers doubled to an estimated 282 million between 1972 and 1986. Indeed, the designation of wilderness areas was very much in sympathy with the growth of the consumer movement in the USA and the demands for quality consumption, whether in terms of goods or leisure time. Arguably, the attachment of National Park status to particular places served to reinforce the signifiers that attracted tourists.

The wilderness emphasis was an attempt to preserve the "natural" element within the national parks. However, as Katz and Kirby (1991: 266) forcefully argue, the national parks are simulacra (copies without originals) of primordial nature: "Yosemite . . . is as much a construction as Disneyland, and perhaps more insidious in that its construction is concealed within a supposedly external nature." As such the present social construction of the national parks can not be taken as fixed and may well shift again as the social construction of rural tourism and leisure changes. In the same way, the use made of them and the values attached to them may shift in response to changes in time–space budgets, accessibility and in the rural opportunity continuum. Not least, that continuum is becoming increasingly internationalized, as increasing numbers of affluent tourists search for wildernesses in locations as remote as the Antarctic.

The European experience of rural tourism and leisure is somewhat different from that of the USA, not least because wilderness (however defined) has hardly existed in Europe in recent decades, or even centuries. Hence, European national parks are mostly attempts to preserve cultural landscapes and are very different from those found in the USA,

Figure 11.3   *The US national wilderness preservation system*

Canada, Australia, and Africa, many of which seek to preserve "primordial" landscapes. Nevertheless, the social construction of some of Europe's remoter rural areas has changed substantially over time, and this provides some parallels with the experiences of the USA (see box 11.2). In broad terms, there have been four phases ranging from aristocratic tourism prior to the nineteenth century to new middle class rural tourism at the end of the twentieth century. Two areas which provide particularly close parallels with North America are the Scottish Highlands and the Alps.

Tourists' social construction of the Highlands has passed through at least five main phases (Butler 1985). Pre 1745 was the "age of the

> **Box 11.2   Changing forms of rural tourism in Europe**
>
> 1. Pre nineteenth century: occasional use of country estates by aristocracy as "second homes"; occasional return visits to family by rural-urban migrants.
> 2. Nineteenth century: romantic "discovery" of "wilderness" areas and particularly valued landscapes, such as the Alps and Scottish Highlands.
> 3. Post 1945: large scale outmigration generates return visiting family and friends (VFR) tourism, combining low cost holidays with the reaffirmation of social relationships.
> 4. Late twentieth century: weakening of outmigration and associated VFR tourism; growth of new middle class rural tourism in response to changes in the tourist gaze.
>
> *Source*: after Cavaco (1995)

explorer." The Highlands were little known and were perceived as an uncivilized and dangerous place. Travel was difficult given the terrain, the lack of accommodation and the language barrier posed by the prevalence of Gaelic. The Highlands had also been the scene of recent bloody revolt against the English crown. These were relatively inaccessible areas, and few potential tourist had the time–space budgets or other resources that were required to travel there. In contrast, the second phase, 1746 to 1810, can be characterized as the age of the "first tourists." Scotland was still perceived as something of a wilderness, but one of growing interest to the naturalist and accessible to the intrepid traveler. There was a growth in visitor numbers, travel became easier and guide books on the region began to be published.

The third phase was "the age of romance, red deer, and royalty." The Highlands were socially reconstructed as a romantic area, not least because of the images painted in Sir Walter Scott's popular writings. Rail services to Glasgow and steamer services up the west coast also opened up access to the Highlands. In 1846 Thomas Cook began to organize accompanied tours to the Highlands for the growing numbers of middle class tourists, effectively reducing risk and uncertainty for the traveler and enhancing their perceived accessibility. The final seal of approval on the romantic but tame wilderness of Scotland was Queen Victoria's leasing of Balmoral Castle in 1848. The fourth phase, 1865 to 1914, can be characterized as the age of "railways, hotels, and sportsmen." The expansion of the railway system into the Highlands was followed by a wave of hotel construction, and the emergence of resorts (really touring centers) such as Oban and Inverness. Individual travel for active tourists, such as hunters, and landscape consumers had now become highly accessible for the middle classes. Finally, in the twentieth century, in the age of the automobile, the Highlands have become "a popular playground for the car owner." The Highlands had become firmly lodged on the rural opportunity continuum, albeit mainly at the long holiday end of this, as a result of changes in accessibility, time–space budgets, growing affluence, and the social reconstruction of the area.

There are parallels between the Scottish and the American experiences. A change in social construction led to and accompanied a growth in tourist numbers. Images of tranquillity and natural beauty attracted large numbers of visitors but, in turn, these threatened to undermine the social constructs that had given appeal to the areas. There is, however, a fundamental difference between them: the Highlands were essentially a cultural landscape with a few areas of wilderness. It has, therefore, not been feasible to return them to even a simulacra of primordial nature. Furthermore, any attempt to freeze the existing cultural landscape would have conflicted with the aspirations and needs of the communities that lived in these areas.

In the late twentieth century, the growth of incomes, leisure time, and mobility, among all except the underclass, has led to more intense demands being made on rural areas as locales for recreation and tourism. At the same time, the social construction of rural areas in the developed world has undergone further, often subtle changes. Perhaps inevitably, this has been the source of increasing conflicts over the use of the wilderness and national park areas: between local communities and tourists, and between different sub-categories of these. The middle classes, in particular, tend to place considerable value on appreciating "nature" and "rurality." Urry (1990) argues that this can be linked to postmodernism and the disillusionment with the effects of modernism, such as regimented and massive architecture (and tourism/leisure spaces). This is also associated with the demand for so-called "alternative" holidays, which are partly defined in terms of their difference to mass tourism and non-reliance on large-scale tour companies (see chapter 12). Not surprisingly, rural areas – and the opportunities they provide for more individualized tourism and recreation – have figured prominently in these new forms of consumption.

Both Urry (1990) and Thrift (1989) believe that the service class has been particularly influential in the new movements. The service class is "a powerful . . . social grouping which has begun to impose its framework upon much of wider society, and hence its distinctions of taste have become highly significant for other classes and social groups" (Urry 1988: 41). The service class has attached particular symbolism to both the countryside and heritage in its value systems. This is reflected in the more than five-fold increase, between 1971 and 1987, in the memberships of organizations such as the National Trust and the Royal Society for the Protection of Birds (Thrift 1989). Further evidence of this cultural shift is provided by the Countryside Commission (1991) which found that frequent users of the countryside tend to be young professionals, who are mobile and wealthy enough to be able to maximize their use of the countryside.

All of this has a strong impact on rural communities, and is also leading to growing pressures to open up access to private and publicly owned land in the countryside – the issue of the politics of countryside ownership and rights that was mentioned in the introduction. It also contributes to the demands for preservation of the "traditional" countryside (itself created by economic and political changes in the eighteenth and nineteenth centuries in many cases), and for stronger controls on modern agriculture and other economic uses of the countryside. Harrison (1991: 157–8) writes that "the pastoral idyll of the post-enclosure landscape is revered – the countryside aesthetic – but scant attention is paid to the conditions of rural society which support it." In other words, the service class demands are for the countryside to be constituted principally as a zone of tourism, leisure, and consumption, rather than as a zone of production. We turn to this theme in the following section.

Trouble in Paradise: Competition and Conflict in Rural Tourism

The construction of the countryside as a zone of consumption necessarily results in a number of sharp contradictions. The first of these is the reality that, in market economies, most rural land is in private ownership, which potentially severely constrains access. Second, there are many social constructions of rural areas – as pastoral idylls, as areas of recreation, and as production zones. All or some of these may come into conflict with each other. There is the potential for host–guest conflict, which is given a special twist in developed societies by second home ownership. But there are also potential conflicts between different groups of tourists and visitors – for example, between those seeking peace and tranquillity and those wanting to practice noisy pursuits (Butler 1998). Finally, there is the question of the rural residents' own access to recreation.

Space is critical to many forms of outdoor recreation, but value may also be attached to land if it possesses particular attributes such as water resources, beautiful landscapes or, for example, areas suitable for mountaineering or hang gliding. Such factors incorporate both the main leisure functions of rural areas: as a setting for space-extensive activities and as an attractive landscape, visiting which is an object in itself. Yet, in practice access to rural areas is often circumscribed by the system of capitalist landownership and the rights attached to this. Restrictions on access are likely to be particularly acute in the case of accessible agricultural areas, where the immediate pressures for recreation are often intense. In the UK, for example, less than 2 percent of the population control and farm more than 70 percent of the land surface, while the bulk of the population live on just 11 percent of the land. The urban dwellers' recreational demands are likely to bring them into conflict with farmers whose main interest is the productive capacity of the land. This is particularly acute in countries with high population densities, such as the UK and Netherlands. In the USA, Canada, and Australia, the conflict over land ownership is less intense as there are large areas which are still relatively little used, and where access is relatively open despite the existence of nominal private ownership. There are also fewer conflicts in Sweden where there is a tradition of allowing recreation on private land, so that customary rights have informed the expectations of both recreation users and land owners. This contrasts with the UK where public access to the countryside has been contested. In the 1930s the Ramblers Association and other groups campaigned to secure access to upland areas such as Kinder Scout; in the 1960s and 1970s there were campaigns to open up access to publicly owned countryside areas such as reservoirs and Forestry Commission land; and in the 1980s and 1990s attention focused on the maintenance of the traditional network of rights of way footpaths, as well as the more general issue of "the right to roam."

One way to resolve the conflict between ownership and use of the countryside is for the state to intervene via purchasing land to be set aside for recreational use. This is the system in much of the USA, as well as in some European countries such as Spain. It is not, however, the approach adopted in the UK, where the national parks were constituted as areas of privately owned lands to which additional development constraints were applied by the state. This is related to the fact that they were preserving cultural and economic landscapes rather than wildernesses; apart from anything else, the costs of outright state purchase was greater than the government of the day was willing to contemplate, giving the existing economic use of and settlement in these areas. In terms of active outdoor recreation, this offered some prospects of greater control over the landscapes in the parks but it did not confer any new rights of access on the public (Patmore 1983: 175).

Even where there is outright purchase or nationalization of land for enclosure in national parks or other reserve areas, this does not obviate the conflict with private capital. The designation of parks as either wilderness or recreational zones may generate conflicts with the owners

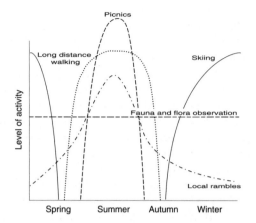

Figure 11.4   *Space–time clustering of rural recreational opportunities*

of adjoining private lands. For example, in Spain the Coto Donana has been set aside as a publicly owned National Park to conserve an internationally important wetland area. However, the attempt to conserve the sensitive eco-system in the delta, which is home to large numbers of wintering birds, is under threat from developments outside the park. More intensive agriculture and the demands of coastal tourism are affecting the water table in the Coto Donana. In this case, there is the added twist that mass tourism is adversely affecting eco-tourism.

The limited supply of available rural recreational spaces inevitably intensifies their multifunctional use. Pigram (1983: 43) writes, with respect to outdoor recreation, that "Pressure on capacity . . . may stimulate multiple use of space over time for varied activities, day and evening, week and weekend and year round rather than seasonal." An upland area may face competing demands from long distance walkers, short distance strollers, climbers, car-borne tourers, horse riders, skiers, and campers. Each of these groups makes demands on the use of the rural space. While they may vary somewhat in their temporal rhythm, there are also time periods and some zones in which they tend to coincide (see figure 11.4). The most accessible or the most attractive zones often generate the greatest conflicts, and this is when there is the greatest degree of overlap in the rural opportunity continuum.

Some of these recreational uses may be complementary, or at least non-conflicting, but some are in direct competition and may generate negative externalities for other activities. This can be understood in terms of the temporal and spatial distribution or "bundling" of activities (figure 11.4). The interests of walkers and hunters may conflict if they require simultaneous use of the same space, say at weekends in "the season." Skiers and mountain walkers may not appear to conflict directly in that they make claims on the same recreational space in different seasons. However, the skiers' activities and associated infrastructure may scar the mountain slopes and detract from their value as a setting for mountain walking. Whether activities do impinge upon each other depends on whether they, individually or collectively, exceed the recreational carrying capacity of an area – that is the level of use beyond which the regenerative capacity of the environment and, or the recreational experience is diminished (Pigram 1983).

This raises important issues of how access to rural recreation sites is or should be regulated. Price mechanisms are, of course, the characteristic mechanism for allocating goods and services in market economies. These do exist, at one level, in terms of the distribution of disposable income and mobility, while the aggregate distribution of free time in a society is also fundamentally determined by its broader politicoeconomic trajectory. These affect who can travel where, when, and the types of leisure equipment they can buy. However, there is generally an absence of direct market mechanisms to control access to rural spaces, for there are usually no "gate" fees to control entry to these. State direct intervention is also limited, as rationing access to rural recreational zones has usually been too politically contentious for most governments. Instead, public policy has largely been confined to less sensitive controls such as creating alternative attractions to divert tourists and recreationalists from the most popular beauty spots. This was the logic behind the UK's 1968 Countryside Act which facilitated the establishment of country parks near the larger cities; the aim was to create intervening recreational opportunities so as to influence the flows of rural recreation. If such policies fail to constrain the pressures on particular recreation sites, then rationing by tolerance is the outcome; those who use the site at peak times are those who are willing or better able to tolerate the presence of large numbers of other users. There is implicitly uneven social access in this resolution of the recreational carrying capacity problem. Those who have more flexible work/leisure arrangements and high disposable incomes – such as some professionals, high salary households without children of school age, and the wealthy active retired – are those most able to avoid the peak usage times at nearby sites, or to travel to more distant ones. In contrast, employees in factories and other workplaces where fixed holiday periods are customary (such as coal mining), are least able to avoid these peak times.

One of the most contentious issues in the use of the countryside is second homes. Place loyalty is often a feature of rural recreation and tourism and, in its most extreme form, this is manifested as second home ownership. Second home ownership is widespread in Europe

---

Box 11.3   German second home ownership

a)   Numbers of second homes owned by Germans in the 1990s

Germany	580,000
Spain	300,000
France	100,000
Italy	80,000
Portugal	65,000

b)   Motivations for buying second homes in Sweden

There are three main types of purchasers:

"Devoted fans of Sweden": have traveled extensively in Sweden, very interested in outdoor activities, and may have friends and relatives living there.
"Dedicated cottagers": primary motivation is to escape the pressures of urban life in Germany, and to have a base for relaxed and tranquil leisure.
"Coincidental and impulsive cottagers": impulse buyers on a first and second trip to Sweden who took advantage of low prices following devaluation of the Swedish currency in the mid 1990s.

Source: based on Müller (1999)

---

although there are significant national differences: second home ownership rates range from 22 percent in Sweden to only 2 percent in the UK (Shucksmith 1983). In terms of international second home ownership, Germany is probably the leading source country in Europe; while the main targets are the southern European countries, there are also many who seek out rural idylls in Austria or Scandinavia (box 11.3). The differences can be explained in part in terms of the economics of the housing market, cultural evaluations of town and country, and the inter-generational links between urban and rural families. For example, late and rapid urbanization in southern Europe means there are large numbers of first or second generation city residents. They often inherit what had previously been family houses in the countryside and these provide them with second homes. But there are also societies, particularly the Scandinavian ones, where second homes or "cottages" have deep cultural attachment. For example, Williams and Kaltenborn (1999: 223) argue that:

The cottage provides continuity of identity and sense of place through symbolic, territorial identification with an emotional home. . . . The cottage provides continuity across generations within the family and across the life course within a generation. The cottage provides for family

Table 11.1 *Contrasting economic and cultural effects of second homes*

	Weekend homes	Second homes
Economic	Greater	Lesser
Housing market	Equal	Equal
Local schools	Equal	Equal
Local services	Greater	Lesser
Cultural	Greater	Lesser

togetherness that is distinct from often segmented lives and schedules that are felt to characterize most urban households.

The use made of second homes is highly variable (Williams and Hall 2000). They can, in effect, be dual first homes with the family dividing its time equally between this and the town residence. This is very much the pattern found around London, New York, and other large cities, where a rural home is used most weekends as a complement to a city apartment. Alternatively, the second home may be located in a more distant region; Parisian families own second homes in the South of France and Madrid families own second homes in distant Spanish provinces. Second home ownership may also be internationalized. For example, there is considerable German ownership of second homes in Sweden (Müller 1999), and British ownership of such dwellings in France (Buller and Hoggart 1994) and the Mediterranean countries (King et al. 2000). In these cases visits may be made less frequently, and involve seasonal long stays. The distribution and intensity of use of second homes, then, can also be understood in terms of accessibility and time–space budgets. They are also embedded into the rural opportunity continuum, although their use spans a large part of this depending on whether they are used for long holidays, dual residences, or places for weekend breaks.

All these different forms of second home ownership have implications for local communities (table 11.1). They have impacts on local school rolls (and hence school viability) and housing markets. However, weekend homes are likely to bring economic benefits to the community, offer more custom to local services and can provide leaders who help to enervate community life. However, where second homes form a large proportion of the local housing stock this can seriously undermine the viability of rural communities as, for example, sometimes happens in the English Lake District, where they outbid locals in the housing market. Similarly, Vincent (1987: 117) notes in the Val de Aosta

(Northern Italy) that the sale of farm houses as second homes can mean that "a culture once meaningful to locals becomes a hollow theatre for tourists." They can, therefore, become an object of political conflict and, where this is combined with cultural and linguistic issues, to violent protests as in North Wales in the 1970s and 1980s.

Finally, there are the often-neglected issues of rural residents' leisure and recreation. Other than in terms of access to the open countryside, there is a hierarchy of recreational facilities that leaves rural residents at a disadvantage. While villages may possess a football pitch and, sometimes, even a swimming pool or a squash court, they will not have cinemas, major spectator arenas, or leisure centres. Access to these will depend on mobility, distance, and the social filter of accessibility. Therefore, in terms of access to facilities, rural leisure deprivation is the mirror image of urban leisure deprivation. The actual extent of rural leisure deprivation is highly variable. This is well documented in the case of the UK: Ventris (1979) has found considerable differences between villages according to their size; Hill (1982) found different patterns between newcomers and locals; and Glyptis (1989) found differences according to location, gender, class, age, and mobility. In general, there is little difference between rural and urban populations in terms of their interests, but considerable variations in terms of the choice and quality of facilities available.

Rural Economies and Restructuring: The Roles of Rural and Farm Tourism

Rural economies have been subject to increasingly strong pressures to restructure in the face of increased competition consequent upon globalization and the gradual weakening of state intervention. With output outstripping demand, and prices being depressed by both market forces and the reduction of state subsidies, there have been consequences not only for farming but for the associated manufacturing sectors (for example, food processing) and producer and consumer services that are dependent on farm and farm household expenditures. Throughout the developed world, rural economies have been restructuring in response to these pressures. Both through the decisions of individual farm capitals and state interventions, there has been a gradual diversification of rural economies. Tourism has often been at the forefront of such restructuring, and is often seen as a panacea for the economic ills of rural areas. In other words, tourism tends to figure large in the productionist-post productionist paradigm shift in rural areas. As Britton (1991: 474) states:

the promotion of domestic tourism, and attraction of overseas visitors where feasible, has become a commonly espoused panacea for economic diversification and revival in peripheral provincial localities in advanced capitalist countries.

A number of functions are ascribed to tourism development: to sustain and create incomes and jobs, to contribute to the costs of economic and social infrastructure such as road improvements, to foster the development of other sectors through horizontal and vertical linkages, to contribute to local residents' amenities (for example, supporting the year round costs of a local leisure center), and to contribute to the conservation of the natural and cultural features of an area (through both direct expenditures, and increased local state tax revenues).

Rural tourism development has a number of features which differentiate it from urban tourism (see chapter 10). First, given its scale, it is more likely to be dependent on endogenous investment and local labor, and less likely to be dependent on external capital. Second, the markets for rural tourism are different, and it is less reliant on business and cultural tourism, and more dependent on nature and relaxation tourism and, arguably, on VFR tourism. Third, although some rural areas are favored above others, rural tourism is generally more geographically dispersed within these than urban tourism is within cities. Fourth, given the scale of rural communities, and the reliance on small scale accommodation providers, the nature and intensity of host–guest relationships are different to those in urban areas; one particular aspect of this, discussed earlier, is the impact of second home ownership on rural communities. Fifth, given the dependency on outdoor activities, rural tourism tends to be more prone to seasonality than urban tourism. Sixth, rural tourism is likely to be closely integrated with rural production, in the form of farm tourism. Farm tourism is probably the most distinctive feature of the rural tourism economy, and this is the subject of the remainder of this section.

Most rural tourism enterprises probably do not differ significantly from tourism enterprises in general (see chapters 5 and 6), although there is less likely to be external or transnational capital, while intermediaries – such as tour companies – play a lesser role. However, farm tourism does constitute a distinctive form of production, because tourism is closely intertwined with farming, and often with the viability of the household economy. In the Developed Countries, the already substantial farm tourism market is expanding strongly. On the demand side, this is fueled by growth in the short break holiday market, reflecting changes in time–space budgets, especially the fragmentation of free time as working hours become more flexible (see chapter 1). There has also been a shift from passive to more activity-based holidays, and rural areas are seen as providing an arena for a range of such activities. Additionally, there has been the growth of more critical consumers reacting against mass tourism, and a tendency to post-Fordist consumption (see chapter 9); farm tourism provides a vehicle for greater individuation and differentiation of tourism experiences. On the supply side, the global crisis of agricultural overproduction is contributing to a drive to farm diversification in both Europe and North America, with tourism being one of the more significant options available to farmers.

There are two main forms of farm tourism, and some farms participate in both of these: non-accommodation and accommodation related activities. Non-accommodation activities include farm trails, farm museums, hunting and fishing, horse riding, and catering (often featuring consumption of food produced on the farm). In effect, the farms are commodifying existing resources, whether nature, their working practices, or simply the "green" and wholesome image of farm life. Accommodation activities are the second form of farm tourism. This may involve letting serviced rooms in the farmhouse, or self catering arrangements, whether camping or farm cottages or villas. This division between the two forms of accommodation tends to involve very different social relationships between the farm family and the tourists: not only in terms of the type of services required, but also the amount of labor input, and the intensity of the host–guest relationship.

Within Europe, Austria has one of the more highly developed farm tourism sectors. For example, Pevetz (1991) considers that 30,000 farms let approximately 250,000 beds in 150,000 guest rooms in Austria. In the UK it is estimated that almost 20 percent of farms in 1990 were involved with farm tourism; 9.5 percent with accommodation, 5.5 percent with leisure activities, and 4.8 percent with horse-related activities. Similarly, farm tourism is a vital element in the household economies of several regions in Canada where there are an estimated 1,000 rural hosts, 70 percent of whom are farmers. In the USA, farm tourism is relatively less important and takes two main forms; dude ranches in the west and vacation farms, such as those found in New England (Vogeler 1977). The dude ranch is usually an enterprise dedicated solely to tourism, but the vacation farm has similarities to European farm tourism.

While there is considerable empirical evidence of the importance of farm tourism, it has proven difficult to conceptualize this. Friedmann (1980) has suggested one possible theoretical framework. She argues that there is a balance between the internal and external relationships of households, between the division of labor within the farm and its involvement in larger divisions of labor beyond the farm (that is, working off the farm). Several different strategies for generating additional income are available to the family farm which is seeking to survive in the face of changing conditions of production. Some family members may work off the farm, some may emigrate or the farm economy may be diversified, perhaps into tourism. Each of these strategies involves a different balance between external and internal relationships and has associated divisions of labor. This is important in contextualizing tourism as just one of the alternative strategies open to families, but also requiring particular divisions of labor. Not only is a certain (probably gendered) division of labor required between farm members, but involvement in farm tourism may obviate the need for, or exclude the possibility of working off the farm.

Friedmann's approach has been criticized. Here we note three criticisms related to the empirical evidence on farm size distribution, internal social relationships, and motivations.

- According to her theory, the diversification of the farm into tourism as part of a survival strategy is likely to be more important in smaller or part time farms where there is presumably a greater need for alternative non-agricultural earnings. Yet, the empirical evidence suggests that farm tourism is more commonplace on larger rather than on smaller farms in most countries.
- Goodman and Redclift (1985) argue that family farms are not an ideal type. Instead, there are many types of family farms and the balance of internal–external relationships changes during the course of the family lifecycle. This is because the amount of time not devoted to looking after dependents, and the availability of potential tourism resources (the number of spare rooms for letting), vary according to the number of children or elderly relatives in the household.
- Another qualification concerns the motivation for diversifying into farm tourism. If it is to generate investment for the agricultural sector rather than household survival, then it should not be expected that farm tourism is necessarily more common on smaller farms. Larger farms simply have more capital to invest in developing their tourism potential.

Despite these reservations, Friedmann's work does highlight the role of tourism as one element in the balance between external and internal relationships on the farm. However, there is also the need to see it as providing only a broad framework, and to take into account other influences as, for example, in Bowler et al.'s (1996) "stress tolerance threshold" approach (box 11.4).

Farm tourism makes demands for additional labor on the farm, although the volume of this and its temporal organization depends on the nature of the tourism activities. Bed and breakfast provision

**Box 11.4   Participation in farm tourism:
a "stress tolerance" approach**

The decision of family farms whether to diversify, and which type of activity to choose is dependent on external and internal stimuli. The most important of these are:

External stimuli
- external capital sources
- state regulation
- market trends
- technological changes
- the role of external agencies
- the physical environment
- broader social trends, such as changing gender relationships

Internal stimuli
- profitability
- time availability within the enterprise
- employment relations
- family life course (and presence of dependents)

Source: after Bowler et al. (1996)

requires relatively fixed labor inputs on a regular basis within largely discrete time periods. In contrast, running a farm shop requires being available, on a flexible basis, for dealing with a highly variable level of demand. While the additional labor can be hired, it is much more likely to be undertaken by family members, usually the women in the household. As Bouquet (1987: 83) writes "in family-based tourist projects, economic relations double with those of kinship." This will generate new gender divisions of labor and may also affect the distribution of power within the family. There is no inevitable outcome to the new gender division of labor; it is contingent upon the nature of the farm economy, the local economy, and culture. It depends also on the role of women within the household prior to the introduction of farm tourism. Gasson (1980), for instance, considers that there are three ideal role types for farm women: as home-centered farm housewives; working farm wives assisting their husbands within a clear division of labor; as women farmers on their own account or jointly. The introduction of farm tourism will have very different impacts on the gender division of labor in each of these ideal types; it is likely to fall largely on women in the first two types, whereas the outcome is uncertain in the third type.

The diversity of experiences of farm tourism is considerable but one constant is that women usually carry the burden of tourism-related work on working farms. In Austria, for example, Dernoi (1991) reports that women have a double and often a triple role in the division of labor: 81 percent of wives involved with farm tourism also have to help with the field work, and almost all do most of the household chores. Similarly in Devon, Bouquet (1982) found that technological changes in milking methods had made it possible for women to redistribute their labor from agricultural activities to farm tourism. Many of the services provided for the tourists – such as cooking or making beds – are similar to those provided for the family. Thus Bouquet (1987: 98) writes that, "the women concerned seem to have professionalised, or commoditised, a portion of their domestic labour, at the same time as defining a new field of domestic competence for themselves." While farm tourism usually involves an increase in the burden of work falling upon the farm wife, it may also increase their power within the family. Bouquet, for example, found that wives could use catering for tourists as a lever to obtain improvements to the family home.

The work implications of farm tourism also touch upon the seasonal rhythm of agricultural work. Farm tourism is usually a summer activity and it may, therefore, clash with the need for agricultural activities at particular times, such as harvest. This does not follow automatically and Neate (1987), for example, observed that on the Isles of Scilly farm and tourism work dovetail together rather than being in competition. From November to March flowers are harvested, from April to May is the season of early potatoes, and from June to October is the peak time for tourism.

Whatever the precise divisions of labor within farms, it seems likely that these are due for further reorganization as the crisis of agricultural overproduction in the Developed Countries leads to further increases in farm tourism. This raises two questions. First, whether markets for farm tourism are likely to become saturated – surely not every farm can offer accommodation or some other tourism service? Second, if there is further expansion of farm tourism and this comes to replace rather than complement farming, then the very nature of the farm and countryside experience will change. In these circumstances – where the landscape is no longer farmed in what has been seen as "traditional" ways – would farms loose some or many of their inherent attractions for tourism? In other words, is farm diversification into tourism constrained by inherent contradictions?

In reality, this may be a distant constraint in many rural areas, because tourism is not able to provide a full time alternative to farming. For example, Garcia-Ramon et al. (1995) comment that in Spain farm tourism is a "supplemental activity" in most cases, although an

Table 11.2 *Earnings from tourism in rural Southern Germany*

Cumulative % of total net income from tourism			
%	Farm	Rural*	Hotel
0–10	53.1	48.7	0
11–20	78.1	68.4	0
21–30	92.7	84.2	14.3
31–50	96.9	94.7	25.0
51–100	100.0	100.0	100.00

* Rural = non-farm, and non-farm accommodation
Source: Oppermann (1996)

important one that leads to enhanced living standards and investment in the homes. Oppermann's (1996) study of farm tourism in Germany provides some quantitative evidence on this question (table 11.2): whereas hotels in rural areas are largely dependent on the income from the accommodation they provide, only 7 percent of farms derive more than 30 percent of their total income from tourism. At one level the demand conditions may not be sufficient to sustain full time tourism enterprises, but there can also be supply side constraints with many of these lacking the required capital and marketing skills. Hjalager's (1996) study of farm tourism in Denmark provides some evidence that this is not the panacea it is often held to be: whereas farm tourism took 18 percent of the labor inputs on farms, it produced only 11 percent of their total income. The key question then is the opportunity cost of the farm tourism activity: does it detract labor from farm work, or does it utilize otherwise under-utlilized labor time? The answer is of course contingent on the circumstances of particular farm enterprises. And this raises a final point: because of the fixed and variable capital requirements of operating a successful farm tourism business, this is likely to exacerbate the already deep cleavages within rural communities. Those farms with the capital and expertise required to prosper are likely to be the larger and more successful farms. In contrast, for most farms, "as typically low entry cost and undercapitalised ventures, where proprietors have little experience, where effective marketing is financially unaffordable, and where reliance is largely on passing trade, there is a high risk of failure" (Britton 1991: 473).

12

Tourism and the Environment: The Challenge of Sustainable Tourism

Tourism and Environment Relationships

In our discussions so far, we have considered the impact of tourism on the economic and sociocultural structures of destination areas in a range of geographical settings. These discussions have, in part, made implicit assumptions about the environmental consequences of tourism which we now consider more explicitly. There are a number of critical issues that warrant attention, namely; the relationship between tourism and the environment, tourism's environmental impacts, and the difficulties in monitoring such impacts.

There is a general assumption in much of the literature that the relationship between tourism and environment is fundamental, with a strong element of mutual dependency. Such a perspective has contributed to the rapid take-up of the notions of sustainability and ecotourism, with the aim of securing this symbiotic relationship (Hunter and Green 1995; Mowforth and Munt 1998). Certainly, increasing numbers of tourists are becoming convinced of the need to preserve and protect particular environments (Holden 2000). Butler (2000) has sought to challenge this "dependency myth," arguing "that there are a number of forms of tourism which have little relationship with the environment" (2000: 339). His point is that the tourism–environment nexus is both complex and variable, and certainly operates within a framework of cost factors (for example, the price of holidays) and general tourism infrastructure. Moreover, there are strong variations in tourism–environment relationships that are contingent on the form of tourism and the type of resort. There is, of course, for any type of tourism, a point beyond which deterioration in the environment becomes a critical factor, even outweighing price economies. In such

Plate 12.1 *Elements of wildlife tourism, in Sri Lanka*

Plate 12.2 *Mass winter tourism extends into Italy's Dolomites*

Plate 12.3 *Visitor pressure and impact on the River Dart, Dartmoor (England). Note the visitor activities and the level of physical erosion along the river*

circumstances, these destinations cease to function as resorts, or at best become marginal tourism areas.

Such debates, as Butler (2000) points out, raise the issue of whether it is possible to identify the specific environmental appeal of a destination from other attracting factors. The nature of these factors is clearly relative and as such they are difficult to assess in a concrete way. Furthermore, such difficulties call into play the need to understand the relationships between tourists, tourism, and the environment. As emphasized in chapter 3, many new forms of tourist consumption revolve around environmental quality and the respect for nature. Macnaughton and Urry (1998: 212) have attempted to explore how perceptions of environmental "threat," "risk," and "loss" are inextricably bound up with wider concerns about social life. Such linkages lie at the heart of shifts in consumption and the growing interest in sustainability. However, as we have debated (chapter 3), there are difficulties in identifying what Krippendorf (1986) termed responsible tourists, and what others have labeled ecotourists or green tourists (Holden 2000). This discourse on sustainable tourism is political, social, and economic and strongly related to the agencies operating in tourism. The importance of environmental quality within the tourism industry is equally difficult to ascertain. For example, while notions of sustainability are on a wide range of government agendas, their impact within the agencies of tourism is far less clear and visible. Many commentators have drawn attention to a "green wash" or a promotional discourse using the language of "greenspeak," which does nothing more than draw attention to the environment as an attraction (Dann 1996b). Finally, consideration must be given to the role of increasing numbers of NGOs and other organizations that present themselves as guardians of the environment. Their rhetoric now shares a common language based on ideas in Brundtland and the various Earth Summits of the 1990s. However, there is lack of clarity in the strategies of many organizations and how they interact with tourism agencies.

The impact of tourism on the environment is a further complex and contested area of debate. This complexity arises because of the inconsistency of tourism impacts, which vary spatially and temporally. It is also extremely difficult to disentangle the impact of tourism from other forms of economic activity in certain destination areas. In essence there are two broad considerations that help unravel the complexity of tourism–environmental impacts, these being: the type of tourism; and the characteristics of the environment.

As discussed in chapter 4, there are a range of tourist types whose motivations, modes of travel, and behavior impact on destination areas. A critical and significant challenge to many destination environments has been the rapid growth and spread of mass tourism since the 1970s. As we have shown, it is usually characterized by being large-scale, relatively low cost and often highly seasonal (see chapter 9). This form of tourism has commodified international travel and, because of its obviousness and scale, has attracted considerable attention from environmentalists. However, it would be wrong to equate the more luxury/elite forms of tourism with having minimal impact. For example, luxury hotels may demand more land, use disproportionately more energy and water, while tourists may expect more facilities, for example marinas, golf courses. Butler (1999) goes further, arguing that many types of ecotourism tended to be based in sensitive environments, where even moderate use may have significant consequences. Of course, set against this is the fact that far fewer tourists are involved, so the aggregate impacts associated with large numbers, which could exceed local carrying capacities, may be avoided.

The complexity of tourism impacts is also conditioned by the scale, character, and diversity of the environment. In terms of the natural environment, it is often the case that tourism activities are drawn to some of the most fragile and sensitive areas, largely because such factors add to environmental attractiveness. For example, in Europe, two of the most popular regions attracting mass tourism are the Alps and the

Mediterranean, both of which contain highly sensitive ecosystems (European Environment Agency 1998).

As we previously argued, the nature of tourism–environment relationships are obviously contingent on the characteristics of the destination areas. In this context, much of the literature on tourism impacts has emphasized negative aspects, constructed around the notion of a tourism industry entering and despoiling some "natural" environment. While this view may reflect the experiences of many countries and regions, it is a simplistic perspective since tourism occurs in a diverse range of environments. In some situations, the environment is so damaged by past industrial processes that tourism development is expected to help upgrade environmental quality. This is certainly true in many inner-city areas, where tourism is being used to promote urban regeneration (chapter 10). In other situations, tourism's role can turn from being negative to positive with regard to the environment. For example, although in a number of older seaside resorts, past tourism developments may have created environmental problems, future improvements can be based on using appropriate tourism developments to aid in enhancing the environment (ETB 1991). The latter example also serves to underline the dynamic nature of tourism–environment relationships and how the balance between perceived negative and positive impacts change over time (Shaw and Williams 1992).

A final factor that adds complexity to the relationship between tourism and environment is that of monitoring and assessing impacts. In much of the debate such measurement and monitoring problems have been consistently neglected. Butler (2000) argues that this neglect is due to the long-term nature of potential impacts which are difficult to accommodate in much of the funded short-term research within tourism. In addition, most tourism impacts occur within uncontrolled settings which make a scientific approach to monitoring difficult and expensive (Butler 2000). To date, where such work has taken place, it has largely been focused on National Parks and examined processes of land degradation (Marion 1995).

The Sustainable Tourism Paradigm

Notions of sustainability are grounded in political discourse and ideologically are part of the rise of a "new" consumerism (see chapter 3; Mowforth and Munt 1998). Within tourism the ideology of sustainability has had a significant impact leading to the emergence of a sub-discipline, sustainable tourism. The ideas surrounding this have largely evolved from two main strands. One is a broader concern linked with the increased awareness of the general environmental consequences of

> **Box 12.1 Key ideas for sustainable development in the Brundtland Report**
>
> - Planning and strategy making should be holistic.
> - The importance of preserving essential ecological processes.
> - The need to protect both human heritage and bio-diversity.
> - Development should occur in such a way that productivity can be sustained for future generations.
> - Inter-generational social considerations.

economic development, as highlighted in the influential Brundtland Report (WCED 1987), which presented a working definition of sustainable development. By contrast, the second strand was much more specific, relating to perspectives on the impacts of mass tourism on the physical, sociocultural, and economic environments of tourism destination areas.

The Brundtland Report established clear, basic principles for sustainable development and, while not entirely new, it gave strong recognition to the issue of equity. It called for a far greater convergence between rich and poor nations in the global system as a condition for stability and sustainability (box 12.1). During the 1990s, certain aspects of the report were criticized, mainly for its message of economic growth through Western-technocentric development (Adams 1990; Sharpley 2000). Clearer ideas concerning sustainable development have been outlined in the IUCN's report (1991) which gives more prominence to the need for developed economies to promote sustainable lifestyles among their citizens. This shifts the emphasis to the human aspects of resource sustainability rather than being solely centered on environmental problems.

Such ideas were, in part, already being loosely debated within tourism following the rise of mass tourism during the 1970s. In this context, a range of commentators had already drawn attention to the destructive force of tourism, while others sought to draw together the various contexts of the impact of tourism in a range of geographical settings (see chapters 3 and 4).

One of the major criticisms of the notion of sustainable tourism is the lack of clarity concerning its definition (Bramwell et al. 1996; Butler 1990; Wheeller 1991). According to the opening editorial of the first volume of the *Journal of Sustainable Tourism* (1993), sustainable tourism is "a positive approach intended to reduce the tensions and frictions created by the complex interactions between the tourism industry, visitors, the environment and communities which are host to holidaymakers." However, there is another key element which is fundamental to the concept and more in line with the definition of sustainable development (de Kadt 1992): it is also an approach which involves working for the long term viability and quality of both natural and human resources. It is not anti-growth but it recognizes that there are limits to growth (Bramwell and Lane, 1993). In this context sustainable development acknowledges that limits to growth will vary geographically and, according to the specific management practices adopted in different areas. Of course, such ideas may be directly applied to sustainable tourism. Sustainable tourism development therefore recognizes that for many areas tourism is an important form of economic development and as such should be managed effectively and in sympathy with indigenous resources. Equally, attention can be directed at tourists themselves and in these terms sustainable tourism development highlights the need to educate tourists to become more concerned about and sensitive to the places and communities they visit (Tourism Concern 1992). Wahab and Pigram (1997) have attempted to encompass all these aspects, arguing it is vital that sustainable tourism is embraced as a valued concept by planners, developers, consumers, and host communities in order for tourism to avoid causing its own destruction.

As a result of the nature of sustainable tourism's development "as a paradigm," the notion itself has unfortunately become associated with a plethora of different terms which refer to tourism development "other" than mass tourism. Some commentators have suggested that sustainable tourism can be viewed as an alternative to mass tourism. A view refuted by Butler (1992) who argues that mass tourism need not be uncontrolled, unplanned, short-term, or unstable. Butler (1999: 13) extends this view by claiming that "it has yet to be proven that all examples of mass tourism are unsustainable" and that such unproven assumptions "have led researchers away from the difficult but much more important task of resolving how mass tourism can be made more sustainable."

There are, unfortunately, a range of terms that relate to forms of alternative tourism which have evolved from the late 1980s. These include ideas of "green" (Dingle 1995), "soft" (Krippendorf 1991), "responsible" (Wheeller 1991), "low-impact" (Lillywhite and Lillywhite 1991), "endemic" (Mill 1996), and "new" (Poon 1989) tourism. There are also a number of more specific forms of alternative tourism including; "nature" (Long 1991) and "eco" (Valentine 1992). The confusion from this range of terms, tourism products, and management philosophies has created a tendency to ignore the fact that these different forms of tourism can potentially have dramatically different effects on the environment of a destination area.

Another legacy of these varied concepts of alternative tourism is that the notions of sustainable tourism have been criticized for being confused and not clearly focused. Other criticisms see the concept as fundamentally misguided (Bramwell and Lane 1993), while Wheeller (1991, 1994) harbors a very pessimistic view of the concept, believing that perhaps there is no answer to all the problems raised by mass tourism. He argues that "unless attempts to solve the ravages of tourism address the central issue of volume, then claims that there are answers to the problems are not only wrong but can be invidiously and dangerously misleading" (Wheeller 1991: 91). This line of reasoning is extreme, but does give a coherent voice to widely perceived notions about the impact of certain types of tourists. Wheeller (1991: 92) raises the argument of which type of tourist is likely to do more harm in the long term, "the mass tourist to the Mediterranean or the sensitive traveller." He points out that, "the new wave, so-called 'aware', educated, I'm going ethnic, individual traveller who is forever seeking the new, the exotic, the unspoilt . . . Inevitably they are paving the way for the prey of the mass package tour." Of course, this argument can be turned around and used as a powerful reason as to why sustainable tourism practises need to be adopted in such circumstances where additional management is required. Critics have also called into question the language and rhetoric used, since some supporters of the concept have used emotive terms such as "appropriate" or "responsible" to define aspects of planning in destination areas (Jones 1992; Wheeller 1994). Wheeller (1991: 93) summarizes part of these views by adding that, "sustainable tourism has burdened itself with conflicting, incompatible objectives."

The debate is not only confused and, as some argue, misplaced (Butler 1999; Wheeler 1994) but is also characterized more by advocacy, and lacks a critical political economy perspective (Williams and Shaw, 1999). As Wall (1996) argues, the term can be an ideology, a process, a concept, or a mere political catch phrase.

Clearly, there are concerns and criticisms over the different terms used to describe aspects of sustainable tourism, while some commentators have also raised doubts about the practicality of the concept. In an effort to overcome such concerns, it is important that we establish a coherent and workable definition of sustainable tourism. The pressure group Tourism Concern have defined sustainable tourism as "tourism and its associated infrastructures that, both now and in the future:

- operate within natural capacities for the regeneration of and future productivity of natural resources;
- recognize the contribution that people and communities, customs and lifestyles make to the tourist experience;

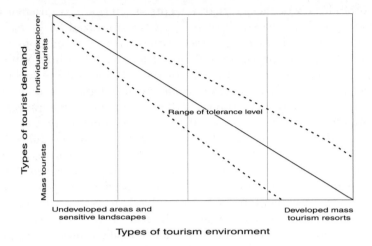

Figure 12.1   *Tourist demand and tourism environments*
Source: modified from Cooper et al. (1998)

- accept that these people must have an equitable share in the economic benefits of tourism;
- are guided by the wishes of local people and communities in host areas (Tourism Concern 1992: 1).

The core element of this definition is that tourism development, if well managed, need not lead to environmental degradation, the alienation of tourists, or members of the host communities. Also implicit in this definition is the notion that tourism will continue to grow as a global activity, but that there are some limits to growth and, more importantly, that these can be managed.

The Environmental Impact of Tourism

As we have previously stressed, tourism is a diverse activity in terms of both production and consumption patterns and consequently its environmental impacts are, in turn, varied (figure 12.1). As with its sociocultural impacts (chapter 4) there is a tendency for much of the literature to emphasize the negative consequences of tourism. Of course, these are significant, but to focus merely on these aspects is to give a partial view. The growth of tourism, especially mass tourism (chapter 9), has had a range of impacts on all types of natural and built environments (table 12.1).

Tourism can lead to the direct destruction of biotopes through the construction of tourist facilities such as hotel complexes, theme parks, and marinas. More significantly, such developments are often set within sensitive landscapes that form the backdrop to the tourism industry, especially coastal, mountain, and heritage environments. Within these different landscapes, a whole range of development processes, pollution, and degradation occur. These impacts can arise either from direct or indirect aspects of tourism developments and visitor pressures. Perhaps the simplest way to view such environmental impacts is to consider tourism developments within specific environments.

Coastal areas hold particular attractions for tourism, and in major playgrounds such as the Mediterranean there has been widespread destruction of local ecosystems. Tourism developments have destroyed sand dunes, while pleasure craft have caused considerable damage to reefs and marine life. Similarly, eutrophication resulting from untreated sewage, much of it from mass tourism resorts, has had widespread consequences for water quality. One report suggests that only about 30 percent of sewage from coastal resorts is treated before being discharged into the Mediterranean (Jenner and Smith 1992). In other cases within the region, tourism has itself been harmed by the impacts of water pollution. Bercheri (1991) highlighted the case of Rimini, where waste produced by agriculture and industrial development led to polluted, algae-strewn water, which in turn reduced visitors to the resort. Such problems have also been reported along the coast of Antigua in the Caribbean, where water quality has greatly diminished (Pattullo 1996). A similar picture emerges from Australia, where water pollution has affected parts of the Great Barrier Reef, leading to the denegration of parts of Queensland's tourism industry. In these cases, tourism is clearly part of a wider system of environmental impacts which have reduced the quality of the tourism environment and the tourist experience. A particular fragile and important ecosystem within coastal margins are wetlands, which contain a high degree of biodiversity. In France, Baron-Yelles (1999) has shown how, along the Aquataine coast, tourism settlements have caused water pollution along the margins of important wetlands. More directly, Klemm (1992) records that the shortage of suitable building land in the Lanquedoc-Rousillon region led to five new coastal resorts being constructed on reclaimed wetlands, directly destroying these ecosystems. Coral reefs are also significant and biologically diverse ecosystems that are affected by tourism and other forms of human activity. These are being destroyed, either directly through the construction of tourist facilities

Table 12.1 *The advocacy and cautionary perspectives of tourism impacts on the environment*

Area of effect	Cautionary	Advocacy
Biodiversity	Disruption of breeding/feeding patterns	Encouragement to conserve animals as attractions
	Killing of animals for leisure (hunting) or to supply souvenir trade	Establishment of protected or conserved areas to meet tourist demands
	Loss of habitats and change in species composition	
	Destruction of vegetation	
Erosion and physical damage	Soil erosion	Tourism revenue to finance ground repair and site restoration
	Damage to sites through trampling	Improvement to infrastructure prompted by tourist demand
	Overloading of key infrastructure (e.g. water supply networks)	
Pollution	Water pollution through sewage or fuel spillage and rubbish from pleasure boats	Cleaning programs to protect the attractiveness of location to tourists
	Air pollution (e.g. vehicle emissions)	
	Noise pollution (e.g. from vehicles or tourist attractions: bars, discos, etc.)	
	Littering	

Resource base	Depletion of ground and surface water	Development of new/improved sources of supply
	Diversion of water supply to meet tourist needs (e.g. golf courses or pools)	
	Depletion of local fuel sources	
	Depletion of local building-material sources	
Visual/structural change	Land transfers to tourism (e.g. from farming)	New uses for marginal or unproductive lands
	Detrimental visual impact on natural and non-natural landscapes through tourism development	Landscape improvement (e.g. to clear urban dereliction)
	Introduction of new architectural styles	Regeneration and/or modernization of built environment
		Reuse of disused buildings
	Changes in (urban) functions	
	Physical expansion of built-up areas	

Source: modified from Hunter and Green 1995, Williams, 1998

or through the pollution caused by poor sewage disposal. Such problems are widespread, affecting the Hawaiian island of Oahu, the Maldives, parts of Tonga, Samoa, and East Africa (Holden 2000). Pattulo (1996) estimates that around 90 percent of coral reef ecosystems have been impacted by developments, although tourism activity probably plays a fairly minor role in most cases. There are exceptions, as along the Kenyan and Egyptian coasts, which again highlights the geographical variations in tourism impacts (Goudie and Viles 1997). For example, along the Kenyan coast, Schoorl and Visser (1991) have shown how overcrowding by tourist boats and related activities, including jet-skiing, have physically damaged the coral reef and disturbed marine life. Furthermore, Sindiga (1999) notes how the collection of shells and coral by large numbers of tourists, together with the impacts of raw sewage from coastal hotels, also degrade the coral.

Mountain landscapes are a second major environment where tourism impacts tend to be especially prominent. This is particularly true in the Alps where the exploitation of landscapes by infrastructures (hotels, ski-lifts, and cable cars) for winter tourism has had marked consequences. For example, it is estimated that in the early 1990s, some 100km^2 of forest had been removed throughout the Alps for tourism developments (see also box 9.4). In the French Alps, the impact of ski tourism on the black grouse population has been highlighted by Jenner and Smith (1992). While the exact causes are still uncertain, they may well include the growth of extensive off-piste skiing, an increase in predators attracted by litter and waste produced by tourists, and the displacement of the grouse by ski activities. On a broader level, the greater use of snow cannon to produce artificial snow to extend the ski season has brought new impacts and increased competition for water supplies. Furthermore, skiing in sparse snow conditions, a growing activity as tourist numbers increase, contributes to the significant damage of sensitive vegetation. As in coastal areas, the problems of pollution and waste treatment are increasing as visitor pressures grow. In the Alps, for example, there are difficulties in disposing of rubbish as the search for new landfill sites is being resisted by a growing number of local communities.

Similar problems are found throughout mountain environments where tourism pressures are growing. Furthermore, not all impacts are associated with mass winter tourism as, for example, the growth of trekking holidays have brought other pressures. This is highlighted by the annual arrival of some 40,000 mountain trekkers and walkers in Nepal which has created marked pressures on the environment as large areas of vegetation have been removed to accommodate tourism facilities (Sparrowhawk and Holden 1999). Increasing numbers of commentators are highlighting such developments and arguing that the growth of eco-tourism may be partially responsible, in that it markets natural environments and unique landscapes. Success brings with it the price of increased numbers which, although far less than mass tourism, involve different pressures as ecotourists are visiting far more sensitive environments (De Alwis 1998; Mowforth and Munt 1998; Shackley 1996). The degradation of mountain landscapes, especially through deforestation also releases destructive geomorphological processes that have impacts on local communities. For example, in the Austrian Alps, it is believed that the creation of 0.7km^2 ski runs for the Winter Olympics contributed to a major mudslide in 1983 (Jenner and Smith 1992).

Other fragile and sensitive landscapes include arid and semi-arid environments where even small numbers of tourists can have large scale impacts (figure 12.1). In areas as diverse as the Antarctic or parts of East Africa, delicate ecologies are easily disturbed by tourists. Even in protected areas such as national reserves in Kenya, tourism practices have conspired to create strongly negative impacts on vegetation and wildlife (Sindiga 1999). Of particular note are the problems caused by day visitors from mass tourism beach resorts to reserves such as the Maasai Mara. These create increased pressures and have led to local carrying capacities being exceeded; as Sindiga (1999: 104) explains, they "make tour drivers chase after only a few animals," as tourists usually want to see lions, leopards, buffalo, elephant, and rhino.

Our discussions so far have focused on the tourism impacts on natural environments but, of course, there are many sensitive built environments, such as historic sites and cities, which suffer from visitor pressures (chapter 10). Venice represents probably one of the most sensitive urban environment as well as being a leading city tourism destination (van der Borg 1998). It therefore serves to highlight some of the key impacts brought by tourism. A significant feature of the city has been the rapid growth of demand in the visitor market from 500,000 in 1952 to 1.45 million arrivals by the mid 1990s (van der Borg 1998). Since the 1980s a combination of factors has resulted in a rapid increase in excursionists. This changed demand was brought about by the increased internationalization of the Venetian market, along with an upgrading of supply facilities. The increased demand from higher market segments to stay within the historic core, along with a static supply of tourist accommodation in this area has driven up prices. In turn this has shifted the lower end of the tourism accommodation market into more peripheral locations in the city's hinterland, resulting in an expansion of demand and to larger numbers of visitors being transported into the historic core on a daily basis. This has produced increased traffic congestion alongside a massive growth in tourist numbers, with the carrying capacity of the core area being consistently exceeded. This reduces not only the quality of life for local people, but also diminishes the tourist experience.

Venice is extreme, but not unique in that most historic cities are suffering from heavy congestion and related aspects of traffic pollution, the increased marginalization of local communities and the commodification of local facilities (chapter 10). Pollution from car traffic obviously contributes to increased amounts of carbon dioxide (CO_2), producing global warming and, on a more localized scale, acid rain – which impacts on historic monuments and buildings.

It can be seen that the negative impacts of tourism on the environment are complex and wide ranging, but in some circumstances problems may be – if not offset – certainly tempered, by potential, environmental benefits. As discussed in the introduction, tourism–environment relationships are symbiotic and, as a consequence, tourism developments may bring some elements of protection. As table 12.1 shows, such tourism benefits include; anti-pollution programmes (for example, the EU Blue Flag scheme to grade coastal water quality), and the use of tourism to help improve run-down landscapes, such as old industrial centers (chapter 10). But, of course, the balance between tourism development and the capacity of an environment to cope with change is critical in determining the outcome.

Managing the Tourism Environment: Applying the Principles of Sustainable Tourism

We have attempted to demonstrate throughout much of this book that tourism is not a simple, monolithic activity, but rather a series of complex circuits of production and consumption. As a consequence, solutions to the negative impacts of tourism must involve a range of concepts and agencies. Much of the literature has characterized tourism development and the environment as an unequal exchange in favor of the former (Krippendorf 1987b). However, the concepts and issues embedded within sustainable tourism provide a framework for re-addressing such imbalances and even empowering local communities. These ideas have been increasingly recognized by a range of organizations in both developed and developing countries (Holden 2000).

There are two broad areas worthy of further attention, in respect of enabling sustainable tourism. The first concerns the key techniques involved in managing the tourism environment, while the second relates to a broad band of concepts involving tourist behavior, development processes, local communities, and the agencies linking these elements.

Table 12.2 *Key techniques in sustainable tourism*

1. *Environmental impact assessment (EIA)*
   - mathematical models
   - cost–benefit analysis (COBA)
   - the materials balance model
   - the planning balance sheet
   - rapid rural appraisal
   - geographic information system (GIS)
   - environmental auditing

2. *Visitor management techniques*
   - Zoning
   - Honeypots
   - visitor dispersion
   - channelled visitor flows
   - restricted entry
   - vehicle restriction
   - differential pricing structures

3. *Carrying capacity calculations*
   - physical carrying capacity
   - ecological carrying capacity
   - social carrying capacity
   - environmental carrying capacity
   - real carrying capacity
   - effective or permissible carrying capacity
   - limits of acceptable change (LACs)

4. *Limits of Acceptable Change (LAC)*
   - review and evaluation of issues in destination area
   - identification of likely changes and suitable indicators of change
   - survey of indicators of change
   - specification of quality standards associated with tourism development
   - desired conditions within development area
   - management to maintain quality

5. *Area protection*
   - national parks
   - wildlife refuges/reserves
   - biosphere reserves
   - country parks
   - biological reserves
   - areas of outstanding natural beauty (AONBs)
   - sites of special scientific interest (SSSIs)

Source: modified from Mowforth and Munt (1998)

In this short chapter, it is not possible to give detailed coverage to all the tools available to sustainable tourism research, although table 12.2 gives a basic overview. As can be seen, these range from fairly basic visitor management techniques of zoning and restricted access, through to more sophisticated tools of environmental analysis (Wight 1998). Of course, these are not mutually exclusive, but rather part of an increasing array of available techniques, which are often complementary.

Environmental impact assessment (EIA) is an overarching and widely used technique for evaluating the possible consequences of tourism and other forms of development. It originated in the USA

Box 12.2   Environmental impact assessment: key principles

Assessments should:
- identify the nature of the proposed and induced activities that are likely to be generated by the project;
- identify the elements of the environment that will be significantly affected;
- evaluate the nature and extent of initial impacts and those that are likely to be generated via secondary effects; and
- propose management strategies to control impacts and ensure maximum benefits from the project.

Source: Adapted from Hunter and Green (1995) and Williams (1998)

---

during the late 1960s following the passing of the National Environmental Policy Act which required EIAs to be made for significant developments (Weston 1997). Within the EU the technique has been given further prominence since the late 1980s and more especially in 1997 when it was recommended that major tourism developments, such as hotel complexes, marinas and ski-lifts be subject to EIA. The technique is not based on any set structure, but rather a number of key principles (box 12.2), and usually involves five main stages. These involve; the identification of impacts, the measurement of impacts, the interpretation of the significance of impacts, the presentation of the assessment results, and the recognition of appropriate schemes of monitoring. As table 12.2 suggests, there are a diverse range of methods used by EIA, including the basic mapping of impacts, through to more sophisticated mathematical models and environmental auditing (Wathern 1988).

Environmental impact assessment techniques are now more widely used in the planning stage of many large-scale tourism developments (Williams and Shaw 1992). However, the technique is not without its drawbacks, which include its costly nature in the early planning stages. This is particularly important within tourism in view of the fact that the cost is often paid for by the developer, which raises questions over objectivity and ownership (Holden 2000; Wight 1998). In addition, many tourism developments are small-scale, but cumulative in their environmental impacts. Such developments are often too small to invoke EIAs, which may, in any case, be too costly. In these situations EIAs may need to be part of the local state's planning response to tourism development.

Another of the long established, though still much contested techniques, is that of carrying capacity. Its origins lie within ecology, but it

---

Box 12.3   The calculation of physical carrying capacity

Physical Carrying Capacity (C) = T/A

Where: C = carrying capacity
T = total area used by tourists
A = average individual standard as measured by the amount of land required for each individual activity

In addition, the number of allowed daily visits can be obtained by:

$$T_d = C \times R_c$$

Where: T_d = total daily visits
C = carrying capacity
R_c = rotation coefficient

$$R_c = N_d/A_v$$

Where: N_d = number of daily hours area is open for visitors
A_v = average time of visit

---

is now a popular idea within tourism management (Cooper et al. 1998). At its most basic, it measures the level of visitor use an area can sustain (see box 12.3). However, there are a range of definitions and there are also measurement problems, as some of the data inputs are rather subjective. For example, the World Tourism Organization (1992: 23) defines carrying capacity as "the maximum use of any site without causing negative effects on the resources, reducing visitor satisfaction, or exerting adverse impact upon the society, economy and culture of the area." This highlights the complexity of the concept in that it can relate to more than just the physical environment. In this context O'Reilly (1986) identified carrying capacities relating to environmental, economic, social, and psychological factors; similarly Farrell (1992) argued that there were at least four types of carrying capacity (table 12.3). Of course, as the WTO definition suggests, these four types of carrying capacity are inter-related. Furthermore, establishing carrying capacities may not only be a subjective exercise, it can also prove extremely difficult. For example, environmental or ecological capacities are difficult to measure and may relate to management practises or even economic factors. Mowforth and Munt (1998: 119) claim carrying capacity calculations can be manipulated by tour operators, officers of conservation organizations, or government officers to promote either a destinations exclusivity (a low carrying capacity) or its ability and potential to absorb more visitors (a high carrying capacity). They also provide one of the few detailed examples of the calculations involved

12.3 *Types of carrying capacity*

Type	Main characteristics
Environmental	the degree of tourism impact on the physical (natural and built) environment
Economic	the degree of dependency the economy has on tourism
Social	the degree of tourism impact on the host community
Psychological	the degree of visitor satisfaction associated with a particular destination

for deriving physical, real, and effective carrying capacities within the context of Guayabo National Monument in Costa Rica (see also Cooper et al. 1998; Butler 1997).

Clearly, the notion of carrying capacity is open to criticism as being both subjective and over-mechanistic. Holden (2000) goes further and highlights those who see the technique as totally discredited, as for example Coccossis and Parpairis (1996). In reality, carrying capacity is still utilized, but does vary according to prevailing management practises and who decides on acceptable levels. These decisions are "subject to multiple determination" although it is possible to give some guidance regarding "the variables that may be measured, the thresholds that be encountered and the effects of over-exploitation" (Cooper et al. 1998: 195).

An important alternative to carrying capacity is the notion of the "limits of acceptable change" (LAC), which grew from attempts within national parks in the USA to resolve visitor–environment conflicts (Holden 2000; Sidaway 1995; Wight 1998). The main advantages of the LAC approach is that, unlike carrying capacity, it does not specify the visitor numbers an area can sustain. In contrast, it attempts to embody some key aspects of sustainable tourism (table 12.4) by recognizing the acceptable environmental limits of a particular area. It is pragmatic in that it also recognizes that some form of change is a consequence of tourism development, but that there are environmental, economic, and social parameters conditioning the limits of such change.

In practical terms, the approach involves identifying suitable indicators of the environmental condition of an area. As argued above, there may be, in effect, a range of indicators including levels of pollution, erosion (land degradation), wildlife disturbance, traffic congestion, and numbers employed within tourism locally. Of course, there are difficulties in both agreeing and measuring some of the variables. Moreover, as Wight (1998) demonstrates, the LAC system is highly

Table 12.4 *Elements of the limits of acceptable change approach*

Initiate and identify issues
- Define issues and concerns

Goals
- Define and describe opportunity classes

Standards and indicators
- Select indicators of resource and social conditions

Inventory and evaluation
- Inventory existing resource and social conditions
- Specify opportunity class standards
- Identify alternative opportunity class allocations

Actions, implementation, and monitoring
- Identify management actions
- Evaluate and select alternative management actions
- Implement and monitor

dependent on a well-structured planning system at both national and local levels.

The key techniques discussed above can only operate within receptive frameworks, both in the public and private sectors. An important issue in this context concerns the notion of stakeholders and partnerships within tourism. The stakeholders within tourism cover a range of geographical scales and are increasingly global in nature. However, in terms of applied, practical action, the main stakeholders very often need to be considered within defined spatial areas, which may vary from the macro-regional scale, as in the Alps or Rocky Mountains, to the micro-scale, such as a sustainable tourism plan for a particular village. The main stakeholders are: host communities; tourism industries; tourists; public bodies; and non-government organizations.

With respect to tourist behavior, it is argued that there is a need to inform and educate visitors about the destinations they are visiting. Such education operates at two levels; the need to change societal values (macro-level) and the need to inform about specific destinations. Both are difficult, but the macro-level changes are the most problematic as well as being most significant. There are signs, as we argued in chapter 3, that there are shifts in the value systems and consumption patterns of some tourists. At the micro-level, the attitude of tourists to

Box 12.4   Codes of conduct for tourists

- Use public transport, or other means of travel that are environmentally friendly, e.g. cycling or walking.
- Avoid peak times of the year or week for a visit, to help ease overcrowding. This is obviously difficult for many tourists, given the institutional constraints of national school holidays, and as such need to involve other organizations.
- Treat the physical environment with care by not leaving litter, keeping off areas not open to the public, staying on footpaths, and being sensitive to the presence of wildlife. For example, a recent survey of beaches in the UK by Beachwatch has shown a major increase in the amounts of litter left by visitors on the country's beaches. It is within this context of beach and marine environments that the EU's "Blue Flag" scheme was mounted.
- Learn about the culture, language and geography of the tourist destination area. This can make it easier to understand and be sensitive to local issues, reducing any potential hostility between hosts and guests.
- Buy local products and eat in locally-owned establishments. This can help to support the local economy. One example of this is the Rhön Biosphere reserve in Germany, which involves produce from local farms being bought by and served in local restaurants.
- Respect the culture of a locality. This involves separating the authentic artistic experiences on offer from the adapted, contrived, commodified experiences developed for tourists.

Source: Croall (1995)

the place they are visiting is important. If respect, care, and tolerance become the hallmarks of tourist behavior, then all aspects of tourism can benefit. The main thrust has been the use of voluntary codes of conduct, which have been developed by a wide range of organizations (box 12.4). For example, there are initiatives by British Airways, which gives information to travelers concerning their potential impact on destinations.

The United Nations Environment Programme (1995) has drawn attention to the codes of conduct which they argue, "are certainly the best way of ensuring long-term commitments and improvements" (1995: 3). They also stress that such codes act as catalysts for a dialogue between government agencies, the tourism industry and community interests. In this respect, such codes have been applied across a range of stakeholders within tourism. They have been outlined for the industry by both national and international organizations as, for example, by the Tourism Association of Canada (Holden 2000). There are signs that many tourism businesses are starting to identify with environmental policies and a number of voluntary codes of practice have been introduced, including the Ecomost programme developed in 1991, and the International Hotels Environment Initiative (IHEI) launched in 1992 (Williams and Shaw 1992). In the case of the IHEI, an international network of hotel companies have come together to promote environmental aspects.

Despite the widespread development of voluntary codes and their seeming ability to influence attitudes, they have not been without their critics. Such critiques encompass three broad areas. First, such codes, especially those developed within the tourism industry, are merely marketing ploys rather than attempts to develop sustainable practices. Second, there are problems associated with evaluating and monitoring voluntary codes which are based on self-regulation (Mowforth and Munt 1998). Finally, there are practical limitations in the use of such codes because of their focus on principles, rather than how environmental practices can be applied (Stabler and Goodall 1996).

It should, however, be recognized that for many tourism businesses the shift to sustainable practises is not easily achievable. Those organizations that have successfully integrated environmental management techniques have done so in a planned and well thought out way. For example, the IHEI has produced a "Green Health Check" covering; energy use, waste management, contractors and suppliers, and business ethics. More specifically, some tourist organizations in the UK have helped fund a "Green Audit Kit" organized around six main sections covering the practical aspects of environmental management (Williams and Shaw 1992). The key to operationalizing such initiatives at the firm level appears to be stimulating motivation for change (usually along economic lines) and then linking this with an action plan.

Marketing and image-making play important roles in tourism (see chapters 4 and 10). It follows, therefore, that such forces can be harnessed in the promotion of sustainable tourism. The basis of this link is that the marketing of tourism needs to be based on providing full and honest information. Strategies for sustainability build on these ideas by identifying, appraising, and constantly reviewing the supply of environmental resources, as well as demand factors. As such, marketing aims to improve the quality of natural environments, the living standards of the local community and at the same time consider the cost of environmental assets. Attempts to extend marketing strategies to embrace environmental policy have mainly centered around establishing "environmental seals of quality" or what can be termed the eco-labeling of tourism products. The principles are simple and based around identifying a range of criteria/best practice that can be applied to products and services. While the concept is simple, organizational aspects tend to be more problematic and require a high degree of co-ordination between different tourism stakeholders. Since the early 1990s such ideas have been supported in Germany, and in 1991 the newly founded organization for "Ecological Tourism in Europe" developed the idea of the "Green Suitcase," which embraced ecolabeling. This is a detailed eco-audit and a range of best practice criteria for accommodation providers as well as tour operators. One successful eco-marketing application has been the "Tyrolean Environmental Seal of Quality," operating in the Austrian Alps, which is marketed under the slogan "Manage with Nature" (Williams and Shaw 1992).

Sustainable Tourism and the Role of the State

A further major issue in the development of sustainable tourism involves the role of the state. The state in all its various forms, is a key stakeholder in the promotion of sustainable practices. It is significant because there is no market for public goods, such as landscapes and ecosystems, which means that at the present time the social costs of environmental damage is not internalized by tourism businesses unless regulations compel them to do so (Hall 2000). In this context, strate-gic and proactive intervention by the state is required to provide overall environmental management. State involvement at the national and local level is also important in ensuring the development of sustainable tourism through promotion (for example, ecolabeling), regulation, and strategic leadership (environmental auditing and management prac-tises). This has been emphasized by the take-up of issues relating to *Agenda 21*, arising from the UN Conference on the Environment and Development in 1992. This was embraced by 182 governments, who agreed to adopt a comprehensive action program for sustainable devel-opment. Within the UK, for example, this has been implemented by the local state through the creation of the *Local Agenda 21* initiative. This and other documents (Friends of the Earth 1994), have stressed the role of the local state as a key partner in implementing sustainable development, since it is best placed to provide a longer term perspec-tive, political legitimacy and a holistic view. However, in reality the local state may come under considerable pressure from a range of influen-tial economic interests. Certainly, this is a strong possibility within the tourism sector with its dominance of commercial interests that are often global in nature, and controlled by large-scale organizations.

At the inter-state level, the European Union has become increasingly involved with tourism, certainly from the 1980s onwards. Major initia-tives have included the "European Year of Tourism" (1991) and in the same year the "Community Action Plan to Assist Tourism." Most

Table 12.5   *EU Review of the Fifth Environmental Action Programme relating to tourism*

Priority actions

A: *Integration*
- Public authorities in Member States should work together to integrate environmental considerations into their tourism policy at the most appropriate level.
- Public authorities in the Member States need to develop integrated land-use planning at local or regional level.
- Public authorities in the Member States need to implement stricter control measures on land-use.
- At EU level approaches to sustainable development in the tourism sector need to be strengthened, building on suggestions in the Green Paper on Tourism and using principal instruments such as the Structural and Cohesion Funds, to support member States in their efforts to protect the quality of the environment, to change attitudes and approaches and to promote sustainable development.

B: *Protection of sensitive areas*
Member States need to develop frameworks for the protection of the environment particularly in sensitive areas such as the Mediterranean, the Baltic, the Alps, and coastal zones.

C: *Information to tourists*
Public authorities in the Member States and the tourist industry should make available to the public better information on the state of the environment in order to enable public pressure to act as a driver towards sustainable tourism; the success of the Blue Flag initiative demonstrates the importance of the public's role.

D: *Management of tourist flow*
Public authorities in Member States and the tourist industry need to examine the carrying capacity of tourist sites and take appropriate measures to manage tourist flows to the lasting benefit of the sector and the environment. The LIFE programme can be used to demonstrate the benefits of more sustainable approaches.

Source: Commission of the European Communities (1996)

important was the DGXXIII report *Taking Account of the Environment in Tourism Development*, which promoted ideas of sustainable tourism. Of greater significance has been the "Fifth Environmental Action Programme" (EAP), which has tourism as one of its five main target areas. The 1996 review established a number of key priority areas relating to tourism (table 12.5). Unfortunately, a major weakness with the EAP is its failure to link its specific aims to policy instruments, and in this context there is a need for a major review of EU policies within this area. In particular, more attention should be given to sustainability in all EU expenditures, particularly structural funds, while there is also a need for greater transparency in the use of such funds.

At the national level, a number of governments have established the basis for sustainable tourism development, if not as yet fully operational policies. For example, within the UK the English Tourist Board and now the English Tourist Council have, since the early 1990s, attempted to promote the ideals of sustainable tourism (for an overview of policy documents see www.wisegrowth.org.uk). The government's strategy for tourism in England, *Tomorrow's Tourism* (1999) has, more recently, highlighted the need to promote sustainable development within tourism and has led to the establishment of a "Sustainable Tourism Task Force." This is charged with helping to produce a sustainable tourism action plan, alongside the identification of national sustainable tourism indicators. These are based around four key themes: visitor satisfaction, industry profitability, community acceptance and benefit, and environmental protection and enhancement. The purpose of these is to give a broad overview of industry trends and developments.

Clearly, attitudes to the environment are changing and such changes are becoming locked into some forms of tourist consumption. However, if sustainable practises are to be fully embraced and made workable within tourism, all the key stakeholders have to recognize the benefits which, in turn, will lead to shifts in production methods. In other words, as emphasized in the introduction (see Ateljevic 2000), there is a need to consider the circuits of tourism production and consumption.

Tourism Internet Resources and Key Websites

Increasing amounts of information and statistics are available on the www – a number of key websites are listed in this section. The addresses given were correct as of 2001, but some may have changed. If in doubt, enter the key words of the organisation. Tourism websites are also being reviewed in some journals; see for example the Web Site Reviews edited by Buhalis in *International Journal of Tourism Research*. It is not possible to cover the vast array of national, regional, and local websites in this short list, therefore we focus on the UK, in the second part, to illustrate the range of available sources. Similar websites exist in most countries.

Topics and Websites	Characteristics
International Tourism and Aspects of Tourism Development	
World Tourism Organization www.world-tourism.org www.world-tourism.org/omt/esta	Gives access to WTO general information centre Gives access to online statistical information.
statserv.htm	Most information needs to be purchased, but free highlights are available
Tourism Concern www.tourismconcern	Established in 1989 to act as a forum for concern over tourism's impact on communities and environment, wide range of resources, including some statistics, and case examples.

Travel and Tourist Intelligence www.t-ti.com/index.cfm	Provides information on travel and tourism, market intelligence reports. Searchable database (free) but all detailed information must be purchased. Online search of TTI Magazine.
ITA Tourism Industries www.t-ti.com/index.cfm	Tourism industries is a special US government site covering aspects of tourism, including development, market research, and policy. Main focus is on international tourism.
Travel Industry Association of America www.tia.org	Wide ranging site covering domestic and international tourism. Detailed information and statistics require payment, but considerable free statistical trends data. Links to other sites.
International Ecotourism Society www.ecotourism.org/data.html	Mainly information on trends in N. America. Contains a range of free statistical information and topic reports.
Bureau of Tourism Research (Australia) www.bra.gov.au	Provides a wide range of statistics on domestic and international tourism, mainly free. Links to related sites.
Pacific Asia Travel Association www.pata.org	Provides information on marketing, research, and education. Links to Green Globe Asia Pacific. Most detailed information limited to members.

World Travel and Tourism Council www.wttc.org	Commercial pressure group for tourism and travel. Role to work with governments to realize the full economic impacts of tourism. Contains a large range of free economic data on international tourism, plus lists of publications for sale.
British Tourism Authority www.britishtouristauthority.org/	Gives range of information on BTA including history of organization, policy statements, and plans, also provides links to other tourism sites.
OECD www.oecd.org www.oecd.org/distri/sti/transpor/ tourism/news/sites.htm	Organization for Economic Cooperation and Development. Wide ranging site offering information statistics on development, labor markets, sustainability, and trade. Provides links to national tourism organizations and statistics for member states.
United Nations Environment Programme (UNEP) www.uneptie.org/	Main site of UNEP Technology, Industry and Economics, and sustainable development. Has a free searchable database and general search engine. Also has links to their tourism site – covering aspects of sustainable tourism including the tour operators initiative. Also access to newsletter *Tourism Focus*.

UK Tourist Boards and Tourism Statistics

Department of Culture, Media and Sport www.culture.gov.uk	Contains range of information and policy statements on leisure, heritage, and tourism. On tourism, main sections include tourism industry, tourism experience, and tourism planning. Has links to other UK sites.
English Tourism Council www.englishtourism.org.uk	Lists information and data, visitor numbers, and earnings. Has special section for students and research. Searchable database. Has links and lists to all regional tourist boards.
www.wisegrowth.org.uk	Information on sustainable tourism in England.
Scottish Tourism Board www.visitscotland.com	This is mainly a site for visitors and contains few statistics or research information. See www.staruk.org.uk for facts and figures on Scotland.
Wales Tourist Board www.tourism.wales.gov.uk	Has links to an industry-based website which contains facts and figures, together with annual reports. Also has a section on market research.
Northern Ireland Tourist Board www.ni.tourism.com	General site for visitors with few statistical data. For research statistics see www.staruk.org.uk
STARUK (Statistics on tourism research) www.staruk.org.uk	Main official site for tourism research. Liaison group of the UK. Gives a wide range of free statistics and publication lists.

Government Statistical Service
www.statistics.gov.uk

National statistical website, information for population and economy is available at a range of spatial scales. Includes statbase – searchable database.

Other UK Organizations Relating to Tourism

English Heritage
www.english-heritage.org.uk

Outlines scope of organization, facilities, and policy statements. Key facts can be accessed via annual reports. Also links to "Images of England" site – constructing a web-based site of England's heritage

National Trust (education site)
www.nationaltrust.org.uk

Broad ranging site, but most useful information is available via education website. Includes visitor numbers under section on marketing.

Recommended Reading

Chapter 1

Ateljevic, I. 2000: Circuits of tourism: stepping beyond the "production/consumption" dichotomy. *Tourism Geographies*, 2, 369–88.

Britton, S. 1991: Tourism, capital and place: towards a critical geography of tourism. *Environment and Planning D: Society and Space*, 9, 451–78.

Hall, C. M. and Page, S. 1999: *The Geography of Tourism and Recreation: Environment, Place and Space*. London: Routledge.

Ioannides, D. and Debbage, K. G. (eds.) 1998: *The Economic Geography of the Tourist Industry: a Supply Side Analysis*. London: Routledge.

Urry, J. 1995: *Consuming Places*. London: Routledge.

Chapter 2

Held, D. (ed.) 2000: *A Globalizing World? Culture, Economics and Politics*. London: Routledge.

Lea, J. 1988: *Tourism and Development in the Third World*. London and New York: Routledge.

Pearce, D. 1995: *Tourism Today: A Geographical Analysis*. Harlow: Longman.

Williams, A. M. and Shaw, G. (eds.) 1998: *Tourism and Economic Development: European Experiences*, 3rd edn. Chichester: Wiley.

Chapter 3

Bramham, P., Henry, I., Mommass, H., and van der Oek, M. (eds.) 1989: *Leisure and Urban Processes: Critical Studies of Leisure Policy in West European Cities*. London and New York: Routledge.

Haukeland, J. 1990: Non-travellers: the flip side of motivation. *Annals of Tourism Research*, 17, 172–84.

Richards, G. 1996: Production and consumption of European cultural tourism. *Annals of Tourism Research*, 23, 261–83.

Urry, J. 1995: *Consuming Places*. London: Routledge.

Chapter 4

Krippendorf, J. 1987: *The Holiday Makers*. London: Heinemann.

Mathieson, A. and Wall, G. 1982: *Tourism: Economic, Physical and Social Impacts*. London: Longman.

Ryan, C. (ed.) 1997: *The Tourist Experience: A New Introduction*. London: Cassell.

Sharpley, R. 1994: *Tourism, Tourists and Society*. Huntingdon: ELM Publications.

Chapter 5

Agarwal, S., Ball, R., Shaw, G., and Williams, A. M. 2000: The geography of tourism production: uneven disciplinary development? *Tourism Geographies*, 2, 241–63.

Dunning, J. H. and McQueen, M. 1982: The eclectic theory of the multinational enterprise and the international hotel industry. In A. M. Rugman (ed.), *New Theories of the Multinational Enterprise*, London and New York: John Wiley, 2nd edn.

Smith, S. 1998: Tourism as an industry: debates and concepts. In D. Ioannides and K. Debbage (eds.), *The Economic Geography of the Tourist Industry: a Supply Side Analysis*, London: Routledge.

Urry, J. 1987: Some social and spatial aspects of services. *Environment and Planning D: Society and Space*, 5, 5–26.

Williams, A. M. 1995: Capital and the transnationalisation of tourism. In A. Montanari and A. M. Williams (eds.), *European Tourism: Regions, Spaces and Restructuring*, Chichester: Wiley.

Chapter 6

Britton, S. 1996: Tourism, dependency and development. In Y. Apostolopoukis, S. Leivadi, and A. Yiannakis (eds.), *The Sociology of Tourism*, London: Routledge.

Dahles, M. and Bras, K. (eds.) 1999: *Tourism and Small Entrepreneurs: Development, National Policy and Entrepreneurial Culture: Indonesian Case*. New York: Cognizant Communications Corporation.

Shaw, G. and Williams, A. M. 1998: Entrepreneurship, small business culture and tourism development. In D. Ioannides and K. Debbage (eds.), *The Economic Geography of the Tourist Industry*, London, Routledge, 235–55.

Williams, A. M., Shaw, G., and Greenwood, J. 1989: From tourist to tourism entrepreneur, from consumption to production: evidence from Cornwall, England. *Environment and Planning A*, 21, 1693–53.

Chapter 7

Bagguley, P. 1990: Gender and labour flexibility in hotel and catering. *Service Industries Journal*, 10, 105–18.

Ioannides, D. and Debbage, K. G. 1998: Neo-Fordism and flexible specialization in the travel industry: dissecting the polyglot. In D. Ioannides and K. G. Debbage (eds.), *The Economic Geography of the Tourist Industry: a Supply Side Analysis*, London: Routledge.

Jordan, F. 1997: An occupational hazard? Sex segregation in tourism employment. *Tourism Management*, 18, 525–34.

King, R. 1995: Tourism, labour and international migration. In A. Montanari and A. M. Williams (eds.), *European Tourism: Regions, Spaces and Restructuring*, Chichester: Wiley.

Chapter 8

Agarwal, S. J. 1997: The resort cycle and seaside tourism. *Tourism Management*, 18, 265–74.

Butler, R. W. 1980: The concept of a tourist area cycle of evolution: implications for management of resources. *Canadian Geographer*, 14, 5–12.

Pearce, D. G. 1995: *Tourism Today: A Geographical Analysis*. London: Longman 2nd edn.

Urry, J. 1995: *Consuming Places*. London: Routledge.

Chapter 9

Knowles, T. and Curtis, S. 1999: The market viability of European mass tourist destinations: a post-stagnation life-cycle analysis. *International Journal of Tourism Research*, 1, 87–96.

Krippendorf, J. 1987: *The Holiday Makers*. London: Heinemann.

Marchena Gómez, M. and Vera Rebollo, F. 1995: Coastal areas: processes, typologies and prospects. In A. Montanari and A. M. Williams (eds.), *European Tourism: Regions, Spaces and Restructuring*, Chichester: Wiley.

Urry, J. 1990: *The Tourist Gaze: Leisure and Travel in Contemporary Societies*. London and Newbury Park, CA: Sage Publications.

Williams, A. M. 1995: Capital and the transnationalisation of tourism. In A. Montanari and A. M. Williams (eds.), *European Tourism: Regions, Spaces and Restructuring*, Chichester: Wiley.

Chapter 10

Judd, D. R. and Fainstein, S. S. (eds.) 1999: *The Tourist City*. New Hoven, Yale University Press.

Law, C. M. 1993: *Urban Tourism*. London: Mansell.

Page, S. J. 1995: *Urban Tourism*. London: Routledge.

Ward, S. V. 1998: *Selling Places: The Marketing and Promotion of Towns and Cities, 1850–2000*. London: E and FN Spon.

Chapter 11

Butler, R. 1998: Rural recreation and tourism. In B. Ilberry (ed.), *The Geography of Rural Change*, Harlow: Addison Wesley Longman.

Butler, R. and Hall, C. M. 1998: *Tourism and Recreation in Rural Areas*. Chichester: Wiley.

Cavaco, C. 1995: Rural tourism: the creation of new tourist spaces. In A. Montanari and A. M. Williams (eds.), *European Tourism: Regions, Spaces and Restructuring*, Chichester: Wiley.

Oppermann, M. 1996: Rural tourism in southern Germany. *Annals of Tourism Research*, 23 (1), 86–102.

Chapter 12

Butler, R. 2000: Tourism and the environment: a geographical perspective. *Tourism Geographies*, 2 (3), 337–58.

Holden, A. 2000: *Environment and Tourism*. London: Routledge.

Hunter, C. and Geen, C. 1995: *Tourism and the Environment: A Sustainable Relationship?* London: Routledge.

Mowforth, M. and Munt, I. 1998: *Tourism and Sustainability: New Tourism in the Third World*. London: Routledge.

Bibliography

Adams, W. M. 1990: *Green Development: Environment and Sustainability in the Third World*. London: Routledge.

Agarwal, S. J. 1997: The resort cycle and seaside tourism. *Tourism Management*, 18, 65–74.

Agarwal, S., Ball, R., Shaw, G., and Williams, A. M. 2000: The geography of tourism production: uneven disciplinary development? *Tourism Geographies*, 2, 241–63.

Airey, D. 1983: European government approaches to tourism. *Tourism Management*, 4, 234–44.

Aitken, C. and Hall, C. M. 2000: Migrant and foreign skills and their relevance to the tourism industry. *Tourism Geographies: an International Journal of Place, Space and the Environment*, 2, 66–86.

Alchain, A. A. 1950: Uncertainty, evolution and economic theory. *Journal of Political Economy*, 58, 211–21.

Allen, J. 1988: Fragmented forms, disorganised labour? In J. Allen and D. Massey (eds.), *The Economy in Question*, London: Sage.

Alvarez, J. R. D. 1988: *Geografia del Turismo*, Madrid: Editorial Sintesis.

American Express 1989: Unique four rations travel study reveals traveller types. London: News release, 25 September.

Amin, A. 1983: The state and uneven development in advanced capitalism. In A. Gillespie (ed.), *Technological Change and Regional Development*. London Papers in Regional Science, 12, London: Pion.

Anderson, G. and Higgs, D. 1976: *A Future to Inherit: the Portuguese Communities of Canada*. Toronto: McClelland and Stewart.

Andrews, F. M. and Withey, S. B. 1976: *Social Indicators of Well-being*. New York: Plenum Press.

Ap, J. and Crompton, J. 1993: Residents strategies for responding to tourism impacts. Journal of Travel Research, 32 (1), 47–50.

Ascher, F. 1985: *Tourism, Transnational Corporations and Cultural Identities*. Paris: UNESCO.

Ashworth, G. J. 1989: Urban tourism: an imbalance in attention. In C. P. Cooper (ed.), *Progress in Tourism, Recreation and Hospitality Management*, London: Belhaven Press.

Ashworth, G. J. and de Haan, T. Z. 1986: *Uses and Users of the Tourist-Historic City: an Evolutionary Model in Norwich*. Field Studies Series 10, Groningen: GIRUG.

Ashworth, G. J. and Tunbridge, J. E. 1990: *The Tourist-Historic City*. London: Belhaven Press.

Ateljevic, I. 2000: Circuits of tourism: stepping beyond the "production/consumption dichotomy." *Tourism Geographies*, 2, 369–88.

Ateljevic, I. and Doorne, S. 2000: Staying within the Fence: Lifestyle Entrepreneurship in Tourism. *Journal of Sustainable Tourism*, 8(5), 378–92.

Atkinson, J. 1984: *Flexibility, Uncertainty and Manpower Management*. Institute of Manpower Studies, Report 89, Falmer: University of Sussex.

Aubrey, P., Herbert D., Carr, P. G., Chambers, D. A., Clark, S. C., and Cook, F. G. 1986: *Work and Leisure in the 1980s: the Significance of Changing Patterns*. London: Sports Council and Economic and Science Research Council.

Augustyn, M. M. and Knowles, T. 2000: Performance of tourism partnership: a focus on York. *Tourism Management*, 21, 341–51.

Bacvarov, M. and Kazacka, D. 1989: Free and recreational time in Bulgaria – geographical aspects. In F. Zimmermann (ed.), *Proceedings of the Austrian Meeting of the IGU Commission of Geography of Tourism and Leisure*, Klagenfurt: Institut für Geographie.

Bagguley, P. 1987: *Flexibility, Restructuring and Gender, Employment in Britain's Hotels*. Lancaster Regionalism Group, Working Paper No. 24, Lancaster: University of Lancaster.

Bagguley, P. 1990: Gender and labour flexibility in hotel and catering. *Service Industries Journal*, 10, 105–18.

Ball, R. J. 1988: Seasonality: a problem for workers in the tourism labor market? *Service Industries Journal*, 8, 501–13

Banks, R. 1985: *New Jobs from Pleasure – a Strategy for Creating New Jobs in the Tourist Industry*. London: HMSO.

Barbaza, Y. 1970: Trois types d'intervention du tourisme dans l'organisation de l'espace littoral. *Annales de Giographie*, 434, 446–69.

Baretje, R. 1982: Tourism's external account and the balance of payments. *Annals of Tourism Research*, 9, 57–67.

Barker, M. L. 1982: Traditional landscape and mass tourism in the Alps, *Geographical Review*, 72, 395–415.

Baron, R. R. 1975: *Seasonality in Tourism*. London: Economist Intelligence Unit.

Baron-Yelles, N. 1999: French coastal wetlands: in search of sustainability. *Tourism Geographies*, 1, 108–20.

Bath City Council 1987: *Economics of Tourism in Bath*. London: Coopers & Lybrand.

Baum, T. 1996: Unskilled work and the hospitality industry: myth or reality? *International Journal of Hospitality Management*, 15, 207–9.

Beechey, V. 1987: *Unequal Work*. London: Verso.

Belisle, J. F. 1983: Tourism and food production in the Caribbean. *Annals of Tourism Research*, 10, 497–513.

Bell, D. 1974: *The Coming of Post-industrial Society*. London: Heinemann.

Bell, M. and Ward, G. 2000: Comparing temporary mobility with permanent migration. *Tourism Geographies*, 2, 87–107.

Bennington, J. and White, J. 1988: Leisure Services at a crossroads. In J. Bennington and J. White, *The Future of Leisure Services*, London: Longman.

Bercheri, E. 1991: Rimini and Co – the end of a legend?: Dealing with the algae effect. *Tourism Management*, 12, 229–35.

Bernardi, R. 1987: The emerging trends in hotel design. In A. Sessa (ed.), *Mega trends in International Tourism*, Rome: Editrice Agnesotti.

Bianchi, R. 1994: Tourism development in resort dynamics: An alternative approach. In C. P. Cooper and A. Lockwood (eds.), *Progress in tourism, recreation and hospitality management*, 181–93, Chichester: Wiley.

Bishop, J. and Hoggett, P. 1989: Leisure and the informal economy. In C. Rojek (ed.), *Leisure for Leisure: Critical Essays*, London: Macmillan.

Bjorkland, E. M. and Philbrick, A. K. 1975: Spatial configurations of mental processes. In M. Belanger and D. G. Janelle (eds.), *Building Regions for the Future: Notes et Documents du Recherche No. 6*, Quebec: University of Laval, Department of Geography.

Blank, U. 1996: Tourism in United States Cities. In C. M. Law (ed.) *Tourism in Major Cities*, London: International Thomson Business Press.

Blank, U. and Petkovich, M. D. 1979: The metropolitan area tourist: a comprehensive analysis, *A Decade of Achievement, Proceedings of Travel and Tourist Research Association*, 227–36.

Blank, U. and Petkovich, M. D. 1987: Research on urban tourism destinations. In J. R. Brent Ritchie and C. R. Goeldner (eds.), *Travel, Tourism and Hospitality Research: a Handbook for Managers and Researchers*, New York: John Wiley, 165–77.

Blasing, A. L. 1982: Prostitution tourism from Japan and other Asian countries, Paper presented to Asian Consultation of Trafficking in Women, Manila.

Böhning, W. R. 1972: *The Migration of Workers in the United Kingdom and the European Community*. Oxford: Oxford University Press.

Bond, M. E. and Ladman, J. R. 1982: A strategy for developing tourism. *Research in Tourism*, 2(2), 45–61.

Bonnain-Moerdyk, R. 1975: L'espace gastronomique. *L'Espace Giographique*, 4, 113–22.

Boorstin, O. J. 1964: *The Image: a Guide to Pseudo-events in America*. New York: Harper and Row.

Bouquet, M. 1982: Production and reproduction of family farms in Southwest England. *Sociologia Ruralis*, 22, 227–44.

Bouquet, M. 1987: Bed, breakfast and an evening meal: commensality in the nineteenth and twentieth century farm household in Hartland. In M. Bouquet and M. Winter (eds.), *Who From Their Labours Rest? Conflict and Practice in Rural Tourism*, Aldershot: Avebury Press.

Bourdieu, P. 1984: *Distinction*. London: Routledge.

Bowler, I., Clark, G., Crockett, A., Ilbery, B., and Shaw, A. 1996: The development of alternative farm enterprises: a study of family labour farms in the Northern Pennines of England. *Journal of Rural Studies*, 12(3), 285–95.

Bramham, P. and Henry, I. 1985: Political ideology and leisure policy in the United Kingdom. *Leisure Studies*, 14, 1–19.

Bramham, P., Henry, I., Mommaas, H., and van der Poel, H. (eds.) 1989: *Leisure and Urban Processes: Critical Studies of Leisure Policy in West European Cities*, London: Routledge.

British Tourist Authority 1988: *Digest of Tourist Statistics No. 12*, London: BTA.

Bramwell, B. and Lane, B. 1993: Sustainable tourism: an evolving global approach. *Journal of Sustainable Tourism*, 1(1), 1–5.

Bramwell, B. and Rawding, L. 1994: Tourism marketing organisations in industrial cities. *Tourism Management*, 15(3), 425–34.

Bramwell, B. and Rawding, L. 1996: Tourism marketing images of industrial cities. Annals of Tourism Research, 23(1), 201–21.

Bramwell, B., Henry, L., Prat, A. G., Richards, G., and van der Straaten, J. (eds.) 1996: *Sustainable Tourism Management: Principles and Practice*, Tilburg: Tilburg University Press.

Britton, S. 1980: A conceptual model of tourism in a peripheral economy. In D. G. Pearce (ed.), *Tourism in the South Pacific: the Contribution of Research to Development and Planning*, Christchurch: University of Canterbury.

Britton, S. 1991: Tourism, capital, and place: towards a critical geography. *Environment and Planning D: Society and Space*, 9, 451–78.

Britton, S. 1996: Tourism, dependency and development: a mode of analysis. In Y, Apastolopoulos, S. Leivadi, and A. Yiannakis, (eds.), *The Sociology of Tourism: Theoretical and Empirical Investigations*, London: Routledge, 155–71.

Britton, S. G. 1981: Tourism, dependency and development: a mode of analysis, Occasional Paper No. 23, Development Studies, Canberra: Australian National University.

Brown, B. 1987: Recent tourism research in S. E. Dorset. In G. Shaw and A. M. Williams (eds.), *Tourism and Development: Overviews and Case studies of the U.K. and the S. W. Region*, Working Paper No. 4, Department of Geography, University of Exeter.

Brown, H. 1974: The impact of the tourist industries on the agricultural sectors, in the competition for resources and the market for food provided by Jamaica. *Proceedings of the 9th West Indies Agricultural Economics Conference*, University of West Indies.

Bryden, J. 1973: *Tourism and Development: a Case Study of the Common-wealth Caribbean*. Cambridge: Cambridge University Press.

Bryden, J. M. 1974: The impact of the tourist industries on the agricultural sectors; the competition for resources and food demand aspects. *Proceedings of the 9th West Indies Agricultural Economics Conference*, University of West Indies.

Buchholtz, C. W. 1983: *Rocky Mountain National Park: a History*. Boulder, CO: Associated University Press.

Buckley, P. J. and Witt, S. F. 1985: Tourism in difficult areas: case studies of Bradford, Bristol, Glasgow and Hamm. *Tourism Management*, 6, 205–13.

Bull, A. 1990: Australian tourism: effects of foreign investment. *Tourism Management*, 11, 325–31.

Bull, P. J. and Church, A. 1996: The London tourism complex. In C. M. Law (ed.), *Tourism in Major Cities*, London: Thomson International Press, 155–78.

Buller, H. and Hoggart, K. 1994: *International Counterurbanisation: British Migrants in Rural France*, Aldershot: Avebury.

Bureau of Transportation Statistics 1979: *US Census of Travel 1997*. US Department of Transportation.

Burkart, A. J. and Medlik, S. 1981: *Tourism: Past, Present and Future*, London: Heinemann.

Burnet, L. and Valeix, M. A. 1967: Equipement hotelier et tourisme. *Atlas de Paris et de la Region Parisienne*. Paris: Berger-Levrault.

Burrell, J., Manfredi, S., Rollin, H., Price, L., and Stead, L. 1997: Equal opportunities for women employees in the hospitality industry: a comparison between France, Italy, Spain and the UK. *Journal of Hospitality Management*, 16, 161–79.

Burtenshaw, D., Bateman, M., and Ashworth, G. J. 1991: *The European City: a Western Perspective*, London: David Fulton.

Butler, R. 1980: The concept of a tourist area cycle of evolution: implications for management of resources. *Canadian Geographer*, 14, 5–12.

Butler, R. 1985: Evolution of tourism in the Scottish Highlands. *Annals of Tourism Research*, 12, 371–91.

Butler, R. 1990: Alternative tourism: pious hope or Trojan horse? *Journal of Travel Research*, 28, 40–5.

Butler, R. 1991: West Edmonton Mall as a tourist attraction. *Canadian Geographer*, 35, 287–95.

Butler, R. 1992: Alternative tourism: the thin edge of the wedge. In V. Smith and W. Eadington (eds.), *Tourism Alternatives: Potentials and Problems in the Development of Tourism*, Philadelphia: University of Pennsylvania Press.

Butler, R. 1997: The concept of carrying capacity for tourism destinations: dead or merely buried? In C. Cooper and S. Wanhill (eds.), *Tourism Development: Environmental and Community Issues*, London: Routledge.

Butler, R. 1998: Rural recreation and tourism. In B. Ilberry (ed.), *The Geography of Rural Change*, Harlow: Addison Wesley Longman.

Butler, R. 1999: Sustainable tourism: a state-of-the-art review. *Tourism Geographies*, 1, 7–25.

Butler, R. 2000: Tourism and the environment: a geographical perspective. *Tourism Geographies*, 2, 337–58.

Butler, R. and Bowlby, S. 1997: Bodies and space: an exploration of disabled people's experiences of public space, *Environment and Planning D: Society and Space*, 15, 411–33.

Carreras i Verdaguer, C. 1995: Mega events, local strategies and global tourist attractions. In A. Montanari and A. M. Williams (eds.), *European Tourism: Regions, Spaces and Restructuring*, Chichester: Wiley.

Carter, S. 2000: Sex in the tourist city: the development of commercial sex as part of the provision of tourist services. In S. Clift and S. Carter (eds.), *Tourism and Sex: Culture, Commerce and Coercion*, London: Pinter.

Castles, S., Booth, H., and Wallace, T. 1984: *Here for Good: Western Europe's New Ethnic Minorities*, London: Pluto Press.

Cater, E. A. 1987: Tourism in the least developed countries. *Annals of Tourism Research*, 14, 202–26.

Cavaco, C. 1980: *Turismo e Demografia no Algarve*. Lisbon: Editorial Progresso Social e Democracia.

Cavaco, C. 1995: Rural tourism: the creation of new tourist spaces. In A. Montanari and A. M. Williams (eds.), *European Tourism: Regions, Spaces and Restructuring*, Chichester: Wiley.

Cazes, G. 1972: Le role du tourisme dans la croissance economique: reflexions partir de trois examplaires Antillais, *The Tourist Review*, 27, 43–7.

Chadefaud, M. 1981: *Lourdes: un pelerinage, une Ville*. Aix-en-Provence: Edisud.

Chadwick, R. A. 1987: Concepts, definitions and measures used in travel and tourism research. In J. R. Brent Ritchie and C. R. Goeldner (eds.), *Travel, Tourism and Hospitality Research: a Handbook for Managers and Researchers*. New York: John Wiley.

Champion, A. G. and Townsend, A. R. 1990: *Contemporary Britain: a Geographical Perspective*. London: Edward Arnold.

Chaney, D. 1990: Subtopia in Gateshead: the Metro centre as a cultural form. *Theory, Culture and Society*, 7(4), 49–68.

Cheek, N. H., Field, D. R., and Burdge, R. J. 1976: *Leisure and Recreation Places*. Ann Arbor: Science Publishers.

Chesney-Lind, M. and Lind, I. Y. 1985: Visitors as victims: crimes against tourists in Hawaii. *Annals of Tourism Research*, 13, 167–91.

Choy, D. L. 1992: Life cycle models for Pacific island destinations. *Journal of Travel Research*, 30, 26–31.

Church, A., Ball, R., Bull, C., and Tyler, D. 2000: Public policy engagement with British tourism: the national, local and the European Union. *Tourism Geographies*, 2, 312–36.

Clark, R. and Stankey, G. 1979: *The Recreation Opportunity Spectrum: a Framework for Planning, Management and Research*. Seattle: US Department of Agriculture Forest Service, General Technical Report, PNW-98.

Clawson, M. and Knetsch, J. L. 1966: *Economics of Outdoor Recreation*. Baltimore: Johns Hopkins Press.

Clevedon, R. 1979: *The Economic and Social Impact of International Tourism on Developing Countries*. E.I.U. Special Report 60, London: Economist Intelligence Unit.

Clevedon, R. 1999: quoted in Holden, A. 2000: *Environment and Tourism*. London: Routledge.

Cliff, S. and Forest, S. 1999: Gay men and tourism: destinations and holiday motivations. *Tourism Management*, 20(5), 615–25.

Clout, H., Blacksell, M., King, R., and Pinder, D. 1989: *Western Europe: Geographical Perspectives*. London: Longman, 2nd edn.

Coates, B. E., Johnston, R. J., and Knox, P. L. 1977: *Geography and Inequality*. Oxford: Oxford University Press.

Coccossis, H. and Parpairis, A. 1996: Tourism and carrying capacity in coastal areas: Mykonos, Greece. In G. K. Priestley, J. A. Edwards, and H. Coccossis (eds.), *Sustainable Tourism: European Experiences*, Wallingford: CAB International.

Cochrane, A. and Pain, K. 2000: A globalizing society. In D. Held (ed.), *A Globalizing World? Culture, Economics and Politics*, London: Routledge.

Cochrane, A., Peck, J., and Tickell, A. 1996: Manchester plays games: exploring the local politics of globalisation. *Urban Studies*, 33, 1319–36.

Cockerell, N. 1988: Skiing in Europe – potential and problems. *Travel and Tourism Analyst*, 68–81. London: Economist Intelligence Unit.

Cohen, E. 1972: Toward a sociology of international tourism. *Social Research*, 39, 164–82.

Cohen, E. 1979a: A phenomenology of tourist experiences. *Sociology*, 13, 179–202.

Cohen, E. 1979b: Rethinking the sociology of tourism. *Annals of Tourism Research*, 6, 18–35.

Cohen, E. 1988a: Traditions in the qualitative sociology of tourism. *Annals of Tourism Research*, special issue, 15, 29–46.

Cohen, E. 1988b: Tourism and AIDS in Thailand. *Annals of Tourism Research*, 15, 467–86.

Cohen, E. 1988c: Authenticity and commoditization in tourism. *Annals of Tourism Research*, 15, 371–87.

Cohen, R. B. 1981: The new international division of labor, multinational corporations and the urban hierarchy. In M. Dear and A. Scott (eds.), *Urbanization and Urban Planning in Capitalist Society*. London: Methuen.

Collinge, M. 1989: *Tourism; a Catalyst for Urban Regeneration*. London: English Tourist Board.

Collins, L. R. 1978: Review of hosts and guests an anthropology of tourism. *Annals of Tourism Research*, 5, 278–80.

Collins, M. F. 1982: *Leisure Research, Current Findings and the Future Challenge*. London: Sports Council, Social Science Research Council and Leisure Studies Association.

Colton, C. W. 1987: Leisure, recreation, tourism: a symbolic interactionism view. *Annals of Tourism Research*, 14, 345–60.

Commission of the European Communities 1987: *Europeans and their Holidays*. vii/165/87-EN, Brussels.

Commission of the European Communities 1996: *Progress Report on Implementation of the European Community Programme of Policy and Action in Relation to the Environment and Sustainable Development*. Brussels: Commission of the European Communities.

Confederation of British Industry 1985: *The Paying Guest*. London: CBI.

Cooke, P. 1983: *Theories of Planning and Spatial Development*. London: Hutchinson.

Cooper, C. and Wanhill, S. (eds.) 1997: *Tourism Development: Environment and Community Issues*. Chichester: Wiley.

Cooper, C., Fletcher, J., Gilbert, D., Wanhill, S., and Shepherd, R., [1993] 1998: *Tourism: Principles and Practices* (2nd edition). Marlow: Longman [1st edn. 1993].

Cooper, C. P. 1981: Spatial and temporal patterns of tourist behaviour. *Regional Studies*, 15, 359–71.

Cooper, C. P. 1990: The life cycle concept and tourism. Conference paper presented at "Tourism Research Into the 1990s," University of Durham.

Cooper, C. P. 1992: The life cycle concept and strategic planning for coastal resorts. *Built Environment*, 18, 57–66.

Cooper, C. P. and Jackson, S. 1985: Changing patterns of Manx tourism. *Geography*, 70, 74–6.

Cordell, H., McLellan, R., and Legg, M. 1980: Managing private rural land as a visual resource. In D. Hawkins, E. Shafer, and J. Rovelsted (eds.), *Tourism Planning and Development Issues; International Symposium on Tourism and the Next Decade*, Washington, DC: George Washington University.

Cornet, J. 1975: African art and authenticity. *African Art*, 9, 52–5.

Corsico, F. 1994: Urban marketing: a tool for cities and business enterprises, a condition for property development, a challenge for urban planning. In G. Ave and F. Corsico (eds.), *Urban Marketing in Europe*, Turin: Torino Incontra, 75–88.

Cosgrove, I. and Jackson, R. 1972: *The Geography of Recreation and Leisure*. London: Hutchinson.

Countryside Commission 1991: *Visitors to the Countryside*. Manchester: Countryside Commission.

Cowan, G. 1977: Cultural impact of tourism with particular reference to the Cook Islands. In B. R. Finney and K. A. Watson (eds.), *A New Kind of Sugar*, Santa Cruz: Center for South Pacific Studies, University of Santa Cruz, 79–85.

Craig, W. 1972: Recreational activity patterns in a small negro urban community: the role of the cultural base. *Economic Geography*, 48, 107–15.

Crandall, J. 1987: The social impact of tourism on developing regions and its measurement. In J. R. B. Ritchie and C. R. Goeldner (eds.), *Travel, Tourism and Hospitality Research: a Handbook for Managers and Researchers*, New York: John Wiley.

Crang, M. 1999: Knowing, tourism and practices of vision. In Crouch, D. (ed.), *Leisure/tourism Geographies: Practices and Geographical Knowledge*, London: Routledge.

Crompton, J. L. 1979: Motivation for pleasure vacation. *Annals of Tourism Research*, 6, 408–24.

Crompton, J. L. 1993: Choice set propositions in destination decisions. *Annals of Tourism Research*, 20(3), 461–77.

Crouch, D. 1999: Introduction: encounters in leisure/tourism. In Crouch, D. (ed.), *Leisure/tourism Geographies: Practices and Geographical Knowledge*, London: Routledge

Culler, J. 1988: *Framing the Sign*. Oxford: Blackwell.

Dahles, H. and Bras, K. (eds.) 1999: *Tourism and Small Entrepreneurs: Development, National Policy and Entrepreneurial Culture: Indonesian Case Studies*. New York: Cognizant Communications Corporation

Damette, F. 1980: The regional framework of monopoly exploitation: new problems and trends. In J. Carney, R. Hudson, and J. R. Lewis (eds.), *Regions in Crisis*, London: Croom Helm.

Dann, G. 1977: Anomie, ego-enhancement and tourism. *Annals of Tourism Research*, 4, 184–94.

Dann, G. 1983: Comment on Iso-Ahola's "Towards a Social Psychological theory of tourism motivation": A rejoinder. *Annals of Tourism Research* 10(2), 273–6.

Dann, G. 1996a: *The Language of Tourism: A Sociolinguistic Perspective.* Oxford: CAB International.

Dann, G. 1996b: St Lucia: sociocultural issues. In L. Briguglio, R. Butler, D. Harrison, and W. L. Filho (eds.), *Sustainable Tourism in Islands and Small States: Case Studies,* London: Pinter, 103–21.

Davidson, R. 1996: Holiday and work experiences of women with young children. *Leisure Studies,* 15, 89–103.

Davidson, T. L. and Maitland, R. 1997: *Tourism Destinations.* London: Hodder and Stoughton.

De Alwis, R. 1998: Globalisation of ecotourism. In P. East, K. Luger, and K. Immann (eds.), *Sustainability in Mountain Tourism: Perspectives for the Himalayan Countries,* Delhi: Book Faith India.

de Grazia, S. 1984: *Of Time Work and Leisure.* New York: Anchor Books.

de Kadt, E. (ed.) 1979: *Tourism: Passport to Development.* Oxford: Oxford University Press.

de Kadt, E. 1990: *Making the Alternative Sustainable: Lessons from Development for Tourism.* Brighton: University of Sussex, Institute of Development Studies, Discussion Paper 272.

de Kadt, E. 1992: Making the alternative sustainable: lessons from development for tourism. In V. Smith and W. Eadington (eds.), *Tourism Alternatives: Potentials and Problems in the Development of Tourism,* Philadelphia, University of Pennsylvania Press, 47–75.

Debbage, K. G. 1990: Oligopoly and the resort cycle in the Bahamas. *Annals of Tourism Research,* 17, 513–27.

Debbage, K. G. and Daniels, P. 1998: The tourist industry and economic geography: missed opportunities. In D. Ioannides and K. G. Debbage (eds.), *The Economic Geography of the Tourist Industry: a Supply-side Analysis,* London: Routledge.

Deem, R. 1996: Women, the city and holidays. *Leisure Studies,* 15, 5–25.

Deitch, L. I. 1977: The impact of tourism upon the arts and crafts of the Indians of the Southwestern United States. In V. L. Smith (ed.), *Hosts and Guests: an Anthropology of Tourism,* Philadelphia: University of Pennsylvania Press.

Dernoi, L. A. 1991: Canadian country vacations: the farm and rural tourism in Canada. *Tourism Recreation Research,* 16, 15–20.

Dex, S. 1985: *The Sexual Division of Labour.* Brighton: Wheatsheaf.

Dicken, P. 1986: *Global Shift: Industrial Change in a Turbulent World.* London: Harper and Row.

Dicken, P. 1986: *Global Shift,* 1st edn. London: Paul Chapman.

Dicken, P. 1998: *Global Shift,* 3rd edn. London: Paul Chapman.

Dickie, P. 2000: *The Political Economy of Tourism Development in Africa.* New York: Cognizant Communication.

Dietvorst, A. 1989: Unemployment and leisure: a case-study of Nijmegen. In P. Braham, I. Henry, H. Mommaas, and H. van der Poel (eds.), *Leisure and*

Urban Processes: Critical Studies of Leisure Policy in West European Cities, London: Routledge.

Dimaggio, P. and Useem, M. 1978: Social class and arts consumption. *Theory and Society*, 5, 141–61.

Din, K. M. 1992: The "involvement stage" in the evolution of a tourist destination. *Tourism Recreational Research*, 17(1), 10–20.

Dinan, C. 1999: A marketing geography of sustainable tourism, with special reference to Devon, England. Unpublished PhD thesis, Department of Geography, University of Exeter.

Dingle, P. 1995: Practical green business. *Insights*, March, London: ETB.

Direcção Geral do Turismo 1996: *O Turismo em 1994*. Lisbon: Direcção Geral do Turismo.

Disability View 1998: *Disability View*, June, 10–12.

Doeringer, P. B. and Piore, M. J. 1971: *Internal Labour Markets and Manpower Analysis*. Lexington: Lexington Books.

Doherty, L. and Stead, L. 1998: The gap between male and female pay: what does the case of hotel and catering tell us? *Service Industries Journal*, 18, 126–44.

Doxey, G. V. 1976: When enough's enough: the natives are restless in Old Niagara. *Heritage Canada*, 2, 26–7.

Drexl, C. and Agel, P. 1987: Tour operators in West Germany. *Travel and Tourism Analyst*, London: Economist Intelligence Unit.

Dubinsky, K. 1994: "The pleasure is exquisite but violent": the imaginary geography of Niagara Falls in the nineteenth century. *Journal of Canadian Studies*, 29(2), 64–88.

Dunning, J. H. and McQueen, M. 1982: The eclectic theory of the multinational enterprise and the international hotel industry. In A. M. Rugman (ed.), *New Theories of the Multinational Enterprise*, London: Croom Helm.

Dwyer, L. and Forsyth, P. 1994: Foreign tourism investment: motivation and impact. *Annals of Tourism Research*, 21, 512–37.

Earl, P. 1986: *Lifestyle Economics: Consumer Behaviour in a Turbulent World*. London: Wheatsheaf.

Eastman, C. M. 1995: Tourism in Kenya and the marginalization of Swahili. *Annals of Tourism Research*, 22, 172–85.

Eco, U. 1986: *Travels in Hyper-Reality*. London: Picador.

Economist Intelligence Unit 1988: *International Tourism Report: Spain and Balearic Islands*. London: Economist Intelligence Unit.

Economist Intelligence Unit 1995: *The International Hotel Industry: Corporate Strategies and Global Opportunities*. London: Economist Intelligence Unit, Research Report R463.

Economist Intelligence Unit 1996: The package holiday market in Europe. *Travel and Tourism Analyst*, 4, 51–71.

ECTARC 1989: *Contribution to the Drafting of a Charter for Cultural Tourism (Tourism and the Environment)*. Llangollen: ECTARC.

Edwards, P. K. 1981: Race, residence and leisure style: some policy implications. *Leisure Sciences*, 4, 95–112.

Ehrlich, B. and Dreier, P. 1999: The new Boston discovers the old: tourism and the struggle for a livable city. In D. R. Judd and S. Fainstein (eds.), *The Tourist City*, New Haven: Yale University Press, 155–78.

Elkington, J. and Hailes, J. 1992: *Holidays That Don't Cost the Earth*. London: Victor Gollancz.

English Tourist Board 1981: *Tourism and the Inner City*. London: ETB.

English Tourist Board 1984: *Chester Tourism Study*. London: ETB.

English Tourist Board 1988: *Visitors in the Countryside*. London: ETB.

English Tourist Board 1989: *The Inner City Challenge: Tourism Development in Inner City Regeneration*. London: ETB.

English Tourist Board 1990: *British Holiday Intentions*. London: ETB.

English Tourist Board 1991a: *The Future for England's Smaller Seaside Resorts*. London: ETB.

English Tourist Board 1991b: *Tourism and the Environment: Maintaining the Balance*. London: ETB.

English Tourist Board 1999: *UK Tourism Facts*. London: ETB.

European Commission Directorate General XXIII 1998: *Facts and Figures on the Europeans on Holidays*. Brussels: Eurostat.

European Environment Agency 1998: *Europe's Environment: The Second Assessment*. Oxford, Elsevier Science.

Evans, N. J. 1989: *Investigating Farm-based Accommodation in England and Wales – Theoretical Framework*. Coventry: University of Coventry, Department of Geography Working Paper 2.

Eversley, D. 1977: The ganglion of tourism: an unresolvable problem for London? *London Journal*, 3, 186–211.

Exhibition Industries Federation 1990: *The UK Exhibition Industry: the Facts*. London: Polytechnic of North London.

Fainstein, S. S. 1983: *Restructuring the City: the Political Economy of Urban Redevelopment*. London: Longman.

Fainstein, S. S. and Judd, D. R. 1999: Cities as places to play. In D. R. Judd and S. S. Fainstein (eds.), *The Tourist City*, New Haven: Yale University Press, 261–72.

Falk, N. 1987: Baltimore and Lowell: two American approaches. *Built Environment*, 12, 145–52.

Falk, P. and Campbell, C. 1997: *The Shopping Experience*. London: Sage.

Farrell, B. 1992: Tourism as an element in sustainable development: Hana Mavi. In V. L. Smith and W. R. Eadington (eds.), *Tourism Alternatives: Potentials and Problems in the Development of Tourism*, Philadelphia: University of Pennsylvania Press.

Featherstone, M. 1987: Leisure, symbolic power and the life course. In J. Horne, D. Iary, and A. Tomlinson (eds.), *Sport, Leisure and Social Relations*, London: Routledge and Kegan Paul.

Featherstone, M. 1990: Perspectives on consumer culture. *Sociology*, 24, 5–22.

Featherstone, M. 1991: *Consumer Culture and Postmodernism*. London: Sage.

Featherstone, M. and Lash, S. (eds.) 1999: *Spaces of Culture*. London: Sage.

Fedler, A. J. 1987: Are leisure, recreation, and tourism interrelated? *Annals of Tourism Research*, 14, 311–13.

Feldman, J. 1989: The growth of international travel service companies. *Travel and Tourism Analyst*, London: Economist Intelligence Unit.

Fenelon, R. 1990: The European and international hotel industry. In M. Quest (ed.), *Howarth Book of Tourism*, London: Macmillan.

Ferrario, F. F. 1988: Emerging leisure market among the South African Black population. *Tourism Management*, 9(1), 23–38.

Fish, M. 1984: On controlling sex sales to tourists: commentary on Graburn and Cohen. *Annals of Tourism Research*, 11, 615–17.

Fitch, A. 1987: Tour operators in the UK. *Travel and Tourism Analyst*, London: Economist Intelligence Unit.

Fjellman, S. 1992: Vinyl Leaves: Walt Disney World and America. Boulder: Westview.

Floyd, M. F. 1998: Getting beyond marginality and ethnicity: the challenge for race and ethnic studies in leisure research, *Journal of Leisure Research*, 30, 3–22.

Ford, K. and Eirowan, D. N. 2000: Tourism and commercial sex in Indonesia. In S. Clift and S. Carter (eds.), *Tourism and Sex: Commerce and Coercion*, London: Pinter.

Franklin, S. H. 1971: *Rural Societies*, London: Macmillan.

Freitag, T. G. 1994: Enclave tourism development: For whom the benefits roll? *Annals of Tourism Research*, 21, 538–54.

Friedmann, H. 1980: Household production and the national economy: concepts for the analysis of agrarian formations, *Journal of Peasant Studies*, 7, 158–84.

Friends of the Earth 1994: *Planning for the Planet: Sustainable Development Policies for Local and Strategic Plans*. London: Friends of the Earth.

Gabriel, Y. 1988: *Working Lives in Catering*. London: Routledge.

Gabriel, Y. and Lang, T. 1995: *The Unmanageable Consumer: Contemporary Consumption and its Fragmentation*. London: Sage.

Gamble, W. P. 1989: *Tourism and Development in Africa*. London, John Murray.

Garcia-Ramon, M. D., Villarion, M., Baylina, M., and Canoves, G. 1995: Farm women, gender relations and household strategies on the Coast of Galicia. *Geoforum*, 24, 5–17.

Gasson, R. 1980: Roles of farm women in England. *Sociologia Ruralis*, 20, 165–80.

Gershuny, J. I. and Jones, S. 1987: The changing work/leisure balance in Britain, 1961–1984. In J. Home, D. Jary, and A. Tomlinson (eds.), *Sport, Leisure and Social Relations*, London: Routledge and Kegan Paul.

Gershuny, J. I. and Miles, I. 1983: *The New Service Economy*. London: Frances Pinter.

Gershuny, J. I. and Thomas, G. S. 1982: Changing leisure patterns in the UK, 1961–1974/5. In M. F. Collins (ed.), *Leisure Research*, London: The Sports Council, The Social Science Research Council, and The Leisure Studies Association.

Getz, D. 1992: Tourism planning and destination life cycle. *Annals of Tourism Research*, 19, 752–70.

Getz, D. and Carlsen, J. 2000: Characteristics and goals of family and owner-operated businesses in the rural tourism and hospitality sectors. *Tourism Management*, 21, 547–60.

Getz, D. and Cheyne, J. 1997: Special event motivation and behaviour. In C. Ryan (ed.), *The Tourist Experience: A New Introduction*, London: Cassell, 136–54.

Gilg, A. 1998: Switzerland: structural change within stability. In A. M. Williams and G. Shaw (eds.), *Tourism and Economic Development: European Experiences*, Chichester: Wiley.

Gill, S. and Law, D. 1988: *The Global Political Economy: Perspectives, Problems and Policies*, London: Harvester-Wheatsheaf.

Gitelson, R. J. and Crompton, J. L. 1983: The planning horizons and sources of information used by pleasure vacationers. *Journal of Travel Research*, 23, 2–7.

Giyduem A. and Viles, H. 1997: *The Earth Transformed: An Introduction to Human Impacts on the Environment*. Oxford: Blackwell.

Glyptis, S. 1989: Recreation in rural areas: a case study in Ryedale and Swaledale. *Leisure Studies*, 1, 49–64.

Glyptis, S. A. and Riddington, A. C. 1983: *Sport for the Unemployed: a Review of Local Authority Projects*. London: Sports Council.

Go, F. 1989: International hotel industry – capitalising on change. *Tourism Management*, 10, 195–9.

Go, F. G. and Pine, R. 1995: *Globalization Strategy in the Hotel Industry*. London: Routledge.

Go, F., Pye, S. S., Uysal, M., and Mihalik, B. J. 1990: Decision criteria for transnational hotel expansion. *Tourism Management*, 11, 297–304.

Go, F. M. 1997: Asian and Australasian dimensions of global tourism development. In F. M. Go and C. L. Jenkins (eds.), *Tourism and Economic Development in Asia and Australasia*, London: Pinter.

Goddard, J. B. 1973: *Office Linkages and Location*. Oxford: Pergamon Press.

Goeldner, C. R., Buchman, T. A., DiPersio, C. E., and Hayden, G. S. 1991: *Economic Analysis of North American Ski Areas 1989–1990*. Boulder, CO: Business Research Division, University of Colorado at Boulder.

Goffee, R. and Scase, R. 1983: Class entrepreneurship and the service sector: towards a conceptual clarification. *Service Industries Journal*, 3, 146–60.

Golbey, G. 1985: *Leisure in Your Life: an Exploration*, New York: CBS College Publishing.

Goodall, B. 1988: How tourists choose their holidays: an analytical framework. In B. Goodall and G. Ashworth (eds.), *Marketing in the Tourism Industry*, London: Croom Helm.

Gooding, E. G. B. 1971: Food production in Barbados with particular reference to tourism. In G. V. Doxey (ed.), *The Tourist Industry in Barbados*, Kitchener: DUSCO Graphics.

Goodman, D. and Redclift, M. 1985: Capitalism, petty commodity production and the farm enterprise. *Sociologia Ruralis*, 15, 231–47.

Gordon, C. 1991: Sustainable leisure. *Ecos*, 12(1), 7–13.

Gordon, I. and Goodall, B. 2000: Localities and tourism. *Tourism Geographies*, 2, 290–311.

Gormsen, E. 1981: The spatio-temporal development of international tourism: attempt at a centre-periphery model. *La Consommation d'Espace par le Tourisme et sa Preservation*, Aix-en-Provence: CHET.

Goss, J. 1993: "The magic of the mall." An analysis of form, function, and meaning in the contemporary retail built environment. *Annals of the Association of American Geographers*, 83(1), 18–47.

Gottlieb, A. 1982: Americans' vacations. *Annals of Tourism Research*, 9, 165–87.

Goudie, A. and Viles, H. 1997: *The Earth Transformed: an Introduction to Human Impacts on the Environment*. Oxford: Blackwell.

Graburn, N. H. H. 1976: The Eskimos and airport art. *Trans-Action*, 4, 28–33.

Graburn, N. H. H. 1983: Tourism and prostitution. *Annals of Tourism Research*, 10, 437–43.

Gratton, C. 1990: Consumer behaviour in tourism: a psycho-economic approach. Conference paper presented at "Tourism Research Into the 1990s," University of Durham.

Gratton, C. and Taylor, P. 1987: *Leisure in Britain*. Letchworth: Leisure Publications.

Gratton, C. and Taylor, P. 1988: *Economics of Leisure Services Management*. London: Longman.

Gray, H. P. 1970: *International Travel: International Trade*. Lexington: Heath Lexington Books.

Greenwood, D. J. 1976: Tourism as an agent of change. *Annals of Tourism Research*, 3, 128–42.

Greenwood, D. J. 1977: Culture by the pound: an anthropological perspective on tourism as cultural commiditisation. In V. L. Smith (ed.), *Hosts and Guests*, Philadelphia: University of Pennsylvania Press.

Greenwood, J. 1993: Business interest groups in tourism governance? *Tourism Management*, 14, 335–48.

Greenwood, J., Williams, A. M., and Shaw, G. 1989: *1988 Cornwall Visitor Survey*, Exeter: University of Exeter, Department of Geography, Tourism Research Group.

Gregson, N. 1995: And now it's all consumption? *Progress in Human Geography*, 19, 135–41.

Griffin, S., Hobson, D., MacIntosh, S., and McCabe, T. 1982: Women and leisure. In I. Hargreaves (ed.), *Sport, Culture and Ideology*, London: Routledge and Kegan Paul.

Guitart, C. 1982: UK charter flight package holidays to the Mediterranean, 1970–78. *Tourism Management*, 3, 16–39.

Gunn, C. 1980: Amendment to Leiper, The framework of tourism. *Annals of Tourism Research*, 7, 253–5.

Gunn, C. A. 1988: *Tourism Planning*. New York: Taylor and Francis, 2nd edn.

Gutiérrez, R. S. 1977: Localizacion actual de la hosteleria madriléna. *Boletin de la Real Sociedad Geografica*, 2, 347–57.

Hall, C. M. 1989: Hallmark tourist events: analysis, definition, methodology and review. In G. J. Syme, B. J. Shaw, D. M. Fenton, and W. S. Muelles (eds.), *The Planning and Evaluation of Hallmark Events*, Aldershot: Avebury.

Hall, C. M. 1996: Tourism prostitution: the control and health implications of sex tourism in South East Asia and Australia. In S. Clift and S. J. Page (eds.), *Health and the International Tourist*, London: Routledge.

Hall, C. M. 1997: *Hallmark Tourist Events: Impacts, Management and Planning*. Chichester: Wiley.

Hall, C. M. 2000: *Tourism Planning: Policies, Processes and Relationships*. Harlow: Prentice Hall.

Hall, C. M. and Page, S. 1999: *The Geography of Tourism and Recreation: Environment, Place and Space*. London: Routledge.

Hall, D. R. (ed.) 1991a: *Tourism and Economic Development in Eastern Europe and the Soviet Union*. London: Belhaven Press.

Hall, D. R. 1991b: Evolutionary pattern of tourism development in Eastern Europe and the Soviet Union. In D. R. Hall (ed.), *Tourism and Economic Development in Eastern Europe and the Soviet Union*, London: Belhaven Press.

Hall, J. A. and Braithwaite, R. 1990: Caribbean cruise tourism: a business of transnational partnerships. *Tourism Management*, 11, 341–7.

Hall, T. D. 1986: Incorporation in the world system: towards a critique. *American Sociological Review*, 51, 390–402.

Hantrais, L. 1989: Central government policy in France under the socialist administration 1981–86. In P. Bramham, I. Henry, H. Mommaas, and H. van der Poel (eds.), *Leisure and Urban Processes: Critical Studies of Leisure Policy in West European Cities*, London: Routledge.

Harper, M. 1984: *Small Businesses in the Third World: Guidelines for Practical Assistance*. Chichester: John Wiley.

Harrison, C. 1991: *Countryside Recreation in a Changing Society*. London: TMS Partnership.

Harrison, D. 1992: The background. In D. Harrison (ed.), *Tourism and Less Developed Countries*, Belhaven (Wiley), London. 1–18.

Hart, C. W., Casserly, G., and Lawless, M. J. 1984: The product life cycle. How useful? *The Cornell Quarterly*, 25, 54–63.

Hartmann, R. 1986: Tourism, seasonality and social change. *Leisure studies*, 5, 25–33.

Hartmann, R. and Hennig, L. 1989: Wilderness recreation, experimental consumerism and the American West – origins, trends and environmental implications. In F. Zimmermann (ed.), *Proceedings of the Austrian Meeting of the IGU Commission of Geography of Tourism and Leisure*, Klagenfurt: University of Klagenfurt.

Harvey, D. 1985: *The Urbanisation of Capital: Studies in the History and Theory of Capitalist Urbanisation*. Oxford: Blackwell.

Harvey, D. 1987: Flexible accumulation through urbanisation. *Antipode*, 19, 260–86.

Harvey, D. 1989: From managerialism to entrepreneurialism: the transformation in urban governance in late capitalism. *Geografiska Annaler B*, 71(1), 3–17.

Haukeland, J. 1990: Non-travellers: the flip side of motivation. *Annals of Tourism Research*, 17, 172–84.

Haylock, R. 1988: Developments in worldwide timeshare. *Travel and Tourism Analysis*, 53–67, London: Economist Intelligence Unit.

Haywood, K. M. 1986: Can the tourist area life cycle be made operational? *Tourism Management*, 7, 154–67.

Held, D. 2000: Introduction. In D. Held (ed.), *A Globalizing World? Culture, Economics and Politics*, London: Routledge.

Henderson, D. M. 1975: *The Economic Impact of Tourism in Edinburgh and the Lothian Region*. Edinburgh: University of Edinburgh, Tourism and Recreation Research Unit.

Henderson, K. A. 1990: The meaning of leisure for women: an integrative review of the research. *Journal of Leisure Research*, 22, 228–43.

Henderson, K. A. 1996: One size doesn't fit all: the meanings of women's leisure. *Journal of Leisure Research*, 26, 139–54.

Henry, E. W. and Deane, B. 1997: The contribution of tourism to the economy of Ireland in 1990 and 1995. *Tourism Management*, 18, 535–53.

Herbert, D. T. 1995: Heritage as literary place. In D. T. Herbert (ed.), *Heritage, Tourism and Society*, London: Mansell.

Herold, E. S. and van Kerkwijk, C. 1992: AIDS and sex tourism. *AIDS and Society: International Research and Policy Bulletin*, 4, 8–9.

Hewison, R. 1987: *The Heritage Industry: Britain in a Climate of Decline*. London: Methuen.

Heyzer, N. 1986: *Working Women in South East Asia*. London: Open University Press.

Hill, C. M. 1982: Newcomers and leisure in Norfolk villages. In M. J. Moseley (ed.), *Social Issues in Rural Norfolk*, Norwich: Centre for East Anglian Studies.

Hills, T. L. and Lundgren, J. 1977: The impact of tourism in the Caribbean: a methodological study. *Annals of Tourism Research*, 4, 248–67.

Hjalager, A. M. 1996: Agricultural diversification into tourism: evidence of a European Community Development Programme. *Tourism Management*, 17 103–11.

Hodgson, A. (ed.) 1987: *The Travel and Tourism Industry: Strategy for the Future*. Oxford: Pergamon Press.

Holcomb, B. 1990: Purveying places: past and present. Centre for Urban Policy, Research working Paper No. 17, Rutgers University.

Holcomb, B. 1999: Marketing cities for tourism. In D. R. Judd and S. Fainstein (eds.), *The Tourist City*, New Haven: Yale University Press, 54–70.

Holden, A. 2000: *Environment and Tourism*. London: Routledge.

Holden, R. 1989: British garden festivals: the first eight years. *Landscape and Urban Planning*, 18, 17–35.

Holder, J. 1988: Pattern and impact of tourism on the environment of the Caribbean. *Tourism Management*, 9, 119–27.

Hollinshead, K. 1997: Heritage tourism under post-modernity: truth and the past. In C. Ryan (ed.), *The Tourist Experience: A New Introduction*, London: Cassell, 170–93.

Hollinshead, K. 1999: Surveillance of the worlds of tourism: Foucault and the eye-of-power. *Tourism Management*, 20(1), 7–23.

Holman, R. 1984: A values and life styles perspective on human behaviour. In R. E. Pitts and A. G. Woodside (eds.), *Personal Values and Consumer Psychology*, Lexington: Lexington Books.

Hopkins, J. 1990: West Edmonton Mall: landscape of myths and elsewhere-ness. *Canadian Geographer*, 34, 2–17.

Horner, A. E. 1993: Tourist arts in Africa before tourism. *Annals of Tourism Research*, 20 52–63.

Horwath and Horwath Ltd 1986: *London's Tourist Accommodation in the 1990s*. London: Horwath and Horwath Ltd.

Hotels 1991: Hotels 300 overview. *Hotels*, July 40–50.

Hotels 2000: 'Top 300', *Hotels*, July, 44–70.

Howard, E. 1990: *Leisure and Retailing*. Harlow: Longman.

Howard, J. A. and Sheth, J. N. 1969: *Theory of Buyer Behavior*. New York: Wiley.

Hudson, R. 1997: The end of mass production and of the mass collective worker? Experimenting with production, employment and their geographies. In R. Lee and J. Wills (eds.), *Geographies of Economies*, London: Edward Arnold.

Hudson, R. and Williams, A. M. 1989: *Divided Britain*. London: Belhaven Press.

Hudson, R. and Williams, A. M. 1995: *Divided Britain*. 2nd edn. Chichester: Wiley.

Hughes, H. 1991: Holidays and the economically disadvantaged. *Tourism Mangement*, 12, 193–96.

✗ Hughes, H. L. 1987: Culture as a tourist resource – a theoretical consideration. *Tourism Management*, 8, 205–16.

Hunter, C. and Green, C. 1995: *Tourism and the Environment: A Sustainable Relationship?* London: Routledge.

Hymer, S. H. 1975: The multinational corporation and the law of uneven development. In H. Radice (ed.), *International Forms and Modern Imperialism*, London: Penguin.

Ioannides, D. and Debbage, K. G. 1998: Neo-Fordism and flexible specialization in the travel industry: dissecting the polyglot. In D. Ioannides and K. G. Debbage (eds.), *The Economic Geography of the Tourist Industry: a Supply Side Analysis*, London: Routledge.

Iso-Ahola, S. E. 1980: *The Social Psychology of Leisure and Recreation*. Dubuque: W. C. Brown.

Iso-Ahola, S. E. 1984: Social psychological foundations of leisure and resultant implications for leisure counselling. In E. T. Dowd (ed.), *Leisure Counselling: Concepts and Applications*, Illinois: C. C. Thomas.

IUCN 1991: *Caring for the Earth: A Strategy for Sustainable Living*, Gland, Switzerland.

Jackson, E. L. 1988: Leisure constraints: a survey of past research. *Leisure Sciences*, 10, 203–15.

Jackson, E. L. 1991: Leisure constraints/constrained leisure: special issue introduction. *Journal of Leisure Research*, 23, 279–85.

Jackson, P. 1995: Changing geographies of consumption. *Environment and Planning A*, 27, 1875–6.

Jafari, J. 1973: *Role of Tourism in the Socio-economic Transformation of Developing Countries*. Ithaca, New York: Cornell University Press.

Jafari, J. 1987: Tourism models: the sociocultural aspects. *Tourism Management*, 8(2), 151–9.

Jafari, J. 1989: Sociocultural dimensions of tourism: an English language literature review. In J. Bustrzanowski (ed.), *Tourism as a Factor of Change: a Sociocultural Study*, Vienna: Economic Coordination Centre for Research and Documentation in Social Sciences, 17–60.

Jakle, J. A. 1985: *The Tourist: Travel in Twentieth-century North America*. Lincoln: University of Nebraska Press.

Jansen-Verbeke, M. 1986: Inner-city tourism: resources, tourists and promoters. *Annals of Tourism Research*, 13, 79–100.

Jansen-Verbeke, M. 1990: Fun shopping: a challenge to planning. In G. J. Ashworth and B. Goodall (eds.), *Marketing Tourism Places*, London: Routledge.

Jansen-Verbeke, M. 1995: A regional analysis of tourist flows within Europe. *Tourism Management*, 16, 73–82.

Jansen-Verbeke, M. and Dietvorst, A. 1987: Leisure, recreation, tourism: a geographic view on integration. *Annals of Tourism Research*, 14, 361–75.

Jenner, P. and Smith, C. 1992: *The Tourism Industry and the Environment*, London: EIU.

Johnson, P. and Thomas, B. 1990: Employment in tourism: a review. *Industrial Relations Journal*, 21, 36–48.

Jones, A. 1992: Is there a real "Alternative" Tourism? *Tourism Management*, 13, 102–3.

Jones, T. 1994: Theme parks in Japan. *Progress in Tourism Recreation and Holiday Management*, 6, 111–25.

Jordan, F. 1997: An occupational hazard? Sex segregation in tourism employment. *Tourism Management*, 18, 525–34.

Jud, G. D. 1975: Tourism and crime in Mexico. *Social Science Quarterly*, 56, 324–30.

Judd, D. R. 1999: Constructing the tourist bubble. In D. R. Judd and S. Fainstein (eds.), *The Tourist City*, New Haven: Yale University Press, 35–53.

Judd, D. R. and Collins, M. 1979: The case of tourism: political coalitions and redevelopment in central cities. In G. A. Tobin (ed.), *The Changing Structure of the City: What Happened to the Urban Crises?*, Urban Affairs Annual Reviews, p. 16.

Kando, T. M. 1975: *Leisure and Popular Culture in Transition*. St. Louis: C. V. Mosby.

Karch, C. A. and Dann, G. 1996: Close encounters of the Third World. In Y. Apostolopoulos, S. Leivadi, and A. Yiannatcis, (eds.), *The Sociology of Tourism*, London: Routledge.

Karn, V. A. 1977: *Retiring to the Seaside*. London: Routledge and Kegan Paul.

Kassé, M. 1973: La théorie du développement de l'industrie touristique dans les pay sous-dévoloppés. *Annales Africaines* (1971–73), 53–72.

Katz, C. and Kirby, A. 1991: In the nature of things: the environment and everyday life. *Transactions, Institute of British Geographers*, new series, 16, 259–71.

Kay, T. and Jackson, G. 1991: Leisure despite constraint: the impact of leisure constraints on leisure participation. *Journal of Leisure Research*, 23, 301–13.

Kelly, J. 1978: Family leisure in three communities. *Journal of Leisure Research*, 10, 38–47.

Kelly, J. R. 1980: Outdoor recreation participation: a comparative analysis. *Leisure Sciences*, 3, 129–54.

Kelly, J. R. 1982: *Leisure*. Englewood Cliffs, NJ: Prentice-Hall.

Kelly, J. R. 1985: *Recreation Business*. New York: John Wiley.

Kenna, M. E. 1993: Return migrants and tourism development: an example from the Cyclades. *Journal of Modern Greek Studies*, 11, 75–95.

Keohane, R. O. and Nye, J. S. 1977: *Power and Interdependence*. Boston: Brown.

Key Note 1986: *Tourism in the UK, Key Note Report, An Industry Sector Overview*. London: Key Note Publications.

Key Note 1988: *Fast Food Outlets, Key Note Report, An Industry Sector Overview*. London: Key Note Publications.

King, B., Pizam, A., and Milman, A. 1993: Social impacts of tourism: host perceptions. *Annals of Tourism Research*, 20, 650–5.

King, R. 1986: Return migration and regional economic development: an overview. In R. King (ed.), *Return Migration and Regional Economic Problems*, London: Croom Helm.

King, R. 1995: Tourism, labour and international migration. In A. Montanari and A. M. Williams (eds.), *European Tourism: Regions, Spaces and Restructuring*, Chichester: Wiley.

King, R., Mortimer, J., and Strachan, A. 1984: Return migration and tertiary development: a Calabrian case study. *Anthropological Quarterly*, 57, 112–24.

King, R., Mortimer, J., Strachan, A., and Trono, A. 1985: Return migration and rural economic change: a south Italian case study. In R. Hudson and J . R. Lewis (eds.), *Uneven Development in Southern Europe*, London: Methuen.

King, R., Warnes, A. M., and Williams, A. M. 2000: *Sunset Lives: British Retirement Migration to the Mediterranean*. Oxford: Berg.

Klemm, M. 1992: Sustainable tourism development: Languedoc and Roussillon. *Tourism Management*, 169–80.

Knoll, G. M. 1988: *Grosstadttourismus der Innenstadt von Ko'ln im 19. und 20. Jahrhundert*. Koln: Hundt Druck.

Knowles, T. and Curtis, S. 1999: The market viability of European mass tourist destinations: a post-stagnation life-cycle analysis. *International Journal of Tourism Research*, 1, 87–96.

Knox, P. and Agnew, J. 1989: *The Geography of the World Economy*. London: Edward Arnold.

Knox, P. and Agnew, J. 1998: *The Geography of the World Economy*. 3rd edn. London: Edward Arnold.

Knox, P. L. 1974: Spatial variations in the level of living in England and Wales. *Transactions, Institute of British Geographers*, 62, 1–24.

Kotler, P., Haider, D. H., and Rein, I. 1993: *Marketing Places: Attracting Investment, Industry, and Tourism to Cities, States, and Nations*. New York: Free Press.

Krakover, S. 2000: Partitioning seasonal employment in the hospitality industry. *Tourism Management*, 21(5), 461–71.

Krippendorf, I. 1986: The new tourist turning point for travel and leisure. *Tourism Management*, 7, 131–5.

Krippendorf, I. 1987a: *The Holiday Makers*. London: Heinemann.

Krippendorf, I. 1987b: *Là-haut sur la Montaigne, Pour un Développement du Tourisme en Harmonie avec l'Homme et la Nature*. Berne: Kummerley and Frey.

Krippendorf, I. 1991: Towards new tourism policies. In S. Medlik (ed.), *Managing Tourism*, London: Butterworth and Heinemann.

Kroon, H. 1995: The dynamics of outgoing tourism: potentials and threats of holiday travel and destination choices. *Tijdschrift voor Economische en Sociale Geografie*, 86, 42–9.

Kuhn, W. 1979: Geschaftsstrassen als Freizeitsraum. *Münchner Geographie*, 42, 22–31.

Kuss, F. R., Graefe, A. R., and Vaske, J. J. 1990: *Visitor Impact Management: A Review of Research*. Washington DC: National Parks and Conservation Service.

Landgren, J. O. J. 1974: On access to recreational lands in dynamic metropolitan hinterlands. *Tourist Review*, 29, 124–31.

Lanfant, M.-F. 1980: Introduction: tourism in the process of internationalisation. *International Social Science Journal*, 23, 14–43.

Lanfant, M.-L. 1989: International tourism resists the crisis. In A. Olszewska and K. Roberts (eds.), *Leisure and Life-Style: a Comparative Analysis of Free Time*, London: Sage Publications.

Latimer, H. 1985: Developing-island economies – tourism v agriculture. *Tourism Management*, 6, 32–42.

Lavery, P. and van Doren, C. 1990: *Travel and Tourism: a North American-European Perspective*. Huntingdon: Elm Publications.

Law, C. M. 1985a: *The British Conference and Exhibition Business, Urban Tourism Project*. University of Salford: Department of Geography.

Law, C. M. 1985b: *Urban Tourism: Selected American Case Studies, Urban Tourism Project*. University of Salford: Department of Geography.

Law, C. M. 1985c: *Urban Tourism: Selected British Case Studies, Urban Tourism Project*. University of Salford: Department of Geography.

Law, C. M. 1987: Conference and exhibition tourism. *Built Environment*, 13, 85–95.

Law, C. M. 1988: Public, private partnerships in urban revitalisation in Britain. *Regional Studies*, 22, 446–51.

Law, C. M. 1991a: Tourism and urban revitalisation. *East Midland Geographer*, 14, 49–60.

Law, C. M. 1991b: *Tourism as a Focus for Urban Regeneration: the Role of Tourism in the Urban and Regional Economy*. London: Regional Studies Association.

Law, C. M. 1992: Urban tourism and its contribution to economic regeneration. *Urban Studies*, 29, 597–616.

Law, C. M. 1993: *Urban Tourism: Attracting Visitors to Large Cities*. London: Mansell.

Law, C. M. 1996: *Tourism in Major Cities*. London: Thomson International Press.

Law, C. M. 2000: Regenerating the city centre through leisure and tourism. *Built Environment*, 26, 117–29.

Laws, E. 1991: *Tourism Marketing: Service and Quality Management Perspectives*. Cheltenham: Stanley Thornes.

Lawson, F. R. 1982: Trends in business tourism management. *Tourism Management*, 3, 298–302.

Lea, J. 1988: *Tourism and Development in the Third World*. London: Routledge.

Lee-Ross, D. 1999: Seasonal hotel jobs: an occupation and a way of life. *International Journal of Tourism Research*, 1, 239–53.

Lehtonen, T.-K. and Mäenpää, P. 1997: Shopping in the East Centre mall. In P. Falk and C. Campbell (eds.), *The Shopping Experience*, London: Sage.

Leiper, N. 1990: Partial industrialisation of tourism systems. *Annals of Tourism Research*, 17, 600–5.

Leontidou, L. 1991: Greece: prospects and contradictions of tourism in the 1980s. In A. M. Williams and G. Shaw (eds.), *Tourism and Economic Development: Western European Experiences*, London: Belhaven Press, 2nd edn.

Leontidou, L. 1998: Greece: hesitant policy and uneven tourism development in the 1990s. In A. M. Williams and G. Shaw (eds.), *Tourism and Economic Development: European Experiences*, Chichester, Wiley (3rd edn.), 101–24.

Lew, A. A. 1987: A framework of tourist attraction research. *Annals of Tourism Research*, 14, 553–75.

Lewis, J. R. and Williams, A. M. 1986: The economic impact of return migration in Central Portugal. In R. King (ed.), *Return Migration and Regional Economic Problems*, London: Croom Helm.

Lewis, J. R. and Williams, A. M. 1988: No longer Europe's best-kept secret: the Algarve's tourist boom. *Geography*, 74, 170–2.

Lewis, J. R. and Williams, A. M. 1991: Portugal: market segmentation and regional specialisation. In A. M. Williams and G. Shaw (eds.), *Tourism and Economic Development: Western European Experiences*, London: Belhaven Press, 2nd edn.

Lewis, J. R. and Williams, A. M. 1998: Portugal: market segmentation and economic development. In A. M. Williams and G. Shaw (eds.), *Tourism and Economic Development: European Experiences*, Chichester: Wiley.

Ley, D. and Olds, K. 1988: Landscape as spectacle: world's fairs and the culture of heroic consumption. *Environment and Planning D: Society and Space*, 6, 191–212.

Lickorish, L. L. 1990: Tourism facing change. In M. Quest (ed.), *Howarth Book of Tourism*, London: Macmillan.

Lillywhite, M. and Lillywhite, L. 1991: Low impact tourism. In S. Medlik (ed.), *Managing Tourism*, London: Butterworth-Heinemann.

Llinas, M. S. 1991: Nature et tourism – l'equilibre indispensable pour l'avenir de l'isle de Majorque. *Miditeranie*, 15–20.

Lloyd, P. E. and Mason, C. M. 1984: Spatial variations in new firm formation in the UK: comparative evidence from Merseyside, Greater Manchester and South Hampshire. *Regional Studies*, 18, 207–20.

Lockwood, A. and Guerrier, Y. 1989: Flexible working in the hospitality industry: current strategies and future potential. *Journal of Contemporary Hospitality Management*, 1, 11–16.

Long, V. H. 1991: Nature tourism: environmental stress or environmental salvation. Paper presented to WLRA World Congress, Sydney (July).

Loverseed, H. 1994: Theme parks in North America. *Progress in Tourism and Tourism Analyst*, 4, 51–63.

Lowyck, E., Van Langenhove, L., and Bollaert, L. 1990: Typologies of tourist roles. Paper presented at "Tourism Research into the 1990s," University of Durham.

Lumley, R. 1988: *The Museum Time-machine: Putting Cultures on Display.* London: Routledge.

Lundberg, D. E. 1972: *The Tourist Business.* Boston: Cahners.

Lundberg, D. E. 1974: Caribbean tourism: social and racial tensions. *Cornell Hotel and Restaurant Administration Quarterly*, 15, 82–7.

Lundgren, D. E., Krishnamoorthy, M., and Stavenga, M. H. 1995: *Tourism Economics.* New York: Wiley.

Lundgren, J. O. J. 1972: The development of tourist travel systems – a metropolitan economic hegemony par excellence. *Jahrbuch fur Fremden- verkehr*, 20, 86–120.

Lundgren, J. O. J. 1973: Tourist impact/island entrepreneurship in the Caribbean. Paper quoted in Mathieson and Wall (1982).

Lury, C. 1996: *Consumer Culture.* Cambridge: Polity.

MacCannell, D. 1973: Staged authenticity: arrangements of social space in tourist settings. *American Sociological Review*, 79, 589–603.

MacCannell, D. 1976: *The Tourist: a New Theory of the Leisure Class.* New York: Sulouker Books; see also revised edn. 1989.

MacCannell, D. 1984: Reconstructed ethnicity: tourism and cultural identity in Third World Communities. *Annals of Tourism Research*, 11, 375–91.

MacKay, J. 1994: Eco tourists take over. *The Times* Feb, 17.

Macnaughton, P. and Urry, J. 1998: *Contested Natures.* London: Sage.

MacNulty, W. K. 1985: U.K. social change through a wide-angle lens. *Futures*, August, 18–25.

McConnell, J. E. 1986: Geography of international trade. *Progress in Human Geography*, 10, 471–83.

McElroy, J. L. and De Albuquerque, K. 1986: The tourism demonstration effect in the Caribbean. *Journal of Travel Research*, 25, 31–4.

McGuire, C. 1984: A factor analytical study of leisure constraints in advanced adulthood. *Leisure Sciences*, 6, 313–26.

McPeters, L. R. and Stronge, W. B. 1974: Crime as an environmental externality of tourism: Florida. *Land Economics*, 50, 288–92.

Mandel, E. 1975: *Late Capitalism.* London: New Left Books.

Mannell, R. C. and Iso-Ahola, S. E. 1987: Psychological nature of leisure and tourism experience. *Annals of Tourism Research*, 14, 314–31.

Mansfield, Y. 1990: Spatial patterns of international tourist flows: towards a theoretical framework. *Progress in Human Geography*, 4, 372–90.

Marchena Gómez, M. 1995: New tourism trends and the future of Mediterranean Europe. *Tijdschrift voor Economische en Sociale Geografie*, 86, 21–31.

Marchena Gómez, M. and Vera Rebollo, F. 1995. Coastal areas: processes, typologies and prospects. In A. Montanari and A. M. Williams (eds.), *European Tourism: Regions, Spaces and Restructuring*, Chichester: Wiley.

Marion, J. 1995: *Monitoring the Impacts of Recreation.* Missoula, MT: USDA Forest Service.

Markusen, A. R. 1985: *Profit Cycles, Oligopoly and Regional Development.* Cambridge, MA: MIT Press.

Mars, G. and Nicod, M. 1984: *The World of Waiters.* London: Allen & Unwin.

Marshall, G. 1986: The workplace culture of a licensed restaurant. *Theory, Culture and Society*, 3, 33–48.

Marshall, J. N. 1989: *Uneven Development in the Service Economy: Understanding the Location and Role of Product Service*. Oxford: Oxford University Press.

Maslow, A. H. 1954: *Motivation and Personality*. New York: Harper and Row.

Mason, P. 2001: The big OE: New Zealanders' overseas experience in Britain. In M. Hall and A. M. Williams (eds.), *Tourism and Migration*, Dordrecht: Kluwer.

Massey, D. 1983: Industrial restructuring as class restructuring: production decentralisation and local uniqueness. *Regional Studies*, 17, 73–90.

Massey, D. 1984: *Spatial Divisions of Labour: Social Structures and the Geography of Production*. London: Macmillan.

Mathieson, A. and Wall, G. 1982: *Tourism: Economic, Physical and Social Impacts*. London: Longman.

Mayo, E. J. 1974: A model of motel-choice. *Cornell Hotel and Restaurant Administration Quarterly*, 15(3), 55–64.

Mazanec, K. (ed.) 1997: *International City Tourism: Analysis and Strategy*. London: Pinter.

Meeker, J. W., Woods, W. K., and Lucas, W. 1973: Red, white and black in the national parks. *North American Review*, Fall, 3–7.

Mendonsa, E. L. 1983: Tourism and income strategies in Nazare, Portugal. *Annals of Tourism Research*, 10, 213–38.

Meyer-Arendt, K. J. 1987: Resort evolution along the Gulf of Mexico litoral: historical, morphological and environmental aspects. Unpublished PhD thesis, Louisiana State University.

Middleton, V. T. C. 1982: Tourism in rural areas. *Tourism Management*, 5, 52–8.

Middleton, V. T. C. 1989: Marketing implications for attractions. *Tourism Management*, 10, 229–34.

Mihovilovic, M. A. 1980: Leisure and tourism in Europe. *International Social Science Journal*, 32, 99–113.

Mill, R. C. 1996: Societal marketing – implications for tourism destinations. *Journal of Vacation Marketing*, 2, 215–21.

Mill, R. C. and Morrison, A. M. 1985: *The Tourism System*. Englewood Cliffs, NJ: Prentice Hall.

Miossec, J. M. 1976: Elements pour une theorie de l'espace touristique. *Les Cahiers du Tourisme*, C-36, Aix-en-Provence.

Mitchell, A. 1983: *The Nine American Life Styles*. New York: Warner.

Mommaas, H. and van der Poel, H. 1989: Changes in economy, politics and lifestyles: an essay on the restructuring of urban leisure. In P. Bramham, I. Henry, H. Mommaas, and H. van der Poel (eds.), *Leisure and Urban Processes: Critical Studies of Leisure Policy in West European Cities*, London: Routledge.

Momsen, J. M. 1986: Linkages between tourism and agriculture: problems the smaller Caribbean economies. Seminar paper No.45, Department of Geography, University of Newcastle-Upon-Tyne.

Monopolies and Mergers Commission 1989: *Thomson Travel Group and Horizon Travel Ltd.* London: HMSO.

Montanari, A. and Williams. A. M. 1995: *European Tourism: Regions, Spaces and Restructuring.* Chichester: Wiley.

Moore, K. 1976: Modernization in a Canary Island village. In J. B. Aceves and W. A. Douglass (eds.), *The Changing Faces of Rural Spain*, New York: Schenkman.

Morgan, N. and Pritchard, A. 1998: *Tourism, Promotion and Power: Creating Images, Creating Identities*, Chichester: Wiley.

Morgan, N. J. and Pritchard, A. 1999: *Power and Politics of the Seaside.* Exeter: University of Exeter Press.

Morrell, J. 1985: *Employment in Tourism.* London: British Tourist Authority.

Morrison, A., Rimmington, M., and Williams, C. 1999: *Entrepreneurship in the Hospitality, Tourism and Leisure Industries.* Oxford: Butterworth-Heinemann.

Morton, A. 1988: 'Tomorrow's yesterdays: science museums and the future. In R. Lumley (ed.), *The Museum Time-machine: Putting Cultures on Display*, London: Routledge.

Mowforth, M. and Munt, I. 1998: *Tourism and Sustainability: New Tourism in the Third World.* London: Routledge.

Müller, D. 1999: *German Second Home Owners in the Swedish Countryside.* Umeå and Östersund: European Tourism Research Institute.

Mullins, P. 1991: Tourism urbanization. *International Journal of Urban and Regional Research*, 15, 326–42.

Munt, I. 1994: The "other" postmodern tourism: culture travel and the new middle classes. *Theory, Culture and Society*, 10, 97–125.

Murakami, K. and Go, F. 1990: Transnational corporations capture Japanese market. *Tourism Management*, 11, 348–53.

Murphy, P. E. 1980: Tourism management using land use planning and landscape design: the Victoria experience. *Canadian Geographer*, 24(1), 60–71.

Murphy, P. E. 1985: *Tourism: a Community Approach.* London: Routledge.

Murphy, P. E. 1988: Community driven tourism planning. *Tourism Management*, 9, 96–104.

Nash, D. 1977: Tourism as a form of imperialism. In V. L. Smith (ed.), *Hosts and Guests: the Anthropology of Tourism*, Philadelphia: University of Pennsylvania Press.

Neate, S. 1987: The role of tourism in sustaining farm structures and communities on the Isles of Scilly. In M. Bouquet and M. Winter (eds.), *Who From Their Labours Rest? Conflict and Practice in Rural Tourism*, Aldershot: Avebury Press

Nelson, J. 1993: An introduction to tourism and sustainable development with special reference to monitoring. In J. Nelson, R. Butler, and G. Wall (eds.), *Tourism and Sustainable Development: Monitoring, Planning, Managing*, University of Waterloo, 3–23.

Newby, P. T. 1981: Literature and the fashioning of tourist taste. In D. C. D. Pocock (ed.), *Humanistic Literature and Geography*, London: Croom Helm.

Newman, O. 1983: The coming of a leisure society? *Leisure Studies*, 2, 97–109.

Nicholls, L. L. 1976: Tourism and crime: a conference. *Annals of Tourism Research*, 3, 176–82.

Nolan, S. D. 1976: Tourists' use and evaluation of travel information sources: summary and conclusions. *Journal of Travel Research*, 14, 6–8.

Nunez, T. A. 1977: Touristic studies in anthropological perspectives. In V. L. Smith (ed.), *Hosts and Guests: an Anthropology of Tourism*, Philadelphia: University of Pennsylvania Press.

OECD 1974: *Government Policy in the Development of Tourism*. Paris: OECD.

OECD 1990: *Tourism Policy and International Tourism*. Paris: OECD.

Ogilvie, F. W. 1933: *The Tourist Movement*. London: P. S. King.

Ohmae, K, 1990: *The Borderless World: Power and Strategy in the Interlinked Economy*. London: Collins.

Opperman, M. 1992: Intranational tourist flows in Malaysia. *Annals of Tourism Research*, 19(3), 482–500.

Opperman, M. 1993: Tourism space in developing countries. *Annals of Tourism Research*, 20(3), 535–60.

Oppermann, M. 1996: Rural tourism in southern Germany. *Annals of Tourism Research*, 23(1), 86–102.

O'Reilly, 1986: Tourism carrying capacity: concepts and issues. *Tourism Management*, 7(4), 254–8.

Page, S. J. 1995: *Urban Tourism*, Routledge: London.

Painter, J. and Goodwin, M. 1995: Local governance and concrete research: investigating the uneven development of regulation. *Economy and Society*, 24, 334–56.

Palloix, C. 1975: *L'Economie Mondiale Capitaliste et Les Firmes Multi-nationals*. Paris: Maspero.

Parker, S. 1983: *Leisure and Work*. London: Allen & Unwin.

Patmore, J. A. 1983: *Recreation and Resources: Leisure Patterns and Leisure Places*. Oxford: Blackwell.

Pattullo, P. 1996: *Last Resorts: The Cost of Tourism in the Caribbean*, London, Cassell.

Pearce, D. G. 1978: Tourist development: two processes. *Journal of Travel Research*, 16, 43–51.

Pearce, D. G. 1987a: Mediterranean charters – a comparative geographic perspective. *Tourism Management*, 8, 291–305.

Pearce, D. G. 1987b: Spatial patterns of package tourism in Europe. *Annals of Tourism Research*, 14, 183–201.

Pearce, D. G. 1987c: *Tourism Today: a Geographical Analysis*. London: Longman.

Pearce, D. G. 1988a: Tourism and regional development in the European Community. *Tourism Management*, 9, 13–22.

Pearce, D. G. 1988b: Tourist time budgets. *Annuals of Tourism Research*, 15, 106–21.

Pearce, D. G. 1989: *Tourist Development*. London: Longman, 2nd edn.

Pearce, D. G. 1995: *Tourism Today, A Geographical Analysis*. Longman: Harlow, 2nd edn.

Pearce, P. 1982: *The Social Psychology of Tourist Behaviour*. Oxford: Pergamon.

Pearce, P. 1993: The fundamentals of tourist motivation. In D. Pearce and R. Butler (eds.), *Tourism Research: Critique and Challenges*, London: Routledge, 113–34.

Pearce, P. L. 1982: *The Social Psychology of Tourist Behaviour*. Oxford: Pergamon Press.

Peck, J. G. and Lepie, A. S. 1977: Tourism and development in three North Carolina coastal towns. In V. L. Smith (ed.), *Hosts and Guests: an Anthropology of Tourism*, Philadelphia: University of Pennsylvania Press.

Peneff, J. 1981: *Industriels Algeriens*. Paris: Editions du CNRS.

Perez, M. 1987: New trends in international tourism viewed in the light of a quantitative interpretation. In A. Sessa (ed.), *Megatrends in International Tourism*, Rome: Editrice Agnesotti.

Perry, M. 1975: Planning and evaluating advertising campaigns related to tourist destinations. In S. P. Ladany (ed.), *Management Science Applications to Leisure Time Operations*. New York: American Elsevier.

Petersen, J. and Belchambers, K. 1990: Business travel – a boom market. In M. Quest (ed.), *Howarth Book of Tourism*, London: Macmillan.

Pevetz, W. 1991: Agriculture and tourism in Austria. *Tourism Recreation Research*, 16, 57–60.

Phelps, A. 1988: Seasonality in tourism and recreation: the study of visitor patterns. A comment on Hartman. *Leisure Studies*, 7, 33–9.

Phongpaichit, P. 1980: Rural women of Thailand. *ISIS International Bulletin*, No.13, Geneva: International Labour Office.

Pigram, J. 1983: *Outdoor Recreation and Resource Management*. London: Croom Helm.

Pimlott, J. 1976: *The Englishman's Holiday: a Social History*. Sussex: Harvester.

Pine, R. 1987: *Management of Technological Change in the Catering Industry*. Aldershot: Avebury Press.

Pitch, A. 1987: Tour operators in the UK. *Travel and Tourism Analyst*, London: Economist Intelligence Unit.

Pizam, A. 1982: Tourism manpower: the state of the art. *Journal of Travel Research*, 21, 5–9.

Pizam, A. 1999: A comprehensive approach to classifying acts of crime and violence in tourism destinations. *Journal of Travel Research*, 38, 5–12.

Pizam, A. and Milman, A. 1986: The social impacts of tourism. *Tourism Recreation Research*, 11, 29–33.

Pizam, A. and Pokela, J. 1988: The perceived impacts of casino gambling on a community. *Annals of Tourism Research*, 12, 117–65.

Pizam, A., Reichel, A., and Shieh, C. F. 1982: Tourism and crime: is there a relationship? *Journal of Travel Research*, 20, 7–11.

Plog, S. C. 1972: Why destination areas rise and fall in popularity. Paper presented at Southern California Chapter of the Travel Research Association.

Plog, S. C. 1987: Understanding psychographics in tourism research. In J. R. Brent Ritchie and C. R. Goeldner (eds.), *Travel, Tourism and Hospi-*

tality Research: a Handbook for Managers and Researchers, New York: John Wiley.

Pocock, D. 1992: Catherine Cookson country: tourist expectation and experience. *Geography*, 77, 236–44.

Poon, A. 1989: Competitive strategies for a new tourism. *Progress in Tourism, Hospitality and Recreation Management*.

Poon, A. 1993: *Tourism, Technology and Competitive Strategies*. Wallingford: CAB International.

Préau, P. 1968: Essai d'une typologie de stations de sporte d'hiver dans les Alpes du Nord. *Revus de Géographie Alpine*, 58, 127–40.

Préau, P. 1970: Principe d'analyse des sites en montagne. *Urbanisme*, 116, 21–5.

Prentice, R. 1994: Heritage: a key sector of the "new" tourism. *Progress in Tourism, Recreation and Hospitality Management*, 6, 308–24.

Prideaux, B. 2000: The resort development spectrum – a new approach to modelling resort development. *Tourism Management*, 21, 225–40.

Pritchard, A., Morgan, N. J., and Sedgely, D. 1998: Reaching out to the gay tourist: opportunities and threats in an emerging market segment. *Tourism Management*, 19(3), 273–82.

Prosser, G. 1995: Tourist detination life cycles: progress, problems and prospects. In R. Shaw (ed.), *Proceedings of the National Tourism & Hospitality Conference, Melbourne*, Canberra: Bureau of Tourism Research.

Pyo, S., Cook, R., and Howell, R. L. 1988: Summer Olympic tours and market-learning from the past. *Tourism Management*, 9, 137–44.

Rajothe, F. 1983: The potential for further tourism development in Kenya's arid lands. *Kenyan Geographer*, 5, 422–40.

Rapoport, R. and Rapoport, R. N. 1975: *Leisure and the Family Lifecycle*. London: Routledge and Kegan Paul.

Relph, E. 1976: *Place and Placelessness*. London: Pion.

Richards, G. 1996: Production and consumption of European cultural tourism. *Annals of Tourism Research*, 23, 261–83.

Richter, L. K. 1983: Tourism politics and political science: a case of not so benign neglect. *Annals of Tourism Research*, 10, 313–35.

Richter, L. K. 1985: Fragmented politics of US tourism. *Tourism Management*, 6, 162–73.

Riley, M. 1991: An analysis of hotel labour markets. In C. P. Cooper (ed.), *Progress in Tourism, Recreation and Hospitality Management vol 3*, London: Belhaven Press.

Ritchie, J. R. B. 1984: Assessing the impact of hallmark events: conceptual and research issues. *Journal of Travel Research*, 23(1), 2–11.

Ritchie, J. R. and Zins, M. 1978: Culture as a determinant of the attractiveness of a tourist region. *Annals of Tourism Research*, 5, 252–67.

Ritzer, G. 1998: *The McDonaldization Thesis*. London: Sage.

Rivers, P. 1973: Tourist troubles, *New Society*, 23, 250.

Roberts, K. 1981: *Leisure*. London: Longman, 2nd edn.

Roberts, K. 1989: Great Britain: socioeconomic polarisation and the implications for leisure. In Olszewska, A. and Roberts, K. (eds.), *Leisure and Life-Style: a Comparative Analysis of Free Time*, London: Sage Publications.

Roberts, K. 1997: Same activities, different meanings: British youth cultures in the 1990s. *Leisure Studies*, London: Allen & Unwin.

Roche, M. 1996: Mega-events and micro-modernisation. In Y. Apostolopoulos, S. Leivadi, and A. Yiannakis (eds.), *The Sociology of Tourism*, London: Routledge.

Rojek, C. 1985: *Capitalism and Leisure Theory*. Andover: Tavistock.

Romeril, M. 1989: Tourism and the environment – accord or discord? *Tourism Management*, 10, 204–8.

Rosemary, J. 1987: *Indigenous Enterprises in Kenya's Tourism Industry*. Geneva: UNESCO.

Rothman, R. A. 1978: Residents and transients: community reaction to seasonal visitors. *Journal of Travel Research*, 16, 8–13.

Ryan, C. 1992: The child as visitor. *World Travel and Tourism Review*, 14, 135–9.

Ryan, C. 1997: Similar motivations – diverse behaviours. In C. Ryan (ed.), *The Tourist Experience: A New Introduction*, London, Cassell, 25–47.

Ryan, C. 1998: The travel career ladder: an appraisal. *Annals of Tourism Research*, 25(4), 936–57.

Ryan, C. 2000: Sex tourism: paradigms of confusion? In S. Clift and S. Carter (eds.), *Tourism and Sex: Culture, Commerce and Coercion*. London: Pinter.

Sawicki, D. S. 1989: The festival marketplace as public policy. *Journal of the American Planning Association*, 55, 347–61.

Schmidhauser, H. 1989: Tourist needs and motivations. In S. F. Witt and L. Moutinho (eds.), *Tourism Marketing and Management*, Hemel Hempstead: Prentice-Hall.

Schofield, P. 1996: Cinematographic images of a city. *Tourism Management*, 15(5), 358–69.

Schoorl, J. and Visser, N. 1991: *Towards Sustainable Coastal Tourism: Environmental Impacts of Tourism on the Kenyan Coast*. Discussion Paper, Netherlands Ministry of Agriculture, Nature, Management and Fisheries.

Seager, J. and Olsen, A. 1986: *Women in the World: an International Atlas*. London: Pan.

Seaton, A. V. 1992: Social stratification in tourism choice and experience since the war: part 1. *Tourism Management*, 13, 106–11.

Seaton, A. V. and Tagg, S. 1995: The European family vacation: paedonomic aspects of choices and satisfactions. *Journal of Travel and Tourism Research*, 4(1), 1–21.

Selwyn, T. 1996: *The Tourist Image: Myths and Myth Making in Tourism*. Chichester: Wiley.

Sessa, A. 1983: *Elements of Tourism Economics*. Rome: Catal.

Shackley, M. 1996: *Wildlife Tourism*. London. International Thomson Business Press.

Sharpley, R. 1994: *Tourism, Tourists and Society*. Huntingdon, ELM Publications.

Sharpley, R. 2000: Tourism and sustainable development: exploring the theoretical divide. *Journal of Sustainable Tourism*, 8, 1–19.

Shaw, B. J. and Shaw, G. 1999: Sun, Sand and Sales: Enclave Tourism and Local Entrepreneurship in Indonesia. *Current Issues in Tourism*, 2, 68–81.

Shaw, G. 1992: Culture and tourism: the economics of nostalgia. *World Futures*, 33, 199–212.

Shaw, G. and Williams, A. 1990: Tourism, economic development and the role of entrepreneurial activity. *Progress in Tourism, Recreation and Hospitality Management*, 2, 67–81.

Shaw, G. and Williams, A. M. 1987: Firm formation and operating characteristics in the Cornish tourism industry. *Tourism Management*, 8, 344–8.

Shaw, G. and Williams, A. M. 1991a: From bathing hut to theme park: tourism development in South West England. *Journal of Regional and Local Studies*, II, 16–32.

Shaw, G. and Williams, A. M. 1991b: Tourism and development. In D. Pinder (ed.), *Western Europe: Challenge and Change*, London: Belhaven Press.

Shaw, G. and Williams, A. M. 1992: Tourism development and the environment: the eternal triangle. *Progress in Tourism, Recreation and Hospitality Management*, 4, 47–59.

Shaw, G. and Williams, A. M. 1997: *The Rise and Fall of British Coastal Resorts*. London: Pinter.

Shaw, G. and Williams, A.M. 1998a: Entrepreneurship, small business culture and tourism development. In D. Ioannides and K. Debbage (eds.), *The Economic Geography of the Tourist Industry*, London, Routledge, 235–55.

Shaw, G. and Williams, A. M. 1998b: Western European tourism in perspective. In A. M. Williams and G. Shaw (eds.), *Tourism and Economic Development: European Experiences*, (3rd edn), Chichester, Wiley, 17–42.

Shaw, G., Agarwal, S., and Bull, P. 2000: Tourism consumption and tourist behaviour: a British perspective. *Tourism Geographies*, 2(3), 264–89.

Shaw, G., Williams, A., Botterill, D., and Greenwood, J. 1990: *Visitor Patterns and Visitor Behaviour in Plymouth*. Exeter: Tourism Research Group, University of Exeter.

Shaw, G., Williams, A. M., and Greenwood, J. 1987: *Tourism and the Economy of Cornwall*. University of Exeter: Tourism Research Group.

Sheldon, P. J. 1983: The impact of technology on the hotel industry. *Tourism Management*, 4, 269–78.

Sheldon, P. J. 1988: The US tour operator industry. *Travel and Tourism Analyst*, London: Economist Intelligence Unit, 25–48.

Shih, D. 1986: VALS as a tool of tourism market research. *Journal of Travel Research*, Spring, 2–11.

Shivers, J. S. 1981: *Leisure and Recreation Concepts: a Critical Analysis*. Boston: Allyn and Bacon.

Shiviji, J. G. 1973: *Tourism and Socialist Development*. Dar-es-Salaam: Tanzania Publishing House.

Short, J. R. and Kim, Y.-H. 1999: *Globalization and the City*. London: Longman.

Shucksmith, D. M. 1983: Second homes, a framework for policy. *Town Planning Review*, 54, 174–93.

Sidaway, R. 1995: Managing the impacts of recreation by agreeing the limits of acceptable change. In G. J. Ashworth and A. Dietvorst (eds.), *Tourism and Spatial Transformations*, Wallingford: CAB International.

Sidaway, R. and Duffield, B. S. 1984: A new look at countryside recreation in the urban fringe. *Leisure Studies*, 3, 249–71.

Sillitoe, K. 1969: *Planning for Leisure*. London: HMSO.

Simms, J., Hales, C. and Riley, M. 1988: Examination of the concept of internal labour markets in UK hotels. *Tourism Management*, 9, 3–12.

Sinclair, T. M., Alizadeh, P., and Onunga, E. 1992: The structure of international tourism and tourism development in Kenya. In D. Harrison (ed.), *Tourism and the Less Developed Countries*, London: Belhaven, 17–63.

Sinclair, M. T. and Stabler, M. 1997: *The Economics of Tourism*, London: Routledge.

Sindiga, I 1999: *Tourism and African Development: Change and Challenge of Tourism in Kenya*. Ashgate, Aldershot.

Slattery, P. and Roper, A. 1988: *UK Hotels Group Directory 1988*, London: Cassell.

Smith, D. 1980: *New to Britain: a Study of Some New Developments in Tourist Attractions*. London: English Tourist Board.

Smith, D. M. 1977: *Human Geography: a Welfare Approach*. London: Edward Arnold.

Smith, G. V. 1989: The European conference market. *Travel and Tourism Analyst*, 4, London: Economist Intelligence Unit, 60–76.

Smith G. V. 1990: The growth of conferences and incentives. In M. Quest (ed.), *Howarth Book of Tourism*, London: Macmillan.

Smith, J. 1987: Men and women at play: gender, lifecycle and leisure. In J. Homes, D. Jary, and A. Tomlinson (eds.), *Sport, Leisure and Social Relations*, London: Routledge and Kegan Paul.

Smith, S. 1998: Tourism as an industry: debates and concepts. In D. Ioannides and K. Debbage (eds.), *The Economic Geography of the Tourist Industry: a Supply Side Analysis*, London: Routledge.

Smith, S. L. J. 1983: Restaurants and dining out: geography of a tourism business. *Annals of Tourism Research*, 10, 515–49.

Smith, V. L. (ed.) 1977: *Hosts and Guests: an Anthropology of Tourism*. Philadelphia: University of Pennsylvania Press.

Smith, V. L. 1994: Privatisation in the Third World: small-scale tourism enterprises. In W. F. Theobald (ed.), *Global Tourism: The Next Decade*, London, Butterworth-Heinemann.

Smith, V. and Hughes, H. 1999: Disadvantaged families and the meaning of holiday. *International Journal of Tourism Research*, 1, 123–33.

Sparrowhawk, J. and Holden, A. 1999: Human development: the role of tourism based NGOs in Nepal. *Tourism Recreation Research*, 24, 37–44.

Spink, J. 1989: Urban development, leisure facilities and the inner city: A case study of inner Leeds and Bradford. In P. Bramham, I. Henry, H. Mommaas, and H. van der Poel (eds.), *Leisure and Urban Processes: Critical Studies of Leisure Policy in West European Cities*, London: Routledge.

Spreitzer, E. and Snyder, E. E. 1987: Educational-occupational fit and leisure orientation as related to life satisfaction. *Journal of Leisure Research*, 19, 149–58.

Stabler, M. and Goodall, B. 1996: Environmental auditing in planning for sustainable island tourism. In L. Briguglio, J. Archer, B. Jafari, and G. Wall (eds.), *Sustainable Tourism in Islands and Small States: Issues and Policies*.

Stallinbrass, C. 1980: Seaside resorts and the hotel accommodation industry. *Progress in Planning*, 13, 103–74.

Stamps, S. M. and Stamps, M. B. 1985: Race, class and leisure activities of urban residents. *Journal of Leisure Research*, 17, 40–56.

Standing Bear, L. 1989: *Your House is Mine*. New York: Storefront for Art and Architecture.

Stansfield, C. A. and Rickert, I. E. 1970: The recreational business district. *Journal of Leisure Research*, 2(4), 213–25.

Stauth, G. and Turner, B. 1988: Nostalgia, postmodernism and the critique of mass culture. *Theory, Culture & Society*, 5, 509–26.

Stephenson, M. and Hughes, H. 1995: Holidays and the UK Afro-Caribbean community. *Tourism Management*, 16, 429–36.

Stockdale, J. 1985: *What Is Leisure?* London: Sports Council and Economic and Social Research Council.

Summary, R. M. 1987: Tourism's contribution to the economy of Kenya. *Annals of Tourism Research*, 14, 531–40.

Sundelin, A. 1983: Tourism trends in Scandinavia. *Tourism Management*, 4, 262–8.

Swarbrooke, J. and Horner, S. 1999: *Consumer Behaviour in Tourism*. Oxford: Butterworth-Heinemann.

Talbot, M. 1979: *Women and Leisure: a Review for the Joint Panel on Recreation and Leisure Research*. London: The Sports Council and Social Science Research Council.

Tarrant, C. 1989: UK hotel industry – market restructuring and the need to respond to customer demands. *Tourism Management*, 10, 187–91.

Taylor, J. 1994: *A Dream of England: Landscape Photography and the Tourist's Imagination*. Manchester: Manchester University Press.

Taylor, M. and Thrift, N. 1986: Introduction: new theories of multi-national corporations. In M. Taylor and N. Thrift (eds.), *Multinationals and the Restructuring of the World Economy*, London: Croom Helm.

Telfer, D. J. and Wall, G. 1996: Linkages between tourism and food production. *Annals of Tourism Research*, 23, 635–53.

Tetley, S. 1999: Visitors attitudes to authenticity at a literary tourist destination. Unpublished PhD thesis, Sheffield: Sheffield Hallam University.

Teuscher, M. 1983: Social tourism for all: the Swiss Travel Savings Fund. *Tourism Management*, 4, 216–19.

Theobold, W. F. 1994: The context, meaning and scope of tourism. In W. F. Theobald (ed.), *Global Tourism: The Next Decade*, Oxford: Butterworth-Heinemann, 3–19.

Theodorson, G. A. and Theodorson, A. C. 1969: *Modern Dictionary of Sociology*. New York: Thomas Crowell.

Thomas, J. 1964: What makes people travel? *Asia Travel News*, August, 64–5.

Thompson, G., O'Hara, G., and Evans, K. 1995: Tourism in the Gambia: problems and proposals. *Tourism Management*, 16, 571–81.

Thornton, P. 1995: Tourism behaviour on holiday: a time–space approach. Unpublished PhD thesis, Department of Geography, University of Exeter.

Thornton, P., Williams, A. M., and Shaw, G. 1996: Revisiting time–space diaries: an exploratory case study of tourist behaviour in Cornwall, England. *Environment and Planning A*, 29(10), 1847–68.

Thrift, N. 1989: Images of social change. In C. Hamnett, L. McDowell, and P. Sarre (eds.), *The Changing Social Structure*, London: Sage Publications.

Thurot, J. and Thurot, G. 1983: The ideology of class and tourism. *Annals of Tourism Research*, 10, 173–89.

Todaro, M. 1977: *Economic Development in the Third World*. London: Longman.

Tourism Concern 1992: *Beyond the Green Horizon: Principles for Sustainable Tourism*. Goldaming: Tourism Concern and WWF.

Towner, J. 1996: *An Historical Geography of Recreation and Tourism in the Western World*, 1540–1940. Chichester: Wiley.

Townsend, A. R. 1992: New directions in the growth of tourism employment? Propositions of the 1980s. *Environment and Planning A*, 24, 821–32.

TPR Associates 1999: *The European Tourist: a Market Profile*. London: TPR Associates.

Travel and Tourism Analyst 1999: The European ski market. *Travel and Tourism Analyst 1999*, 2, 42–58.

Travel and Tourism Analyst 2000: Winter sports in North America. *Travel and Tourism Analyst 2000*, 6, 25–44.

Travis, A. S. 1982: Leisure, recreation and tourism in W. Europe. *Tourism Management*, 3, 3–15.

Truett, D. B. and Truett, L. J. 1987: The response of tourism to international economic conditions: Greece, Mexico and Spain. *Journal of Developing Areas*, 21, 177–90.

Truong, T. D. 1990: *Sex, Money and Morality: Prostitution and Tourism in Southeast Asia*. London: Zed Books.

Turner, L. and Ash, J. 1975: *The Golden Hordes: International Tourism and the Pleasure Periphery*. London: Constable.

Tuynte, J. C. M. and Dietvorst, A. G. J. 1988: Musea anders bekeken: vier Nijmegse musea bezien naar vitstralingseffecten en complexvoming. Quoted in Ashworth and Tunbridge (1990).

Tyrell, B. 1982: Work, leisure and social change. In M. F. Collins (ed.), *Leisure Research*, London: The Sports Council, The Social Science Research Council and The Leisure Studies Association.

UNESCO 1976: The effects of tourism on sociocultural values. *Annals of Tourism Research*, 4, 74–105.

Unger, K. 1986: Return migration and regional characteristics: the case of Greece. In R. L. King (ed.), *Return Migration and Regional Economic Problems*, London: Croom Helm.

United Nations 1982: *Transnational Corporations in International Tourism*. New York: UN.

United Nations Environment 1995: *Environmental Codes of Conduct for Tourism*, Technical Report No. 29. Paris: UNEP.

Urry, J. 1987: Some social and spatial aspects of services. *Environment and Planning D: Society and Space*, 5, 5–26.

Urry, J. 1988: Cultural change and contemporary holiday-making. *Theory, Culture and Society*, 5, 35–55.

Urry, J. 1990: *The Tourist Gaze: Leisure and Travel in Contemporary Societies*. London: Sage Publications.

Urry, J. 1992: The tourist gaze revisited. *American Behavioral Scientist*, 36(2), 172–86.

Urry, J. 1995: *Consuming Places*. London: Routledge.

Valentine, P. S. 1992: Ecotourism and nature conservation: a definition with some recent developments in Micronesia. In B. Weiler (ed.), *Ecotourism*, Canberra: Bureau of Tourism.

Valenzuela, M. 1991: Spain: the phenomenon of mass tourism. In A. M. Williams and G. Shaw (eds.), *Tourism and Economic Development: Western European Experience*, London: Belhaven Press, 2nd edn.

Valenzuela, M. 1998: Spain: from the phenomenon of mass tourism to the search for a more diversified model. In A. M. Williams and G. Shaw (eds.), *Tourism and Economic Development: European Experiences*, Chichester: Wiley.

van den Berg, L. and Braun, E. 1999: Urban competitiveness, marketing and the need for organising capacity. *Urban Studies*, 35(5–6), 987–99.

van den Berg, L., van der Borg, J., and van der Meer, J. 1995: *Urban Tourism: Performance and Strategies in Eight European Cities*. Aldershot: Avebury.

van der Borg, J. 1998: Tourism management in Venice, or how to deal with success. In D. Tyler, Y. Guerrier, and M. Robertson, (eds.), *Managing Tourism in Cities*, Chichester: Wiley.

van Doom, I. W. M. 1979: The developing countries: are they really affected by tourism? Some critical notes on socio-cultural impact studies. Paper presented at Leisure Studies and Tourism Seminar, Warsaw, December.

van Duijn, J. J. 1983: *The Long Wave in Economic Life*. London: Allen & Unwin.

Vandermey, A. 1984: Assessing the importance of urban tourism. *Tourism Management*, 5, 123–35.

Vaughan, R. 1990: *Assessing the Economic Impact of Tourism: the Role of Tourism in the Urban and Regional Economy*. London: Regional Studies Association.

Veal, A. J. 1987a: *Leisure and the Future*. London: Allen & Unwin.

Veal, A. J. 1987b: *Using Sports Centres*. London: Sports Council.

Veblen, T. 1925: *The Theory of the Leisure Class*. London: Allen & Unwin.

Ventris, N. 1979: Recreational and cultural provision in rural areas. In J. M. Shaw (ed.), *Rural Deprivation and Planning*, Norwich: Geo Books.

Vetter, F. (ed.) 1985: *Big City Tourism*. Berlin: Reimer Verlag.

Vickerman, R. W. 1980: The new leisure society – an economic analysis. *Futures*, 10, 191–200.

Vincent, J. 1987: Work and play in an Alpine community. In M. Bouquet and M. Winter (eds.), *Who From Their Labours Rest? Conflict and Practice in Rural Tourism*, Aldershot: Avebury Press.

Vogeler, J. 1977: Farm and ranch vacationing. *Journal of Leisure Research*, 9, 291–300.

Wahab, S. and Pigram, J. J. 1997: *Tourism Development and Growth: the Challenge of Sustainability*. London: Routledge.

Waitt, G. 1999: Playing games with Sydney: marketing Sydney for the 2000 Olympics. *Urban Studies*, 36, 1055–77.

Wall, G. 1996: Is ecotourism sustainable? *Environmental Management*, 2, 207–16.

Walvin, J. 1978: *Leisure and Society, 1830–1950*. London: Longman.

Ward, C. and Hardy, D. 1986: *Goodnight Campers! The History of the British Holiday Group*. London: Mansell.

Ward, S. V. 1998: *Selling Places: The Marketing and Promotion of Towns and Cities, 1850–2000*. London: E & FN Spon.

Washburne, R. F. 1978: Black under-participation in wildland recreation: alternative explanations. *Leisure Sciences*, 1, 175–89.

Wathern, P. (ed.) 1988: *Environment Impact Assessment: Theory and Practice*. London: Routledge.

Watson, G. L. and Kopachevsky, J. P. 1994: Interpretation of tourism as commodity. *Annals of Tourism Research*, 21, 643–60.

Waycott, R. 1999: Marvels of the millennium or millennium madness. *Insights* November, D15–D20.

WCED 1987: *Our Common Future, The World Commission on Environment and Development*. Oxford: Oxford University Press.

Wearing, S. and Neil, J. 1999: *Ecotourism: Impacts, Potentials and Possibilities*. Oxford: Butterworth-Heinemann.

Weber, M. 1968: *Economy and Society*. New York: Bedminster Press.

Weiler, B. and Hall, C. M. (eds.) 1992: *Special Interest Tourism*. London: Bellhaven.

Weston, J. 1997: *Planning and Environmental Impact Assessment*. Harlow: Addison Wesley Longman.

Whatmore, S., Munton, R., Little, J., and Marsden, T. 1987: Towards a typology of farm businesses in contemporary British agriculture. *Sociologia Ruralis*, 27, 21–37.

Wheatcroft, S. 1982: The changing economies of international air transport. *Tourism Management*, 3, 71–82.

Wheatcroft, S. 1990: Towards transnational airlines. *Tourism Management*, 11, 353–8.

Wheeller, B. 1991: Tourism's troubled times – Responsible tourism is not the answer. *Tourism Management*, 12, 91–6.

Wheeller, B. 1994: Ecotourism: A ruse by any other name. *Progress in Tourism, Recreation and Hospitality Management*, 6, 3–11.

White, P. E. 1974: The social impact of tourism on host communities: a study of language change in Switzerland. Research paper No. 9, School of Geography, University of Oxford.

White, P., Wall, G., and Priddle, G. 1978: Anti-social behaviour in Ontario provincial parks. *Recreational Research Review*, 2, 13–25.

Wight, P. 1998: Tools for sustainability analysis in planning and managing tourism and recreation in a destination. In C. Hall and A. Lew (eds.). *Sustainable Tourism: A Geographical Perspective*. London: Longman. 75–91.

Wilensky, C. H. 1960: Work, careers and social integration. *International Social Science Journal*, 4, 543–60.

Williams, A. M. 1995: Capital and the transnationalisation of tourism. In

A. Montanari and A. M. Williams (eds.), *European Tourism: Regions, Spaces and Restructuring*, Chichester: Wiley.

Williams, A. M. 2001: Tourism on the fabled shore. In R. King, P. de Mas, and J. M. Beck (eds.), *Geography, Environment and Development in the Mediterranean*, Brighton: Sussex Academic Press.

Williams, A. M. and Balaz, V. 2000a: *Tourism in Transition: Economic Change in Central Europe*. London: I. B. Tauris.

Williams, A. M. and Balaz, V. 2000b: Privatisation and the development of tourism in the Czech Republic and Slovakia: property rights, firm performance and recombinant property. *Environment and Planning A*, 32, 715–34.

Williams, A. M. and Balaz, V. 2001: From collective provision to commodification of tourism? *Annals of Tourism Research*, 28, 27–49.

Williams, A. M. and Hall, M. 2000: Tourism and migration: new relationships between production and consumption, *Tourism Geographies*, 2, 5–27.

Williams, A. M. and Shaw, G. 1988: Tourism: candy floss industry or job generator? *Town Planning Review*, 59, 81–104.

Williams, A. M. and Shaw, G. 1990: Tourism in urban and regional development Western European experiences. In S. Hardy, T. Hart, and T. Shaw (eds.), *The Role of Tourism in the Urban and Regional Economy*, London: Regional Studies.

Williams, A. M. and Shaw, G. 1991: *Tourism and Economic Development: Western European Experiences*, London: Belhaven Press, 2nd edn.

Williams, A. M. and Shaw, G. 1992: *Tourism, Leisure, Nature Protection and Agri-Tourism: Principles, Partnerships and Practice*. Exeter, European Partners for the Environment/Tourism Research Group: University of Exeter.

Williams, A. M. and Shaw, G. 1998a: Introduction: tourism and uneven economic development. In A. M. Williams and G. Shaw (eds.), *Tourism and Economic Development: European Experiences*, Chichester: Wiley.

Williams, A. M. and Shaw, G. 1998b: Tourism policies in a changing economic environment. In A. M. Williams and G. Shaw (eds.), *Tourism and Economic Development: European Experiences*, Chichester: Wiley.

Williams, A. M. and Shaw, G. 1999: Tourism and the environment: sustainability and economic restructuring. In C. M. Hall and A. A. Lew (eds.), *Sustainable Tourism: A Geographical Perspective*, London: Longman.

Williams, A. M., King, R, Warnes, A. M., and Patterson, G. 2000: Tourism and international retirement migration: new forms of an old relationship in southern Europe. *Tourism Geographies*, 2, 28–49.

Williams, A. M., Greenwood, J., and Shaw, G. 1989a: *Tourism in the Isles of Scilly: a Study of Small Firms on Small Islands*, University of Exeter: Tourism Research Group.

Williams, A. M., Shaw, G., and Greenwood, J. 1989b: From tourist to tourism entrepreneur, from consumption to production: evidence from Cornwall, England. *Environment and Planning A*, 21, 1639–53.

Williams, A. V. and Zelinsky, W. 1970: On some patterns in international tourist flows, *Economic Geography*, 46, 549–67.

Williams, D. R. and Kaltenborn, B. P. 1999: Leisure places and modernity: the use and meaning of recreational cottages in Norway and the USA. In

D. Crouch (ed.), *Leisure/Tourism Geographies: Practices and Geographical Knowledge*, London: Routledge.

Williams, R. 1975: The Country and the City London: Chatto and Windus.

Williams, S. 1998: *Tourism Geography*, London: Routledge.

Willits, W. L. and Willits, F. K. 1986: Adolescent participation in leisure activities: "the less, the more or the more, the more." *Leisure Sciences*, 8, 189–206.

Wilson, K. 1998: Market/ industry confusion in tourism economic analyses. *Annals of Tourism Research*, 25, 803–17.

Winpenny, J. T. 1982: Some issues in the identification and appraisal of tourism projects in developing countries. *Tourism Management*, 3, 218–21.

Wöber, K. 1997: International city tourism flows. In J. A. Mazanec (ed.), *International City Tourism*, London: Pinter, 39–53.

Wolfe, R. I. 1983: Recreational travel, the new migration revisited. *Ontario Geography*, 19, 103–24.

Wood, S. 1981: A tale of two markets: contrasting approaches to developments in Covent Garden and Les Banes. Paper given at PTRC summer meeting.

World Tourism Organization 1981: *Estudio Piloto Sobre las Consecuencias Sociales y Culturales de los Movimentos Turistocos*. Madrid: WTO.

World Tourism Organization 1983: *Development of Leisure Time and the Right to Holidays*. Madrid: WTO.

World Tourism Organization 1984: *Economic Review of World Tourism*. Madrid: WTO.

World Tourism Organization 1985: *The Role of Transnational Tourism Enterprises in the Development of Tourism*. Madrid: WTO.

World Tourism Organization 1989a: *Yearbook of Tourism Statistics, Volume 1*. Madrid: WTO.

World Tourism Organization 1989b: *Yearbook of Tourism Statistics. Volume 2*. Madrid: WTO.

World Tourism Organization 1990: *Current Travel and Tourism Indicators, January 1990*, Madrid: WTO.

World Tourism Organization 1991: *Tourism to the Year 2000: Qualitative Aspects Affecting Global Growth, A Discussion Paper (Executive Summary)*. Madrid: WTO.

World Tourism Organization 1992: *Tourism Carrying Capacity: Report on the Senior-level Expert Group Meeting, June 1990*. Madrid: WTO.

World Tourism Organization 1998: Yearbook of Tourism Statistics. Madrid: WTO.

World Tourism Organization 1999: *Yearbook of Tourism Statistics*. Madrid: WTO.

World Tourism Organization 2000a: *Tourism Highlights 2000*. Madrid: World Tourism Organization

World Tourism Organization 2000b: *Yearbook of Tourism Statistics*, Madrid: WTO.

Wynne, D. 1990: Leisure lifestyle and the construction of social space. *Leisure Studies*, 9, 21–34.

Yokeno, N. 1968: La localisation de l'industrie touristique: application de l'analyse de Thunen-Weber. *Les Cahiers du Tourisme*, C-9, Aix-en-Provence.

Young, G. 1973: *Tourism: Blessing or Blight?* London: Penguin.

Young, Lord 1985: *Pleasure, Leisure and Jobs – the Business of Tourism.* London: HMSO.

Young, M. and Winmott, P. 1973: *The Symmetrical Family.* London: Routledge and Kegan Paul.

Zalatan, A. 1998: Wives' involvement in tourism decision processes. *Annals of Tourism Research*, 25(4), 890–903.

Zimmermann, F. 1991: Austria: contrasting tourist seasons and contrasting regions. In A. M. Williams and G. Shaw (eds.), *Tourism and Economic Development: Western European Experiences*, London: Belhaven Press, 2nd edn.

Zimmermann, F. 1995: The Alpine region: regional restructuring opportunities and constraints in a fragile environment. In A. Montanari and A. M. Williams (eds.), *European Tourism: Regions, Spaces and Restructuring*, Chichester: Wiley.

Zimmermann, F. 1998: Austria: contrasting tourist seasons and contrasting regions. In A. M. Williams and G. Shaw (eds.), *Tourism and Economic Development: European Experiences,* Chichester: Wiley.

Zukin, S. 1990: Socio-spatial prototypes of a new organisation of consumption: the role of real cultural capital. *Sociology*, 24, 37–56.

Zukin, S. 1991: *Landscapes of Power: From Detroit to Disney World.* Berkeley: University of California.

Index